AF821749

Imperfect Collusion in the Cement Industry

This is the fourth in a series of studies on competition and monopoly in American industry financed by a grant from the Merrill Foundation for the Advancement of Financial Knowledge. The series has been planned to include a number of studies focusing on the effectiveness of competition in particular industrial markets accompanied by certain investigations into the effect on competition of various elements of market structure and business practice common to many industries. Although each volume is an independent study representing only the views of its author, all are expected to contribute to the central objective of the whole project: an evaluation of monopoly policy in the United States.

Imperfect Collusion in the Cement Industry

SAMUEL M. LOESCHER

HARVARD UNIVERSITY PRESS · CAMBRIDGE
1959

© Copyright 1959 by the President and Fellows of Harvard College

Distributed in Great Britain by
Oxford University Press, London

Library of Congress Catalog Card Number: 59–11512

Printed in the United States of America

Preface

Dean Edward S. Mason in 1950 suggested that I redevelop my Harvard dissertation on the cement industry for publication, including an examination of the economic consequences of the *Cement* decision. I waited patiently for several years for a re-emergence of excess capacity in order to test the impact upon the industry's market behavior of the FTC order to cease and desist. However, the persistence of a continuously expanding demand for cement since World War II has nullified the effects of capacity expansion, and an empirical test of the market still lies in the future. In fact, recent enactment of the federal highway program is likely to delay further a plentiful supply of cement. In the meantime I have had ample time in which to rethink and refine my concepts of imperfect collusion and formula pricing as applicable to the cement industry, and to study the superficial responses of the cement industry to the *Cement* decision and the industry's market structure as it has evolved since 1950. Thus I believe that notwithstanding the absence of an empirical test, it is possible to forecast the response which the industry is likely to make to an eventual softening in cement markets, and that little would be gained by postponing further the publication of this study.

Credit for suggesting its title should be given to Lynn C. Paulson, assistant counsel of the Federal Trade Commission during the *Cement* case. In the *Record,* I discovered that Mr. Paulson asked an expert economist for the Cement Institute: "Is it not true there might be imperfect collusion just as well as there might be imperfect competition?"

Correspondence and conversations with many individuals have sharpened my thinking about formula pricing and collusion in recent years. Especially helpful have been Clair Wilcox, Corwin D. Edwards, Ward S. Bowman, Jr., William S. Johnson, Morris A. Adelman, Ralph F. Fuchs, and Ivan C. Rutledge.

To Carl Kaysen are due particular thanks for having read and criticized the entire manuscript. Professor Kaysen's comments were very helpful, but he must, of course, be freed from any guilt by association. His criticisms, like those of others, were possibly too frequently treated as "suggestions."

The Graduate School of Indiana University provided funds to finance a summer's research and the typing of the manuscript. The Merrill Foundation is financing publication.

Greatest credit must go to Aase, my wife, who pressed me unceasingly to clarify my propositions for the lay reader.

S.M.L.
Bloomington, Indiana
June 25, 1957

Contents

I The Concept of Imperfect Collusion Analyzed 1

II Technological Factors Conditioning Development, Entry, Location, and Market Structure in the American Cement Industry 31

III Nature of Costs and Demand — Consequences: A Quest for Defensive Monopoly 58

IV The Evolution of an Effective Delivered Pricing Formula 87

V Market Behavior Under the Basing-Point System 143

VI Economic Performance Under the Basing-Point System 191

VII Remedial Proposals and the *Cement* Case 226

VIII Developments Since the *Cement* Decision and Policy Recommendations 264

Appendix 305

Works Cited 315

Index 323

Tables

1 Number of American Cement Mills and Companies within Short and Long Range Supply Areas of the Fifty Leading Metropolitan Areas in the United States, Circa 1956 50–51

2 Elements of Cost as Percentages of Total Cost (Exclusive of Financial Return on Investment) and Percentage of Practical Capacity Operated in the Cement Industry, 1925–1938 64

3 Estimated Elements of Cost as Percentages of Full Cost (Inclusive of a 5% Return on Total Investment) and Percentage of Practical Capacity Operated in the Cement Industry, 1925–1938 66

4 Miles of First Class Roads Surfaced by State Highway Departments and Average Mill Prices of Petroleum Asphalt and Portland Cement, 1928–1942 82

5 Portland Cement Produced in the Lehigh Valley and All the United States, 1895–1915 89

6 Capacity and Production of United States Portland Cement Mills, 1909–1955 168–169

7 Average Price Per Barrel, F.O.B. Plant, of Portland Cement Shipped from U.S. Cement Plants, 1900–1955 171

8 Annual Rate of Return After Taxes on Stockholders' Equity for Selected Samples of Cement Corporations, 1919–1955 173

9 Cement Shipments Received and Made by Mills in Nine Southern States: Comparisons with Practical Capacity, 1936–43, 1946–48 206

10 Capacity of the Ten Largest Producers of Cement in the United States, 1952 291

Illustrations

Figures

Figure 1 Schematic Diagram of Basing-Point System 7

Charts

Chart 1 Cement Consumption in Ohio Compared with Consumption in Pennsylvania, Michigan, and Indiana and Average Consumption in the Three Major Adjoining States 75

Chart 2 Selected Base Price Movements, 1925–1940 157

Chart 3 The Estimated Rate of Practical Capacity Utilization, 1910–1955, Estimated After Taxes, Rate of Return on Net Worth, 1910–1955, and Average Realized Mill Price, 1909–1955 in the United States Cement Industry 174

Maps

Map 1 Cement Plants and Cement Producing Districts in Relation to Sources of Limestone and Bituminous Coal, 1940 123

Map 2 Geographical Relationships of the Plants of Six of the Largest Producers of Portland Cement, 1937 124

Map 3 Portland Cement Basing-Points in the United States, excluding Washington, Oregon, and California, 1937 145

Imperfect Collusion in the Cement Industry

CHAPTER I

The Concept of Imperfect Collusion Analyzed

Introduction

In April 1948 the Supreme Court decided that collusive use of a basing-point system violated American antitrust law, and the defendant cement companies were enjoined from continuing such action.[1] Now major court decisions tend to produce controversy as to their meaning, consequences, and wisdom; and the *Cement* decision was no exception. However, the excited discussions in the press, trade, and Congress were both trifling and legalistic, concentrating on such questions as the meaning of "collusion," "system," and "independent meeting of competition." These are important questions and, indeed, receive extensive discussion in Chapters I, VII, and VIII. Yet a host of underlying economic questions went either unasked or unanalyzed in the popular discussions. The writer believes that these economic issues will share the limelight in any future basing-point debates — when cement producers once again seek to sell appreciably more cement than buyers will take at the price asked.

It is hoped that this economic study of the American cement industry between circa 1900 and 1956 — giving special emphasis to the place of the basing-point system — will add light and reduce heat in any renewed public debate. The study is based heavily on the wealth of economic data found scattered in the testimony and exhibits of the Federal Trade Commission's *Cement*[2] case. The other major sources of information are reports of the Federal Trade Commission and Congressional Committees, the Bureau of Mines' *Minerals Yearbook* (and predecessor volumes), the cement industry's two major trade journals, *Pit and*

[1] *Federal Trade Commission* v. *Cement Institute,* 333 U.S. 683 (1948).

[2] *Transcript of Record, Cement Institute,* 37 FTC 87 (1943). Hereafter cited as *Record.*

Quarry and *Rock Products,* and information obtained by the writer from cement producers and consumers through interviews and questionnaires.

The central theme of this study is that imperfect collusion best describes the industry's behavior, and the concept of imperfect collusion is developed analytically in Chapter I. The chapter's basic question is whether the basing-point system reflects anything more than the spatial working of imperfect competition — with all sellers merely meeting the lower prices quoted by rivals more advantageously located. Following a detailed analysis of the mechanics and principles of the basing-point formula, the writer argues that overt collusion would almost inevitably be involved in the institution and perfecting of such a formula, while the continued absence of departures from the formula would provide strong grounds for inferring strict adherence to some agreement. The chapter concludes by distinguishing between the pricing-formula variety of imperfect collusion and Fellner's concept of imperfect spontaneous coordination, and between the spatial uncertainties of the cement industry and the Chamberlinian variety of uncertainty. The general reader will undoubtedly find Chapter I the most difficult in the book, and he is urged to skip the concluding portions of the chapter.

Factors which have shaped the cement industry's market structure are explored in Chapter II. What has been the impact of technology and institutional factors upon location, entry and economies of scale? Have technological factors produced a number of sellers so small as to render spontaneous coordination inevitable? If not, does the total concentration in the relevant geographic markets, nevertheless, exceed that induced by the economies of scale in production, thereby increasing the likelihood of adherence to a geographic pricing formula — once the details, mechanics, and rules have been collusively formulated? Moreover, what market pattern exists among the buyers? May schemes have been developed among the sellers to nullify the bargaining power of particular groups which would otherwise have disrupted the confirmed adherence to an accepted formula?

In Chapter III the nature of costs and demand is examined to discover why the cement industry, believing that it could not withstand price competition, was determined to effect a geographic system of defensive monopoly. The examination shows that actually supply and demand conditions in the industry were not as inelastic as industry spokesmen believed. Therefore, if cyclically flexible pricing tendencies were not restrained, it is argued that most cement enterprises could expect to avoid bankruptcy if the federal government were also to institute a vigorous monetary-fiscal policy to lessen future declines in construction and therefore in cement demand. However, heavy losses and strains would still recur throughout the industry, and defensive efforts against effective competition could be expected to persist. Whether significant anti-social effects would outweigh the comforting private effects of defensive monopoly is examined in Chapter VI.

A documentation of practices used by the industry in effecting a system of defensive monopoly constitutes the body of Chapter IV. The extensive recital of collective efforts supports the writer's thesis that the basing-point system was no natural development, save to the extent that it is natural to collude and to try to increase the permanency of the collusive behavior through merger. The detailed examination of the collusive practices shows that most important schemes were used to institute certainty-creating marketing procedures. Once instituted, little or no continuing collaboration or formal exchange of information was required in order to make use of the pricing system — except in 1932 when some damaged gates in the industry's flood wall had to be replaced.

Market behavior associated with the basing-point system is examined in Chapter V; for example, the behavior of base and non-base mills, and evidence concerning adherence to the pricing formula. The chapter concludes with a chronological summary as registered by prices, capacity utilization, and profits, in an effort to gauge and explain the industry's historical success in resisting the market forces of supply and demand.

Performance under the basing-point system is studied in Chapter VI. Attempts are made to analyze and, where possible, measure the structural waste of resources resulting from the basing-point system — as it operated in the cement industry.

The magnitude of structural waste is primarily attributed to the price stabilizing effects of the system. However, the lack of cyclical price flexibility in the industry is not only charged with raising the average level of cement costs and prices over the course of the cycle, but it is also charged with lowering the average level of resource use within the entire economy during periods of recession, through the effects of money flow.

Alternatives to the basing-point system are considered in Chapter VII, as is the shifting remedial objective of the Federal Trade Commission in prosecuting the *Cement* case. The writer argues that the alternative behavior most likely to promote price flexibility is that which is characterized by unsystematic discrimination, itself a term requiring considerable explanation. In turn, several methods for inducing unsystematic price behavior are evaluated in terms of their probable feasibility legally and administratively; and the Commission's Cement Order, in the light of the Supreme Court decision, is put to the same test.

The concluding chapter examines the industry's response to the 1948 *Cement* decision, examines subsequent structural changes in the industry, and attempts to evaluate the impact of the decision on the industry's behavior and performance. The writer concludes that so far the antitrust decision has been encouraging, but he predicts that effective price competition will not be restored in the industry unless vigorous efforts are taken to win compliance with a bold interpretation of the Cement Order. Of some seven policies recommended, the two most novel, and in many respects the most important, concern the elimination of certain controls affecting the trucking of cement by buyers and the direct purchase of cement by contractors. These controls are believed to be crucial in effecting a pricing formula and maintaining producer adherence in the commercial, non-governmental, cement market.

Indeed most of the policy conclusions are logical by-products of the theoretical structure presented in the first chapter. To help the reader to appreciate more readily the relevance of the analysis of imperfect collusion in Chapter I, this introduction closes with a simplified preview of the industry's economic structure.

Cement is a highly standardized product subject to appreciable transportation costs. There are over fifty non-affiliated manufacturers in the United States. Although several large "chain" companies exist, during the past twenty years the leading five have held less than 40 per cent and the leading ten less than 60 per cent of the nation's productive capacity. None of the leading firms sells in every section of the United States, however, so seller concentration is appreciably greater in certain geographic markets. Concentration ratios are not available for the regional markets, but the writer has estimated that the "typical" community can be supplied by about six producers practicing little or no freight absorption and fourteen producers when allowance is made for customary, cost-price margins. Although some large clusters of mills exist at a few locations, cement mills are widely dispersed and most communities can choose between several alternative sources. Because cement is a product of derived demand, the technological and economic behavior of the construction market tends to make the demand for it rather price inelastic, geographically mobile, and cyclically unstable. In the absence of flexibility in the basic price at each cement mill, producers in some or all areas are likely to find themselves confronted from time to time with appreciable excess capacity. Given a cost structure composed of high overhead, producers with excess capacity are tempted at given times to reduce their asking price appreciably for those buyers who appear to guarantee some extra sales, i.e., they are tempted to practice price discrimination. Finally, in most of the separated consumption markets, government, large contractors, and building supply dealers constitute the major potential wholesale customers of cement.

The Basing-Point System

Although the formal characteristics of the basing-point system have been stated in previous discussions *ad nauseum,* there may be some readers to whom the formula is unfamiliar. Moreover, the very mechanical aspects of the formula so frequently presented in the past have served to hide some of the assumptions implicit in this form of imperfect collusion. So, let us repeat once more the mechanics of the basing-point pricing formula. As usually employed, the formula can be shown to be extremely simple, even elementary. Stated mathematically, it might read:

delivered price = lowest combination of base price + "published" freight rate

That is, all quoted prices are delivered prices, and the delivered price to be quoted by any seller interested in a given transaction is the minimum combination from alternative mills of base price at the mill plus "published" freight rate from the mill to the given destination. In the event that the base price is not published in a trade journal, posted at the mill, or listed separately on price circulars, it can easily be ascertained by subtracting from the delivered price quotation the corresponding "published" freight rate from the mill. With the base price known and with freight rates readily accessible, the "proper" delivered price for any new destination can be derived by using the formula. Figure 1 presents a simplified picture of the operation of the formula involving only two sellers, with particular destinations being arranged along one dimension. Only three concessions to the complex reality are offered in the diagram: first, identical base prices do not exist at the rival mills; second, the destinations where frequent sales are made (labeled A through K), including those at the mill locations X and Y are shown as not being spaced equally distant from one another; third, published freight rates are shown to be non-proportional with distance, and include a substantial rail switching charge or a minimum transportation charge on "regulated" truck delivery to market destinations in mill towns.

Employing the terminology that will be used frequently hereafter, we read from Figure 1 that, given the assumed base mill prices and the published freight rates, destination prices will be "controlled" west of G by mill X and east of G by mill Y, G constituting the boundary separating the "natural markets"[3] of

[3] The term "natural market" refers to an admittedly variable phenomenon. A relative shift in the base price of a mill will tend to shift the natural market of that mill. Were we to rely strictly on the theory that mill prices are and should be established on a "cost plus basis," and if such prices are identical at each mill, the boundary separating natural markets would be that point where the freight rate from each mill is the same. However, "cost" and "plus" are not completely objective terms, and empirical information regarding them is not readily available. Therefore we shall continue to refer to "natural markets" in the manner treated

Figure 1. Schematic Diagram of Basing-Point System

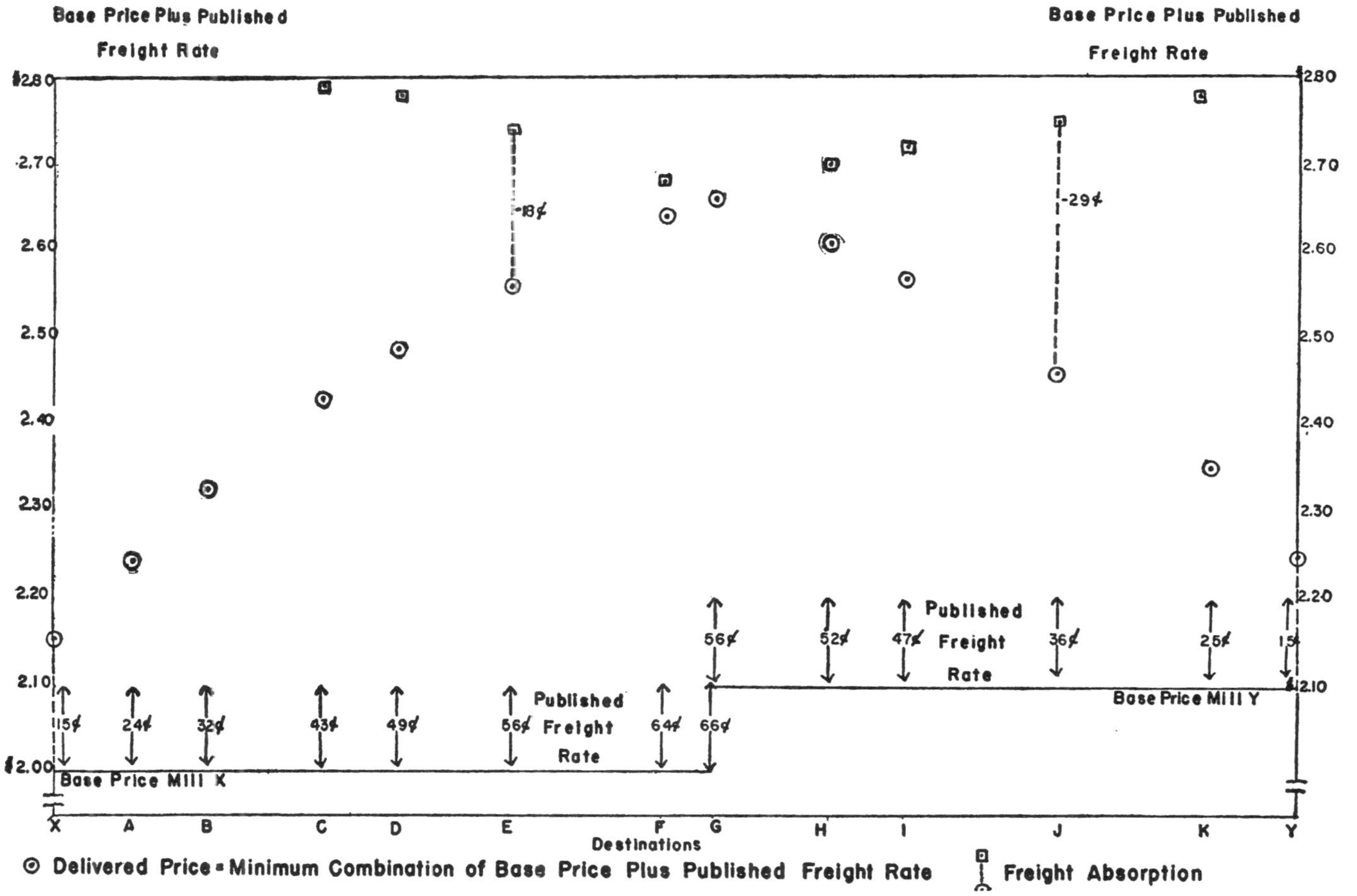

the respective mills. At E in the natural market of mill X, the formula price is $2.56 ($2.00 base price at mill X plus 56¢ published freight rate). Should mill Y have some unutilized capacity after selling nearby and seek to make a sale at E, it would have to absorb some freight. Its destination price of base price plus freight would amount to $2.74 ($2.10 plus 64¢) or 18¢ more than the figure for mill X. Or alternatively, mill Y would have to reduce its mill net from the base price of $2.10 to $1.92. Similarly, should mill X attempt to make a sale at J, controlled by mill Y, mill X would have to absorb 29¢ of freight in order to equal the price of $2.46 set by mill Y. So long as all firms adhere to the formula in computing their delivered prices, all destination prices will be identical, and freight absorption will take place systematically.

The characteristic operation of the system in the cement industry has been such that mills have been free to change their base prices.[4] When a mill has elected to lower or to raise its base price, all destination prices in the mill's natural market (except those in the area of the boundary) will be raised or lowered proportionally to the amount of the change in the base price. Mutual adherence to the formula will assure this result. In fact, unless the basing-point formula is modified by the adoption of zone pricing within limited areas,[5] the pattern of destination prices within any natural market (again excepting destinations affected by a shifting boundary) will be influenced *only* by changes in the published freight rate structure. Any mill could elect to become a non-base mill[6] simply by raising its base price so high that the formula became non-operative. Should mill Y in Figure 1 elect to become a non-base mill, prices at all destina-

---

in the text. It should also be noted that a mill with a base price too high to control effectively any destination prices will, by definition, have no "natural market."

[4] Of course, when two or more mills are located at the same production location, as is frequently the case, barometric price leadership or overt agreement among firms at that particular location will usually be necessary to facilitate a price increase during periods of unutilized capacity.

[5] E.g., large metropolitan areas have frequently been quoted a single delivered price in spite of differing freight rates from various sections of the territory.

[6] A non-base mill is one which does not quote a base price. Such a mill *always* calculates delivered prices on the basis of the base price plus freight from a rival mill.

tions would be controlled by mill X and the maximum mill net for mill Y would be obtained only at destinations in its immediate vicinity. Using the hypothetical data in Figure 1, if the destination price at Y were to rise to $2.80, mill Y would derive a maximum mill net of $2.65 (after deducting the 15¢ minimum rail switching charge), and the mill nets would progressively decrease as Y attempted to sell toward the west in the direction of the steadily decreasing destination prices established by mill X.

So much for the purely formal characteristics of the basing-point system. As stated, and I believe that the presentation rendered is fairly typical of most treatments, it is little wonder that many people have come to accept the basing-point system as merely a natural outgrowth of imperfectly competitive pressures. In the face of unutilized capacity it seems natural for a mill to reach out for potential additional sales by absorbing freight so as to meet the low price quoted by a competitor. That identical destination prices should develop and persist, they attribute merely to the self-restraint imposed by oligopolistic rationality. However, careful examination of the development and implementation of the basing-point system in the cement industry has revealed that the system is a good deal more complex than a simple diagram might indicate, and an introductory treatment of the elements of imperfect collusion — overt, tacit, or implied — is herewith presented.

Elements of Imperfect Collusion

1. All price quotations are delivered prices

There are at best two reasons why individual versus group interest might induce a mill to quote some of its prices on a delivered basis. In the first place buyers are interested in their destination cost, and not all buyers are equally well informed about freight rates so as to compare the price offers of rival sellers in terms of destination costs. In some circumstances delivered prices may, therefore, constitute a convenience to the purchaser. A more important reason for quoting delivered prices is the opportunity this affords sellers to separate markets and thereby practice geographic price discrimination without fear of arbitrage operations. By means of the delivered price, freight absorption can be employed to make a sale to distant buyers by meeting or "beating" the rival offer, and the buyers will have no opportunity to divert for resale into the natural market of the seller the product obtained at reduced mill nets. In the absence of the delivered price, a seller might hesitate to vary selectively his f.o.b. mill price in the attempt to penetrate more distant markets, for fear that the buyers, securing control of the product at the mill, might make an arbitrage profit by reselling it in the higher-priced local market of the manufacturer. Since extensive diversion of shipments for arbitrage purposes would inevitably have the effect of lowering the producer's base price, the development of delivered prices was a perfectly natural phenomenon when quoting to distant buyers.

Why individual manufacturers, however, should have insisted that all price offers be made on a delivered basis is another matter. Why would quotation of the established base price, f.o.b. mill, to buyers in the natural market of the mill be contrary to the individual interest of the seller? Certainly buyers who paid the posted base price and arranged their own transportation from the mill would not be in a position to practice arbitrage. When local buyers could purchase at the posted mill price and arrange their own transportation, they frequently found a saving in using private or contract truck or water transportation instead of rail or common carrier truck. Why should manufacturers seek to deny such savings to their customers, since their mill prices were not directly undermined by the process? Indeed, the transportation savings made available to local buyers lowered the destination costs in the local markets and thereby tended to make these markets somewhat less attractive to distant sellers. The penetrating rivals would need to absorb even more freight (accept lower mill nets) on their long haul rail shipments in attempting to offer such buyers equally attractive destination prices. Unregulated buyer transportation served to lower short haul costs of transportation and therefore reduced the downward concavity in the freight rate structure with respect to distance (see Figure 1). These transporation economies promised a larger share of such markets to those mills located close to large consuming areas without requiring them to reduce their base prices.

Why, therefore, did cement manufacturers in most areas of the United States collude to eliminate or control trucking (i.e., refuse buyers the opportunity of arranging their own transportation and purchasing at the posted mill base price)?

Later chapters will show that uncontrolled trucking caused the industry to experience disorderly pricing so extensive as to endanger general adherence to the pricing formula. But how does this come about? The explanation most frequently offered is that the presence of alternative methods of transportation complicates the determination of the minimum freight rate to be applied in the formula in calculating the delivered price. It is true that multiple transportation media make more complex the application of a common formula, but if the rates of alternative methods of transportation are published, the possibility of applying a formula still remains. For example, when efforts were undertaken to control trucking in the cement industry, a few sections of the country continued to make extensive use of truck transportation; *but* this type of delivery almost invariably moved to destinations at delivered prices.[7] In these areas trucking was controlled by limiting such deliveries to common carrier trucks, those operated by exclusive contractors of the selling mill, or those owned by the selling mill — all deliveries being made at "published" freight rates. Common carrier truck rates were, of course, on file at regulatory agencies, while in all other cases of controlled trucking the freight rates were actually published by mills in advertising circulars.

The reason, therefore, that buyers were denied the opportunity to purchase at the posted f.o.b. mill price and to haul in their privately selected contractor's trucks or in their own, was that definite freight rates in such cases were not available. When buyers were free to arrange their own transportation from local mills, the distant mills which absorbed freight on long haul rail transportation could not know what delivered price to quote so

[7] The term delivered price is broadly construed by the writer to include quotations of mill base prices allegedly on a f.o.b. mill basis, but which circumscribe the freedom of buyers to arrange their own transportation.

as to meet identically the destination cost to such buyers. The freight charged by a contract trucker to a buyer was negotiated, and, although close guesses might be made about the cost, certainty was impossible. Of course, when the buyer trucked in his privately owned facilities knowledge of the hauling costs became even more uncertain. (What would be the buyer's private opportunity cost for hauling cement from a local mill to destination, particularly when he possessed trucks which were not being fully utilized?) The effect of uncontrolled trucking would be to destroy an automatic geographic pricing formula. Moreover, the very uncertainties of uncontrolled trucking would place buyers in a strategic bargaining position. The final consequences would be such that the distant sellers would either forego the opportunities of making such sales or accept the likelihood that they would "beat" competition in making sales.

As will be discussed in a later chapter,[8] cement producers offered several private business reasons for eliminating buyers' trucking. The two most significant explanations were that the loading of buyers' trucks at the mill was an inconvenience and more costly than loading a uniform type of transportation more easily scheduled by the seller; and that the majority of dealers complained that certain rivals, particularly new and smaller dealers, could more readily avail themselves of the economies of truck transportation and use the savings to reduce prices. As to the first reason, however, the evidence presented to show alleged greater costs of loading buyers' trucks was inconclusive. Yet even if substantiated those costs would only have justified a differential base price proportional to the demonstrated *additional* cost. In answer to the second reason it should be stated that the interest of individual manufacturers need not compel action to restrain competitive pressures at the resale level, although there may be a common interest among producers to restrain price competition at the resale level so as to abate bargaining pressures by disadvantaged dealers for price concessions from rival manufacturers.

If the invading mill accepted the risk of "beating" competition in order to maintain patronage, such lowered pricing would

[8] See Chapter IV.

in turn frequently lead to additional unsystematic price reductions on the part of the local mill. The history of the cement industry during the period of uncontrolled trucking shows that penetrating mills frequently "beat" competition and that uncertainties so generated must have contributed to breaking through the formula pricing system even in areas outside the range of economical trucking. The disharmony and distrust engendered by chaotic pricing in the local areas of mills probably induced some of them to seek additional sales by cutting prices in areas where the formula still held, cuts which ultimately led to wide-scale open reductions in base mill prices.

Unlike the purely *individual* purpose of preventing arbitrage disruptions, a purpose logically to be inferred when sellers elected to quote delivered prices on freight absorbing sales, the *common* purpose of implementing an industry-wide pricing formula was the prime motive in adopting the *exclusive* use of delivered pricing. In fact, ample evidence will be presented later to indicate both implicit and tacit agreements within the cement industry to discontinue posted f.o.b. mill prices to buyers' trucks, as well as overt agreement in the case of a few mills.

The collusion involved in selling at delivered prices *exclusively* was imperfect in two senses. No action was taken to check the wastes of cross-hauling. But, of even greater interest, the very elimination of uncontrolled trucking increased the magnitude of this cross-hauling. To the extent that buyers in the local areas of mills were denied the opportunity of reducing their destination cost via privately arranged truck transportation, the attractiveness of these particular markets to the more distant mills was increased since the amount of freight that had to be absorbed would be lessened. However, in spite of the increased waste resulting from such imperfect collusion, the adoption of this trade practice constituted effective collusion since the greater costs resulting from non-price competition were more than offset by the larger revenues flowing from a stabilized price structure.[9]

[9] A similar attitude seems to prevail on the part of almost all retailers operating under a system of effectively enforced resale price maintenance. They would probably admit that the greater pressures for non-price competition in the form of store appointments, salesmen's expenditures, and advertising serve to increase unit costs. But they believe that the resulting reduction in total profit is less than that which would follow if there were no restraints on price competition.

2. Common freight rate books

Historically, the bulk of cement shipments moved by rail. With only a small proportion of cement mills and construction sites located on navigable waterways, water transportation has inevitably accounted for but a small fraction of total cement shipments. Although modern trucking has made substantial inroads, the range of its potential economy relative to rail transportation is generally under 100 miles and most frequently under 50 miles. Furthermore, because many mills refuse to ship by truck, even in carriers controlled by the mill and moving under published rates, most shipments are by rail.

It so happens that with the exception of the Pacific Coast and some of the Rocky Mountain states, railroad freight rates in the United States are extremely complex. And this, too, is where the bulk of the nation's cement is produced and shipped. Diagrams such as Figure 1, therefore, oversimplify the nature of the problem with respect to computing minimum freight rates from several alternative production points to innumerable potential destinations, destinations which include not only major cities and a host of small towns but also rail sidings in isolated areas where sizable construction activity may be taking place. Considering the large number of rail freight rates which must be ascertained in order to apply the basing-point formula, it would be surprising if errors in transcribing were not made occasionally by individual companies when compiling freight books for their salesmen. Moreover, at times of particular or general changes in freight rates the traffic departments of rival companies might make additional errors as to the amount or effective date of the changed rates, or might fail to discover promptly that certain rates had been changed. Consequently, when relying merely upon the rate books prepared by his own company's traffic department, a salesman might at times inadvertently quote below the "correct" formula price at specific destinations. Such "beating" of competition, even if only occasional, could in some degree disturb the harmony of an industry-wide pricing policy by leading to bad feeling, recriminations, and general uncertainty. (Uncertainty would result from the lack of knowing whether the price cut was intentional or accidental; even claims of "accident" might be considered mere rationalization.)

In order to minimize such uncertainties, freight rate books were compiled by a single organization with the understanding that all mills would use them for purposes of quoting delivered prices, thus avoiding the chances of accidental errors in quotations. There were also indications that detailed rules of the game were developed to handle problems that arose when errors were discovered in the common freight rate books. Prices were to be quoted on the basis of the rates listed in the books until such time as all firms could be supplied by the common organization with a corrected freight table.

It seems best not to make too much of common freight rate books as a crucial collusive element in increasing the effective implementation of a common pricing formula. The use of common freight factors was of significance in quoting "proper" delivered prices to isolated places where there were no dealers, yet where construction projects occasionally created a large demand for cement. However, in other areas the manufacturers regularly distributed advertising circulars to dealers within the territory controlled by their base price, listing the delivered price applicable to the dealer's city or town. Such circulars were shown or offered to salesmen of rival concerns. So even in the absence of common freight rate books, uncertainties as to "correct" freight factors would rarely cause an unintended "beating" of competition in metropolitan areas. Penetrating mills had only to meet the price quoted to dealers in the particular towns.

Nevertheless, it can scarcely be denied that collusion was entailed in the implicit understanding that all mills would use the rates published in the freight books commonly supplied to all rivals. Moreover, given the collective purpose of the freight rate books, it is not difficult to infer collusion from the mere distribution to all sellers in a given area of the rate books prepared by a commonly selected organization, even though some firms may have achieved certain minor economies by supplying salesmen with rate books so prepared.

3. Identical sealed bidding to governmental agencies

Most governmental agencies are required, when it is administratively feasible, to solicit sealed bids before procuring materials. Excepting the period 1929–31, when there were many departures from the basing-point pricing system, governmental agencies have nearly always received identical bids of delivered prices. In the few cases where f.o.b. mill prices were quoted, they were systematically varied at the respective bidding mills so that, upon adding freight rates in accordance with the formula, identical destination prices were obtained. Mills would almost invariably refuse to quote f.o.b. mill prices to governmental agencies if the destination were not made known. And where land grant freight rates were involved, firms developed a complicated "destination cost" bid which involved use of commonly circulated *estimates* of land grant rates available to the federal government. The typical situation, however, simply involved the quotation of identical delivered prices to governmental agencies — mill nets of the disadvantageously located mills having been systematically reduced to meet exactly the delivered price of the controlling mill.

Identical sealed bids might be expected occasionally on the basis of chance. But when over time sellers repeatedly quoted identically on sealed bids, or when sellers simultaneously offered identical bids at each of ten to thirty different destinations, chance had nothing to do with it. Company representatives admitted that in sealed bidding to governmental agencies, except where land grant freight rates applied, their concerns simply quoted what would have been their regular commercial price for the given destination. As the former president of the largest cement company testified, "We would naturally assume, and correctly assume, that other companies do their marketing in an equally orderly fashion." [10]

The mechanical procedure used in calculating prices for commercial buyers usually differs substantially from the mechanics of sealed bidding, and the significance of identical quotations differs accordingly. When a penetrating mill quotes to a dealer

[10] *Record,* Transcript p. 34840.

in another mill's natural market, the penetrator might very well match the delivered price which the dealer shows to have been offered in a recent advertising circular or to have been recently charged in an invoice. But on sales involving simultaneously deposited sealed bids from sellers at different locations, how can each firm know the price that the other will quote if there is no understanding? How does the penetrating mill know that the controlling mill will not shade its delivered price below the usual commercial price in order to assure a final sale (frequently a very large one) in its maximum mill net territory? Hence, if penetrating mills are anxious to make some additional sales, even at mill nets below maximum, why do they not attempt to "beat" the competition of the local mill? By the same token, and with even greater force of logic, why does not fear that an invading mill will "beat" the formula price induce the local mill to cut its price in order to garner a sale when the potential mill net is inevitably higher for the local mill? It is inconceivable that secret quotations could have continued to be identical, if there had been no understanding between the mills as to the delivered price to be quoted. Whether or not the understanding was bolstered by telephonic reassurances, it was undoubtedly reinforced at least by the experience of common adherence to a formula in the past when making sealed bids. Given the conditions of uncertainty which surround the mechanics of sealed bidding, repeated identical quotations of sealed bids scarcely permit any inference other than one of collusion to adhere to a common pricing formula.

Opinion prevailed in the cement industry that during depression periods, when governmental agencies constituted a much larger proportion of total demand than usual, the industry could not gamble on making exceptions from its formula method of pricing — even on sealed bidding to governmental agencies despite the inferences of collusion inevitably to be drawn therefrom. It was held that independent price-making on sealed bids would not remain isolated from pricing practices on commercial sales: an unchecked virus of non-identical sealed bids would inevitably spread to quotations below the formula on commercial sales. Hence, non-collusive sealed bidding raised the specter of a delivered price system destroyed.

4. Rigid adherence to the formula pricing system and reciprocal price leadership

Great controversy has arisen over the inference of collusion based solely on a market behavior which showed persistent industry-wide adherence in commercial sales to a rigid geographic price pattern. Such sustained adherence indicates that when producers penetrate markets they simultaneously reduce mill nets by the exact amounts necessary to meet competition at particular destinations, while reciprocally facilitating the precise meeting of competition by others by refraining from reducing mill nets at any particular destinations in their own natural market. The question under debate is: If we exclude from consideration sealed bidding to governmental agencies and collective practices employed to make freight rates known, may concerted action be inferred from continued adherence to a common geographic formula?

Following a brief period of severe price competition which abated in the spring of 1932, base mill prices were raised sharply in most regions one or more times between July 1932 and July 1933. These base prices were increased while mill operations were substantially below 50 per cent of their practical capacity and prior to official approval of an N.R.A. code for the cement industry. Most of them remained unchanged for the next four or five years although the rate of mill operations climbed only slightly above 50 per cent of practical capacity throughout the period. Evidence points to the existence of unusually strict adherence to formula prices on commercial sales following the spring of 1932. There was little indication that penetrating mills "beat" competition when they absorbed freight, or that local mills undercut the penetrators selectively at particular destinations in their natural market.

One obvious feature of the basing-point formula is that it facilitates price leadership by base mills, which are enabled to raise prices in the face of adverse market conditions. If a mill is confident that the formula principle will be adhered to by penetrating concerns,[11] it may readily advance its base price without

[11] Adherence to formula price alone, however, cannot explain effective price leadership upward at such multiple mill locations as exist in the cement industry

fear that a "kink" in its demand curve [12] will result in a loss of its share of market in areas controlled by its base price. Following such an increase, penetrating mills pricing mechanically in accordance with the basing-point formula find it unnecessary to absorb as much freight as before in order to meet the lower delivered prices within the market of the competitor advantageously located. Once the various mills have established base prices at a pre-determined propitious level (considering such factors as potential threats of entry, potential substitution of other products, and potential access to the natural market by more distantly located rivals), they may leave them unchanged for a considerable period of time.

The question posed is whether the increase in the base prices, their subsequent rigidity, and the unchallenged evidence of marked adherence to the geographic pattern of formula prices may be attributed merely to oligopolistic self-restraint. Those who thus argue may conceivably be correct. However, there are others who believe that uncertainties resulting from a complex pattern of geographic and temporal demand are so great that, if it were not for implicit collusion, adherence to the delivered price pattern would be less perfect than it actually has been. The writer counts himself among the latter group.

Let us examine first the matter of market destinations. In an effort to deny the existence of a pricing formula, representatives for the cement industry have urged repeatedly that the only market for cement is at destination, and that each destination constitutes a distinct market unrelated to others. Certain unintentional implications, however, follow from their position. It will be recalled that one concession to reality was made in Figure 1 by showing that these destination markets were not equally distant from one another, and that certain of them were a considerable distance from neighboring markets. Furthermore, because short haul transportation rates are higher per ton mile than longer haul rates, the total transportation cost for shipping a product from destination C to destination D is greater than the

---

in the Lehigh Valley of Pennsylvania, the Hudson Valley of New York, the Gas-Belt area of Kansas, and the Birmingham, Alabama area, to name some of the most important.

[12] See Paul M. Sweezy, "Demand Under Conditions of Oligopoly," JPE, 47:568–573 (August 1939).

difference in cost in shipping from mill X to destination D, compared to shipping to C. Thus, the delivered price could be reduced, within limits, at destination C without tempting buyers at C to reship and affect the delivered price at destination D. One consequence is that a seller could initiate a delivered price reduction in one small section of its marketing territory provided no formula existed which tied together separate destination prices into a geographic pattern.

It is also important to realize that the temporal pattern of cement demand provides strong incentives for mills to initiate selective price reductions. One peculiar feature of the demand is that large construction jobs entailing very large cement requirements frequently occur at places which are not centers of a continuing large demand for cement.[13] Therefore, a net gain, over even a long period, could be realized from initiating a selective price reduction although rival mills may meet this delivered price in future sales at this particular destination. Moreover, even if the place of the unusually large contract is one where there is a moderately large, regular demand, a selective reduction in the delivered price at this particular market would constitute an anticipated *ultimate* gain if the initiating firm expects in the not too distant future an increase in the general demand sufficient to create a tight market. Industry members, of course, considered such selective quotations to be a "discriminatory" practice and a violation of the "equitable" system of pricing.

It was considered unethical for a penetrating mill to reduce the delivered price below that determined by the formula at a given destination in the invaded market. It was also thought unfair for a penetrating seller not to increase his delivered prices at all destinations in the invaded market when the mill controlling that territory initiated an increase in its base price. (Such "unethical" unsystematic dumping is what many new-car dealers have done in recent years when they have disposed of their oversupply of cars by reselling in distant markets at prices below those of the established dealers in the dumping ground.) If a penetrating firm desired a large contract at a destination controlled

[13] E.g., power plants, highways, bridges, and dams in small towns and rural areas.

by a rival, the rules of formula pricing permitted only one method of assuring such a contract, the initiation of a *base* price change. The base price of the would-be price cutter would have to be reduced sufficiently to convert the penetrating mill into the controlling mill at this destination. The guaranteed winning of very large contracts at particular destinations in the rivals' natural markets was rarely sufficiently attractive to compensate the initiator for reducing his base price, applicable to his entire natural market.

By the same token, a base mill had an obligation to penetrating rivals to facilitate their meeting of destination prices within the natural market controlled by its base price. Although a very large contract could be won at some particular destination in the natural market, the controlling mill was not supposed to initiate a delivered price reduction in that market alone, thereby "beating" in an unsystematic manner the delivered price quotation of penetrating mills.[14] Orderly pricing as established by the formula required that any "beating" of competition be undertaken by initiating a *base* price reduction which would lower uniformly the delivered prices at all markets controlled by the initiator. Again, it would not be very frequent that an opportunity to capture a particular very large contract would justify the controlling mill in making a relatively permanent reduction in its base price.

Thus, to lessen the incentive to initiate price reductions at particular destinations, the system of formula pricing came to be accepted as a desirable variety of open pricing. The absence of such mutually accepted checks upon incentives to initiate unsystematic selective price reductions might have played havoc with the geographic price structure, and there would have been general uncertainty as to what prices would be quoted on particular large construction jobs.

[14] The point was neatly developed by Charles Weston, of the solicitor general's office, in his rebuttal argument before the Supreme Court. Mr. Weston argued that collusion could be inferred from the fact that mills were always willing to accept very low mill nets in the course of penetrating markets while refusing to initiate a price reduction at particular destinations in their natural market. See *Transcript of Proceedings*, pp. 180–181, *FTC* v. *Cement Institute*, 333 U.S. 683 (1948). Robinson-Patman Act difficulties could scarcely arise from such selective

In all oligopolistic producer-goods industries there are potential incentives for breaching price structures, stemming from secret price quotations and pressures of threatened illiquidity. In the basing-point industries there is the additional, overriding incentive springing from the complex geographic pattern of demand. It is probably the nullification of this latter incentive, in the manner described above, which has led one group of economists to argue that rigid adherence to a basing-point formula requires a system of pricing which implies collusion. The Supreme Court also took under consideration the possibility that oligopolistic reasoning alone might explain the self-restraint inherent in this rigid adherence, but believed that in the light of the economic record of the case such an explanation was improbable:

It may possibly be true, as respondents' economists testified, that cement producers will, without agreement express or implied and without understanding explicit or tacit, always and at all times (for such has been substantially the case here) charge for their cement precisely, to the fractional part of a penny, the price their competitors charge. Certainly it runs counter to what many people have believed, namely, that without agreement, prices will vary — that the desire to sell will *sometimes* be so strong that a seller will be willing to lower his prices and take his chances.[15] (Italics added.)

5. *Automatic enforcement mechanism — the punitive base*

In the preceding section we have indicated that adherence to the basing-point formula required a firm to make a reduction in its base price whenever it desired to quote below the existing formula-derived delivered price at a particular destination. Under the circumstances it is not surprising that many firms, especially the geographically diversified chain mill companies, believed that each had the right, in accord with the pricing convention, to use methods to transform the disorderly pricing by rivals into orderly pricing. Typical of this attitude was the opinion expressed in March 1935 by the president of Lehigh Cement Company:

It is my contention that any manufacturer finding such competitive price cuts in the field has every right not only to meet the cut prices as discovered but

---

pricing in the cement industry since buyers in one area — fabricators of concrete construction goods — are not in substantial competition with those in other areas.

[15] *FTC* v. *Cement Institute,* 333 U.S. 683, 715–16 (1948).

also to quote prices generally in that territory predicated on the assumption that the competitor had in fact reduced his base price. Furthermore, before taking such action to meet competitive cut prices, according to my theory it would not be incumbent upon a manufacturer to inquire of his unfriendly competitor whether or not the cut prices in the field constituted a reduction in the base price.[16]

This is what is known as imposing a punitive base: A price cutter is forced to accept as the maximum mill net on all future business, commercial as well as governmental, the mill net received on the special quotation.

It is obvious that the mill on which the involuntary punitive base price was imposed suffered most from that disciplinary action since presumably it would be making most of its sales in the area controlled by its base price, while the mill enforcing the formula invariably made but a fraction of its sales in those same destinations.[17] (Of course, if the mill applying the punitive base belonged to a geographically diversified chain, the relative disparity in the impact of disciplinary action on the profits of the two concerns would be even greater.)

Although the mill being disciplined is an unwilling party to the practice, and although other surrounding mills in the region need not be consulted in the decision, the very application of a punitive base in a systematic manner implies the existence of a collusive pricing formula, compliance to which is being compelled. The inference that an understanding exists to employ a basing-point system is quite compelling when one considers, as we shall in a later chapter, the attitude of those firms which imposed the punitive bases. It can only be described as self-righteous indignation and a "good faith" apologia against those less ethical rivals who priced in a "discriminatory" manner.

Although there is evidence that punitive bases were applied at least twice during the 1920's, it is probable that during this period several departures from the basing-point system went unchecked or that the reduced prices were met at the specific

[16] *Record,* Commission Exhibit 971 4Q–4R.

[17] The above statement is not strictly correct since many disciplined mills had maintained a non-base status prior to the imposition of the punitive base. Nevertheless, it is reasonable to suppose that a larger proportion of total sales in the territory affected by the newly imposed base price was being made by the non-base mill than by the disciplinarian.

destinations. In this case the punitive base initially constituted only a potential, automatic enforcement mechanism. However, following a period of extensive unsystematic pricing during 1931–32, which led in turn to a series of voluntary reductions by major firms of their own base mill prices, an effort was made to halt the formula violations in sealed bids to state highway departments and in secret commercial quotations. During this time over ten punitive base mill prices were applied. By the summer of 1932 they had played an effective role in eliminating unsystematic pricing, and although cement production was well below 50 per cent of practical capacity, the stage was set for a general increase in base prices throughout the country.

The punitive base experience of 1931–32 undoubtedly made an impression upon firms (especially smaller ones) which might otherwise have been tempted subsequently to depart from the formula price understanding. The basing-point formula itself indicated the exact magnitude of a punitive base price which could be anticipated if recriminatory action consistent with the system were applied by a rival mill. There is evidence which indicates unusually high adherence to the formula and of the imposition of only one punitive base after 1932. It might be added that the president of a firm previously disciplined by a punitive base wrote to the Cement Institute in December 1935 approving of the principle of the retaliatory generalizing of an unsystematic mill net reduction into a reduced base price. He believed it to be valuable in preventing a nibbling away at the price structure. However, he recommended that regional industry committees be established to evaluate the evidence of alleged price cutting prior to the imposition of the punitive base.[18] Commenting upon this proposal, the president of one of the largest chain mill companies which had been the principal disciplinarian, disapproved of the latter plan because the contemplated joint action would constitute illegal conspiracy. Moreover, he reasoned, the same result of market stabilization could be achieved by the decision of an individual firm to force rivals to adhere to the formula, as he believed any firm was legally free to do.[19]

18 *Record,* Commission Exhibit 817 G–H.
19 *Ibid.,* Commission Exhibit 817 I–J.

Though the action was taken by individual companies, punitive bases were applied for the purpose of maintaining an industry-wide geographic formula, and the reductions made in the base price were completely consistent with the customary pricing formula. It is logical, then, to conclude that collusion was implicit in the application of punitive bases, as practiced in the cement industry.

6. Sundry collective activities not directly related to the basing-point pricing formula

In order to minimize the competitive difficulties on other fronts, additional cooperative activities were engaged in from time to time by the cement mills. In this chapter these practices, except for the last, are listed without comment.

A. Standardizing of discounts and terms of sale
B. Reporting, checking, and eliminating duplicated specific job contracts (options to buy)
C. Collecting and disseminating individual plant statistics on production, stocks, and shipments
D. Trading of sales contracts between firms more advantageously located with respect to customers' destinations
E. Boycotting the dealers of imported foreign cement
F. Promoting the belief that all so-called standard cements are identical in quality and suppressing incentives to raise quality
G. Restricting the territorial jurisdictions of dealers
H. Refusing to sell directly to contractors in cities or towns where dealers were located

To this last practice, I believe, can be attributed the fact that secret price quotations were so infrequent in the cement industry. Dealers continually in the market to purchase several brands of cement served as ready exchange posts of comparative price quotations, thus eliminating opportunities for secret price concessions by cement manufacturers. By contrast, large contractors were highly irregular both in the timing and location of their cement demand. The possibility of making isolated secret price shadings to such contractors was unusually great, thus giving to such contractors strong bargaining powers when trying to wrench substantial price concessions from cement manufacturers. Had manufacturers sold directly to contractors, a formalized price reporting scheme would have been necessary to insure adherence to the pricing formula. Instead, by selling to dealers exclusively, producers established a buffer to absorb the shock of the contractors' bargaining pressures. Had no cooperative approach been adopted to handle marketing to contractors, it is very possible that manufacturers' secret concessions could have resulted in scattered delivered price reductions sufficient to threaten the general adherence to the geographic pricing formula.

Imperfect Collusion and the Elimination of Oligopolistic Uncertainty

The following theoretical proposition is predicated upon the existence of collusive practices as described above. In order to control uncertainties unleashed by interpenetration of markets, an interpenetration which producers are administratively and legally unable to eliminate, imperfect collusion is adopted to perfect a common geographic pricing formula which will enable rational oligopolists to make the best of a difficult situation and to realize the benefits which accrue from the recognition of their interdependence.

The concept of imperfect collusion used by the writer differs markedly with the concept of incomplete "spontaneous coordination," collusion in the broad sense, propounded by William J. Fellner.[20] Not only does the writer's concept of collusion refer to the clear use of collaboration in establishing a system of behavior, but also to the *accentuation* of wasteful selling and transportation costs which result from the particular collusive system adopted. Fellner's incomplete collusion refers to assumed impediments to circumspect coordination, impediments which merely prevent oligopolists from *maximizing* the industry's joint monopoly profit.

Fellner suggests that oligopolists can easily avoid price competition, save for its occasional use in an aggressive testing of

[20] See W. J. Fellner, *Competition Among the Few* (New York, 1949).

strength. However, he shows that oligopolists will be unable to achieve the full monopoly profit and price unless they are willing to pool outlays and revenues. His thesis is that production and promotional costs relative to revenues will be somewhat higher than could be achieved through monopoly-like coordination of all market variables because of: first, static differences in costs and product and/or spatial differentiation; second, fears that price policies will be misinterpreted; and third, unpredictable degrees of success from rivalry on the quality, advertising, and technological cost-saving fronts. Fellner intimates that the persistence of incomplete coordination of all market variables stems partly from legal considerations. (Overt collaboration in a pool may be difficult to keep secret.) However, his principal explanation rests upon the unwillingness of firms to accept the vulnerability to which reduced contacts with customers and production staff would leave them, should the pool break up in the future. Hence he concludes that under oligopoly an inevitable, but incomplete, "spontaneous coordination" will result in a cartel-like rather than a monopoly level of profit and price.

The writer contends, however, that in certain oligopolistic industries both fundamental economic and institutional considerations militate against the achievement of even the cartel-like price and profit solution solely by means of "spontaneous coordination" in the area of price. He argues that the same uncertainties and hopes which impel or induce the skillful outdoing of rivals in the area of product variation and advertising [21] (at the calculated risk of reducing the aggregate level of industry profit), also induce selective ventures with competitive price in *particular* industries. Therefore collusive *planning* as distinct from mere "spontaneous coordination" will be necessary to eliminate the incentives to use price as an effective weapon. Should a collusive plan such as the basing-point formula be selected, a formula which incidentally tends to bring higher marketing costs, the phrase imperfect collusion would apply.

It is this writer's view that many economists believe that the mere recognition of interdependence by oligopolists will lead inevitably to the adoption of cartel-like pricing without any as-

[21] *Ibid.*, especially pp. 185–190, 219–222.

sistance from collusion. Such a conclusion usually rests upon a misapplication of a special hypothesis proposed by Edward H. Chamberlin.[22]

The Chamberlinian cartel-like solution of the oligopoly problem assumes a very perfect type of market in all respects other than number of sellers, and, where applicable, product differentiation. Many economists have disregarded the reservations which Professor Chamberlin has raised with respect to effects which frictions (time lags in price adjustments) and uncertainties as to rival behavior have upon the prediction of a determinate outcome.[23] Moreover, even the Chamberlinian discussion does not consider the uncertainties present in situations where common markets may be compartmentalized into several sub-markets, where each sub-market may consist of only a few buyers, where secret price concessions may be feasible, where sealed bidding may be required, and where ignorance as to transportation charges makes destination "prices" unascertainable.

A review of how collusion was used in the cement industry to eliminate these uncertainties may be helpful. Probably the most important certainty created by the institution of the basing-point pricing formula came from the agreement to ship only in transportation moving at published freight rates. Only by resorting to such a practice could penetrating sellers know the exact price at each destination served by rival mills. If buyers were permitted to arrange their own truck transportation from a local mill, the penetrating mill could not know the destination cost (price) to such buyers. And even should he desire merely to meet and not to "beat" his competitor's prices, without knowledge of the buyer's transportation cost he would either have to run the risk of underquoting his rival when giving a delivered price or to withdraw from that market. This would not be a Chamberlinian uncertainty as to when and in what manner the rival would react to

22 E. H. Chamberlin, *The Theory of Monopolistic Competition*, 5th ed. (Cambridge, Mass., 1946), pp. 46–51.

23 *Ibid.*, pp. 50–53, 101–102. Moreover, after discussing the excess capacity outcome which might be brought about by independent, monopolistic pricing on the part of non-conspiring oligopolists, he admits that in practice the outcome is likely to be bolstered by something more: "But it is fortified in actuality by formal or tacit agreements, open price associations, trade association activities in building up an *esprit de corps*, 'price maintenance', . . ." (p. 106).

a delivered price reduction by the penetrating firm, but rather an uncertainty over the very "price" the buyer paid for the product at his destination.

The distribution and use of common freight rate books, although probably of rather minor significance, were designed to serve the same purpose. Uncertainty as to the freight rate to be applied was to be removed in order that accidental cutting of delivered prices might be eliminated.

Because sealed bidding precluded the use of a posted price exchange, and because governmental agencies were neither purchasing cement continuously nor a part of the regular commercial market in particular localities, there would be great uncertainty as to what each seller would quote when there was no agreement to use a common pricing formula. However, any uncertainty as to the consequence of violating the agreement was eliminated by the practice of imposing punitive bases.

Although there would have been strong incentives to initiate delivered-price reductions at special sub-market destinations in order to assure the winning of certain large commercial contracts, and although the winning of such large contracts promised ultimate economic gain even if rival concerns were to meet quickly any particular price reduction, participation in an agreement to price according to the basing-point formula eliminated unsystematic price reductions. Thus, given assurance that no rival would reduce prices in this market only, firms did not need to fear that, by adhering to the formula price, they would lose an equality of opportunity in winning a strategically located large contract. And again, the practice of imposing punitive bases increased the certainty of general adherence to the understanding.

Finally, in order to minimize the possibility that one or more sellers might be tempted to make secret price concessions to large contractors, the mills agreed to refuse to quote directly to those wielders of bargaining power in cities and towns where dealers were located. Certainty as to the delivered prices which rivals would really quote was thereby greatly increased.

The Task Ahead

A later chapter (IV) will attempt to trace, through documentation and interpretation, the evolution of the industry's collusive full-blown formula pricing system. But the political economist's role extends beyond mere description and explanation. He must evaluate and recommend. Given the fact that firms are free to exercise their individual judgment in changing their base prices openly, the imperfect collusion entailed in developing and adhering to an orderly method of quoting prices is not necessarily undesirable nor contrary to public interest.[24]

There is reason to believe that Professor John M. Clark, one of the nation's basing-point experts and early exponents of the natural evolution hypothesis, might now agree that collusion of the imperfect variety was used in the cement industry to achieve an orderly method of price quotation.[25] However, he would also probably suggest that the orderly practices flowing therefrom have not been totally objectionable, because the characteristics of the industry generate economic pressures which threaten chaos much of the time. He would agree that compulsory modification in trade practices could be effected to increase the workability of competition in this industry, but would at the same time insist that any proposed modifications should recognize the necessity of preserving a modicum of orderly price quotation.[26] His reasoning must be examined with great care, although one may not arrive at his conclusion. In fact, after the writer's examination of the industry's economic foundation in the succeeding two chapters and of the social costs of the stabilizing practices in Chapter VI, he advances proposals aimed at making the pricing process quite flexible, or disorderly.

24 Few topics in the field of industrial economics have produced so much controversy and literature as the basing-point issue. Selectivity is difficult, but in the list of works cited at the end of the book the writer has indicated by an asterisk those which he believes to constitute the most significant and representative contributions.

25 See J. M. Clark, "Rejoinder," AER, 33:618 (September 1943); "The Law and Economics of Basing Points: Appraisal and Proposals," *ibid.*, 39:435, 438, 439 (March 1949); "Machlup," QJE, 63:317 (August 1949); and his dissenting opinion in the *Report* of the Attorney General's National Committee to Study the Antitrust Laws (Washington, 1955), p. 219.

26 See Clark, "Basing Point Method . . . ," *Canadian Journal of Economics and Political Science*, 4:477–489 (November 1938); "Toward a Concept of Workable Competition," AER, 30:241–256 (June 1940); and "The Law . . . ," AER 39:439–440 (March 1949).

CHAPTER II

Technological Factors Conditioning Development, Entry, Location, and Market Structure in the American Cement Industry

Domestic Portland Cement Emerges as the Major American Cement

When one speaks of cement today, in the absence of adjectives, one invariably refers to portland cement. A mineral mixture, scientifically proportioned and burned,[1] portland cement was so named because the manufactured product originally resembled in color and texture a famous building stone quarried on the Isle of Portland in the English Channel.

The American portland cement industry passed quickly from infancy to late adolescence around 1901 when consumption of domestic portland cement in the United States first exceeded the combined consumption of imported portland cement and domestic natural cement, and thereafter proceeded to outstrip its major rivals rapidly.[2] The McKinley Tariff of 1890 [3] served to slow

[1] Unlike natural and puzzolan (slag-lime) cements, portland cement is made by combining in a specific proportion calcareous (lime) and argillaceous (clayey) materials and is burned at extremely high temperatures (about 2700° F.) to the point of incipient vitrification (fusion). "The most commonly used portland cements of today contain approximately these proportions of mineral oxides: calcium oxide, 64.5%; silicon dioxide, 21.1%; aluminum oxide, 5.9%; iron oxide, 2.7%." H. C. Persons, *The Portland Cement Industry* (Boston, 1950), p. 11.

[2] American consumption of domestic natural cement, domestic portland cement, and imported portland cement (measured in 1000 barrels) between 1880 and 1910 is shown in the following table:

Year	Domestic natural cement	Domestic portland cement	Imported portland cement	Total consumption
1880	2,031	43	187	2,061
1881	2,440	60	221	2,721
1882	3,165	85	370	3,620
1883	4,100	90	456	4,646
1884	3,900	100	586	4,586

down the growing rate of imports, but it was a series of technological breakthroughs[4] which permitted domestic portland cement to put to rout the less expensive natural cement as well as the imported portland cement. The development of massive crushing machinery during the 1880's had brought the initial processing costs of American hard rock lime materials into line with that for European marl. However, dependence upon the vertical kiln resulted in high labor costs. Extensive, relatively high-wage, manual labor was required to mold briquettes of kiln feed and also to sort out inferior clinker from the kiln product. The gradual perfection of the rotary kiln during the 1890's re-

1885	4,000	150	554	4,704
1886	4,350	150	915	5,415
1887	6,693	250	1,514	8,457
1888	6,253	250	1,836	8,339
1889	6,532	300	1,740	8,572
1890	7,441	335	1,941	9,717
1891	7,768	454	2,988	11,210
1892	8,211	547	2,441	11,199
1893	7,412	591	2,674	10,677
1894	7,563	799	2,638	11,000
1895	7,741	990	2,997	11,728
1896	7,950	1,543	2,989	12,482
1897	8,312	2,678	2,091	13,080
1898	8,419	4,316	1,153	13,888
1899	9,868	5,652	2,108	17,629
1900	8,384	8,483	2,387	19,254
1901	7,085	12,711	939	20,735
1902	8,044	17,231	1,963	27,238
1903	7,030	22,343	2,252	31,625
1904	4,866	26,506	968	32,340
1905	4,473	35,247	897	40,617
1906	4,056	46,463	2,273	52,792
1907	2,888	48,785	2,033	53,696
1908	1,698	51,073	843	53,614
1909	1,538	64,991	434	66,963
1910	1,139	76,550	307	77,996

Source: U.S. Geological Survey, *Mineral Resources of the United States.*

[3] The duty of 30.4 cents per barrel constituted 15 to 30 per cent of the average realized price at domestic portland cement mills during the ensuing decade, as this average domestic mill net declined from $2.09 in 1890, to $1.57 in 1895 and $1.09 in 1910.

[4] See R. W. Lesley, *History of the Portland Cement Industry in the United States* (Chicago, 1924), for a good discussion of early technological developments.

sulted in a drastic reduction in man-hours per barrel of finished cement. Not only did the superior burning process produce uniform quality clinker, but, most importantly, a feed of finely ground powder or damp slurry which could be poured directly into the kiln. Two other cost-saving developments during the early 1900's hastened the virtually complete domination of American cement markets by domestic portland that existed by 1910. The introduction of longer kilns produced substantial savings in unit capital and fuel costs; and the Hurry-Seaman process, for burning powdered coal with an air blast, permitted the substitution of inexpensive bituminous coal slack for Ohio oil which was rapidly increasing in price.[5]

The Technological Process

The technology of manufacturing portland cement is relatively simple.[6] It is frequently described as "putting a mountain through a sieve" before and after burning in the chemistry center of cement mills — the rotary kiln.

1. Raw materials and their preparation

Some source of calcium carbonate provides approximately 75 per cent of the raw material fed into cement kilns, and almost invariably cement mills "mine" their own raw materials. Typical production begins in a quarry, since at least 80 per cent of American cement production has always used cement rock or pure limestone as its source of calcareous material. In the Lehigh Valley region of eastern Pennyslvania and northwestern New Jersey lies an impure limestone known as cement rock. Originally much of this cement rock contained almost a perfect proportioning of the minerals required for portland cement. However, most of it today contains less than 75 per cent calcium

[5] *Ibid.*, pp. 119, 123.

[6] Much of the ensuing technological discussion is based upon: (1) *Transcript of Record, Cement Institute* 37 FTC 87 (1943) (Hereafter cited as *Record*), pp. 22516–52, 22676–778, testimony of J. R. Magee, Vice-President in Charge of Operations, Alpha Portland Cement Co.; (2) H. E. Hilts, *The Manufacturing, Volume, and Costs of Portland Cement in the United States* (Washington 1934), (3) Nicholas Yaworski et al., *Fuel Efficiency in Cement Manufacture, 1909–35* (Philadelphia, 1938); (4) George Perazich et al., *Mechanization in the Cement Industry* (Philadelphia, 1939); and (5) various issues of the trade journals, *Rock Products* and *Pit and Quarry.*

carbonate and so must be supplemented by quarried pure limestone or be beneficiated. Conversely, where pure limestone is used, it is supplemented by quarried argillaceous materials (clay, slate, or shale). Quarried pure limestone is the major source of calcareous material today.

Alternative sources of lime material for the American industry have been marl, sea shells, and blast furnace slag. Cement produced from marl in the Michigan area once constituted a significant proportion of national output, but even in this region the dredged marl has largely been supplanted by the quarried limestone. Some mills along the Gulf Coast have used dredged oyster shells for about thirty years, while a new mill in northeastern Florida uses dredged coquina shells. Both marl and sea shells are supplemented by clayey materials in preparing the kiln feed. Blast furnace slag constitutes the major raw material at few cement mills, for only in steel centers using relatively pure ores is such slag chemically suitable for portland cement, and most mills must import pure limestone to increase the calcium content of the kiln feed.

Cement manufacturing today is divided about equally between dry and wet process mills. Where the dry process is employed, the crushed raw material must be dried before mixing; where the wet process is employed, water must be added to make a slurry before mixing. Originally the wet process was used for raw materials of high moisture content, such as marl and certain damp limestones, so as to obviate the expense of preliminary drying and to facilitate grinding. During the twenties and thirties, the wet process came into special favor since it was believed to facilitate quality control because it permitted a more exact proportioning of raw materials. However, the development of air separators and of dry blending systems have increased quality control in dry process mills also. So once again, the water content of the basic raw material appears to be the principal consideration in selecting the process to be used.

After the materials have been chemically analyzed and proportioned into either a slurry or a dry mixture, two stages of grinding pulverize the mixture into a refined powder which then passes through a sieve much finer than that in kitchen use.

2. Kiln burning

Cement kilns are expensive and are among the largest pieces of moving machinery used in industry. Some modern kilns exceed 450 feet in length. They are also costly to operate in terms of daily fuel requirements and of periodic maintenance of their firebrick linings.

The kilns, installed in batteries in the larger mills, are set up at a slight incline (approximately one half inch to each foot of length) to expedite the flow of material. At the lower end, flames 30 to 40 feet long are blown into the kilns under pressure. These kilns are fed with powdered coal in most American mills, although as mill locations have shifted (relatively) toward the deep South and West, and as the price of coal has increased in comparison with rival fuels, increasing proportions of oil and natural gas have been employed. However, the substantial part of American cement continues to be produced in kilns fed with powdered coal.

The raw mixture is fed automatically and continuously into the upper end of the kilns where hot gases drive out all of the moisture. In the middle portion, a major loss in weight takes place in the raw material as carbon dioxide is driven off, a loss amounting to about 40 per cent of the calcium carbonate component. Finally, in the intense heat of the lower third of the kiln where temperatures exceed 2700° F., incipient fusion of the calcium and silicon takes place. It is in this "clinkering" zone that the crucial chemical and physical changes occur. The red hot clinker discharged from the kiln is typically cooled in heat-recovering devices. After cooling, cement clinker is chemically inert and may be stored for several months during the slack season.

3. Clinker grinding and preparation for shipment

Prior to grinding the clinker into cement, approximately 3 per cent gypsum is added to retard the "setting" time. There follow two stages of grinding, after which the finished cement is stored in silos until time for shipment. Slightly over half of the product today is shipped in paper bags, each holding one cubic foot of cement. The wooden barrel and the cloth bag have become obsolete, but four 94-pound paper bags equal the standard American measuring unit still used: the 376-pound barrel. With large consumers bulk cement has become increasingly popular, and is shipped in special hopper rail cars or tank trucks.

Technological Progress

The real costs of manufacturing American cement have been greatly reduced during the last half century, but individual technological developments have been neither so dramatic nor so crucially innovative as was the rotary kiln. Mechanization of the mill was mainly accomplished during the second and third decades of this century. Significant improvements in output per man-hour and per fuel-unit have continued; the increased efficiency has apparently resulted from a multitude of small refinements. In all probability manufacturers of machines have been more influential in developing the improvements in machinery and in technological processes than have the cement producers. A brief account will indicate the more salient technological developments.

The second decade of the twentieth century was characterized by the enlargement of equipment capacity and the mechanization of operations. During this decade the usual length of kiln was increased from 60 to 250 feet. Quarrying operations were improved by the introduction of "well drilling" for blasting and of larger steam shovels and locomotives for handling material. In the plant proper, crushing and grinding equipment was enlarged, while bucket and belt conveyors as well as pumping systems were devised which expedited the flow of the increased volume of material. Automatic equipment was developed for packing the cement into sacks. Moreover, electrically operated machinery gradually replaced the more cumbersome steam-driven equipment.

During the third decade kilns were lengthened again, some up to 400 feet. Improved kiln linings of high-alumina or magnetite firebrick reduced maintenance costs, as did a further enlargement of crushing and grinding equipment. The method of handling the material was simplified through the introduction of closed circuit grinding and of air separating equipment. Auxiliary devices were developed for the burning department which facilitated the partial recovery of heat from flue gases and clinker.

Again, during the thirties, when the potential supply of cement exceeded demand, efforts were made to economize on unit labor and fuel costs without increasing capacity. One result was the introduction of direct-firing-unit coal pulverizers which reduced substantially the investment, operating, and maintenance costs in the preparation of coal for kiln burning.

During and after World War II, there have been no reports of major innovations affecting the technology of cement manufacture.[7] Nevertheless, the industry has continued to achieve modest increases in output per man-hour and per fuel-unit through improved equipment for handling material, new methods of flue dust recovery, the use of control instruments in kiln operation, and so on.

If a major innovation is ever to be made, it will be found most likely in stepping up fuel efficiency. Various writers have commented upon the low thermal efficiency of the rotary kiln. Writing in 1934 when fuel costs averaged almost 20 per cent of revenue from cement sales, two sympathetic critics pointed out that little attention had been given to heat losses due to radiation.[8] Substantial progress has been made in recovering heat from flue escapes and clinker cooling, but no solution has yet been found for the problem of kiln radiation.

Entry Conditions and Economies of Scale

Throughout the twentieth century economies of scale of manufacture have made entry far from easy, although the technological conditions have apparently made it only moderately difficult. Moreover, institutional considerations have never

[7] The suspension type preheater developed in Germany probably constitutes the closest approximation to a major technological development. See W. M. Avery, "First Published Report of American Experience with Suspension Type Preheater," *Pit and Quarry*, Vol. 47, No. 1:88–90 (July 1954).

[8] H. H. Hughes and B. W. Bagley, *Minerals Yearbook 1934* (Washington, 1934), pp. 785–786.

created formal restrictions to entry. As to the effect which certain commercial developments, namely the full-flowered basing-point system and the creation of diversified chain mill companies, may have had in conditioning entrance of new mills in the period since 1932, we withhold judgment in this chapter.

As already described, the technology of cement manufacture is relatively simple. There appears to have been no significant pre-emption of know-how by a few; and projected new firms have always been free to bid for experienced production men from existing American and European cement firms. Many manufacturers of specialized cement machinery have also served as plant designers. Moreover, process patents have never blocked significantly the entrance of newcomers. No strategically important innovations were introduced during the twentieth century, and most of the mechanical elaborations were developed by suppliers of machinery. It is true that in 1907 a group of American cement producers who acquired the patent rights of the widely used Hurry-Seaman process for the air-blast burning of pulverized coal in cement kilns, attempted to use the patent as a licensing device to restrict further entry and to effect legalized price fixing. Membership in the Association of Licensed Cement Manufacturers was offered to all cement manufacturers who would adhere to the terms of the license agreement. However, not all producers took licenses; and in 1910 the patent pool collapsed after the patent was declared in a contested infringement suit to be invalid.[9] Access to raw materials and markets also appears to have been unrestricted. Deposits of suitable lime and clayey raw materials are widely scattered throughout the country. It has been virtually impossible for cement producers to pre-empt strategic raw materials as did the steel and aluminum industries whose superior deposits of iron ore and bauxite were highly localized. Finally, the introductory marketing by a new producer of a relatively standardized article such as cement could be easily accomplished by a slight price concession. Hence significant cost

[9] Information concerning entry conditions and economies of scale during the first decade of the twentieth century is based upon U.S. Geological Survey, *Mineral Resources of the United States* (Washington, 1900–1911) and Lesley, *supra*, fn. 4.

disadvantages would not restrict the entry of a firm which could achieve compensating economies of scale.

The speculative boom in entry of new firms which characterized the first decade of the century demonstrates that economies of scale alone could have made entrance only moderately difficult during the period. It is not known how many companies owned the 50 mills which operated in 1900, but by 1905 the eighty-seven plants in operation were owned by 78 companies.[10] It was estimated in 1906 that a 500,000 barrel-per-year plant, costing approximately $550,000, would be necessary to achieve economies of scale.[11] Mills of this size produced slightly more than 1 per cent of the total United States output in 1906, and somewhat less than 2½ per cent of that in the Lehigh Valley area where twenty mills were located. In other sections of the country, where productive capacity and market demand were lower, a 500,000 barrel mill would have represented a much larger proportion of regional capacity, but the prospective addition to total supply would scarcely consitute a major barrier to entry. Moreover, promoters appeared to have little difficulty in floating stock for the construction of mills of new companies. In fact, most discussion during the period was concerned with the excessive expansion of mill capacity, as 111 mills were in operation by 1910.[12]

Although the industry's productive capacity increased by about 50 per cent during the second decade of the century, most of the expansion resulted from mechanization and the installation of larger sized equipment at existing mills. Between 1910 and 1920 there was a net addition of only six new mills.

It was during the twenties that a new wave of mill construction and entry broke upon the industry. Capacity was virtually doubled as fifty-one new mills were constructed and thirty new companies entered the industry. The newly con-

[10] U.S. Geological Survey, *Mineral Resources of the United States 1905* (Washington, 1906), p. 923.

[11] U.S. Geological Survey, *Mineral Resources of the United States 1906* (Washington, 1907), pp. 903–904.

[12] See e.g., U.S. Geological Survey, *Mineral Resources of the United States 1910*, Part II, Nonmetals (Washington, 1911), pp. 438–441.

structed mills reflected increased economies of scale, as the size of the typical mill was found to be in the 1,000,000 barrel-per-year class, while certain mills placed in less isolated areas averaged 1,500,000 barrels. However, because of the growth of the industry's capacity, even a mill capable of producing 1,500,000 barrels annually represented appreciably less than 1 per cent of total capacity in 1925 and less than 0.7 per cent in 1930. A more meaningful regional picture would show that a 1,500,000 barrel-mill would represent as little as 3 per cent of the 1930 installed capacity in the Lehigh Valley and Maryland region but as much as 25 per cent of that in the Rocky Mountain producing region.[13] With construction costs amounting to about $3.00 per barrel of installed annual capacity during the twenties, a 1,500,000 barrel company could probably have been made a going concern for $5,000,000, after allowing a liberal $500,000 for working capital. Such a sum undoubtedly constituted a substantial financial outlay, but investors were optimistic during the roaring twenties. The birth of thirty additional cement firms during the period bears evidence to the fact that the problems of entry were no more than moderately difficult either for those firms in other industries which entered laterally[14] or for the many promoters who fashioned truly new firms.

All evidence concerning current economies of plant scale in the cement industry suggests that a plateau in size was attained in the late twenties, which ensuing technological developments have as yet failed to raise significantly. Most of the new mills constructed during the postwar period have been installed with annual capacities of 1,500,000 barrels or moderately less. Officers of cement companies, when questioned, have suggested that the bulk of production economies are reached in mills of 1,500,000, or at most, 2,000,000 barrels of annual capacity. The distribution of cement plants according to theoretical annual

[13] However, even the percentage figure for the Rocky Mountain region exaggerates the potential displacement problem inherent in certain regions, since the barriers of cost in such territories will frequently permit the continued profitable existence of high cost production mills, designed for only 500,000 barrels annually.

[14] E.g., Pittsburgh Plate Glass Co., Diamond Alkali Co., and Davidson Coke and Iron Co., each entered the cement industry with a new mill in an area close to the Pennsylvania-Ohio border.

capacity in 1952 (when the figure for the nation was 284,000,000 barrels) was as follows: [15]

Theoretical annual capacity (bbls.)	*Number of plants*
Less than 1,000,000	21
1,000,000 to 1,999,000	88
2,000,000 to 2,999,000	33
3,000,000 to 10,000,000	15
	157

An engineering firm, supplying cement-making equipment and machinery as well as technical advice on plant design, has written:

[The difference in] the cost of production of a barrel of cement in a plant rated 2 million barrels per year [and] unit cost in a plant with a production rating of 1½ to 2 million barrels per annum is not appreciable.

The cement plants of 1½ to 2 million capacity would not be constructed unless market conditions definitely warranted the substantial capital investment required. Plants of this size would not be built primarily for saving in cost of production.

We have made studies that show that the average capacity of the 150 odd cement plants operating in the United States have a capacity of from 1,200,000 to 1,400,000 barrels per annum. We can take this range of capacity to represent the most economic size. Cement plants of much higher rating than the range indicated generally result from expansion of the original plant for the purpose of meeting a growing demand.[16]

As of 1954, when the total capacity of all cement mills in the nation was estimated to be 290,000,000 barrels, a single 1,500,000 barrel mill would have constituted less than 0.6 per cent of national capacity. Regional cement markets are difficult to define, since their geographic extensiveness varies with the allowance made for potential freight absorption. However, arbitrarily treating as regional markets the current Bureau of Mines producing districts, the output of a 1,500,000 barrel mill would range from less than 4 per cent of the 1954 installed capacity in eastern Pennsylvania and Maryland to more than 18 per cent in Tennessee. However, if contiguous Alabama were added to Tennessee

[15] Bureau of Mines, *Minerals Yearbook, 1952,* Vol. I, p. 255.

[16] This conclusion was stated in a letter received by the writer in 1949 from the Basic Industries Department of Allis-Chalmers Manufacturing Co. The Traylor Engineering and Manufacturing Co. has written to similar effect.

such a mill could produce but slightly more than 7 per cent of the combined possible output in this area.

Further inquiries concerning capital costs for a new cement mill of 1,500,000 barrel capacity have brought fairly consistent replies from cement producers that, as of 1954, $7.00 must be invested for each barrel of annual capacity. Should $1,000,000 be required for working capital, one could estimate that today about $12,000,000 would be required to open a new enterprise in the cement industry on an efficient scale. In view of the inflation since World War II, a $12,000,000 investment would not appear a much greater barrier to entrance today than did a $5,000,000 investment in the twenties. Yet it is not easy to confirm this hypothesis by the industry's entry experience. Only three of the eighteen mills built between World War II and 1957 were constructed by firms entering the industry for the first time, and of these enterprises two represented entrants from allied industries rather than newly promoted firms.

Finally there is the matter of the potential scale economies of the multiple plant firm. Although difficult to substantiate, significant production economies seem unlikely to redound to the multiple plant firm. As previously described, the production process is relatively simple and the machinery manufacturers appear to be the principal developers and promoters of the important technical elaborations. So long as a single plant firm is able to finance the purchase of improved equipment economically, the single, local firm should be able to keep pace with its largest chain competitor in terms of production costs at similar percentages of operating capacity. Of course, marketing considerations (which have been excluded from this chapter) may favor the multiple plant cement firm cost-wise, if extensive cross-hauling and selling expenditures, incident to non-price competition, characterize the marketing process. In an investigation of economies of scale, Joe S. Bain has reported that executives in the cement industry whom he queried estimated the extent of multi-plant economies to be "small, or 2 or 3" per cent of total costs.[17] In an industry like cement with slow capital turnover,

[17] J. S. Bain, "Economies of Scale, Concentration, and the Conditions of Entry in Twenty Manufacturing Industries," AER, 44:15–39, esp. 30–31 (March 1954).

even a 2 or 3 per cent saving in total costs would be relatively minor. Moreover, since Bain's estimated multi-plant economies include distribution costs (other than sales promotion) which are affected by non-price competition, his estimates may very well be consistent with the assumed absence of production cost economies of the multi-plant firm. In any event, a financial survey comparing the rate of return of the five largest chain-mill companies with that of forty-five other cement companies (possibly as many as ten of these being multiple plant concerns) for the period 1928–37 showed the rate of return on net investment after taxes of the five largest chain companies to be 2.75 per cent as compared with 3.24 per cent for the others.[18] Moreover, a recent, but more limited, study of 1954 financial data showed no significant difference in the profit rates of multiple versus single mill cement companies.[19] Technical economies of scale, as such,

---

It might be added that the capital requirements estimated by cement executives for an efficient cement plant of 1.5 to 1.85 million barrels of annual capacity appear to be excessively high. Bain reported estimates of $20 to $25 million. *Ibid.*, p. 36.

[18] *Record*, Transcript pp. 47470–77, Survey prepared by Price, Waterhouse & Co. The modestly inferior profit record of the largest chains may possibly be attributable to the acquisition of overvalued corporate assets during the merger movement of the twenties. It may possibly also be attributable to the poorer profits (greater losses) suffered by the chains during 1929–32, when many independents were actively engaged in price competition (and presumably increased their relative share of the market).

[19] See H.R. Select Committee on Small Business, 84th Cong., 2d Sess., Report No. 2965, *The Portland Cement Industry: Supply-Demand Outlook* (Washington, 1956), pp. 36–40. The Committee reported the following rates of profits, before taxes, on sales for "ten of the smallest" and "six of the seven largest" cement companies:

Ten of the smallest	Six of the seven largest
12.7%	22.5%
22.5%	23.3%
23.4%	28.6%
27.9%	29.3%
28.6%	31.6%
28.7%	38.2%
29.0%	
33.4%	
35.5%	
39.2%	

(In 1954 there were twenty single-mill cement companies with rated annual capacities of 2 million bbls. or less. Ten of these supplied profit and sales data to the Committee. The largest cement company, U.S. Steel's Universal Atlas subsidiary, was omitted since financial data were not available on a segregated basis.

either of the plant or the company, would not appear to raise more than moderate difficulties of entry for the firm contemplating a single plant.

Locational Factors

Cement is a transportation-oriented industry because of the relatively high transfer costs entailed in the assembling of heavy and bulky raw material and the distribution of a low value finished product. Moreover, the deposits of essential raw materials are sufficiently widespread to have induced the establishment of production centers at a multitude of locations throughout the United States. Map 1 shows the distribution of cement plants in 1940 in relation to most deposits of the key raw material, chemically suitable limestone, as well as the major fuel source, coal. The savings in transport costs on this highly standardized product are sufficiently great relative to production cost economies of plant scale to create many regional cement markets. In the territory east of the Rocky Mountains, rail freight rates for shipping cement 100 miles ranged from 40 to 57 cents per barrel in the late

---

The next six largest cement chains were reported to have rated annual capacities in the 10 to 30 million bbls. range.)

To avoid disclosure of nonpublic information, the Committee did not publish the profit margins with the associated sales, profits, capacity or name of the company. The Committee provided only a summary statement for the two groups, reporting that the aggregate before taxes profits to sales was 29.3% for the "largest" group and 24.7% for the "smallest." The Committee took some cognizance of the great range in the samples of profit margins, especially for the "smallest" group, and noted that the effect of excluding the 12.7% firm was to raise to 30.5% the aggregative rate for the remaining nine "smallest." However, the Committee's staff made no statistical test of significance of the difference in the two averages.

The writer has made three statistical tests of the unweighted profit ratios, and each test failed to indicate any significant difference between the two series. The Mann-Whitney test, the test of the geometric means ("largest" g.m. = 28.5%, "smallest" g.m. = 27.1%), and the test of the medians ("largest" med. = 28.65%, "smallest" med. = 28.65%) fell very short of statistical significance at the 10% level.

The Committee also compared the ratio of profits, before taxes, to net property account for the *seven* of the "smallest" companies submitting both profit and property account data with the *same* six of the "largest." Individual profit rates were not reported, but the aggregative rates were 54% for the "smallest" and 41% for the "largest." Although the sample composition of the "smallest" group in the profits/net property account ratio differs from that in the previous profits ratio, the extent of divergence between the means of the "smallest" and "largest" undermine further any proposition that multiple-mill companies on average yield higher profit rates than single-mill companies.

1930's as compared with base mill prices ranging from $1.35 to $1.85. The following approximate rail rates prevailed in the Central Freight Association (covering western Pennsylvania, Ohio, Indiana, Michigan, and Illinois) during the same period: [20]

Distance in Miles	*Cents per Barrel*
5	28
50	34
100	40
200	53
300	65
400	76

In areas east of the Rocky Mountains mills usually shipped less than 300 miles, although there were cases where shipments exceeded 500 miles.

Since the cement industry is characterized by regional markets, let us examine the locational forces operating within such regions. During World War II Paul E. Sweeney made an excellent study of the locational forces acting upon the cement industry,[21] and his findings will be briefly summarized. For the purpose of examining conversion weight losses Sweeney used limestone (including cement rock) and coal as the representative raw material and fuel source. Employing the 1941 industry average of 643 pounds of raw material needed to produce each 376-pound barrel of cement, the ratio of raw material weight to finished cement was found to be 1.71. In plants using only coal the average weight of coal used per pound of cement was found to be 0.32 pounds. These weight ratios were virtually unchanged in 1952, raw materials having increased to 1.72 and coal having decreased to 0.30. If freight rates per ton were equal on each of these commodities, mill location would necessarily be attracted to the limestone quarry, even if the coal supply and the cement market were coterminous, since 1.71 pounds of limestone would have to move to the coal-market area, while only 1.32 pounds of coal and cement would have to move to production at the quarry site.

Although cement is a more valuable product than limestone

[20] *Record,* Respondent Exhibit 2899.

[21] P. E. Sweeney, "Economics of Cement Traffic Flow," Record Group No. 198, Board of Investigation and Research — Transportation.

and also requires more elaborate shipping equipment to prevent deterioration from the weather, rate differentials are limited because cement is more compact and more tons of it can be shipped per car than of bulky limestone rock, unless the latter is previously subjected to extensive crushing and grinding. Sweeney examined the freight rate structure in various regions of the United States and discovered that only rarely would rate differentials on cement compensate sufficiently for the high cost of moving limestone to pull plant location away from the limestone quarry.

Nevertheless, some exceptions do exist. Sweeney noted the cases of Pittsburgh and Des Moines where unusually low rail rates on limestone attracted mill location to these two coal-market centers. The case of New Orleans is somewhat similar. Not only did New Orleans constitute the focal center of a large market, but also as a port city had cheap fuel oil made available from nearby refining centers while at the same time economical assemblage of limestone was facilitated by barge shipments from deposits up an Alabama river.[22] The only other important exceptions to the locational rule occurred at certain Great Lakes ports. Giant lake carriers made economical the assembling of coal and Michigan limestone for mill production at the central market points of Manitowoc, Wisconsin and Detroit, Michigan. Other producing mills not located at limestone quarries constituted no real exception to the tendency to locate at the site of lime deposits since they are located at sources of marl, sea shells, or blast furnace slag.

The feasibility of constructing a cement mill in some portion of a regional cement market believed to be inadequately supplied usually depends upon the availability of suitable limestone. Unlike the virtually ubiquitous clayey raw material, suitable limestone deposits are highly localized within some regions although found throughout the United States. To be suitable, a limestone deposit should meet three requirements. Quarrying or mining costs should be low, the quantity of stone available should guarantee a forty to fifty year supply, and the chemical composition of the limestone must be suitable for cement. The first considera-

[22] Oliver Bowles, *The Stone Industries*, 2d ed. (New York, 1939), p. 407.

tion raises the fewest problems, while the last frequently rules out completely the use of a particular limestone deposit for the manufacture of cement. In terms of chemical characteristics, only small percentages of magnesium carbonate, free silica, alkalies, and sulphides are tolerable for cement manufacture.

When alternative suitable limestone deposits are available, the mill which can be built closest to large city markets, or which can be placed in an extensive consuming area previously supplied only by distant mills, will possess a significant transportation advantage over its rivals. Shifting locational advantages not only result from differing rates of growth of cement consumption geographically but also from the discovery of alternative calcareous deposits. For example, a subsidiary of the California Portland Cement Company opened a new mill near Tucson, Arizona, in 1949, following the discovery of suitable limestone. A tremendous transportation advantage was available to this mill in the growing Arizona market which formerly had been supplied from El Paso, Texas, and southern California. Moreover, in this case the barrier of distance from the nearest rival permitted the initial construction of only a 700,000 barrel mill.[23] Transportation advantages more than compensated for the diseconomies of small scale operation.

In addition to possible future discoveries of new resources it seems likely that technological developments will also increase the number of possible locations. For example, flotation and beneficiation, a technological development which substantially increased the supply of satisfactory limestone, were first applied in the cement industry in 1927 by the Valley Forge Cement Company at its new plant located in a suburb of the large Philadelphia market. Flotation constituted a radically new method of disintegrating raw material and separating out many of the undesirable elements, and permitted the proper mixture of the desired elements for the kiln mix. Thus, low grade cement rock could be used without the expensive importation of additional high grade limestone.[24] It was the newly found possibility of using

[23] *Rock Products* (July 1948), p. 59.

[24] N. C. Rockwood, "Chemistry Applied to Cement Manufacture," *Rock Products,* Vol. 41, No. 8:32–36 (August 1938).

low grade limestone which enabled the Valley Forge Company to establish a mill within 15 miles of the Philadelphia City Hall, giving it a substantial transportation advantage over the mills concentrated in the Lehigh Valley area, 50 or more miles away. The limited deposit of limestone at Conshohocken, Pennsylvania, deterred any significant expansion in capacity of the Valley Forge mill, and there was no possibility that the company would attempt to become the dominant supplier of the Philadelphia market. But the new mill was able to profit handsomely from its favorable location, and, as will be mentioned in a later chapter, the differential advantage of trucking cement from this mill to the Philadelphia market was in large part the cause of the breakdown of the basing-point system in the Lehigh Valley area between 1929 and 1932.

The flotation process also made possible the placing of a cement mill in the Sunnyvale Valley area of northern California by Henry J. Kaiser's Permanente Cement Company in 1940.[25] Other producers had believed it impossible to locate a mill in the area because of excessive impurities in the limestone. However, the flotation process permitted removal of an excessive amount of chert from the limestone. Incidentally, the building of this mill also permitted Kaiser to fulfill an obligation to supply a tremendous volume of cement for the Shasta Dam on which, prior to entering the cement industry, he had submitted a bid substantially below the formula-quotation of regular producers.

Market Structure

No one should be surprised to find some degree of concentration on the seller side of cement markets. Production economies of scale limit the minimum practical plant size, and appreciable transfer costs limit the feasible distance of shipment from the scattered economically-situated plants. Difficulties confront efforts to describe from empirical data relevant geographic markets in the cement industry, but the writer believes that Table 1 provides a more meaningful picture than that given in the conventional Bureau of Mines production districts. The writer selected the fifty leading metropolitan areas in the United States

[25] *Rock Products* (October 1941), p. 36.

as of 1950, and estimated the number of American companies[26] and mills, circa 1956, within the "short" and "long" range supply areas of these centers. The "short" range (established at approximately 75 or somewhat more air miles) was designed to cover the supply area within which little or no freight absorption would be necessary. The "long" range (established at approximately 275 air miles)[27] was also expected to include the supply area entailing appreciable, though not prohibitive, freight absorption relative to the gross margins (above marginal costs) which have characterized the cement industry during most of the past forty years. Given the conventional gross margins, overland shipments exceeding the designated "long" range radius will probably still yield some minor contributions to overhead. However in periods of sharp reductions in the price level relative to marginal costs, the "long" range supply area would be found far too large.

The fifty leading metropolitan areas in Table 1 included 42 per cent of the total United States population in 1950 and communities whose "long" range supply areas appear typical of the market situations for the whole country except for northern New England, the Dakotas, western Texas, and the Rocky Mountain and Southwest areas where the "long" range supply area, as defined, is likely to include three or fewer companies. On the average, each of the fifty leading metropolitan areas was supplied by 5.2 companies within "short" range and by 13.6 companies within "long" range, although the dispersion was considerable. Within the "short" range most listed metropolitan areas in Ohio and Pennsylvania, as well as New York City, Boston, Chicago, and Kansas City, were supplied by seven to fifteen companies, a figure appreciably above the average; while most listed metropolitan communities in the South (excluding Birmingham), Texas, Indiana–Kentucky, and western New York, as well as Denver, Omaha, and Portland (Oregon) were supplied by one to three companies.

26 Although two Puerto Rican producers were included in the "long" range Florida markets, neither Canadian, Mexican, nor other foreign producers were included in Table 1's supply areas. Foreign imports have been relatively small since 1907.

27 Mills located beyond the designated distances were included in the supply areas when they were believed capable of making economical shipment by water.

Table 1

Number of American Cement Mills and Companies Within Short and Long Range Supply Areas of the Fifty Leading Metropolitan Areas in the United States, Circa 1956

Standard metropolitan area	1950 Census of population (000 omitted)	"Short" range supply area [a]		"Long" range supply area [b]	
		Mills [c]	Companies [d]	Mills [c]	Companies [d]
1. New York, New York–N.E. New Jersey	12,912	26	15	40	18
2. Chicago, Illinois	5,495	9	7	29	16
3. Los Angeles, California	4,368	7	5	11	7
4. Philadelphia, Pennsylvania	3,671	20	15	41	18
5. Detroit, Michigan	3,016	10	6	32	18
6. Boston, Massachusetts	2,370	8	7	28	15
7. San Francisco–Oakland, California	2,241	5	4	6	5
8. Pittsburgh, Pennsylvania	2,213	8	8	52	27
9. St. Louis, Missouri	1,681	4	4	22	12
10. Cleveland, Ohio	1,466	13	9	31	18
11. Washington, D. C.	1,464	5	5	41	20
12. Baltimore, Maryland	1,337	6	6	40	19
13. Minneapolis–St. Paul, Minnesota	1,117	4	4	19	12
14. Buffalo, New York	1,089	2	2	51	26
15. Cincinnati, Ohio	904	7	7	41	21
16. Milwaukee, Wisconsin	871	5	5	21	13
17. Kansas City, Missouri	814	7	7	17	12
18. Houston, Texas	807	3	3	12	7
19. Providence, Rhode Island	737	5	5	28	15
20. Seattle, Washington	733	5	4	12	9
21. Portland, Oregon	705	1	1	12	8
22. New Orleans, Louisiana	685	2	2	6	5
23. Atlanta, Georgia	672	2	2	16	11
24. Dallas, Texas	615	4	3	12	6
25. Louisville, Kentucky	577	3	3	26	14
26. Denver, Colorado	564	3	2	4	3
27. Birmingham, Alabama	559	7	6	16	11
28. San Diego, California	557	7	5	11	7
29. Indianapolis, Indiana	552	3	3	30	18

30. Youngstown, Ohio	528	7	7	50	27
31. Albany–Schenectady–Troy, New York	514	7	6	30	17
32. Columbus, Ohio	503	7	7	30	19
33. San Antonio, Texas	500	2	2	11	7
34. Miami, Florida	495	2	2	7	6
35. Rochester, New York	488	3	3	50	20
36. Memphis, Tennessee	482	4	3	18	12
37. Dayton, Ohio	457	6	6	28	20
38. Norfolk–Portsmouth, Virginia	446	1	1	27	16
39. Allentown–Bethlehem–Easton, Pennsylvania	438	20	15	39	19
40. Akron, Ohio	410	6	5	29	21
41. Tampa–St. Petersburg, Florida	409	1	1	6	6
42. Springfield–Holyoke, Massachusetts	407	6	5	29	16
43. Toledo, Ohio	396	6	4	30	20
44. Wilkes-Barre–Hazleton, Pennsylvania	392	19	14	39	19
45. Omaha, Nebraska	366	1	1	15	11
46. Fort Worth, Texas	361	4	3	12	6
47. Hartford, Connecticut	358	6	5	29	16
48. Wheeling, West Virginia	354	8	8	48	28
49. Syracuse, New York	342	2	2	36	19
50. Knoxville, Tennessee	337	3	3	22	13
Total for Leading 50 Metropolitan Areas	63,768	312	258	1292	679
Unweighted average for leading 50 metropolitan areas		6.2	5.2	25.8	13.6
Median for same		5	5	28	15.5
Range for same		1–6	1–15	4–52	3–28

[a] Approximately 75 air miles from the metropolitan area. However, when the closest mill is an appreciable distance from the metropolitan market, or would be unable to meet the market's total requirements, a somewhat greater area has been used, especially in the case of mills capable of shipping economically by water. Furthermore, when a group of freight rates is known to exist (e.g., the Lehigh Valley of eastern Pennsylvania, and the Gas Belt of eastern Kansas), the entire group of mills is included in the supply area, although one or more may be beyond the designated range.

[b] Approximately 275 air miles from the metropolitan area. Mills capable of shipping economically by water on appreciably longer hauls are also included.

[c] Where a company operates two adjacent mills in a community, the production facility is treated as one mill.

[d] Includes two cement producers in Puerto Rico.

Except under conditions of a shortage in cement, the "long" range supply area is likely to be the more meaningful market for these metropolitan districts. When allowance is made for considerable freight absorption, supply areas on an average showed substantially less company concentration, although variation from the average was again considerable. On the "long" range market basis, most listed metropolitan areas in the Middle Atlantic states (including Washington, D.C.), Ohio, Indiana, and Michigan were supplied by eighteen to twenty-eight companies; those in the Pacific Coast, southeastern Coast, Texas, as well as Denver, by only three to nine companies; and those in the middle and upper South, western Middle West (plus Chicago and Milwaukee), and southern New England (plus Albany), by eleven to seventeen companies.

Of course, technological considerations alone fail to explain the relatively small number of companies found in certain metropolitan market areas. In some supply areas, the size of mills appreciably exceeds the minimum necessary to achieve substantial economies of scale of production. A significant public policy consideration, however, is the extent to which multiple mill companies operate within given supply areas. Looking at the number of mills serving each area, as shown in Table 1, we find a mean of 6.2 mills as against 5.2 companies within the "short" range supply areas and 25.8 mills as against 13.6 companies within the "long" range supply areas. The presence of multiple mill operations does not significantly reduce the number of independent producing companies within "short" range in most of the listed metropolitan areas. Within the "short" range supply areas, the number of mills exceed the number of companies in only twenty-two cities, and, in twelve of these only by one mill. In twenty-eight cities there was no excess.

However, when we analyze both the absolute and relative excess of mills to companies within the "long" range supply areas of the leading fifty cities, the role played by multiple mill operations in furthering market concentration looms large. Ranking the metropolitan areas in terms of the excess number of mills over companies, the median figure was found to be ten and a half mills in absolute terms and 70 per cent relatively. There were only eleven metropolitan areas (principally in the Pacific Coast, southeast Coast, Denver, and Omaha regions) where the number of mills exceeded the number of companies by as little as four mills in absolute terms and 50 per cent relatively. By contrast, there were ten metropolitan areas (principally in the Middle Atlantic states) where the number of mills exceeded companies by as much as twenty mills in absolute terms and 90 per cent relatively.

Some of the multiple mill ownership within the "long" range market areas resulted from internal expansion. Companies installed an additional mill to serve more economically a metropolitan market within the fringe territory of an existing mill. However, mergers accounted for the largest share of the greatly increased seller concentration in the "long" range supply areas. This subject is discussed later, in Chapter IV for the period preceding 1930 and in Chapter VIII for more recent times.

It seems sufficient here to state that the concentration of sellers in the "long" range supply areas is great enough to facilitate the collusive adoption of a geographic pricing formula and of marketing practices which tend to promote adherence to it.

Turning to the purchasing side of cement markets, potential buyers of cement may be classified as follows:

A. Government

1. United States — for public works (including conservation and power projects) and military construction
2. States — for highway pavements and other public works construction
3. Counties — for highway pavements and other public works construction
4. Cities and towns — for street pavements and other public works construction

B. Commercial

1. Railroads — for roadbed groutings and bridges
2. Private waterpower and water supply projects
3. Large contractors — for contract awards on any of the above, plus construction of industrial plants, office

buildings, apartment houses, and suburban residential developments

4. Concrete products manufacturers — for blocks, pipe, prestressed units, et cetera
5. Building supply and ready-mix concrete dealers
6. Small contractors, farmers, "Do it yourself" householders

By the early thirties the cement producers had developed a distribution policy, which apparently still persists, of confining direct sales to the following:

A. Government

1. United States — all projects, except those undertaken by emergency agencies (e.g., W.P.A.) in cities and towns
2. States — projects located *outside* cities and towns
3. County — projects located *outside* cities and towns

B. Commercial

1. Railroads
2. Private water power and water supply — projects located *outside* cities and towns
3. Large contractors — contract awards on the above projects *only*
4. Concrete products manufacturers
5. Building supply and ready-mix concrete dealers

A restriction on direct sales to contractors was the key to the cement producers' distribution policy. Government sales produced little price disturbance, at least before the 1948 *Cement* decision. Although government agencies required sealed bids, the usual practice was to bid the delivered price derived by formula. Commercial sales went primarily to established dealers and to contractors. Sales to the dealer group caused little difficulty since here too the "posted" delivered price was quoted. Direct sales to contractors, however, were ticklish and made difficult adherence to the pricing formula. Because of the irregular occurrence and changing location of construction awards to the large contractors, the latter tended to shop around and bargain for secret concessions, and cement producers were often tempted to negotiate a shaded price on a single large deal.[28]

As early as 1913 cement manufacturers initiated measures to reduce direct sales to large contractors and by the early thirties had established a system of dealer protection.[29] Contractors were sold to directly only on projects located outside cities and towns, with dealer distribution margins absorbing the shocks engendered by any bargaining on cement sales in the cities.

The number and size of cement dealers in localized urban markets undoubtedly tend to vary with the size of the city or town. Manufacturers testified during the thirties that dealers characteristically handled several brands of cement; served as trading posts of delivered price quotations in their respective communities; and were rarely offered price concessions. It is possible, of course, that the recent rapid growth of ready-mix concrete sales (absorbing approximately one third of the United States cement production in 1956) has also resulted in the creation of powerful dealers [30] in major metropolitan markets. However, there are reasons to doubt if sales through large established dealers would pose as grave a threat to an orderly pricing system as do direct sales to contractors. It is true that during future periods of excess cement capacity the bigger dealers in large metropolitan markets may threaten to shift their patronage in hopes of obtaining price concessions, but it is doubtful if such threats can ever be as effective as the isolated concession to the large contractor. A cement manufacturer cannot expect to discriminate temporarily in a metropolitan market when he makes a concession to an established dealer: a price concession made to

[28] Unlike marketing to small contractors (farmers and household consumers), both the large contractor and manufacturer found it saved costs to by-pass the general building supply dealer. Moreover, the large contractor frequently found it economical to "roll his own" and thus by-pass the ready-mix concrete dealers.

[29] See Chapter IV for an extended treatment and documentation of the development of distribution policy.

[30] Economies of scale of ready-mix production are not appreciable relative to the size of major metropolitan markets, but mergers and pre-emptive acquisition of strategically located aggregate quarries have facilitated concentration in many of the local markets. However, no firm is believed to have significant geographic diversification in the ready-mix field.

one dealer is bound to persist in this community on all future sales, so long as demand is depressed. Moreover, although the annual cement requirements of a leading ready-mix producer frequently exceed the annual capacity of a single mill achieving substantial economies of scale, it is unlikely that many ready-mix concrete producers could effectively bargain for concessions by threatening to integrate backward. Not only would the ready-mix producer be reluctant to jeopardize his commercial relationships with his usual alternative sources of supply, but he would find the financing of a $12,000,000 cement mill a heavy burden. For example, only twelve of the ready-mix concrete companies are of sufficient importance to be listed in *Moody's Industrials,* and only four of these had a net worth exceeding $10,000,000 at the end of 1955.[31]

The cement industry is virtually free of vertical integration, with the exception of northern California.[32] The Permanente cement mill was constructed in 1940 when the Henry J. Kaiser Company, with an appreciable aggregates and ready-mix enterprise in the Bay Region, was low bidder on the cement requirements for the Shasta Dam. During 1956 two of the other three cement companies in northern California integrated vertically. Calaveras acquired stock control of six relatively small ready-mix and crushed stone producers in California's Central Valley,

[31] The four largest were the Maule Industries in Miami (net worth = $12.6 million), Warner in Philadelphia (net worth = $23.0 million), Materials Service in Chicago (net worth = $38.2 million), and Dravo in Pittsburgh (net worth = $39.3 million), with the bulk of the latter's assets being employed in other industries. Of course, the writer may have appreciably underestimated the number of large enterprises in the ready-mix field by employing the *Moody's* classification. Some ready-mix enterprises may be buried in the financial web of other large corporations, while more than one large ready-mix enterprise (e.g., Henry J. Kaiser Co.) may be a non-public corporation.

More recent information (*Pit and Quarry,* January 1959) discloses that the Colonial Sand and Stone Co., an aggregates and ready-mix enterprise in the New York metropolitan area, erected during 1958 a $3,500,000 cement mill at Kingston, New York. It is further reported that this mill, operated by Colonial's newly formed subsidiary, the Hudson Cement Co., may soon double its present 825,000 barrels of annual capacity.

[32] Blue Diamond, in Los Angeles, is not considered fully integrated. This ready-mix producer purchases clinker from Riverside Cement (after the greatest portion of value has been added) and grinds cement in its own grinding mill. Blue Diamond had originally established this grinding mill in the twenties to grind clinker imported from Japan.

while Santa Cruz was acquired by a San Francisco crushed stone and ready-mix producer. These latter two may well have been sports springing from a lagging response to the marketing challenge posed by Kaiser's integration.

In summary, the market structure in the typical modern cement market might best be described as having relatively few sellers with an appreciable divergence in spatial advantage. Producers sell cement directly to government buyers on a sealed bid basis; to contractors in non-urban areas on a secretly negotiated basis; or to a sheltered and probably small number of dealers in each of the separated urban markets at list prices. The existence of relatively few sellers makes feasible the attempt at effective collusion, and Chapter III explains why the quest has been so strongly motivated in the cement industry.

CHAPTER III

Nature of Costs and Demand — Consequences: A Quest for Defensive Monopoly

The Hypothesis

As we have seen, entry into the cement industry has been free from traditional forms of institutional restrictions. And at least during the first three decades of the twentieth century, plant scale economies in terms of market displacement and capital requirements made entry only moderately difficult. Entry, both potential and actual, checked the prospects and realization of super-monopoly rates of return by mills already in the industry. However, lively expectations of an ever-growing demand and a "highly satisfactory" rate of return engendered an optimism which characteristically resulted in an expansion of capacity faster than full production could be absorbed — at least at prices which would yield the hoped-for rate of return. Formal estimates of capacity in the entire industry made only since 1909 are given in Table 6. These global estimates, moreover, conceal regional changes in relative capacity resulting from shifts in the locational pattern of demand, both temporary and more persistent. However, government reports refer to the development of excess capacity along with the quadrupling of production during the first five years of the twentieth century and a further doubling during the next five.[1] Save for the decade following World War

[1] See U.S. Geological Survey, *Mineral Resources of the United States, 1906* (Washington, 1907), pp. 902–905. In this portion of the chapter on "Cement," Edwin C. Eckel wrote, "As already stated, there is nothing in existence at present even remotely approaching a cement trust. The trouble is in the other direction. The prosperity of the last few years, with reports of enormous profits earned by existing companies, has led to the building of many new cement plants. A fair proportion of these are either too small, badly located, faulty in design, or badly managed; and with the first general business depression and the commencement of falling prices such plants will necessarily become a danger to the entire industry. The condition at present is therefore marked by excess rather than lack of competition."

II, the middle twenties, and a few scattered years preceding World War I, the industry was characterized by considerable structural excess capacity. Competitive pressures of this excess capacity threatened to reduce the level of profit and so to encourage cooperative activity which would stabilize prices by regulating trade practices.

However, the very nature of demand and cost relationships impinging upon the industry may have created incentives to restrain independent action that were far more powerful. The demand and cost functions for cement may have been such that unchecked competitive behavior would from time to time have subjected the industry to severe losses of uncertain duration. Not only may the short period total demand for cement have been inelastic, but, more importantly, the demand may also have been subject to recurring declines. Downward shifts in cement demand, sometimes severe, may have occasionally left the industry stranded with extensive cyclical surplus capacity despite the general upward trend of cement production and shipments during the past half century. If recurring declines in an inelastic demand were added to existing structural excess capacity, general as well as regional, producers might find that the accentuated surplus capacity could be fully utilized only by quoting prices well below "fair" figures.

Moreover, if overhead costs had constituted a very large proportion of total costs at designed capacity rates of operation, the bottom limit of potential price reductions might have appeared disastrously low. The predicament would be aggravated if the technological process resulted in approximately constant marginal costs at most output levels below peak capacity. Within a considerable range of contraction, reductions in output from peak levels would fail to maintain the possibility that marginal costs would exceed average operating expenditures (variable and overhead cash outlays). Producers might fear that a slight disturbance of the price level could lead to a sequence of price cutting down to (or close to) the limit of marginal costs. Such a price level would preclude not only any return for depreciation and implicit interest but also, as we have seen, any return to cover operating overhead, thus producing a cash drain.[2]

[2] See J. M. Clark, "Toward a Concept," AER, 30:241–256 (June 1940).

Under such circumstances, fear of loss of control or bankruptcy would probably loom large on the horizon for managements of the less liquid firms. The desire to minimize loss and to assure managerial or ownership survival would probably be a far stronger incentive for setting up a collective development of orderly marketing practices than that of merely preserving profits at a "satisfactory" level.

Of course the presence of relatively few sellers would have eased the development of defensive monopoly schemes to guard against recurrent losses. However, if such schemes were in use it would require more then fewness of sellers to explain the stalemate and inertia in the industry's price structure. Were overhead costs to constitute a relatively small proportion of total costs, the reluctance to reduce prices, either openly or secretly, would be far less.[3] The expected immediate gain from the capture of major sales contracts would appear more enticing if at the same time the extent of potential future loss could be appreciably reduced. Moreover, were overhead costs relatively small, a period of operations at reduced prices and sustained losses would more readily lead marginal firms, or firms less optimistic as to the future's outlook for demand, to discontinue production either temporarily or permanently.[4] Even if the exit of rivals were only temporary, the firms continuing production would operate at least with larger shares of the market during the period of reduced prices. Should the exit prove permanent, the remaining firms would benefit also from the higher prices which would follow when demand revived. If the more efficient firms believed that their marginal costs were considerably below those of their rivals, while overhead costs were modest, reluctance to reduce prices would be substantially lessened.

In short, technological conditions of high overhead costs in an industry with unstable demand and few sellers will promote

[3] See C. R. Daugherty et al., *The Economies of the Iron and Steel Industry* (New York, 1937), p. 1098 and A. C. Neal, *Industrial Concentration and Price Flexibility* (Washington, 1942) for contrasting views of the significance of overhead costs in affecting price policies.

[4] For example, the flour milling industry where overhead costs form a small proportion of total costs, contains "many submarginal mills which can operate only during very prosperous periods," E. B. Alderfer and H. E. Michl, *Economics of American Industry*, 2d ed. (New York, 1950), p. 519.

fraternal attitudes and cautious behavior in the price arena. However, it should not be construed that this situation makes unnecessary the development of subtle collusive practices to convert the mere recognition and fear of potential rival reactions into the price stalemate characteristic of the basing-point system. Nor should the fact that the business cycle magnifies the amplitude and duration of price instability necessarily condone price rigidity. Perhaps here the following proposition will suffice: To the extent that the national policy of counter-cyclical or counter-secular monetary expansion and public spending is penurious or hesitant in providing at least *relative* stability of demand, the threat of extremely low prices can be expected to lead industry members toward collective action to maintain stable prices.[5] Fear of huge losses and of bankruptcy will induce individual members in high overhead cost industries to try to eliminate the temptation of sporadic price cutting, whether open or secret. Collusive group action to achieve certainty of defensive monopoly will thus be encouraged.

Cost Conditions

Let us examine the nature of costs confronting the cement industry. Available data are extremely meager, and suggest only the general nature of cost conditions; they do not demonstrate the firm and inter-firm cost relationships. Professors Arthur R. Burns and John M. Clark probably had at their disposal more concrete data on accounting costs in the cement industry than any other economists outside the industry, since as consultants for the Cement Institute between 1934 and 1937 they studied and evaluated the marketing practices of the cement industry. But neither their study nor their findings have been released.[6] However, in an article published in 1938 Professor Clark made

[5] See K. E. Boulding, "In Defense of Monopoly," QJE, 59:524–542 (August, 1945).

[6] See *Brief for Respondent*, App. A, Vol. III, pp. 2056–2098, *FTC* v. *Cement Institute*, 333 U.S. 683 (1948) for a description of the Cement Institute's efforts to have an independent evaluation of basing-point pricing in the cement industry. From the listing of the twelve chapter titles, it appears that the completed study, "The Basing Point System in the Cement Industry 1925–1934," constituted a comprehensive economic study of the industry. Efforts to obtain a copy of the report have been unsuccessful.

the statement, presumably based on his investigation, that marginal costs at a "reasonable average level of capacity" are about one-half of average full costs including a moderate return on investment.[7] Unfortunately, there was no explanation of the methods employed in estimating marginal costs and no explicit definition of "moderate return on investment," nor most importantly, of a "reasonable level of capacity."

There does exist superficial confirmation of the thesis that unit capital costs are relatively greater in the manufacture of cement than in most other industries. Sample data collected by Ralph C. Epstein show that capital turnover (the ratio of sales to net worth) averaged only 0.66 in the cement industry between 1919 and 1928, with that industry ranking fifth from the bottom among some seventy-three industries in capital turnover.[8] That marginal costs were a small proportion of total costs is partially suggested by the experience of the Hercules Cement Corporation. During the middle thirties this firm shipped several hundred thousand barrels of cement annually for the account of another Lehigh Valley company which had discontinued the manufacture of its own cement, transferring the cement at prices ranging from 65¢ to 80¢ per barrel while the Lehigh Valley base price ranged from $1.50 to $1.65.[9] Shipments to Hercules' own accounts, however, averaged less than 44 per cent of its practical capacity.[10] This was a typical operating capacity for the region and reflected the structural excess capacity as well as cyclical unutilized capacity of the industry. As will be discussed in Chapter VI, 91 per cent utilization of the industry's practical capacity in 1926 would have taken care of the peak year production in 1928, yet in 1930 practical capacity had risen to 25 per cent above

[7] Clark, "Basing Point," *Canadian Journal of Economics and Political Science*, 4:478 (November 1938). "In the case of cement, for which fairly adequate data have been analyzed, this added cost appears to be not much more than half the minimum necessary long-run supply price (including a moderate return on investment) for a plant working at a reasonable average percentage of capacity in an industry of very highly fluctuating demand. To take purely illustrative figures, if the minimum supply price under average conditions of operation were $1.50 per barrel, the marginal cost would not be more than 80 cents and possibly less."

[8] R. C. Epstein, *Industrial Profits in the United States* (New York, 1934), pp. 121–123.

[9] *Record*, Transcript p. 26272, Respondent Exhibit 2487.

[10] *Ibid.*, Commission Exhibit 3203–A, 3205–A.

the 1926 level. To what extent, if any, the large structural excess capacity of the cement industry due to overbuilding in the latter 1920's was discounted by Professor Clark to arrive at a legitimate overhead burden is not known. But even if one were adequately to discount overhead to allow for overbuilding, the question of "reasonable average percentage of capacity" operation remains a troublesome concept. For if one assumes constant marginal cost, as does Clark,[11] average total costs at 80 per cent of practical capacity will be greatly reduced when compared with that of 50 or 30 per cent. The more significant relationship is that of the proportion of marginal costs to total costs — assuming little or no structural excess capacity — at various levels of operation.

The author, unfortunately, has been unable to obtain convincing information on which to build such a concept. But he does offer some crude economic data which, while confirming the relatively great burden of overhead in the cement industry, suggest that marginal costs may have been at least appreciably more than half of the necessary full costs at reasonably average levels of capacity. In 1940 the editor of an industry trade journal published the results of a cost study covering the period 1925–38.[12] He had undertaken this study with the assistance of cement manufacturers who represented one-third to one-half of the nation's capacity. Cost data supplied by the companies were averaged for the whole industry and each cost element was presented as a percentage of unit costs exclusive of either contractural or imputed interest.[13] Although we have no method of ascertaining the direction or extent of bias in the sample, the editor believed his averages to be representative of the entire industry. The following cost categories were presented: (1) labor costs; (2) nonlabor manufacturing costs (raw materials, fuel, power, operating and repair materials); (3) selling cost; (4) overhead including depreciation, depletion, and administration; (5) tax costs, na-

[11] Clark, "Basing Point," *Canadian Journal of Economics and Political Science,* 4:478 (November 1938).

[12] N. C. Rockwood, "Elements of Cost in a Barrel of Portland Cement," *Rock Products,* Vol. 43, No. 1:20–21 (January 1940).

[13] The current editor (1957) of *Rock Products,* B. Nordberg, in a letter to the author dated August 2, 1955, transmitted a message from Nathan C. Rockwood stating that the overhead element in costs was exclusive of "any profit or interest money."

tional, state, and local. Table 2 presents the editor's findings plus the writer's estimate of the corresponding percentage of practical capacity operated in each of the years 1925–38.

Table 2

Elements of Cost as Percentages of Total Cost (Exclusive of Financial Return on Investment) and Percentage of Practical Capacity Operated in the Cement Industry, 1925–1938

Year	Labor %	Non-labor manufacturing %	Selling %	Overhead %	Taxes %	Total %	Labor plus non-labor manufacturing %	Percentage of practical capacity operated %
1925	29	45	9	13	4	100	74	92.8
1926	28	43	11	14	4	100	71	84.9
1927	27	44	12	14	3	100	71	84.7
1928	26	42	13	15	4	100	68	80.4
1929	25	41	14	17	3	100	66	73.2
1930	27	37	15	18	3	100	64	66.3
1931	26	36	16	20	2	100	62	51.3
1932	21	32	18	25	4	100	53	31.4
1933	22	29	17	27	5	100	51	26.3
1934	26	32	16	22	4	100	58	32.9
1935	26	32	18	21	3	100	58	32.5
1936	25	35	15	19	6	100	60	49.0
1937	28	35	14	18	5	100	63	50.6
1938	27	34	15	19	5	100	61	45.8

Source: Nathan C. Rockwood, "Elements of Cost in a Barrel of Portland Cement," *Rock Products,* Vol. 43, No. 1:20–21 (January 1940); and Table 6 of this volume.

Even if we accept labor and non-labor manufacturing costs as constituting a reasonable approximation of both average variable and marginal costs, the breakdown provided by the trade journal study does not offer for our purposes a fully satisfactory estimate of variable costs as a share of the total, exclusive of return on investment. In a cement plant there is a large element of overhead supervisory and skilled production labor employed in the highly mechanized kiln and grinding operation, and this particular segment of factory labor does not differ much with variations in the rate of yearly output.[14] Yet offsetting somewhat this classification error is the portion of selling and admin-

[14] See B. H. Topkis, "Labor Requirements in Cement Production," *Monthly Labor Review,* 42:576–577 (March 1936).

istrative expenditures which does increase with volume, and the particular share of use depreciation (not compensated for by maintenance expenditures) which might technically be some function of the rate of operations during the year. But, on the whole, manufacturing costs ("labor" plus "non-labor") can probably be accepted as approximating the changing proportion of variable to total costs at different levels of practical capacity utilization.[15] Of course the underlying accounting data also reflected varying relationships resulting from changes in factor prices and technology.

Table 3 attempts to re-define the percentage cost elements as shown in Table 2 in terms of full unit costs, inclusive of a "moderate return" on invested capital. In an industry in which the capital turnover is relatively slow, an appreciable profit margin must be built into full unit costs in order to yield a moderate return on investment, arbitrarily established by the writer at 5 per cent. And perforce the percentage profit margin must rise significantly at rates of operation substantially below practical capacity. As explained in the footnote to Table 3, a series of simplifying assumptions necessarily had to be made in order to express the cost elements as a percentage of full costs per barrel at specified rates of practical capacity utilization.

From a free-hand interpolation in a scatter diagram, which related the percentages of average variable costs (labor plus non-labor manufacturing) in full costs to the corresponding percentages of practical capacity operated in the cement industry, the following estimates were drawn for the period 1925–38:

Practical capacity utilized	*Average variable costs as percentages of average full costs*
90%	66.5%
80%	62.0%
70%	58.5%
60%	56.0%
50%	54.0%

15 Practical capacity, for reasons to be explained in Chapter V, has been defined by the writer as 90 per cent of theoretical capacity as published by the Bureau of Mines. Table 6, pp. 168–69, for each year since 1909 shows theoretical capacity, practical capacity, production, and percentage of practical capacity operated in the United States.

Table 3

Estimated Elements of Cost as Percentages of Full Cost (Inclusive of a 5% Return on Total Investment [a]) and Percentage of Practical Capacity Operated in the Cement Industry, 1925–1938

Year	Labor	Non-labor manu-facturing	Selling	Overhead	Taxes	5% rate of return	Total	Labor plus non-labor manufacturing	Percentage of capacity operated
	%	%	%	%	%	%	%	%	%
1925	26	41	8	12	4	9	100	67	92.8
1926	25	39	10	13	4	9	100	64	84.9
1927	24	40	11	13	3	9	100	64	84.7
1928	23	38	12	13	4	10	100	61	80.4
1929	22	37	12	15	3	11	100	59	73.2
1930	24	32	13	16	3	12	100	56	66.3
1931	23	31	14	17	2	13	100	54	51.3
1932	17	27	15	21	3	17	100	44	31.4
1933	18	24	14	22	4	18	100	42	26.3
1934	22	27	14	19	3	15	100	49	32.9
1935	22	28	15	18	3	14	100	50	32.5
1936	22	30	13	17	5	13	100	52	49.0
1937	25	31	12	16	4	12	100	56	50.6
1938	23	30	13	17	4	13	100	53	45.8

[a] The 21 portland cement manufacturers in Epstein's sample possessed in 1928 a total investment (stockholders' equity plus funded debt) of $245,660,000. Investors' income (after-taxes net income plus estimated contractual interest) amounted to $26,030,000 in 1928, or approximately 11% on total investment. Total sales of these 21 firms for the same year were $119,000,000. Thus, net income (after taxes) plus estimated interest constituted about 22% of total sales. Disregarding the impact of changing net income upon taxes, an investment return of approximately 10% of total sales in 1928 would have yielded a 5% return on total investment. Assuming the percentage cost elements in Table 2 to be reasonably representative for the entire cement industry, each element of cost for 1928 would have approximated 90% of total full costs (inclusive of a return to capital yielding 5% on total investment). The investment return margin on total full costs for other years was estimated by varying the 10% 1928 margin in proportion to the variation of each year's overhead margin relative to the 1928 overhead margin as expressed in Table 2. In turn, every percentage cost element shown in Table 2 has been appropriately reduced to express its proportion of full cost for the year. In computing these estimates no allowance has been made for the fact that investment per barrel of annual capacity remaining in the industry probably declined during the decade of the 1930's, since it is unlikely that replacement capital expenditures offset the real (or accounting) depreciation which took place cumulatively. Therefore, some overstatement of the investment return margin (and full cost) probably exists for the decade of the 1930's, with the inevitable consequence that other cost elements expressed as a percentage of full costs are somewhat understated.

Source: Table 2 and R. C. Epstein, *Industrial Profits in the United States,* Appendix B, Table 6, pp. 617–633.

From these relationships the writer offers some suggestions as to what may have constituted the proportion of variable to full costs at alternative "reasonable average levels" of practical capacity utilization. In terms of the industry's experience during the twenty-year period 1920–39, the actual unweighted average annual level of practical capacity utilized amounted to 64 per cent. At this level, variable costs may have constituted at best 57 per cent of full costs, no allowance being made for the considerable structural excess capacity which developed after 1926. By recomputing for subsequent years what practical capacity would have been utilized had there been no structural increase beyond the 1926 figure,[16] the average annual level of practical capacity would have risen to 70.5 per cent during the twenty-year period, with average variable costs constituting at best 58.5 per cent of full costs. And of course, had a more vigorous government counter-cyclical fiscal policy been employed to moderate declines significantly, average variable costs would have constituted an even higher percentage. For example, even if a cement industry without structural excess capacity had had its demand stabilized to permit operations at only 80 per cent of practical capacity, variable costs would have approximated about 62 per cent of full costs. Finally, had greater price competition been induced in the industry, selling costs might have been substantially reduced (as will be discussed in Chapter VI). Even at 80 per cent of practical capacity, selling costs constituted about 11 per cent of estimated full costs. Since under effectively competitive conditions the selling costs of a standardized producers' good would scarcely constitute more than a small fraction of long run supply price, a reduction of the proportion of selling costs by about six points would have raised average variable costs to approximately 66 per cent of full costs with operating levels at only 80 per cent of practical capacity. Although the data and assumptions employed in making these estimates are subject to serious question, there seems reason to believe that

[16] Even the 1926 level of practical capacity would have permitted production during the peak output year of the interwar period (1928) at 91 per cent of practical capacity, a rate of operation significantly exceeded during 1923–24 and substantially exceeded between 1951 and 1954.

Professor Clark's estimate concerning the proportion of marginal cost to long run supply price during the interwar period was unduly low.

Nevertheless, the facts themselves would appear to substantiate Clark's fundamental point. Overhead costs, broadly defined, constitute a large proportion of total full costs, even at "reasonable" average levels of capacity operation. And this overhead burden may be expected to condition the attitude of industry members concerning the dangers of price competition. Yet the dangers of prolonged price competition to financial solvency in the short run would appear at least to be slightly less extreme than pictured by Professor Clark, particularly if structural excess capacity can be avoided and if cyclical declines in demand can be considerably moderated in amplitude and duration.

Turning attention to the nature of marginal costs in the cement industry, it should be remembered that Clark believed them to be constant up to full capacity. There are no modern statistical studies of cost functions in the cement industry,[17] yet the nature of the mill's technology, depending as it does on full and continuous kiln operation, suggests that the comparative lack of "adaptability" of the kiln with labor would lead to relatively constant marginal costs with respect to annual rates of operation. Nevertheless, output can probably be increased beyond the engineered, or designed, level of capacity. At times of abnormally high demand, greater output can be gained by sacrificing fuel efficiency.[18] And to supply the larger amounts of limestone needed to meet these abnormal demands, either the firm's quarrying operations must be enlarged by hiring additional labor with some attendant diminishing returns, or overtime wages must be paid. Moreover, attempts to meet abnormal demand by forced-draft rates of kiln operation and/or by continuing uninterrupted production without normal shutdowns for maintenance result in

[17] K. Ehrke, *Die Uebererzeugung in der Zementindustrie von 1858–1913* (Jena, 1933), covers a period prior to the development of the modern long rotary kilns, conveyor systems, etc.

[18] J. C. Buckbee, "Volume Delusion in the Cement Industry," *Rock Products,* Vol. 35, No. 9:30–32 (May 7, 1932); B. Nordberg, "Operates Kiln for Best Efficiency Rather than Overcapacity," *Rock Products,* Vol. 47, No. 1:70 (July 1954).

higher cost repair and replacements at a later date.[19] The production official of one of the nation's largest cement chains told the writer that possibilities exist for increasing output beyond the designed capacity, but that his firm determines on a minimum operating cost rate for each kiln and maintains that rate as long as the kiln is operated. Uncertainties as to the potential fuel diseconomies and potential increases in maintenance costs explain the adoption of the standard operations policy, although some additional profit *may* admittedly have to be given up as a consequence. But to the extent that other firms expand output at increased average variable costs during periods of peak demand, there exists some element of flexibility in cement output beyond designed capacity, an additional output which otherwise would be possible only through the installation of additional kilns or new mills.

It seems safe to assume, however, that with the possible exception of periods of peak capacity operation, marginal costs are approximately constant during wide variations in a kiln's annual rate of operation. In fact, most reductions in output are accomplished by shutting down the kiln for a few weeks or months; and average variable costs remain constant. Therefore, if a reduction in price accompanies declines in demand, no easing of the squeeze on gross overhead margins will result from smaller output of a single-kiln plant. Some lessening in average variable costs within the typical cement mill there still may be, since most mills operate with two or more kilns. If one of the kilns is older, shorter, and generally less efficient, as is frequently the case, the more obsolete or depreciated kiln will be the first to be closed down when output is reduced because of decreased demand. In such mills, marginal costs, to some unknown degree, decrease discontinuously at annual output levels appreciably below design capacity. There is no information available to show the differential kiln efficiency within a mill, however, so we shall continue to assume, along with Clark, that marginal costs within

19 See B. Nordberg, "Producers Forecast Capacity Production in 1949," *Rock Products*, Vol. 52, No. 1:76 (January 1949). Nordberg reports a very large "eastern manufacturer" as having written, "A number of high-cost operations will remain in service only while the demand for cement is so great, but will be abandoned when it falls off."

a mill are approximately constant at annual operating rates below designed volume.

Unless there are a number of marginal mills, declines in price toward marginal cost, following a lessening of demand, would be extremely painful and financially disastrous to all firms in the industry. The losses from such low prices, simulating purely competitive market behavior, would *continue* until either demand revived or operating capacity contracted. However, if there are several marginal mills, and if the decline in demand is not severe, the pressure of continued losses need not be intolerable. In the first place, even purely competitive prices would not decline to the minimum marginal cost level of those mills technically most efficient and economically best located. In the second place, the pressure of prices which fail to cover the operating overhead (as distinct from mere financial overhead) of the less efficient mills will encourage at least their temporary exit from the industry. Whether or not the more marginal mills discontinue operations will depend on the management expectations concerning both the length of time before demand revives and the probable extent of revival.

Mills which discontinue as operating units may *permanently* remove their productive capacity from a region for whatever return can be obtained. They may use their strategic personnel and their plant in other lines of production, although this is not a promising possibility considering the relatively specialized character of cement producing equipment. They may sell their productive facilities to firms in other regions or countries. In the case of chain companies they may transfer usable equipment to sister mills. Lastly, they may sell their equipment to second-hand dealers. Alternatively, the mills may discontinue as active producers *temporarily* by dismissing all personnel, save those needed to maintain the plant in satisfactory repair, if management expects an adequate revival of business in a reasonable number of years. Temporary exit will be deemed economically preferable to continued operation, if the out-of-pocket losses of sustaining operations as compared to those of a shutdown are likely to be greater than the costs involved in building up later a new administrative, technical, and skilled worker organization and customer good will.

Has there been a significant number of marginal mills in the cement industry? To answer this question for an industry where locational factors are important, one ought to be able to examine the spreads between average mill price and average variable cost among mills located in the same region. Such data, unfortunately, are not available. But there do exist economic date which suggest that considerable variation in unit production costs (exclusive of selling costs) prevailed during the year 1929.[20] For the twenty mills of the Lehigh Valley territory, such costs ranged from $.88 to $1.50 per barrel, with costs of the ten plants in the middle of the array ranging from $1.00 to $1.24. The range in the ten plants in the southeastern section of the United States was only from $1.14 to $1.65, although the spread between the middle four mills, $1.17 to $1.41, was close to the Valley differential. For the twenty mills in the Lake states the range was somewhat greater, extending from $.96 to $1.68 per barrel, although the spread between the ten plants in the middle of the array, $1.15 to $1.37, was slightly less than in the Valley. In the case of these latter mills, some crude estimates of diversity in over-all economic effectiveness are possible, including the influence of location as partially reflected by the average mill net realized. When the twenty Lake states mills were arrayed in terms of the average margin realized (between unit production costs and average mill net realized), the range in unit margin varied from minus 15¢ to 64¢ per barrel, while that for the ten plants in the middle of the array ranged from 13¢ to 33¢ per barrel. The data presented for the various regions are, of course, merely suggestive, and the differences shown in unit production costs per barrel are influenced by variations in the rates of utilized capacity, although the distortion caused by diverse rates of overhead is somewhat reduced by the omission of selling expenses. To be sure, the variability in unit production costs (or unit margins for that matter) is probably greater between firms in any single year than would be the

[20] T.N.E.C. Monograph No. 13, "Relative Efficiency of Large, Medium-Sized, and Small Business" (Washington, 1941), pp. 24–25.

case over two or more years. Moreover, it is possible that disparities in mill efficiency were unusually great in 1929.

In spite of all of these qualifications, the spread in unit costs or margins of mills in selected regions appears to be great enough to suggest that if declines in demand are not paralyzingly large, a period of low prices may well induce some marginal mills to leave the cement industry within a reasonable span of time. Then the pressure of excess capacity, with its attendant huge losses, need not last overly long. Nevertheless, despite the probable presence of marginal mills which could cushion the impact of competitive prices in times of excess capacity, the nature of the cost structure in the industry indicates that uncontrolled price competition might still be quite severe. And given a powerful predisposition to avoid the threat of any short-run losses, even though profits in the preceding boom have been extensive and the liquidity position carried forward substantial, firms in the cement industry may be expected to promote and maintain a system of pricing conducive to stability.

Demand Conditions

Our principal concern in this chapter with respect to demand conditions is with the aggregative demand for cement in the nation. Nevertheless, it may be desirable first to consider the nature of the demand as seen by an individual producer in a particular geographic location. In the first place, he considers the product so highly standardized that a difference in price of a few cents a barrel will command the buyer's business. Yet the product is not so standardized that the customer is necessarily indifferent to brands when prices are identical. From time to time quality rivalry has emerged when minimum engineering specifications as to fineness of grind or quality control standards have been exceeded. By the same token particular firms have managed to build up good will through service to customers, the cultivation of buyers through salesmen, and the establishment of a reputation for reliability. Under these circumstances, and in the absence of boomtime non-price rationing, new firms must frequently shade prices in order to establish themselves in a market. An established firm in turn is reluctant to surrender the markets it has built up. Given some excess capacity, or early prospects of it, the established seller is likely to meet the price competition in the natural market of the new rivals, in order to maintain his investment in customer good will and thus protect his stake in a "guaranteed" market. Thus freight absorption and delivered prices develop. Only as the amount of freight absorption becomes excessive, will the established seller reluctantly surrender a long term customer to his rival. In turn, new producers, whose natural markets continue to be invaded via freight absorption by established mills, will invade the natural markets of other established mills in an effort to utilize their own excess capacity. Of course the new mills, lacking prestige and established customer relationships, are at a disadvantage in winning sales, and so are tempted to dump unsystematically, rather than to make capital investments in building up a market by means of salesmanship.

Second, the producer is confronted by a complex pattern of geographic destination prices because of the substantial transportation charges involved in distributing the product to buyers in many localities. Because long haul transportation charges are less than short haul rates per ton mile, reductions in delivered price can be offered for particular destinations, without giving buyers an incentive to reship the product to surrounding areas. Moreover, many rural destinations, usually with low demand for cement, will occasionally loom as temporary markets with a great demand when a new highway or a conservation project involving a dam or water supply conduit is being built. Under such circumstances the urge to grant a price reduction to the contractor is particularly strong, and it was to offset this that the common basing-point formula was designed.

Third, the density of demand is continually shifting between larger areas, such as states, both secularly and, in the short run, capriciously. Not only have the various regions of the United States developed at different rates, but the rates of growth of concomitant construction activity within regions have also differed. To counteract the consequent instability in the demand for their product, producers have sought to cultivate even wider markets. Mills located in areas where the local market has increased less rapidly than in other areas and where the former geographic natural market has shrunk because of the installation of new mills, have a special incentive to continue sales in earlier markets through the practice of freight absorption. The same incentive appears when a concentration of mills and supply develops in a particular location at a rate faster than the growth of their natural market. (Both of these phenomena occurred in the Lehigh Valley early in the twentieth century.) Freight absorption constitutes a long-run differential security advantage to mills less advantageously located than their competitors. Of course, market penetration is a two-way street, but shifts in the geographic distribution in demand relative to the location of producing units make freight absorption much more important for the mills less advantageously located.

The short-run fluctuations in geographic demand in the cement industry, conditioned as it is by the mobility of construction activity, encourage freight absorption as a flexible technique for promoting greater short-run stability in the level of sales of every firm. George J. Stigler, in an article which assumes that geographic fluctuations in demand are primarily responsible for the development of the basing-point system, has shown that between 1921 and 1940 the annual cement consumption in each of the adjoining states of Illinois, Iowa, Kansas, and Missouri was substantially more variable than the corresponding annual rate of cement production relative to the nation as a whole.[21] The geographic fluctuations in demand are also illustrated in Chart 1. This chart shows, on a logarithmic scale, cement consumption in Ohio and in the three major consuming bordering states, Pennsylvania, Michigan, and Indiana, between 1914, the initial year of published data, and 1930, prior to the precipitous decline in demand. Although the year-to-year percentage changes in consumption in Ohio compared with the average of the three major bordering states are relatively stable, seven of the sixteen (1916–

[21] G. J. Stigler, "A Theory of Delivered Price Systems," AER, 39:1154 (December 1949).

CEMENT CONSUMPTION IN OHIO COMPARED WITH CONSUMPTION IN
PENNSYLVANIA, MICHIGAN, AND INDIANA
AND AVERAGE CONSUMPTION IN THE THREE MAJOR ADJOINING STATES

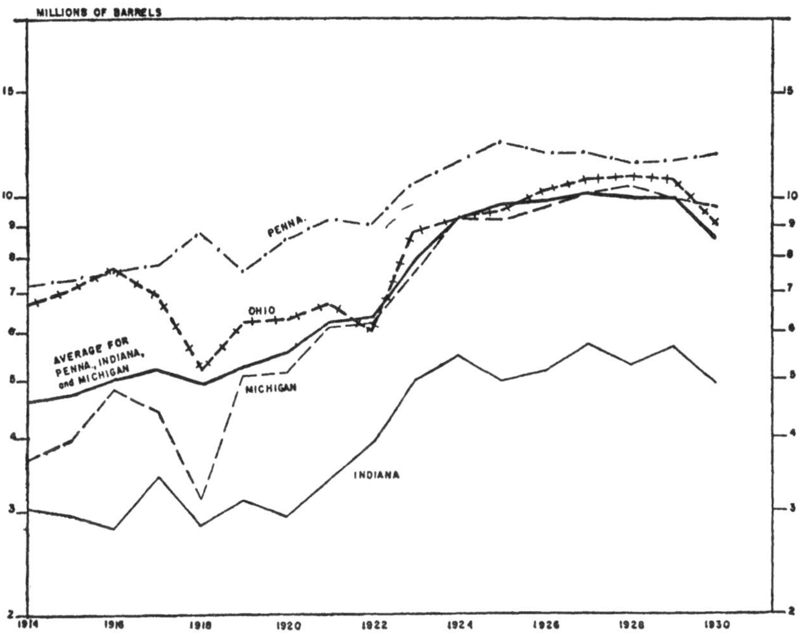

Chart 1

17, 1917–18, 1918–19, 1921–22, 1922–23, 1927–28, and 1928–29) differed by at least ten points, and the divergence in two of the year-to-year changes exceeded twenty points.

Geographic fluctuations in construction activity and cement demand are probably even greater within sections of a single state than between states. Nine executives testified during the Commission hearings as to the "indiscriminate" location of large construction projects, the testimony of John C. Bowen, vice-president of the Lehigh Cement Company being quite definite on this point:

It is also very noticeable that frequently even in small consuming areas, these areas that are ordinarily small consuming areas, the existence of a large road project, hydroelectric project, or water supply project, may, in some years, cause that very small market to use more cement than is used in the same year in the nearest metropolitan market.[22]

Whereas differential success in customer cultivation and differential disadvantage in plant location provide special inducements for some manufacturers to initiate market penetration, *all* sellers have an incentive to practice freight absorption in order to compensate for geographic fluctuations in demand. Once begun, this practice can scarcely be abandoned without complex collusive machinery involving compromises over initial market divisions and periodic revisions of territorial allotments. However, save in periods of high levels of sales relative to capacity, the very process of freight absorption, per se, may prove a very upsetting element. When unsystematically employed, it may lead to successive breaches in the geographic price structure, and these, in turn, to reductions in the industry's base price level.

The characteristics of the geographic structure of demand described above encouraged the adoption of the particular system of imperfect collusion involved in the basing-point formula. That the members of the industry felt so strongly impelled to achieve and maintain a collusive system is in large part explained by the cost structure previously discussed as well as by the aggregate demand schedule for the industry.

The short period total demand for cement has been relatively inelastic with respect to price, and, even more importantly, has shifted appreciably in response to fluctuations in business activity, especially construction activity. From time to time the upward trend in demand for cement over the past half century has been interrupted by reversals. Mild declines were experienced in 1914–15, 1921, and 1929; substantial contraction had to be faced in 1918–19 and 1943–45 because of wartime restrictions on construction activity; and, of course, there was the catastrophic shrinkage between 1930 and 1940. Unlike some other materials employed in the construction industry, cement is used almost exclusively in construction. For example, the estimated distribu-

[22] *Record*, Transcript p. 26594.

tion of cement consumption to various types of users in the United States for 1939 was as follows:[23]

	Percentage	*1000 Barrels*
Pavings: Roads, streets, airports	20	24,530
Structural: Building (including multiple buildings), bridges, railroads	30	36,796
Conservation: Reclamation, water supply, sewage	18	22,077
Housing: (1- and 2-family dwellings) and miscellaneous uses	22	26,953
Farm:	10	12,265
Total	100	122,651

The proportion of cement destined for different types of construction purposes varies over time. Paving, which had absorbed 35 per cent of cement shipments in 1928, took as little as 15 per cent in 1951. The highly variable construction expenditures have been reflected quite directly in the derived demand for cement. The Bureau of Mines found a fairly close relationship between the time series of cement consumption and of construction awards between 1928 and 1940 for the whole United States as well as for most regions.[24] A much more sophisticated technique for estimating the demand for cement from construction expenditures has been presented recently by Nathan H. Schein of the Department of Commerce.[25] The period covered was 1939–52 during which cement shipments varied from a low of 94.3 million barrels in 1944 to a high of 251.4 million in 1952. In order to estimate consumption (shipments) of cement in millions of barrels, x_1, Mr. Schein employed three independent variables. Total new construction expenditures in billions of constant dollars (1947–49 prices) for each year were divided into three categories: x_2, new residential buildings; x_3, new non-residential

[23] Portland Cement Association, *Cement and Concrete Reference Book, 1940* (Chicago, 1940). Based on limited available information.

[24] *Minerals Yearbook, Review of 1940* (Washington, 1941), pp. 1128–1132.

[25] N. H. Schein, "1954 Cement Demand to Set New Record," *Pit and Quarry*, Vol. 47, No. 2:77–79 (August 1954).

building; and x_4, "all other" new construction (non-building, e.g., highways, airfields, military construction, farm construction, and conservation). Having found an upward shift in cement consumption relative to total construction expenditures in the postwar period, the following separate estimating equations were derived for the two parts of the period:

For 1939–1945:

$$x_1 = 49.03058 + 1.34068x_2 + 10.92365x_3 + 4.60529x_4$$

For 1946–1952:

$$x_1 = 2.69190 + .53720x_2 + 11.18254x_3 + 159.04123 \log x_4$$

These two equations, using the three categories of deflated construction expenditures, yield very close estimates, despite their restricted statistical significance because of the limited number of observations:

	1939–1945	*1946–1952*
Standard error of estimate (after adjustment for 3 degrees of freedom)	± 7.5 million bbls.	± 4.0 million bbls.
Coefficient of multiple correlation	.936	.997
Maximum variation in shipments (from estimated consumption)	6.4 per cent in 1939	3.0 per cent in 1949

Given the strong relationship which exists between deflated construction expenditures and cement consumption and recalling the notorious variability in deflated construction expenditures which has characterized American economic history, at least prior to World War II, it is little wonder that cement demand has been subject to violent swings. In turn, the constant fears of precipitous declines in cement demand, even in the absence of structural excess capacity, have produced strong desires to stabilize the industry by some form of collective action.

Short period responsiveness of cement demand to changes in price is most probably inelastic, just as industry executives and their economic experts claimed during the Commission hearings. Data based on material supplied by the Bureau of Labor Statistics were introduced to show that cement rarely exceeded 10 per cent of the total costs of construction work; indeed, with the exception of massive projects such as highways and dams, it generally amounted to much less.[26] Moreover, the demand for public and for many private construction projects is probably fairly inelastic with respect to price. Political objectives of social welfare and of counter-cyclical spending programs form the primary influence in determining the volume of public projects, while expectations as to future business opportunities are mainly responsible for the volume of private construction.

Nevertheless, it is quite likely that the degree of inelasticity in the demand schedule has been exaggerated by the cement industry because it failed at times to consider adequately the possibility of substituting cement for cheaper rival products. Admittedly, lower cement prices during long depression periods would probably fail to bring even a proportionate increase in units sold, and total revenues would be decreased while total costs increased. The disposition of the cement industry during depression to refrain from *deliberate* downward price adjustments is readily explained. Yet if the cement price level were forced down *inadvertently* through competitive pressures (perhaps induced by some uncertainty), some immediate increase in volume might be expected. And some gradual, appreciable increase in sales is particularly likely to occur, if price stays down for more than a year. The full effects of substituting cement for rival construction materials by price reductions are rarely brought about at once.

Three reasons are suggested for a difference in the demand elasticity between a very short period and an intermediate period of a few years. First, there exist certain technological commitments in construction projects previously planned, specifications for material having been incorporated in the "blue prints"; and some engineers and contractors cling to customary construction methods so that time is needed to overcome friction and inertia. Second, even when the technological possibilities of substitute materials are fully recognized, time is sometimes required to shift complementary construction equipment in order to take advantage of the relative decline in price of the substitute material. Third, even if the above conditions do not exist, additional time is often necessary to re-evaluate the economic alternatives in terms

26 *Record,* Transcript pp. 47523, 47528–34, Respondent Exhibit 3663–70.

of multi-dimensional end-product differences. Using a different production material will often result in an end-product which varies from the more conventional finished product in terms of initial cost, durability, functionalism, and attractiveness. In the case of cement, this involves the merits of concrete roads compared with those of high quality asphalt; house walls made of concrete block, with those of brick, lumber, or stone; and reinforced concrete office buildings, apartment houses, or factories, with those made of structural steel. The comparison of qualitative differences in the end-product which will follow changes in relative prices, entails new policy judgments on the part of business or public officials, and considerable time may elapse before changes in decisions are forthcoming.

The importance of substitution possibilities for these intermediate periods is difficult to ascertain. But the relative growth of high-type asphalt road surfacing during the 1930's and early 1940's suggests that the relative price movements of the major raw material in each type of surface were not unimportant.[27] High-type asphalt is the major rival of concrete in surfacing arterial highways designed for heavy-duty traffic.[28] The finished concrete road need not be priced as low as its high-type asphalt competitor, since the greater durability and lower maintenance cost of concrete (plus qualitative advantages in skid resistance and nocturnal visibility) will compensate for somewhat greater initial costs. The key raw materials for these two substitute highway surfaces are, of course, portland cement and petroleum asphalt, the latter a refinery by-product. The annual shrinkage in concrete surfacing relative to high-type asphalt after 1932, as shown in Table 4, undoubtedly reflects, at least in part,[29] the

[27] The relative expansion of high-type asphalt surfacing at the expense of concrete has also been emphasized in a financial study by E. W. Axe & Co., *Cement Company Common Stocks in 1947* (New York, 1947), pp. 7–10.

[28] In contrast to high-type, low-type asphalt roads are light-duty surfaces for rural and less industrialized areas. The annual surfacing of the low-type road experienced a fantastic expansion during the thirties, rising to well above ten times the 1928 rate in most years. But because of their markedly different function and initial cost, low-type asphalt roads do not constitute a significant substitute for concrete.

[29] Various non-price reasons have been suggested to the author to explain the substitution of high-type bituminous surfaces for concrete during the 1930's. An official of a large ready-mix concrete firm in Philadelphia stated that the petroleum

effect of increases in base mill cement prices during 1932 and 1933, increases in spite of the existence of tremendous excess capacity. By 1934 the average mill price had practically reached the 1928 level, the peak year of cement production, and cement prices persisted close to that level for the remainder of the thirties and early forties. By comparison, prices of petroleum asphalt seem to have behaved quite competitively; at least they exhibited a flexibility which might *prima facie* be expected of workable competition in the marketing of a highly standardized producers good. Annual mileage of surfacing made of high-type asphalt remained fairly constant during the thirties, contributing to the demand for petroleum asphalt, a demand already growing because of a boom in low-type asphalt surfacing.[30] To the extent that the progressive decline in concrete road surfacing was caused by a differing relative price pattern, it can be argued that cooperative price stabilization in the portland cement industry contributed to a large expansion in the production of petroleum asphalt.

This analysis of the relative trends in consumption between cement and one of its important substitutes merely suggests the extent to which short-run defensive thinking can lead firms to overstate the degree of price inelasticity of demand for their product. More aggressive exploring of the possibilities of expanding consumption through selective price reductions might have led some firms to initiate an especially low price policy to state highway departments,[31] thereby stemming the relative encroach-

asphalt roads employed a larger proportion of visible, on-the-job labor per dollar of expenditure. He suggested that this factor, plus an allegedly more powerful petroleum industry lobby, supplied political pressure for high-type bituminous road construction during the Great Depression. And an official of the Public Roads Administration, although admitting the importance of price trends, also suggested that decreased state budgets created incentives for immediate economy in road-building, with the emphasis being placed upon reconstructing depreciated roads with a bituminous surface, widening existing roads with that same surface, and achieving low initial costs whenever extensions in arterial highways were contemplated. In economic parlance, we might say that pressures induced by the depression led highway commissions to discount the future by placing less emphasis upon durability and future savings in maintenance expense.

30 See footnote 28.

31 Special reductions in delivered prices might have been granted to those highway departments distantly located from any cement mill, since freight charges made cement use particularly expensive to such consumers. Such "purposive"

Table 4

Miles of First Class Roads Surfaced by State Highway Departments and Average Mill Prices of Petroleum Asphalt and Portland Cement, annually, 1928–1942

Year	Actual figures				Relative figures: 1928 = 100			
	Miles surfaced		Average mill price		Miles surfaced		Average mill price	
	Concrete	High-type asphalt	Portland cement per bbl.	Petroleum asphalt per ton	Concrete	High-type asphalt	Portland cement	Petroleum asphalt
1928	6055	2577	$1.57	$12.95	100	100	100	100
1929	6991	1756	1.48	11.29	116	68	94	87
1930	8651	1973	1.44	10.74	143	77	90	82
1931	9664	2688	1.11	8.66	160	104	71	67
1932	6914	2942	1.01	7.81	114	114	64	60
1933	4688	2615	1.33	9.71	77	102	85	75
1934	3681	2596	1.54	10.96	60	101	98	85
1935	2282	1456	1.51	9.98	38	68	96	77
1936	2568	2096	1.48	10.10	42	81	94	78
1937	3515	2815	1.45	10.66	58	109	92	82
1938	2929	2633	1.45	9.24	48	102	92	71
1939	2183	2577	1.47	8.47	36	100	94	65
1940	1603	3264	1.48	9.14	27	127	93	70
1941	1900	4098	1.47	9.72	31	159	94	75
1942	1160	2751	1.53	10.35	19	107	97	80

Source: U.S. Bureau of Mines, Public Roads Administration.

ment of asphalt in the heavy-duty road field. Moreover, in the absence of a basing-point *system*, competitive downward pressures on the price structure of the entire cement industry might have maintained a far larger volume of concrete road construction unintentionally, that is, from the viewpoint of cement executives.

For reasons already suggested, total cement demand may well be extremely inelastic in a static sense, and even fairly inelastic for the intermediate period of a few years. Nevertheless, there is good reason to believe that production of portland cement would have been substantially larger, and employment in the industry therefore greater, had prices remained closer to the average level of 1932, or even of 1933. No doubt substantial losses would have continued because of the relative inelasticity of demand. Yet substitution might have been expected to expand the sales of cement, and thereby reduce somewhat the magnitude of losses which the industry anticipated would accompany price competition.

Significance — The Quest for Defensive Monopoly

The significance of cost and demand functions in the portland cement industry may be summarized as follows: (1) if extremely large variations in construction activity persist, making for huge shifts in the derived demand for cement, producers operating under marginal costs both relatively constant and comparatively small in proportion to total costs, may be expected to concentrate upon the extreme price inelasticity of the short period demand schedule for the industry. (2) With price competition for the highly standardized commodity promising extreme financial losses from time to time (possibly of long duration and entailing also the loss of managerial control in many firms), and with fairly concentrated oligopolistic market structures in every regional market, the management of each firm will usually operate under powerful incentives to identify its interest with that of the whole industry. (3) However, because of the significant element of transportation costs, there exists a myriad of separated con-

price discrimination, however, in contrast to the "incidental" variety, would have been contrary to the principles of the basing-point price formula.

sumer markets with a complicated pattern of uncertain destination prices, whose very uncertainty operates ultimately to tear down the posted prices at the various mills. The willingness and desire to refrain from competitive price behavior is thwarted by an inability to cope with the complexities of geographic price differentials, at least in the absence of some common plan to put order into the structure of destination prices.

Development and refinement of the basing-point system of formula pricing constituted the collective action chosen by the cement industry. The common use of the system is best described by the euphemism "defensive monopoly" since its purpose was to systematize the process of quoting prices for a multitude of geographically dispersed destinations, so that all sellers would *know* the competition to be met and could exercise the kind of self-restraint in pricing policy posited by simple oligopoly theory. That the cement industry should have come to insist upon adopting and adhering to a system with so many arbitrary features despite prolonged and incisive criticism from academic writers and public officials alike, stems, I believe, from fear of and a determination to defend itself against recurring large losses, even though the stigma of trust or monopoly was thereby attached to the industry.

Two letters written during the middle of the Great Depression by John Treanor, a trustee of the Cement Institute and president of the Riverside Cement Company, express with great clarity and candor the view held by a cement industrialist of the basing-point system as a technique of defensive monopoly. On March 5, 1934 in a letter to Bernard Kilgore of the *Wall Street Journal*, Treanor wrote in part:

> The meaning of this [the large percentage of idle equipment in the form of standby capacity] is that the cement market is practically always a buyer's market, the potential supply practically always exceeding the demand. In these circumstances, under the theory of unrestrained competition the price is cut by one producer after another and comes to rest at some irreducible minimum. This eventual minimum resulting from competition is not of course the price which will yield a fair return upon the average investment. Competition goes further than this, wipes out all profit margin, all reserves for maintenance and depreciation, exhausts the producer's working capital and finally consumes the funds of his creditors, in so far as they fall tem-

porarily within the control of the producer struggling for survival. Receivership and bankruptcy do not end the cycle of destruction. . .

The point I would like to make is that this aspect is more constantly threatening in the cement business than in any other that I know about, owing to its standardized product, its perennial excess capacity, and to the large proportion of bookkeeping charges entering into cost. When a company is in a fight and in distress it ignores bookkeeping. The indirect capital, or bookkeeping part of cost representing the fixed capital of the industry, becomes then, in effect, a war fund, a subsidy for the injury or destruction of its competitors.

Now it is to the credit of the men responsible for the capital invested in the cement business that, in the face of the peculiar menace, they have been as successful as they have been in avoiding the extreme evils of such a system; that, foreseeing the dismal end-product of unrestrained competition, they have by forebearance and skill, consciously obtained equilibrium at something above the level of ruin, even sometimes within the zone of profit.

They have done this, where it has been done through the open price system and I beg leave to say that in such an industry as ours, it cannot be done in any other way. The open price system enables sensible men, acting within the law, to avoid ruin and sometimes to make a fair profit. Its successful operation depends upon the virtues of self-restraint, and of intelligent consideration for the needs of other competing factors in the industry. It would be a real calamity for this and for other industries, to have this reasonable system of price making misunderstood and discredited, as it is by some of the current comment.

Of course the basing-point method of fixing destination prices is a necessary complement to the open price system in the cement industry.[32]

On May 17, 1934 Treanor wrote to the chairman of the NRA Code Authority for the cement industry. A portion of one paragraph of this letter has been quoted frequently, but to emphasize the argument of this chapter, I shall quote the entire paragraph italicizing that portion of it which is usually omitted:

Do you think any of the arguments for the basing-point system, which we have thus far advanced, will arouse anything but derision in and out of the government? I have read them all recently. They amount to this however: that we price this way in order to discourage monopolistic practices and to preserve free competition, etc. This is sheer bunk and hypocrisy. The truth is of course — and there can be no serious, respectable discussion of our case unless this is acknowledged — that ours is an industry that cannot stand free competition, that must systematically restrain competition or be ruined. *We sell in a buyer's market all the time. The capital cost, as distin-*

[32] *Record,* Commission Exhibit 553–3D, 3E.

guished from the out-of-pocket cost, of producing cement is extraordinarily large. In free competition this capital cost is whittled away and this means loss and ruin.[33]

Some Perspective

Even should buyers' markets in cement develop less frequently and with less intensity in the future, it is probable that recurring competitive pressures downward on price would still be strenuously resisted by the natural *private* desire of firms in the industry to avoid *any* annual loss. Yet, both because in the "intermediate period" demand is probably only mildly inelastic because of substitution possibilities, and because marginal facilities in varying degrees of obsolescence are usually present, the pressures of large losses for the majority of firms may be only temporary, if prices actually decline toward marginal costs. Should the amplitude of cyclical declines in construction activity and the derived demand for cement come to be lessened through future monetary-fiscal policy, there is no reason to assume that the majority of firms in the cement industry will not be able to withstand the induced short-run insecurity, although they still would not like it.

[33] *Ibid.*, Commission Exhibit 7.

CHAPTER IV

The Evolution of an Effective Delivered Pricing Formula

Early Concentration of Location in the Lehigh Valley

The Lehigh Valley of eastern Pennsylvania and western New Jersey has always been a favorable location for the production of cement because of an abundant supply of lime and clayey raw materials, proximity to sources of fuel, and nearness to large East Coast markets. In the early days of the industry, the Valley was considered to have special locational advantage because of the nature of its cement rock deposits and of a persistent preference among consumers for Lehigh Valley portland cement.

At the beginning of the twentieth century when the tensile strength standards set by engineers were not very high, much of the Lehigh Valley cement rock supplied a raw material satisfactory in its natural state, not needing any supplementary pure limestone. Also, the rock was of a peculiarly low moisture content and so required little preliminary drying before grinding. This made dry process manufacture much more economical in fuel consumption during the period of short-kiln technology than did the wet process of manufacture from marl used in the Michigan area. Moreover, the Valley rock, being sedimentary in character, was only moderately hard and therefore very easy to grind. In New York and certain other states, early attempts to manufacture portland cement out of crystalline limestone and clay were rather unsuccessful until improved machinery permitted grinding of hard limes to adequate fineness. Technological factors (simplicity of quarrying, fuel economy, and ease of grinding) were thus important in giving differential processing economies to the Lehigh Valley.[1]

Expansion in this relatively small region was also encouraged by consumer preferences for its product. Even after fully im-

[1] Lesley, *supra*, II fn. 4, pp. 100–102.

proved grinding methods had been introduced, a prejudice against cement made from pure limestone is said to have continued for a number of years.[2] Producers in the Chicago and Pittsburgh areas were faced with another prejudice, that against portland cement made partly from blast furnace slag, because consumers continued to think of its product as a mere puzzolan cement.[3] Thus, in developing a market demand, producers outside the Lehigh Valley were at a disadvantage similar to that originally faced by Lehigh Valley producers themselves when they were competing with imported European cement. At the turn of the century, over 70 per cent of the American production of portland cement was made in the Lehigh Valley, and the area had become almost synonymous with the product.

With the gradual overcoming of technical disadvantages in using non-Valley calcareous raw material, with the gradual lessening of consumer preferences for the Valley product, and with the expansion of cement markets in the area west and south of Pennsylvania, a large number of mills came into existence which were better located with respect to these developing markets. Several new mills were also established in the Hudson Valley of New York, being in a slightly better situation freight-wise with respect to New York City and substantially better with respect to other markets in the state and in New England. Notwithstanding, the capacity of Lehigh Valley mills continued to expand rapidly, quadrupling between 1900 and 1910. But in the remainder of the country, growth was at an even faster rate and the Lehigh Valley's percentage of the national production declined to 49 per cent by 1905 and to 37 per cent by 1910, as shown in Table 5.

During much of the first decade of the twentieth century and especially during summer months, the surplus production of the Lehigh Valley tended to establish prices for the rest of the country at levels approximately equal to the Lehigh Valley prices plus freight to destination. During periods of relative shortages, producers in the West and South charged prices equal to those

[2] E. C. Eckel, *Cement Materials and Industry of the United States* (Washington, 1905), pp. 31–33.

[3] E. J. Hadley, *The Magic Powder* (New York, 1945), pp. 46–54.

established by the Valley producers. However, when demand was weak, producers in the hinterland frequently shaded their prices at delivery points below the f.o.b. Lehigh Valley price plus freight. Much of the initial shading was needed to overcome the prejudice of consumers for the Lehigh Valley product and their long-term attachments to particular Valley producers.[4] These producers, who directly or through distributors had gained customers in the western and southern markets, were not to be removed easily from these markets. Customarily they met the reduced destination prices by absorbing freight as long as mill nets realized on otherwise unutilized capacity were satisfactory. The first formal base prices outside the Lehigh Valley, however, were not established until set up at Hannibal, Missouri, and Iola, Kansas, about 1908.[5]

Table 5

Portland Cement Produced in the Lehigh Valley in the United States, annually, 1895–1915

Year	Lehigh Valley (barrels)	United States (barrels)	Percentage made in Lehigh Valley
1895	634,276	990,224	64.1
1896	1,048,154	1,543,023	67.9
1897	2,002,059	2,677,775	74.8
1898	2,674,394	3,692,284	72.4
1899	4,110,132	5,642,266	72.8
1900	6,153,629	8,482,020	72.5
1901	8,595,340	12,711,225	67.7
1902	10,829,922	17,230,644	62.9
1903	12,324,922	22,342,973	55.2
1904	14,211,039	26,505,881	53.6
1905	17,368,687	35,246,812	49.3
1906	22,784,613	46,463,424	49.0
1907	24,417,686	48,785,390	50.1
1908	20,200,387	51,072,612	39.6
1909	24,246,706	64,991,431	37.3
1910	26,315,359	76,549,951	34.4
1911	25,972,108	78,528,637	33.1
1912	24,762,083	82,438,096	30.0
1913	27,139,701	92,097,131	29.5
1914	24,614,933	88,230,170	27.9
1915	24,876,442	85,917,907	29.0

Source: U.S. Geological Survey, *Mineral Resources of the United States.*

[4] *Record,* Transcript p. 32650.

[5] *Ibid.,* Commission Exhibit 2878 K–L, Respondent Exhibit 3743 A–B, 3745 B.

Promoters, Excess Capacity, and Unsystematic Pricing

As the rapidly expanding portland cement industry spread westward and new mills were opened in the marl fields of Michigan and in the natural gas belt of eastern Kansas, investor optimism over prospects for profit encouraged promoters to step in and multiply the number of new producers, particularly in these two territories. With the moderate financial barriers to entry overcome by investor optimism and promoter persuasion, and with no important institutional barriers blocking entry, a huge plant capacity was constructed well ahead even of the expanding demand. This success on the part of the promoters added to the problem of maintaining prices which plagued the industry during and after the financial crisis of 1907 and the mild recession in 1911. The average price realized for cement, which had held at a level of $1.12 a barrel during 1906 and 1907, fell to 90 cents and remained below that figure for the next five years before climbing back to $1.00 in 1913.[6] It was the desire to stabilize prices during this period that led to the development of various trade association activities.

But even during the period of reduced prices, capacity continued to expand as did the decentralization of the industry, and there developed an increasing number of complaints that some producers were dumping cement unsystematically in territory logically the domain of their competitors.[7] In the face of extremely low average realized prices between 1908 and 1912, thirty-two cement mills were put into the hands of creditors.[8] This prolonged siege of demoralization, plus another but milder "trade war" in 1914 and 1915,[9] led to greater discipline in the industry, to the evolution of protective devices, and to the circularization of more information. These stabilizing measures were to protect the industry through much, but not all, of the next period of overexpansion, the later 1920's.

Pricing Practices 1900–1910

Documentation of the pricing practices of the portland cement industry during the first decade of the twentieth century is

[6] Lesley, *supra*, II fn. 4, pp. 270–275.
[7] *Ibid.*, p. 274. [8] *Ibid.*, p. 165. [9] *Ibid.*, p. 277

practically non-existent. To explain the origin and evolution of the basing-point pricing system one can only draw upon the recollections of certain witnesses during the Commission hearings, on some memoranda remaining in corporation files, on excerpts from minutes of early trade associations, and on the interpretation given these by a knowledge of the geographic pattern of demand and productive capacity during the period.

Until 1900 the American portland cement industry was scarcely in a position to attempt any kind of market control activity. As late as 1896 importation of portland cement was double the quantity produced in the United States, but in 1900 it had dropped to about 28 per cent of American production. During 1901–03, it amounted to but 10 per cent of domestic production and during the remaining years of the decade never reached as much as 5 per cent.

The first documentary evidence of delivered prices appears in a letter of June 3, 1901, sent to a St. Louis cement dealer from the Atlas Portland Cement Company, then the largest cement manufacturer in the United States:

> We take pleasure in advising you that our company has decided to establish a large plant in the West, from which point we believe we can supply our product to many of our agents on a better basis than we have been able to do from our mills located in Pennsylvania.
>
> We have purchased 1,000 acres of cement land at Hannibal, Missouri, and will start at once the erection of a plant there, the capacity of which will equal or exceed 1,000,000 barrels for the first year and be increased to 2,000,000 the second year. We confidently expect to commence shipping therefrom on or before May, 1902.
>
> In establishing this plant we desire it to be understood that sales will be made f.o.b. cars destination in all cases, and this policy will be adopted on our sales from our Pennsylvania mills as rapidly as arrangements can be consummated.[10]

For approximately its first five years, the delivered prices from the new mill were based on the company's Pennsylvania mill price plus freight from the Lehigh Valley. Given the relative shortage of productive capacity which existed in the territory of the new mill, it is not surprising that the company took advantage of the opportunity to sell at high mill nets. Nor is it surprising that the Hannibal mill chose to sell at delivered prices when

[10] Federal Trade Commission, *Price Bases Inquiry* (Washington, 1932), p. 30.

selling eastward to markets in Illinois or Indiana in order to prevent diversion in transit into its higher mill net territory. But why was the policy adopted of making *all* sales at delivered prices in *railcars*? No explanation was given by the company, but two possible reasons may be suggested. First, a basing-point system was developing in the steel industry, and perhaps Atlas, the leading cement firm, wanted to introduce a similar system in the cement industry. Second, being located on the Mississippi River, Atlas may have desired to prevent the unsettling of destination prices which would have resulted if a posted mill price were to be quoted to buyers free to arrange their own water transportation, with characteristically variable freight charges.

The Atlas letter also indicated the firm's intention to quote only delivered prices at its Lehigh Valley mills at Northampton. As Atlas was a leading producer in the Valley, the motives behind this new policy merit close scrutiny. Buyers were interested, of course, in comparing prices at their destination, and many buyers may not have been equipped to handle the complexities of freight rates. Testimony given at the Commission hearings is replete with this explanation for the development of delivered prices. However, buyers could have been informed of the posted mill price and the applicable freight rate, without being required to purchase at the delivered price. Four possible explanations are offered here for the shift in pricing policy at Atlas's Lehigh Valley mills: (1) Until some time after 1920, no group freight rate existed for all mills in the Lehigh Valley so that freight rates could be equalized on shipments to all destinations outside the territory.[11] To the extent that f.o.b. mill prices had occasionally been varied to equalize freight costs from a rival Valley mill, delivered prices may have been adopted to prevent occasional arbitrage by favored buyers. (2) Desire to prevent diversion in transit would also have prompted the quotation of delivered prices in the effort to meet isolated price cuts in particular markets, irrespective of location. Of course, the addition of base prices in other areas in 1908 would inevitably have encouraged

[11] *Record*, Transcript pp. 38078–81, 38555, 48260–63. After the formal grouping of rates, all rates outside a territory approximately 70 miles long and 30 miles wide were made identical from any mill within this territory, although rates continued to differ from various mill locations to points within the territory.

Valley mills to quote delivered prices on sales where reduced mill nets were being accepted regularly. (3) In order to assure *known* destination prices in southern coastal cities and surrounding towns, Atlas may have wished to discourage large southern dealers from buying cement in railcars at Valley mills and reshipping it by water from the ports of Philadelphia and New York at uncertain coastal shipping rates. (4) In order to facilitate *known* destination prices even in the very small consumption territory surrounding its mills at Northampton, Atlas may have wished to eliminate shipment by customers' own wagon teams. Such customers might have found it more economical to deliver the product by team directly to the construction job five or ten miles away, than to pay a rail switching charge plus a wagon haul from the rail siding to the construction site. Unlike the first two explanations which furnish purely private reasons for adopting delivered prices when discriminating in mill nets, a policy of selling exclusively on a rail delivered basis suggests that Atlas wished to enable its rivals to meet its destination prices. Perhaps Atlas was tendering an invitation to other firms to follow a more orderly marketing policy.

At the beginning of the twentieth century most of the other Lehigh Valley cement firms were quoting prices on a variable f.o.b. mill basis at least superficially. Unlike Atlas, which maintained its own sale force, most Valley mills sold to dealers through a sales agent or distributor. Although the distributor would purchase at an f.o.b. mill price, negotiating reductions when necessary to meet competition at particular destinations, he generally made his sales at destination prices. At the same time some mills also made direct sales to dealers and contractors at f.o.b. mill prices.[12] As the need grew to quote special f.o.b. mill prices to distributors and dealers, opening a wedge for arbitrage, most concerns decided to integrate forward, having their own sales departments sell directly to dealers at delivered prices. However, there is no way to gauge the extent to which these Lehigh Valley mills quoted prices *exclusively* on a delivered basis prior to 1908. By that date most producers in the Lehigh Valley had joined forces in a patent licensing price agreement.

[12] *Ibid.*, Transcript pp. 27196–97.

Marketing practices of producers located outside the Lehigh Valley appear to have differed somewhat from those in the Valley. Producers located outside generally organized their own sales departments when their firms were established,[13] thereby eliminating the necessity of quoting variable f.o.b. mill prices to distributors. Furthermore, since the non-Valley mills had no formally established base prices, the pattern of rising destination prices north, south, and west of the Lehigh Valley established at least a ceiling price for the hinterland mills, and in order to avoid diversion delivered prices were almost surely quoted by these mills whenever they solicited sales at destinations in the direction of the Valley. It is not known to what extent, if any, mills located close to cities and waterways offered a mill price to dealers and contractors who wished to arrange their own wagon transportation to a local job or their own water transportation for a long distance haul. However, testimony during the Commission hearings showed that both a cement-producing subsidiary of United States Steel with mills close to waterways in the Pittsburgh and Chicago areas and an independent cement mill on the Ohio River in Kentucky quoted only delivered prices during this early period.[14]

Early Collective Activity Directed at Standardizing Conditions of Sale

The Association of American Portland Cement Manufacturers was organized in 1902 and continued until May 1916 when it became the Portland Cement Association. At the 1916 reorganization, activities relating to scientific inquiry and to the joint promotion of the use of cement were separated from those concerned with "marketing ethics." From that time on, the Portland Cement Association would handle the former while separate organizations were to be established to deal with trade practices. The very first meeting, in 1903, was designed to develop a standardized method of handling the cloth sacks and compensating buyers for their return.

By 1904 membership had climbed until it included mills ac-

[13] *Ibid.*, Transcript pp. 23047–48.
[14] *Ibid.*, Transcript pp. 35875–79, 36879.

counting for 90 per cent of total productive capacity. This level of membership was equaled or exceeded every year except for 1911 when there was a slight decline. The first reference to pricing practices to appear in the minutes came in the December 1904 session. Following an exhortation that they should develop a uniform price for cement, since the price had apparently been fluctuating seasonally as well as in particular markets, the members adopted a resolution formally making the Lehigh Valley a single basing-point for the industry:

> Resolved, that the members of this Association in answering inquiries for prices, confine deliveries up to April 1st, 1905, and quote a higher price for deliveries after that date, and that it is the sense of this meeting that the price should not be less than $1.00 per barrel at the mill for the Lehigh Valley.[15]

The agreement does not appear to have been kept entirely, however, because the minutes of the April 1905 meeting referred to prices in some sections of the country as being below the Lehigh Valley formula. But it was expected that prices, where below the formula, would rise by summer, since a shortage in production in the Middle West would call for additional shipments from the Lehigh Valley at destination prices based upon "Valley plus." At the same meeting the assembly voted unanimously to form a special committee to develop uniformity in "prices and business methods." [16] The committee's report, details of which are not available, was accepted and signed by forty-six of the forty-nine Association members. At the December 1905 meeting the formal report was censored to eliminate reference to uniform prices, but the modified report disclosed an agreement to standardize contracts (involving future deliveries), terms of payment, cash discounts, and credits for returned bags.[17] Apparently the agreement was not well kept and in September 1908 the chairman of the special committee, which had become known as the Trade Relations Committee, recommended a new one including terms of sale similar to the earlier agreement plus the explicit provision: "All prices quoted for portland cement shall be the

[15] *Ibid.*, Commission Exhibit 3235 W.
[16] *Ibid.*, Commission Exhibit 3235–Z1–Z2.
[17] *Ibid.*, Commission Exhibit 3235–Z6–Z7.

prices for delivery at the point required by the purchaser." [18] The minutes of this and subsequent meetings of the AAPCM fail to disclose any action on the matter. It has been impossible to determine whether the recommendation concerning exclusive delivered pricing was prompted by instability resulting from occasional diversion of shipments in transit when some sellers sold at variable f.o.b. mill prices, or by uncertainty about particular destination prices when sellers allowed buyers to arrange their own transportation in situations not involving diversion.

Marketing policy was not discussed at the 1909 meetings of the AAPCM apparently, but by this time a new, and potentially more effective, price agreement together with a patent pool had become well established with many of the members.[19] To stave off litigation over the use of a patented process for burning pulverized coal, six of the largest manufacturers in the Lehigh Valley formed a holding company in 1906 to purchase the Hurry-Seaman patent from Atlas, one of the group. Once formed, the patent holding company sought to control the erection of new plants.[20] However, the major objective of the patent holders changed at the end of 1907 when they formed the Association of Licensed Cement Manufacturers and offered membership and patent licenses to all existing cement companies. Sixteen manufacturers in the Lehigh Valley and Hudson Valley areas joined the licensing association and in January 1909 established a minimum pricing agreement with a scale of liquidated damages. Initially the pricing agreement applied only to "Territory A," covering the eastern seaboard from Maine to South Carolina and extending westward to a line through Rochester, New York, and a point midway between Northampton (in the Lehigh Valley) and Pittsburgh, Pennsylvania. The provisions stated specifically that all prices should be made on a delivered basis and spelled out a formula for price quotations: "Prices in Territory A shall not be less than $1.20 in wood and cotton [containers] and 95 cents in paper plus the Northampton all-rail rate. . . ." [21]

In Territory B (all other territory covered by the rights of the

[18] *Ibid.*, Commission Exhibit 3235–Z34–Z36.
[19] *Ibid.*, Commission Exhibit 3196–AA–PP.
[20] *Ibid.*, Transcript pp. 24024–25.
[21] *Ibid.*, Commission Exhibit 3196–2Y.

patent), members of the license agreement were free to price as they chose, but provisions were made for extending the pricing formula to this area at a later date.

That the primary purpose of the license agreement was to fix prices through a delivered price formula was admitted by the president of the Alpha Portland Cement Company in 1929:

> The Hurry & Seaman patent-licensing agreement, which provided among other things that the licensee should sell only at delivered prices, was frankly an attempt to stabilize conditions in the cement business. It was an agreement, however, though entered into in good faith as to its lawfulness at the time, based upon what was then thought to be legal under the patent law.[22]

The price-fixing experiment was of short duration, however. When a lower federal court refused to uphold an infringement suit against a mid-western cement manufacturer in 1910 (ruling that the claims of the Hurry-Seaman patent were too broad), the licensing agreement collapsed. The Association of Licensed Cement Manufacturers dissolved itself in January 1911. Firms in the Northeast had found adherence to delivered prices during the two year experiment very beneficial, and the acquisition of mills in other areas by some of these same firms facilitated the future institution of the system on a national basis.

It is impossible to ascertain the exact date when general adherence to the basing-point formula was finally achieved in the United States. However, the minutes of the AAPCM meetings of 1910 (the last year in which the minutes carried post-mortem discussions of pricing conditions) suggest that a considerable amount of unsystematic dumping still prevailed in many sections of the country. Although in June a member of an association of producers in the Michigan area mentioned that local producers had agreed to base all prices in their territory on the Lehigh Valley price,[23] six months later he was lamenting that one-third of the cement entering the Detroit market came from the East at dumped prices.[24] A Lehigh Valley producer, in turn, referred to dumping in the New York City market by a Michigan firm.[25]

22 *Ibid.*, Commission Exhibit 1174–I.
23 *Ibid.*, Commission Exhibit 3235–Z59.
24 *Ibid.*, Commission Exhibit 3235–Z67.
25 *Ibid.*, Commission Exhibit 3235–Z59–Z69.

Also complaints were registered during the 1910 meetings by producers in Virginia and Alabama against unsystematic dumping by Lehigh Valley producers in southern markets.[26] Thus, until sometime after 1910, formula pricing, bolstered by tacit or explicit agreement, was apparently adhered to by firms in their home markets better than in more distant ones.

Common Freight Factors

By 1915 a concerted effort to comply with the basing-point formula was apparent in most areas of the country. Not only had a Rocky Mountain chain issued instructions to its affiliates to begin quoting delivered prices exclusively, based upon those of the Lehigh's chain of western mills in Washington, Iowa, and Kansas; [27] but several regional freight rate associations were being established. The use of common freight factors would serve, of course, to prevent unintentional deviations in pricing for particular markets, deviations which could lead to antagonisms and retaliatory selective price reductions.

In the northeastern section of the country most if not all competitors were using freight rate books made available by the Alpha Portland Cement Company between 1911 and 1916. An excerpt from the minutes of one of the earliest meetings of the Sales Managers' Branch of the Cement Manufacturers Protective Association, held in January 1916, contained the following colloquy between F. M. Coogan of Alpha and B. L. Swett of Lehigh:

> Mr. Coogan: We have felt until the Association gets in working order that we had better continue notifying everybody for say another month, at least, and by that time things here will be in such shape as to handle it from this office. So until then, gentlemen, we will continue to notify you of all changes. In connection with those freight rate books we believe that with the corrections that we have made on them that at the present time they are correct. I guess practically all of the companies are using the book as a basis and it seems to me that if any company notices any difference from what it shows in those books . . . notify us at once. . . .
>
> Mr. Swett: It is further understood that the member companies use these freight rates until they are notified of the change in the rates by our secretary regardless from what source they secure information as to a change in rate. . . .[28]

[26] *Ibid.* [27] *Ibid.*, Commission Exhibit 3210–A, B, C.
[28] *Ibid.*, Commission Exhibit 3191–A, B.

The Alpha freight books were superseded later that year by books assembled and distributed by the Cement Manufacturers Protective Association, which operated in the Northeast. Four other regional associations also were organized to distribute common freight factors: Southeastern Portland Cement Association, Kansas City Cement Bureau, Chicago Statistical Bureau, and an organization for the Rocky Mountains. Some of these regional freight rate services were reorganized from time to time. For example, when the Cement Manufacturers Protective Association was dissolved in 1922, pending a Supreme Court decision to determine the legality of its activities (which also included distribution of individual company statistics on production and shipments and the common checking of specific job contracts), producers in the Northeast subscribed first to the Nazareth Traffic Bureau from 1922 to 1928 and then to the National Traffic Bureau from 1928 to 1930. In the latter year the newly-formed Cement Institute began to issue freight rate books covering all states except those on the Pacific Coast and in the Rocky Mountain area, where rail rates on commercial freight were relatively simple.

Despite the repetitious testimony offered during the hearings that purposes of mere economy dictated the use of freight books produced and sold by a common agency, the fact remains that formula pricing was thereby facilitated because otherwise errors could easily be made in computing the highly complex rail rates,[29] particularly to stations where relatively few prices were quoted. The following excerpts from correspondence of cement companies illustrate the real purpose of the common freight factors.

An inter-office communication in November 1929 of a holding company of southern cement mills read: "One of the principal features of this service is that our principal competitors will be using the same books as we are, resulting in uniformity." [30]

In reply to a division manager who wished to economize by eliminating a subscription to the Cement Institute's freight rate service, the vice-president of the Lone Star Cement Company

[29] My colleague, Paul Blomgrem has told me of the extensive and expensive double checking of freight rates done by several pharmaceutical houses when outright economy rather than identical pricing was the objective.

[30] *Record*, Commission Exhibit 988A.

(formerly called International Cement Company) wrote in September 1931:

> From this you will learn that we in this office feel that the freight rate service is well worth the money that the Institute charges, in that it has a distinct advantage over any individual company record, because it disseminates freight rate information to practically all of the companies in a given territory, and thereby serves to prevent variations in quotations by the various companies, which might be due entirely to incorrect freight information.[31]

There was apparently an understanding that when a rate reduction was discovered by a particular producer, he should inform the issuer of the common freight books and refrain from using the lower rate until the corrected rate had been issued to the entire industry by the issuing agency. For example, after a district sales manager at Norfolk, Virginia, effected a low bid in the fall of 1936 by quoting on the basis of a special rail rate which reduced freight by 3 cents a barrel, he received the following statement from his home office:

> You are aware of the conditions surrounding the issuance and maintenance of these *price books* [italics added]. The Freight Rate Bureau depends to a great extent upon the member companies to furnish them with information having to do with rate changes. The Rate Bureau cannot be expected to maintain the close scrutiny over cement rates that is possible by members of the industry. On the other hand the freight rate books are furnished to members of the industry as the official rate bases and, as such, they are accepted by the industry as containing the rates on which prices are based.
>
> The reason for this is perfectly obvious. To do otherwise would quickly result in a chaotic condition due to local changes in rates which would be known to those companies most deeply concerned and would probably be overlooked by the companies whose interest was not quite as great.
>
> So far as our company is concerned, we have always worked on the policy that the freight rates shown in the rate books are the only rates we will use in the computation of prices. If we have knowledge of any rates that are different from those in the rate book, then we have an obligation to inform the Rate Bureau of the new rate before such a rate is used in computing a price.[32]

The unguarded reference to the freight rate books as "price

[31] *Ibid.*, Commission Exhibit 2461.
[32] *Ibid.*, Commission Exhibit 287–B, C.

books" paralleled a request made to the Cement Manufacturers Protective Association in July 1918 by the eastern sales manager of the Lehigh chain for "an extra West Virginia price book." [33] That the industry had long been sensitive to the connotation, however, may be seen in the reply made by an officer of the Association to that request:

> Responding to your letter of July 1st, file 65414–C, we are sending you under separate cover a copy of the West Virginia Rate Book which I take it is what you want.
>
> In your letter you request a price book, which is no doubt a typographical error, inasmuch as you are aware of the fact that this Association does not issue any books in any way connected with price matters.[34]

The importance of freight rate books as "price books" for a smoothly working basing-point system should not be exaggerated, however. In the first place, cement companies could have simply broadcast advertising circulars to dealers showing destination prices (base prices plus freight), with the proviso that in territories where the destination price quotations of some rival mills were lower than those being issued by a particular concern, the lower advertised destination prices would be met. Of course, this method would have been somewhat less manageable administratively, and complications could have arisen at rural destinations where no dealers were located. Secondly, and most importantly, the great concern expressed over the elimination of occasional, unintentional differences in delivered prices due to freight rate errors, demonstrated that more serious forms of unsystematic pricing had been brought under control. By the more serious errors, I have in mind the uncertainties resulting from buyers arranging their own transportation, an insufficient general willingness to adhere to a pattern of delivered prices as derived from a commonly accepted formula, lack of a technique for disciplining unsystematic pricing of the recalcitrant minority, and direct sales to contractors. Difficulties over all of these uncertainties had developed during the twenties, and techniques were developed in the industry to minimize or eliminate them, thus conferring once more on common freight rate books their function as simple "price books."

[33] *Ibid.*, Commission 3200. [34] *Ibid.*

Control Over Destination Prices

1. Elimination of sales to buyers' trucks

The policy of quoting delivered prices exclusively was relaxed at many mills between 1918 and 1920, a period of severe shortage of railroad cars. To facilitate shipments to buyers in general and to retain the patronage of particular buyers, many companies offered to load the trucks of buyers at the mill. Mills made no special marketing adjustment to the new situation, and simply invoiced the sale at the delivered price minus full allowance for the rail rate. Later, as railroad transportation service returned to a fairly normal basis in 1923, comparatively little trucking took place, and not until 1925 did trucking begin to expand on a significant scale because of its own economic merits. The vice president of Lehigh testified before the Commission: "It was a time when there had been a great expansion of good highways, and growing of motor transportation, and a great many buyers who felt that this mode of transportation offered them convenience and economy." [35] With the door left open to buyers' trucks from the period of car shortage and with the cement industry operating in 1925 at production levels close to or exceeding "practical" capacity, producers offered no apparent resistance to requests that they load buyers' trucks.

Trucking offered substantial economies to local buyers, and it increased greatly between 1925 and 1931. Not only were trucking costs on short hauls considerably below rail rates, but further savings were effected through delivering cement directly to the construction job, thereby eliminating the extra truck haul from the rail siding. For many newly established dealers without rail sidings there was a similar economy. Moreover, trucking had the advantage of faster delivery. In an emergency, delivery could be made by truck in a few hours, whereas rail delivery required at least a day. Finally, small dealers found a further benefit from trucking because they could obtain smaller orders and were not required to maintain large inventories.

Trucking, of course, contained the seeds of serious instability in the future, although the industry did not show concern until about 1927 when an excess capacity developed. Price instability

[35] *Ibid.*, Transcript p. 26839.

due to trucking took five principal forms, although the first was the most important. (1) Uncontrolled trucking resulted in uncertain transportation costs. Rates of contract truckers fluctuated markedly and frequently. They were negotiated between the cement buyer and the trucker, and for cement producers destination prices became uncertain quantities. Moreover, when a buyer did his own trucking the opportunity cost of such truck transportation became even more uncertain. As a consequence, the more distantly situated sellers, who absorbed freight when shipping by rail into the local territory of a rival, did not know what delivered price to quote in order to offer the buyer the same cost. The buyers from local mills possessed unusual bargaining power against the penetrating seller. As a result the penetrator would almost certainly need to "beat" competition in these markets, thereby unsettling the geographic pattern of prices, or else to forego entirely any attempt to make such a sale. (2) The non-base mill in selling to buyers' trucks at the formula destination price minus an allowance of rail freight from the mill also subjected itself to the dangers of arbitrage. Buyers might divert cement from their alleged more distant destination to markets closer to the mill, where other buyers were paying higher mill-net prices.[36] Thus, trucking controlled by buyers had the effect of converting nominally non-base mills into base mills within a radius of approximately 50 miles, a distance where trucking was apparently economical. It should be emphasized, however, that base mills were not confronted with this arbitrage problem so long as they quoted their posted base price to truckers. (3) Where mills were located relatively close together, as in the Lehigh Valley, Pittsburgh, Detroit, and Cleveland areas, even mills with base prices were occasionally subjected to arbitrage diversions by buyers. In order to make a sale to buyers located within an economical trucking radius but also closer to another mill, a special f.o.b. mill price was occasionally quoted. Then these favored buyers would sometimes direct their truck shipments into the base price territory of the seller.[37] (4) Trucking of cement disturbed the highly

[36] *Ibid.*, Commission Exhibit 976–10T.

[37] *Ibid.*, Commission Exhibit 969–14M, 14N, 14D. A situation is described at Bethlehem, Pa., in the Lehigh Valley. This city of 50,000 population was about five miles from one group of mills at Bath and twelve miles from another group at Northampton.

rigid system of dealerships which was maintained in the industry. The older building-supply dealers, with warehouses established on rail sidings, objected to savings made available to their newer rivals through truck transportation and to the propensity of these trucking dealers to share their savings by cutting prices to consumers.[38] The old-line dealers also objected to the breakdown in exclusive territories which occurred when a dealer acquired the product at a mill and delivered it to a market "belonging" to another dealer. Even where the invading dealer paid the posted mill price and arbitrage was not an issue (the typical case), he frequently cut his price to consumers below that being quoted by established local dealers who used trucks.[39] Dealers faced with increased competition in their retail market attempted to bargain more vigorously with rival cement suppliers for price concessions.[40] (5) Truck delivery frequently offered important qualitative advantages which could not be matched by rail shippers. In such cases, even when truck-delivered prices were known, as in the case of trucks controlled by the manufacturer, the penetrating rail shippers were at a competitive disadvantage, and buyers sought price concessions from them.[41]

Between 1927 and 1932 there was a boom in trucking from mills and silos[42] located within an economical range (40 to 60 miles) of large cities. The earliest areas to be affected were the state of Michigan and various cities located close to mills and silos along the Great Lakes. For example, the Huron Portland Cement Company, with a mill at Alpena, Michigan, shipped by water to port silos along the Great Lakes in Minnesota, Wisconsin, Michigan, Ohio, and New York. Distribution from these silos was primarily by truck. As early as 1927, about 75 per cent of the total shipments from Huron's silos at Detroit and Grand Haven, Michigan, Milwaukee, Wisconsin, and Cleveland, Ohio, moved by truck.[43] Other producers, in turn, with mills in Michi-

[38] *Ibid.*, Commission Exhibit 970–6G. [39] *Ibid.*, Commission Exhibit 976–6X.

[40] *Ibid.*, Commission Exhibit 971–9A, B.

[41] *Ibid.*, Commission Exhibits 969–3V, 971–202–21A. Rail shippers into the Toledo area, during the summer of 1935, reduced their rail delivered price by 8¢ per barrel below the delivered price based on controlled truck prices, so as to offset the advantage of delivery direct to the job.

[42] Silos are warehouses on waterways, especially along the Great Lakes.

[43] *Record*, Respondent Exhibit 63–2391.

gan and in territories close to the Great Lakes cities greatly increased their shipment by truck. S. T. Crapo, president of Huron, testified during the Commission hearings that Benjamin Affleck, president of United States Steel's cement subsidiary, Universal, had come directly to him during the twenties to urge that his concern and others in the area eliminate trucking. He said that Universal (with a large mill near Chicago) was complaining because it did not know how to make uniform delivered prices when selling in Michigan.[44]

By the early thirties very substantial truck shipments were also being made from mills or silos in different areas: eastern New York close to Albany and metropolitan New York; central and western New York near Rochester, Syracuse, and Buffalo; western Pennsylvania around Pittsburgh; eastern Virginia near Norfolk and Washington, D.C.; northern Ohio, including Cleveland and Toledo; Michigan; northwestern Indiana and Chicago; western Tennessee near Nashville; Iowa close to Des Moines and Davenport; and eastern Kansas near Kansas City.

Although all mills in the Lehigh Valley did some trucking, the percentage of such shipments was small compared with that in almost all other areas, and most of it went to the New Jersey portion of metropolitan New York and to Pennsylvania cities within the Valley area. New York City and Philadelphia were generally outside the economic trucking range of the Valley mills, and yet trucking severely disturbed the Valley's market in Philadelphia. The Valley Forge Cement Company, which had opened in 1927 within fifteen miles of downtown Philadelphia, by June 1932 was shipping over 50 per cent of its output in buyers' trucks.[45] In an effort to offset Valley Forge's advantage, the Lehigh Cement Company, market leader of the Lehigh Valley, established a warehouse close to the Valley Forge mill to which it shipped, by rail, cement to be subsequently transshipped in buyers' trucks. The warehouse was presumably designed to induce the Valley Forge mill to discontinue trucking, although a Lehigh executive testified that its function was simply to protect the company's Philadelphia business.[46]

44 *Ibid.*, Transcript pp. 11077–82.

45 *Ibid.*, Commission Exhibit 973–3G.

46 *Ibid.*, Transcript pp. 26853–56.

Warehouses were installed and serviced at great expense in the late twenties and early thirties by some firms that wished to continue to sell in more distant markets, refraining at the same time from quoting unsystematic delivered prices based on rail shipment. In 1928 when the Basic Products Company offered to sell to buyers' trucks at its new mill at Neville Island, Pennsylvania, four or five miles from the heart of Pittsburgh, the Universal Cement Company established a trucking warehouse within the city limits at a cost of $200,000.[47] The Universal mill was some sixteen miles northeast of its city warehouse which now superseded Universal as the basing-point for western Pennsylvania. Between 1929 and 1931, over 60 per cent of the shipments of Basic Products and Universal moved by truck,[48] virtually forcing other mills in western Pennsylvania and eastern Ohio to establish small warehouses in Pittsburgh. In addition, rather than breach the "delivered price" on a rail shipment, several inland mills set up warehouses at Great Lakes points so as to meet directly the truck prices offered by lake mills and port silos. Again, in an effort to equalize marketing conditions in the nation's capital where the Lone Star Cement Company was shipping by water from its Norfolk, Virginia, mill to its silo in Georgetown, D.C., six producers (four from the Lehigh Valley) shipped by rail to rented warehouses in Georgetown from which they met the truck price quoted by Lone Star.

There seem to have been only two producing states in which truck sales were never made, Alabama and Florida. This may well be explained by the fact that five of the six mills in these states belonged to chain companies, always strongly opposed to trucking.

The earliest attempt to control trucking was made by Texas mills in March 1926. At that time, loading of customers' trucks was discontinued and superseded by delivery through a single truck contractor at published transportation rates. Later when the Riverside Cement Company, the largest producer in southern California, experienced marketing difficulties from selling at the mill to buyers' trucks, the company took only two months after

[47] *Ibid.*, Transcript pp. 35184–85.
[48] *Ibid.*, Commission Exhibit 1320, pp. 70, 113.

learning about the Texas plan to follow the same procedure. This change in policy, which came to be adopted by all southern California mills, followed the receipt of a letter sent on November 29, 1929 by the president of the Lone Star Cement Company, the third largest chain in the United States, with mills scattered east of the Rocky Mountains. The letter is worthy of extensive quotation.

I could write you a thesis on trucking. Properly handled, in territories of small consumption, trucking is a very satisfactory means of transportation. Under all other conditions it exerts a most demoralizing influence over the market affected. There are several large trucking markets in the territory. Universal puts about 6,000,000 barrels into the city of Chicago annually on trucks. The Medusa Company supplies the major requirements of the city of Toledo under a very vicious trucking arrangement from their Silica mill. The Detroit market is demoralized by trucking from Peerless and Wyandotte. Cleveland has suffered for years as a result of indiscriminate trucking from the bulk warehouses and packing station there maintained by the Huron Company. Pittsburgh has been upset by the Universal trucking from their plant at Universal, Pa., and now from the Basic Products Company's plant on Neville Island. I understand that the Bessemer Company is adding to the confusion in that market by putting up a new plant which will be located on the court house steps. Syracuse has for years been dominated by trucking from the Jamesville plant of Alpha.

We have been trucking for years from our Houston and Dallas plants in Texas without difficulty. These markets are also served by the Trinity Company. The only trucks served are those operated by a trucking concern which has a published line of rates to the various parts of the cities, which have been zoned and priced for the information of all consumers and producers alike. This trucking company is bonded both for performance and against manipulation. It acts in exactly the same capacity as a Railroad Company or an electric line. The delivered prices in various parts of the cities are based on the mill price to the manufacturer, plus the published cost of transportation from the producer's plant to the zone of the city in question.

Eastern Pennsylvania and Northern New Jersey have for the past few years been a veritable madhouse. Indiscriminate trucking has brought forth greater and greater concessions by producers, until it finally reached the point at which manufacturers were absorbing thirty and forty cents a barrel in order to lay cement down by truck on the job. Whenever a manufacturer makes a delivered price by truck, or employs a trucker, only trouble and suspicion can result. An attempt has been made to correct this condition by placing a truck price on the various mills. This price is generally 15¢ a barrel higher than the carload price. Most manufacturers have now refrained from employing trucks but allow the contractor or the dealer to engage transportation from the mill to the job. The charge is the mill truck price on board the customer's trucks. The tendency of this method is to limit trucking to within 12 or 15 miles of the mill. In the case of Philadelphia, with a mill at West Conshohocken, about twelve or fourteen miles from City Hall, a 5,000,000 barrel market is pretty well shot to pieces by this practice.

The question has not yet been solved. I believe that we will not reach a solution until trucking is entirely eliminated or else a plan similar to the one which we have followed for years in Texas is adopted. . . .[49]

The fifteen cents premium imposed on buyers' trucks loaded at the mill was initially adopted in the Lehigh Valley area during the fall of 1929. The differential was extended to most other eastern, southern, and midwestern mills by the summer of 1930, although several mills and silos, particularly in the Pittsburgh and Great Lakes areas refused to adopt the practice intended to deter trucking. Even where the truck differential applied, however, buyer trucking continued in sufficient volume to perpetuate uncertainty in destination prices in many important markets. Cooperative negotiation to eliminate trucking completely was therefore begun in the summer of 1931.

Established dealers in building supplies took the lead, at least nominally, in the movement to eliminate trucking in an area north of the Ohio River. These dealers had found that unregulated trucking increased the severity of price competition at the retail level. There is also evidence, however, that many cement manufacturers encouraged the dealers' movement to eliminate trucking. For example, following receipt of a letter circulated by a Youngstown, Ohio, dealer urging that trucking of cement from manufacturers' plants be discontinued, the Pittsburgh sales manager of Universal Atlas wrote to the home office on June 12, 1931:

You can see the fine handwriting of Bob Long of Lehigh, McKee of West Penn, and Denkle of Bessemer. All of these companies are continually urging the dealers to have trucking discontinued in Pittsburgh, giving them the impression that if this were done it would clean up the situation throughout the entire country.[50]

[49] *Ibid.*, Commission Exhibit 1203 TT–UU.

[50] *Ibid.*, Commission Exhibit 2654. Each of the three firms referred to had a plant in northwestern Pennsylvania disadvantageously located for truck shipments to Pittsburgh.

The president of the National Builders Supply Association called meetings in July 1931 and January 1932, attended by the president of the Cement Institute and representatives of various railroad companies and railroad associations. The general plan adopted called for agents of various railroads to interview officers of cement companies in an effort to negotiate an elimination of trucking. The only evidence of a *specific* agreement resulting from the series of interviews was of the one developed at a Chicago meeting of cement manufacturers on November 17–19, 1931, to eliminate trucking in Pittsburgh on December 1, 1931.[51] Other mills in western Pennsylvania and Ohio (except the Ohio mills close to Lake ports) discontinued trucking on the same day, or a few days thereafter.

Mills in Maryland, southern Pennsylvania, western Virginia, and West Virginia (most of which belonged to chains) discontinued trucking in the middle of June 1932. Mills in the Lehigh Valley and all in New York State (except those near Lake Erie) accepted the July 28, 1932 invitation of the price leader, Lehigh, and during the first few days of August both eliminated trucking and announced price increases of sixteen cents per barrel.[52] By late summer of 1932 practically every mill east of the Rocky Mountains had given up truck delivery (including Texas, where even controlled trucking had been eliminated). The principal exceptions were all the mills in Michigan, port silos along the Great Lakes, and certain mills in the Great Lake states located very close to those silos.

In the Great Lakes region, where Huron refused to give up trucking from its strategically located silos at large port cities, trucking was gradually put on a *regulated* basis. Companies in this region usually either operated their own trucking departments or employed exclusive contract truckers.[53] By hauling at

[51] *Ibid.*, Commission Exhibits 1348 A–B, 2260, 2658.

[52] *Ibid.*, Transcript pp. 23693–95, 27362–67, 33845–46, 35153–54, 38151–52. Firms in the area denied agreement or understanding, but admitted to following Lehigh's leadership.

[53] One major exception was Chicago, where buyers could send their trucks to the port silos and purchase at silo prices. The huge Universal Atlas mill in an Indiana suburb of Chicago also sold to trucks destined for Chicago (at a 15¢ premium above its base price). This same mill, however, refused truck delivery to consumers located in Indiana, and employed a controlled contract trucker to meet

"'published" rates, destination prices of truck shipments were regulated. The typical marketing procedure was to circulate a schedule of delivered prices at various points served by controlled trucks from a silo or mill. If the buyer wanted possession at the mill or silo in his own truck, he had to pay the full delivered price at his destination and bear his own trucking expenses.[54] Moreover, Huron even had to restrict the area of its controlled trucking to a few counties surrounding its silos in New York, Ohio, Wisconsin, and Minnesota, because of pressure exerted by inland mills unable to offer the superior service advantage of truck delivery.[55]

In the remainder of the country (the Mountain and Pacific Coast states) trucking continued. In southern California controlled trucking was used in conjunction with a system of zone delivered prices. However, the *Record* is not clear as to the extent to which in other parts of the West it remained free or controlled, either partially through the adoption of arbitrary premium mill prices on truck loadings, or completely through exclusive use of a trucking organization which delivered at published rates.

It may well be that some small premium charge for loading trucks, rather than rail cars, was justified. But ample evidence exists to suggest that the conventional fifteen cent premium was excessive in terms of possible additional costs of loading and invoicing sales to buyer trucks, and was designed primarily to restrict the area of economical trucking.[56] The *Record* is replete with evidence concerning the "unstabilizing" and "demoralizing" effect of unregulated trucking upon the cement market. Most of these company statements were made in 1935 in reply to questionnaires prepared by Professors Arthur R. Burns and John M.

---

the formula prices established by controlled truck competition in southern Michigan.

[54] *Record,* Commission Exhibit 422.

[55] E.g., under pressure from Alpha and Lehigh, Huron decided in 1932 not to truck from its Oswego, N.Y. silo to Syracuse, only 35 miles away. *Ibid.,* Transcript pp. 11050–66, 11124, 11262–63. In the case of its Cleveland silo, Huron subsequently agreed to confine its trucking to Cuyahoga County. *Ibid.,* Transcript pp. 11065–68, 11278–79.

[56] *Ibid.,* Transcript pp. 8777, 12467; Commission Exhibits 968–6W, 975–6Y; and Respondent Exhibit 2112.

Clark, then employed to make an economic study of the cement industry.[57] This discussion of trucking may profitably be concluded by quoting part of the reply to the Burns-Clark questionnaire by the Lehigh Portland Cement Company, a leader in the industry:

> The manufacturer, striving to figure his prices on indeterminate and fluctuating trucking rates and to meet the equally fluctuating and independent rates from his competitor's plants, quickly found himself engaged in blind, reckless and destructive competition.
>
> [*Two paragraphs omitted.*]
>
> . . . It is our firm belief that the trucking practices of the cement industry from 1925 to 1932 were not fair to the consumer. The apparent price advantage was more frequently the result of guerilla warfare among the manufacturers engaged in blind competition on unknown and often fictitious truck delivery costs, rather than an economy inherent in the method of transportation. This guerilla competition was waged most fiercely after a construction contract had been awarded, with the result that the larger part of its fruits did not reach the consumer, the advantage being retained as an added profit by the contractor or by the retailer who supplied the contract.
>
> [*One paragraph omitted.*]
>
> By 1932 it was clear that trucking practices were one of the chief contributory causes of the state of chaos and demoralization in which the industry found itself. When about August 1932, one manufacturer announced he would no longer load trucks but would sell only in carload lots, his action was met by practically all manufacturers in the Lehigh Valley area. The action was primarily the result of the desperate condition of the industry and the general realization that only by the elimination of the destructive practices associated with trucking could there be any hope of improvement. . . .[58]

2. *Refusal to sell at f.o.b. mill prices to government agencies and the control-clause-destination-cost bid*

By 1929 an increasing number of state governments began to purchase their large cement requirements for highways directly from the manufacturer, hoping to reap quantity discounts. But although cement manufacturers would quote to state governments just as to dealers, discounts below the formula price even for quantity were contrary to the industry's marketing code.

[57] *Ibid.*, Commission Exhibits 967–76. These exhibits include the voluminous replies to the questionnaires.

[58] *Ibid.*, Commission Exhibit 969–14M.

Because of the political necessity of avoiding charges of corruption or favoritism, governmental agencies were generally kept from undertaking the kind of individual negotiation and bargaining employed by contractors. In an effort to secure lower prices for their huge cement requirements, therefore, the states experimented with the policy of requesting sealed bids on prices for cement delivered at various destinations. This proved a signal failure, save for a brief flurry of competitive bidding in 1931 and early 1932, coincident with a short period of vigorous price competition in the industry's commercial sales. Before 1931 and after July 1932, cement manufacturers in these sealed bids simply quoted the identical formula prices that would have been given on commercial sales to dealers at the same destinations. The fact that any price cutting would be exposed at the public opening of the bids, and the mill involved subjected to a punitive base, strengthened the solidarity in uniform bidding. Overt collusion was not absolutely necessary to account for uniform bidding, but in the light of testimony concerning the frequency of telephone discussions about sealed bids between one firm and its competitors,[59] it is likely that certainty was often strengthened by stated reassurances that the price formula would be followed.

In an effort to circumvent the quoting of identical destination prices by all bidders, the governor of Illinois attempted in 1933 to get each cement manufacturer in his area to bid an f.o.b. mill price for the state's huge requirement of 3,300,000 barrels. This invitation was refused by all the manufacturers. They were unwilling to gamble on the possibility that independently determined, selective reductions in their f.o.b. mill price to the state of Illinois could be made without destroying the satisfactory base price level for commercial sales.[60]

Faced with identical bids, many states, including Illinois and Indiana, gave up their efforts of trying to obtain genuinely competitive bids on cement for new highway construction.[61] After

59 *Ibid.*, Transcript pp. 843–45; testimony of L. V. Fowley, former office secretary in the Aetna Portland Cement Co.

60 *Ibid.*, Commission Exhibits 2607, 2189A–B; letters of Kosmos and Marquette to Governor Horner of Illinois explaining their failure to bid f.o.b. mill.

61 *Ibid.*, Transcript pp. 11825–26, 11736–37. Illinois and Indiana did continue to purchase directly small quantities of cement for maintenance work.

1933 these states awarded an entire construction job to a contractor who then made his own arrangement for cement. As we shall see in a later section of this chapter, on highway work a contractor could occasionally obtain better prices than could the state government.

Prior to the development of the NRA Cement Code in the summer of 1933 the federal government experienced little difficulty in getting f.o.b. mill bids on practically all of its work.[62] However, with the deepening of depression and the growing volume of federal cement buying for reclamation and other public works projects, the industry adopted the policy of quoting the government only at destination prices. Renewed requests by the federal government for f.o.b. mill bids both during and following the NRA period were refused because of the impossibility of achieving identical prices without knowing the place of consumption. Consequently, in most areas the federal government, like the state governments, found itself caught with no alternative to identical delivered prices quoted in accordance with the formula used by the industry.

But in certain sections of the South, Middle West, and Far West where land grant freight rates prevailed on federal government shipments, cement producers found it impossible, at first, to quote precisely identical prices. To avail itself of the lower land grant rates, the government had to use federal bills of lading which required taking possession of the cement shipment at the mill. Land grant rates, in turn, were generally not published and extremely difficult to ascertain correctly because of the complicated formula used in dividing the base rate among the railroad carriers involved on the haul. Although close estimates of land grant rates between particular points could be obtained from the railroads or from records of past hauls, the estimates usually differed from the final figure determined by the government for a particular haul. Moreover, the government could upset efforts of cement firms to quote identical destination prices on the basis of collectively "estimated" land grant rates, by subtracting the cost of commercial freight from the delivered price bid in order to arrive at a mill net price. To the derived mill nets of various

62 *Ibid.*, Transcript pp. 1245, 1258.

bidding concerns, the government then added its own calculation of "true" land grant rates and invariably developed a diversity of destination costs. The contract could then be given to the lowest bidder instead of being awarded by lot among a number of identical bidders or, in accordance with the formula used by Harold Ickes, to the firm absorbing the most freight. The system of known prices at delivery points was thereby threatened, and producers feared waves of unsystematic cutting of mill prices by individual concerns who hoped to win government awards.

The dilemma was sidestepped in 1934 when William Storey, president of Consolidated, worked out a system of bidding "destination cost" to the government with an accompanying "control clause."[63] Under his system, "estimated" land grant rates were to be circulated among the industry, and all bidders were to quote the lowest combination of base price plus "estimated" land grant rate (or commercial freight rate, where applicable) to destination. This would give an identical "destination cost" to the government. The "control clause" which accompanied each competitor's bid specified how to subtract the freight rate in calculating the mill price at which the government would be permitted to take possession of the carload:

> Quotations to the United States Government at bidder's mill on the basis of such "destination costs" shall be determined by subtracting from such "destination costs to the Government" the land grant rate from bidder's mill to destination, or where there is no land grant rate, by subtracting the actual commercial freight rate from bidder's mill to destination.[64]

The result was a method by which identical prices could be quoted to the government, while permitting the government to take possession at the mill and so to realize a saving in freight amounting to the *approximate* land grant rate.

The NRA Code Authority (operated by the Cement Institute) adopted Storey's plan, and "destination cost" bids were filed with the Authority. Following the demise of the NRA, cooperative action was taken by the Cement Institute to gather a mass of "estimated" land grant rates from cement manufacturers and railroads and circulate them. Without knowing what "estimated" land grant rates were being used by others, the

[63] *Ibid.*, Transcript p. 47953.

[64] *Ibid.*, Commission Exhibit 716B.

"control clause" bidding would have been of little avail, since divergent "destination cost" prices would have been received by the government.[65] No further reference will be made to collective activities to circumvent the uncertainties inherent in land grant rates, since after World War II Congress enacted legislation which eliminated the federal government's earlier rail rate privilege.

Acquisitions, Mergers, and the Development of Concentration

Acquisitions and mergers have been frequent in the cement industry. By reducing the number of independent decision-making centers, they have undoubtedly made much easier the mutual recognition of interdependence, self-restraint, and price leadership. Systematic disciplining of mavericks who violate the basing-point formula has also been facilitated by the presence of geographically diversified chain companies. It is true that many early acquisitions were made by concerns which wished to remain in distant markets after new mill installations and the ensuing price reductions in these territories had made access less attractive or even prohibitive on a freight-absorption basis. And the later geographic diversifications through acquisition of plants in areas not regularly served by the concerns undoubtedly offered them the financial advantages of more stable earnings by reducing the shocks of slumps due to shifts in regional construction.[66] However, diversification by acquisition also eliminated the potential increase in competition which would have accompanied

[65] That many bids to the federal government during the 1930's and early 1940's were identical to as many as seven decimal points is attributable to common use of "estimated" land grant rates. Whereas bids involving commercial freight were usually identical only to the nearest penny (or, at most, the nearest mill) per barrel, the land grant rates, as calculated by the federal government, were carried to many decimal places. Cement manufacturers in developing their "estimated" rates attempted to follow the government's calculating procedures to the greatest extent possible.

[66] See C. E. Fraser, and G. F. Doriot, *Analyzing Our Industries* (New York, 1932), pp. 286–317. In the chapter on "Cement," these authors stressed the financial advantages of geographic diversification through mergers. More stable earnings and more ready access to capital were considered the principal advantages. They suggested that mergers in cement offered meager production advantages; that decentralized managements were required; and that product development research was primarily carried on by the Portland Cement Association.

diversification merely through self-expansion. Moreover, in an industry characterized by substantial interpenetration of markets by means of freight absorption, acquisitions of mills in surrounding production territories reduced the number of alternative sources of supply. Acquisitions, therefore, have had the effect of lessening competition either direct or potential, even when this was not the principal motive.

Market stabilization, however, appears to have been the aim of many early efforts to form combinations. In 1908 Edwin C. Eckel, a geologist and an acknowledged expert on the economics of the cement industry, depicted the plight of the newly maturing industry, plagued with cutthroat competition in the face of excess capacity. He cited the formation of ten financial "groupings" which he believed would facilitate price regulation.[67] However, four of these loose stock associations expired during the next few years. A super, $40,000,000 consolidation of thirteen cement companies in the mid-continent area (Missouri, Kansas, Oklahoma, and Texas) was also attempted, but negotiations collapsed in 1912.[68] The development of major multi-plant firms on a significant scale was not to come about until the decade of the twenties, although several of them began their series of acquisitions in the previous decade.

During the first decade of the twentieth century much of the expansion of the larger firms was consummated "naturally," by the direct construction of new plants in more remote areas in order to enlarge the effective marketing territory of the firm. Expansion by internal growth is illustrated in the case of two large Lehigh Valley firms: Lehigh built at Mitchell, Indiana, and Atlas built at Hannibal, Missouri. In the case of two large midwestern concerns, Universal (with plants in South Chicago, Illinois, and Buffington, Indiana) built one close to Pittsburgh; while Sandusky, subsequently renamed Medusa (with a plant in Bay Bridge, Ohio), built additional mills at York, Pennsylvania, Syracuse, Indiana, and Dixon, Illinois. A few Lehigh Valley firms purchased some rival plants within the Valley, but

[67] E. C. Eckel, *The Portland Cement Industry from a Financial Standpoint* (New York, 1908). Eckel saw little prospect of effective price control in pools and thought that patent control or closer consolidation offered the best prospect.

[68] U.S. Geological Survey, *Mineral Resources of the United States, Nonmetals, 1912* (Washington, 1913), p. 516.

internal growth was the typical form of expansion of the multi-plant concern during the first decade.[69]

The next period, 1910–1930, saw the major growth of the multi-plant firms, largely a story of buying up existing mills; but there were a few notable exceptions. Construction of additional new plants was undertaken by the following major producers: (1) Universal at Duluth, Minnesota, in 1916; (2) Lehigh at New Castle, Pennsylvania, in 1910, Mason City, Iowa, in 1911; and Birmingham, Alabama, in 1923; (3) Atlas at Birmingham, Alabama, in 1923, and Waco, Texas, in 1929; (4) Lone Star at New Orleans, Louisiana, in 1927; and (5) Ideal at Boettcher, Colorado, in 1926, and at Okay, Arkansas, in 1928. However, purchase of existing mills, generally in exchange for the stock of the buyer, constituted the usual method of growth. A listing of acquisitions made by the largest concerns will illustrate the point.

The Lehigh Portland Cement Company made acquisitions in the following new territories: Fordwick, Virginia, in 1915; Iola, Kansas, in 1916; and Buffalo, New York, in 1928.[70] In 1924 and 1925 Lehigh also purchased much additional capacity in the northeastern producing area where it operated as the barometric leader on price and marketing policies. The mills acquired were one each at Alsen, New York, and Union Bridge, Maryland; and two in the heart of the Lehigh Valley.[71]

The Ideal Cement Company, which dominated the Rocky Mountain region in 1937 with approximately 70 per cent of the

[69] The material concerning company expansion in the above and following paragraphs is based upon scattered references in the *Record;* the U.S. Geological Survey, *Mineral Resources of the United States* (Washington, various years); as well as the Federal Trade Commission, *Price Bases Inquiry,* pp. 147–157, "Exhibit 1 — Formation and Growth of Important Cement Companies."

[70] In the case of the Buffalo, N.Y., mill, Lehigh purchased 50 per cent of the controlling stock and marketed the entire output under the Lehigh label.

[71] A vice-president of Lehigh went out of his way to deny allegations that these mills in and around the Lehigh Valley area were acquired to remove them from the market, claiming that Lehigh's only desire was to supply under its own label more cement for an expanding eastern market. (See *Record,* Transcript pp. 26585–6.) However, an executive of Penn-Dixie, during a conversation with this writer in December 1948, described Lehigh's purchase of the Bath Portland Cement Company's plants at Bath, Pa. and Sandt's Eddy, Pa. (newly constructed) as a means of clearing from the market a promoter's expansion. Fred Parks, the promoter formerly connected with the Bath Company, then proceeded to organize two more companies and construct two more plants (one during the depression of the thirties). This time, however, neither Lehigh nor any other firm would buy out the concerns.

productive capacity there, developed as a holding and operating company by acquiring cement mills at Portland, Colorado, and Devil's Slide, Utah, in 1908. Later it acquired mills at Trident, Montana, in 1911; at Yocemento, (western) Kansas, in 1916; and Superior, Nebraska, Ada, Oklahoma, and Concrete, Colorado, 1917.

The Alpha Portland Cement Company, with several mills in the Lehigh Valley, secured other mills in the following order: Manheim, West Virginia, in 1909; Catskill, New York, in 1912; Ironton, Ohio, Bellevue, Michigan, La Salle, Illinois, and St. Louis, Missouri, in 1922; and Birmingham, Alabama, in 1928.

The Lone Star Cement Company (known as the International Cement Company until the early thirties) was organized in 1919. Functioning as an operating holding company, it controlled in that year three South American mills and two in Texas. Acquisitions of scattered plants throughout the country proceeded rapidly during the twenties: Hudson, New York, in 1921; Bonner Springs, Kansas, in 1923; Norfolk, Virginia, in 1924; Greencastle, Indiana, in 1925; Birmingham, Alabama, in 1925; Nazareth (Lehigh Valley), Pennsylvania, and Spocari, Alabama, in 1928.

The Pennsylvania-Dixie Cement Corporation was formed in 1926 to merge the properties of four companies: (1) Pennsylvania's mills in the Lehigh Valley and in Portland Point, New York; (2) Dexter's two mills in the Lehigh Valley (one of which Dexter acquired in 1925 by absorbing Penn-Allen); (3) Clinchfield's mills in Kingsport, Tennessee, and Clinchfield, Georgia; and (4) Dixie's mill at Richard City, Tennessee. The new firm acquired another Lehigh Valley producer that same year, as well as a mill in Des Moines, Iowa, in 1928.

The Atlas Portland Cement Company, a major producer in the Lehigh Valley, took over mills at Hudson, New York, sometime before 1917; Leeds, Alabama, in 1919; and Independence, Kansas, in the early 1920's.

In 1929 the greatest consolidation in the history of the cement industry was accomplished when the United States Steel Corporation acquired the properties of the Atlas Portland Cement Company, appraised at over $31,000,000, through an exchange of shares of United States Steel common stock. The approximately

20,000,000-barrel annual cement capacity of Atlas was somewhat greater than that of the Universal Cement Company, the Steel Corporation's cement subsidiary. The new subsidiary was renamed Universal Atlas Cement Company and became the nation's largest producer. In the hands of one concern were 35.3 million barrels of annual capacity, approximately 13.6 per cent of the entire national cement capacity and 15.9 per cent of the capacity east of the Rocky Mountains. Through the merger, Universal's mills at Duluth, Minnesota, Buffington, Indiana, and Pittsburgh, Pennsylvania, were joined with mills serving competitive territories from Lehigh Valley, Pennsylvania, Hudson Valley, New York, and northeastern Missouri. Only the mills acquired in Alabama, Kansas, and Texas appear to have been supplying territories which rarely overlapped with those of Universal. It may be true, as a former president of Universal Atlas testified, that Atlas was purchased because it offered Universal the opportunity to reach large territories remote from its mills,[72] but approximately 50 per cent of Atlas's sales had been made to the same nine states in which Universal made 85 per cent of its shipments,[73] and many consumers in Pennsylvania and Illinois undoubtedly found the number of alternative sources of supply appreciably reduced and prices stabilized.

The formation of these several large multi-plant companies has undoubtedly contributed to stabilization and a rigid adherence to the basing-point pricing formula. That the principal objective in their formation may frequently have been some other purpose does not alter the social consequence.[74] The most obvious result of acquisitions has been the reduction in the number of economically feasible sources of supply for a particular area. Geographic marketing areas cannot be easily defined, but in order to give an illustration of the effect of cement mergers in increasing concentration in a "relevant" marketing area, let us group together producers in eastern Pennsylvania, Maryland, and New York State east of Buffalo. All producers in this arbi-

72 *Record,* Transcript p. 34764.

73 Federal Trade Commission, *Price Bases Inquiry,* p. 96.

74 Stabilization of earning power through geographic diversification and reduction in the wastes of non-price competition (cross-hauling and salesmanship) constitute private advantages which, in the absence of competitive pressures, do not redound to the general public.

trarily defined territory were presumably selling in some common markets. In 1937, there were some nineteen separate manufacturers operating the thirty-five mills in this area, but *ceteris paribus,* there would have been thirty-two companies without the acquisitions made between 1910 and 1928. Such a diminution in the number of decision-makers undoubtedly encouraged and facilitated cooperation in marketing practices.

A second result of the merger movement was the transformation of the pricing behavior of some of the independent companies after absorption into a chain. Testimony before the Commission suggested that independents had been the most frequent price shaders,[75] and more than one producer implied that there had been an elimination of price cutting after certain independents had been acquired.[76]

[75] J. L. Dankel, sales manager of Bessemer until 1936, testified concerning the price cutting period of 1930–31 in the area serviced by his company's mill near Youngstown, O. He stated that he never recalled the majors (Lehigh, Alpha, Medusa, Universal Atlas, and Lone Star) deviating from quoted prices, while the smaller companies (Standard, Pittsburgh, Castalia, Southwestern, and Huron) were frequently cutting prices unsystematically. (*Record,* Transcript pp. 11343–44.)

[76] In reply to the Burns-Clark questionnaire in 1935, Penn–Dixie stated that after nine independents had been absorbed by chains, price conditions had improved, "generally speaking, by the adoption of sounder merchandising methods, more ethical practices and the one price policy." The nine mills mentioned, and their acquirers, were as follows: (1) Spocari, Ala., (2) Birmingham, Ala., and (3) Nazareth, Pa., all acquired by Lone Star; (4) Union Bridge, Md., (5) Bath, Pa., and (6) Alsen, N.Y., all acquired by Lehigh; (7) Birmingham, Ala., acquired by Alpha; (8) Manitowoc, Wis., by Medusa; and (9) Fredonia, Kan., by Consolidated (Cowham Engineering Group). *Ibid.,* Commission Exhibits 975–7H, 8P, 9G, 10N.

Moreover, the president of Southwestern (with mills in southern California, Texas, and Ohio) wrote on April 25, 1928 to the president of Trinity (with mills in Texas, but affiliated with a holding company with mills in Tennessee, Florida, Kansas, and Michigan):

"It is very interesting to hear of the Eastern consolidations and recent purchases of the outlaw plants by some of the larger companies. It is proven that the most effective way to cure a bad situation is to buy up the offenders. I have always understood that there was a hot-bed of bad actors through Alabama and some of the adjoining Southern states, and for a time it looked as though conditions would never adjust themselves. The demoralized market backed up and we felt it in our Osborn [Ohio] territory. At the time the Birmingham base was dropped to $1.45, it trimmed us out of 10¢ a barrel in our Cincinnati territory, and we felt this quite keenly as this was our home town market. We are all hoping that the Southern situation is in good hands and that we soon can look for a more stable situation.

"Lindley Morton has always been inclined to jump over the traces, and has made trouble wherever his organization lands. It was surely welcome news to know that he is out of the game." (*Ibid.,* Commission Exhibit 1274–C.)

Third, the formation of a few large chains brought a price leadership which the remaining independents were induced to follow, the chains operating to force adherence to the delivered price system by imposing selective base price reductions on violators.[77]

As a consequence of the mergers enumerated above, as well as others, substantial concentration in the portland cement industry had developed by 1930. Inevitably there would be a limited number of firms in any marketing area because of the minimum size of plant necessary for economical production; but both within particular marketing areas and on a national basis, concentration had become even greater, primarily because of corporate acquisitions. According to the Federal Trade Commission, concentration of control of the 251,986,000 barrels of theoretical annual cement capacity was as follows in 1937: [78]

	Aggregate capacity in barrels	*Percentage of total U.S. capacity*
1. Five largest producers	96,237,000	39.0%
Alpha		
Lehigh (including Great Lakes)		
Lone Star		
Penn-Dixie		
Universal Atlas		
2. Next five largest producers	39,166,000	15.5%
Cowham Engineering Group (Consolidated, Florida, Trinity, Signal Mountain)		
Huron		
Ideal Group		
Marquette		
Medusa		
Total	135,403,000	54.5%

The letter referred to both the prospective sale of an independent mill at Spocari, Ala. to Lone Star, and Lindley Morton's agreement to quit the cement business, following his sale of a new Alabama plant to Alpha and his previous sale of another in Alabama and one in Pennsylvania to Lone Star. (*Ibid.*, Commission Exhibit 1274.)

[77] Dankel (see footnote 75) explained that price cutting came to an end when Alpha and Lehigh quoted disastrously low base (open) prices at their own and other mills in this area during 1931. The pressure of these uniformly low prices forced the "chiselers" to halt their unsystematic pricing and return to the "ethical practice" of adhering to open prices. (*Ibid.*, Transcript pp. 11343–44.)

[78] *Ibid.*, Commission Exhibit 562–8A, 3205.

The Commission reported further that out of a total of the 164 mills in existence in 1937, the five largest producers controlled 47 mills. In several of the largest producing districts, the percentage of the capacity controlled by the nation's five largest manufacturers was close to or exceeded 50 per cent: [79]

Bureau of mines producing district	*Percentage controlled by the nation's five largest producers*
Districts 1 and 2	51.7%
District 5	61.8
District 6	66.6
District 7	46.1

The geographic location of the Bureau of Mines producing districts is illustrated on Map 1. And the geographic sweep of the six largest producers is illustrated on Map 2. The position of the nation's largest producers in the various Bureau of Mines districts shows that only the Pacific Coast was free from domination by chains (although not oligopoly) in 1937:

	Percentage controlled by the nation's ten largest producers [80]	*Total number of producers* [81]	*Total number of mills* [82]
Districts 1 & 2	52.9	20	38
District 3	43.6	16	19
District 4	45.3	8	10
District 5	88.4	9	11
District 6	79.3	12	19
District 7	52.9	10	12
District 8	57.1	9	12
District 9	66.3	6	9
District 10	69.8	5	8
District 11	none	9	11
District 12	small	7	9
			158

[79] *Ibid.*, Commission Exhibit 3205.

[80] *Ibid.*

[81] Prepared by the writer on the basis of testimony and exhibits scattered throughout the *Record*.

[82] *Ibid.* The total number of mills in this table is fewer than the 164 mills previously reported, because a company operating more than one plant in a single town is treated as operating a single mill.

Map 1. Cement Plants and Cement Producing Districts in Relation to Sources of Limestone and Bituminous Coal, 1940

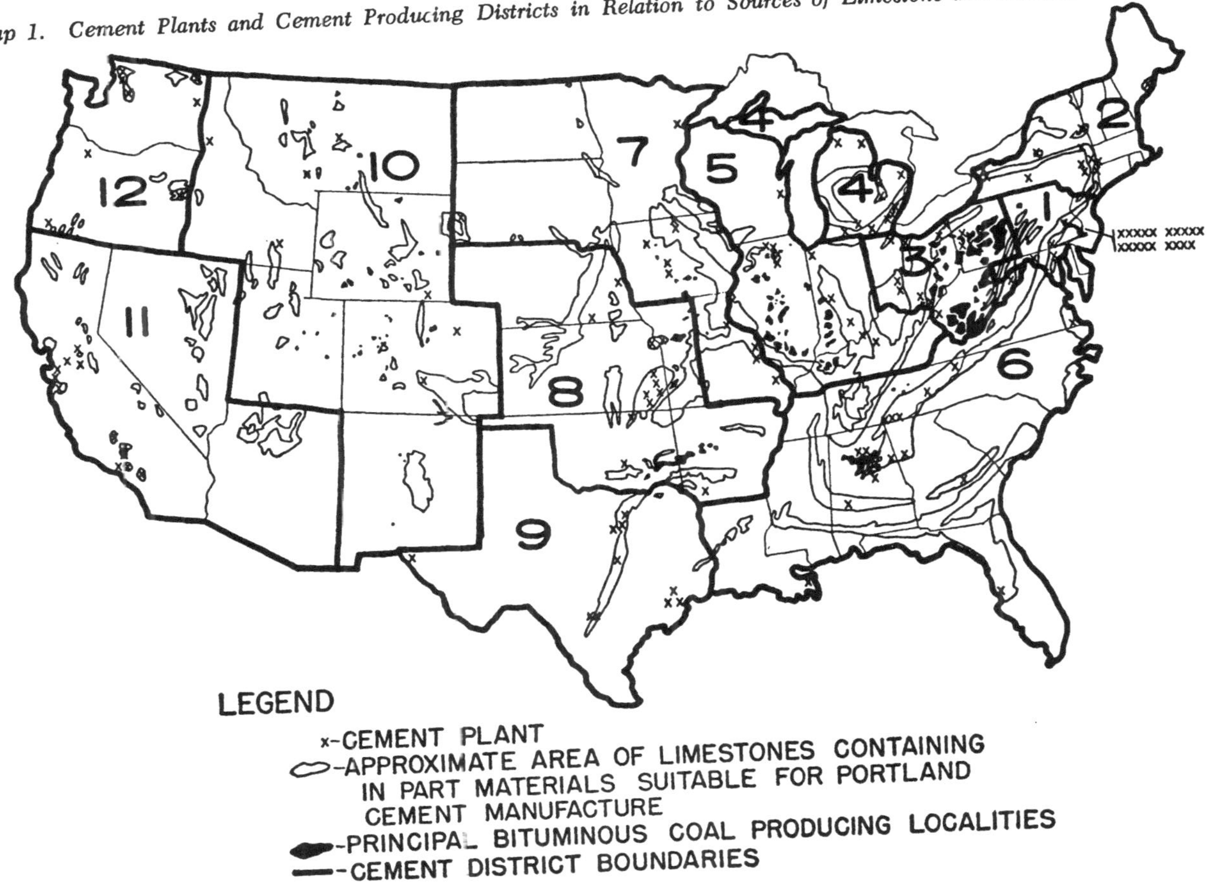

Map 2. *Geographical Relationship of the Plants of Six of the Largest Producers of Portland Cement, 1937*

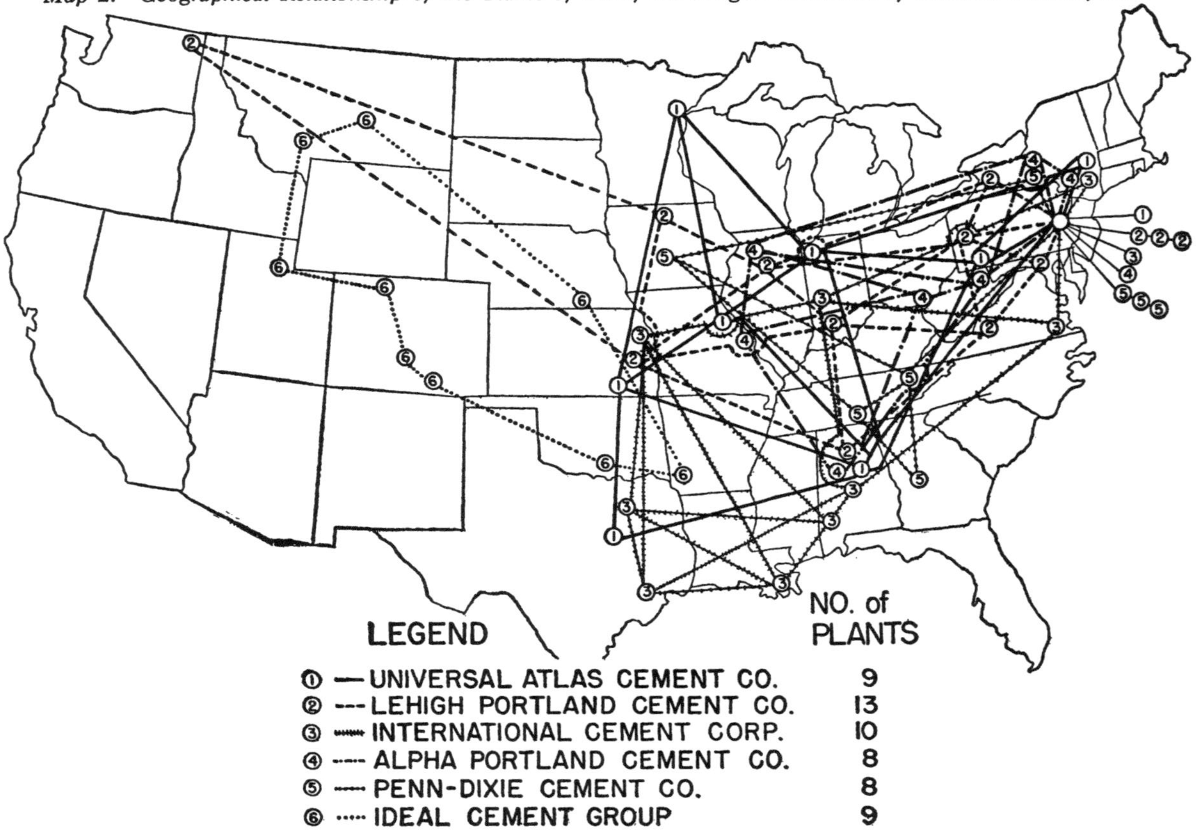

Such concentration undoubtedly contributed to "ethical adherence" to the collusively developed devices required to maintain a system of delivered pricing.

The Punitive Base — A Disciplinary Weapon to Enforce Adherence to the Formula

It is generally acknowledged that whenever a firm produces at scattered geographic locations, it is possible for it to reduce selectively its own base mill price in particular production centers where less diversified firms are situated in an effort to drive the latter out of business, or (and more likely) to coerce them to adhere to higher prices. This type of geographic price discrimination (which could be used in conjunction with uniform mill net pricing) does not appear to have been employed for predatory purposes in the cement industry, although some use has been made of it as a disciplinary device. Strategic geographic pricing in the cement industry has primarily taken the form of a special pattern of discriminatory mill nets designed to reduce the effective base price at a rival's mill alone.

The punitive base has been used to enforce adherence to the basing-point formula. In fact, as many cement firms (particularly the geographically diversified price leaders) interpreted the logic of the basing-point system, any delivered price quotation which breached the formula could be taken as evidence that the price cutter had reduced his base price. When a non-base mill violated the formula on a particular delivered price sale, a base price might be established equivalent to the mill net produced by that sale (delivered price minus commercial freight from the shipping mill). By the same token, if a firm with an established base price abandoned the formula in either his own natural market or his rival's, a base price might be imposed equivalent to the mill net derived on the unsystematic sale. The penalty of such a generalized ("open") price reduction affected mainly the offending mill. The mill which imposed the punitive base suffered comparatively little since the majority of its sales were presumably being made in that portion of its natural market unaffected by the base price reduction at the rival mill.

The usual result of an imposition of a punitive base was the cessation of further price cutting by the offending mill. And the awareness that certain mills were being thus disciplined served to deter other competitors from selective cutting of prices. An expectation that a concession on a delivered price would be met on future price quotations only at the specific destination would not necessarily have deterred such a price cut if thereby a large order could be won. But where there was danger that a particular price concession might be generalized, via the punitive base, into a maximum mill net for all future sales, the potential long-period losses were likely to exceed by far the gain expected from capturing one large contract.

In times of excess capacity, the independent producers have been the ones which exercised price independence most frequently.[83] But under an institutional system which enabled the leaders in the industry to impose these retributive bases, an excellent weapon was at hand to enforce systematic adherence to the basing-point formula among the independents. And the traditional usefulness of this group in introducing uncertainty and flexibility into the pricing structure was thereby nullified.

It seems important to emphasize that not freight absorption, per se, but the strategic pattern of the price discrimination was the culprit which stifled independent pricing and induced collectivism. The anti-competitive "purpose," of course, can be inferred from the systematic process by which the imposer of the punitive base generalized the unsystematically derived mill net to conform to the principles of the basing-point formula. It is true that while the punitive bases remained in effect, prices to many consumers in the areas affected were generally lower than they would otherwise have been *during that period.* But the reduced prices lasted only until the offending mill gave assurances to the leaders in the industry that it would follow the pricing formula.[84]

The exact year in which punitive base mill prices were first established in the cement industry is uncertain. The first evidence of the use of the punitive base was of one applied in 1926 to a new

[83] See, for example, footnotes 75 and 76 of this chapter.

[84] *Record,* Commission Exhibit 2247. This is a letter from a disciplined firm requesting Lehigh to remove the punitive base at Ada, Okla.

plant at Rapid City, owned by the state of South Dakota. The state plant had begun operations in 1925 as a non-base mill, and the effect of the punitive base was to reduce the maximum mill net at Rapid City by 60 or 70 cents.[85] A Lehigh executive testified before the Commission that his firm had applied the base in order to generalize the secret quotations of the state plant, and thereby to protect itself from "a great many prices made by the Rapid City plant lower than its public quotations." [86] In 1927 the Lone Star chain (two of its mills being at Birmingham and New Orleans) quoted to its customers delivered prices based on an assumed price of the Warrior mill at Spocari, Alabama, a practice which converted that mill into a base mill. The president of Lone Star testified that Spocari had "undersold Lone Star so persistently by quoting special prices that Lone Star finally quoted its whole territory on the basis of these special prices." [87] Under the pressure from the drastically lowered base price at Spocari, the Warrior Company sold its plant there to Lone Star in April 1928. This Alabama incident furnishes the only documented example of a punitive base having been maintained long enough to induce an independent firm to sell out.

A great rash of punitive bases broke out between December 1930 and May 1932. Severe price competition, much of it unsystematic, developed in the industry in the fall of 1930 as excess capacity began to pile up. In several midwestern states some unsystematic bids were made to highway commissions, and special delivered prices to commercial customers. Marquette was the principal price cutter on highway bids in Indiana and Illinois. This firm operated one mill at the La Salle, Illinois, basing-point where Lehigh, Alpha, and Medusa also had mills, as well as one non-base mill in relatively isolated Cape Girardeau, Missouri. The maximum mill net of approximately $1.85 per barrel at Cape Girardeau was reduced to $1.35 in December 1930 when Alpha imposed the punitive base price. It was subsequently reduced still further reaching a low of 75 cents which was set up as the base price by Lone Star in June 1932. Price stability returned to the Middle West on July 16, 1932 when Marquette at the same

[85] *Ibid.*, Transcript pp. 12747–50.
[86] *Ibid.*, Transcript pp. 26905–06.
[87] *Ibid.*, Transcript p. 34674.

time joined the Portland Cement Association and raised its base price at Cape Girardeau by 40 cents. (This action was especially important for pricing harmony since several competitors had announced that they would not rejoin the Association until Marquette did.) Marquette's competitors did not meet the advance in price at Cape Girardeau for several days, and so Marquette had to pay further penance for its transgressions.[88]

Although Lehigh did not play a central role in the Cape Girardeau affair, it was the principal instigator and remover of punitive bases in the rest of the Middle West.[89] Between December 1930 and July 1932 Lehigh imposed punitive bases at the following mill locations: Harrys, Texas; Ada and Dewey, Oklahoma; Louisville, Nebraska; Kosmosdale, Kentucky; Speed, Indiana; and Painesville, Ohio. And although Lehigh did not initiate the punitive base at Superior, Nebraska, its removal was delayed until Lehigh was prepared to discontinue quoting prices based on Superior. The only other punitive bases were those applied by Alpha at Fultonham and Osborn, Ohio, in 1931.[90]

The last of the punitive bases was removed by August 1932,[91] at which time trucking was being eliminated or controlled and base prices in most production centers were being increased. It appears that the disciplinary experience had a lasting effect. Dr. Arthur E. Morgan, chairman of the Tennessee Valley Authority, testified in 1934 that during the negotiations to purchase cement for TVA at a reasonable price, representatives of Marquette stated that they could sell cement for a lower price but hesitated to do so because they feared the displeasure of others in the industry.[92] Morgan stated that a sales representative of Volunteer (located at Knoxville, Tennessee, and also famous as a price cutter in 1931) had made a similar statement.[93]

88 *Ibid.*, Commission Exhibits 2268–2358, 2965, 2982–88, 2998, 3000–07.

89 *Ibid.*, Commission Exhibits 2248, 3321, 971–23 N–O–P; Transcript pp. 12412, 12993–94, 27282–83.

90 *Ibid.*, Commission Exhibit 970–15–Y–2.

91 One exception occurred in 1937. Wabash, a small firm with mills in northeastern Indiana and southwestern Ohio, became petulant when Aetna, another small firm with a mill at Bay City, Mich., "high-jacked" an important Wabash contract. For a short period Wabash reduced the Bay City base price by 10 cents per barrel, until intervention by some of the region's largest firms settled the feud. *Ibid.*, Transcript pp. 11100–11, 11196–97.

92 *Ibid.*, Transcript pp. 11290–304.

93 *Ibid.*

The punitive base was one of the most insidious features of a full-flowered basing-point system of pricing by formula. Firms, which had come to accept orderly pricing as part of the "trade ethics" of the industry, felt morally justified in forcing rivals to generalize their price concessions. The self-righteous attitude of Lehigh's president is seen in his correspondence with Dr. Arthur R. Burns in 1935, concerning preparation of an industry questionnaire:

The addition of the phrase "although it subsequently emerges that no base price had been installed by the mill there" seems unfortunate in that an answer to the question in this form might be interpreted as an admission on the part of the company meeting lower competitive delivered prices in the field that no base price had been installed at the mill of the price cutter. Whether or not cuts made by a competitor in the field result in a lowering of his base price is a moot point. It is my contention that any manufacturer finding such competitive cut prices in the field has every right not only to meet the cut prices as discovered but also to quote prices generally in that territory predicated on the assumption that the competitor has in fact reduced his base price. Furthermore, before taking such action to meet competitive cut prices, according to my theory it would not be incumbent upon a manufacturer to inquire of his unfriendly competitor whether or not the cut prices in the field constitute a reduction in the base price.[94]

The basic morality which Lehigh conceived to be tied up in the open price system of the basing-point formula is also illustrated in a brief exchange between the trial examiner and the testimony of one of Lehigh's vice-presidents:

Trial Examiner Norwood: "Were they cutting below your base price?"
The Witness: "Cutting below their own base quoted destination price, and below ours, and because we would make our prices only openly we were unable to match that sort of competition; we were compelled to make public the prices which we hoped would enable us to sell." [95]

Protected Dealer Marketing System: Minimization of Secret Pricing

In restricting to dealers sales of cement destined for use in cities and towns, cement manufacturers had devised a marketing method to encourage adherence to the basing-point pricing formula. Because the dealer buys both continuously and from sev-

[94] *Ibid.*, Commission Exhibit 971 4Q–4R.
[95] *Ibid.*, Transcript p 27272.

eral sources simultaneously, a trading post is maintained to make public delivered prices quoted for various destinations. Numerous manufacturers testified that a dealer, being friendly with company salesmen, would usually inform them as soon as a rival had quoted secretly below the list, formula price.[96] In this respect the marketing position of the dealer is in striking contrast to that of most large contractors. Not only is such a contractor continually changing the geographic destination of his cement requirements, but his large lump sum orders are made in a discontinuous manner, as awards for construction jobs come his way. He is in a peculiarly advantageous position to shop around and bargain to obtain a special price from manufacturers' representatives. When a contractor places a large order for a specific spot at a special price, not only does the sale constitute a single deal at this place with this purchaser, but also there is less likelihood that rivals will learn about the price concession. The uncertainty surrounding isolated sales to contractors ominously threatened strict adherence to the basing-point pricing formula. By the early thirties a trade practice was finally developed allowing direct sales to contractors only in territories outside of cities and towns where dealers were not operating.

The Federal Trade Commission, in its complaint, hearings, findings, and order, took cognizance of the cooperative efforts of cement manufacturers to classify buyers and the channels of direct sales, but the Commission apparently interpreted these endeavors as merely one of many other subsidiary activities designed to standardize trade practices in the industry. Testimony and exhibits persuasively suggested that the policy of dealer protection was primarily designed to curtail the unsettling bargaining power of the large contractor. But representatives of the Commission seem never to have quite come to grips with the problem.[97] At least there is no discussion of the threat posed by

[96] In fact, counsel for the Commission heard so many executives of cement companies testify as to the difficulty of keeping prices to dealers secret that he conceded that an unspecified number of respondent executives would testify to the same effect. *Ibid.*, Transcript pp. 39231–32.

[97] At two points in the Hearings, representatives of the Commission made the following concessions:

"*Mr. Wooden:* I will make it unnecessary [to introduce additional respondent

direct sales to large contractors in the Commission's lengthy statement of the "Findings as to Facts and Conclusion."[98]

Confining direct sales to dealers was clearly an arbitrary arrangement since a dealer served no real economic function when he operated as a middleman between a manufacturer and a very large contractor. The firm which was to construct a large factory, office building, apartment house, or city bridge requiring several thousand barrels of cement was in a position to do its own servicing of the order (i.e., arranging a rail siding, trucking to the job, and guaranteeing payment to the manufacturer). Cement producers typically would wine and dine such a contractor and perform various technical services for him, so as to induce him to specify their brands to the dealer. But unless forced by competition (as sometimes happened in the very early thirties), producers would not talk prices but instead would require the contractor to buy through their dealer in his locality. The president of Hercules explained that when his firm received requests from contractors for direct sales, ". . . we either refer them to a dealer in the vicinity or we refer them to the salesman who takes it up with the dealer to see if he can secure the business for the dealer."[99] While manufacturers continued to sell to their dealers at the delivered price posted for each particular locality, the bargaining power of the contractor would be turned only against the dealers whose conventional mark-ups would thus be subject to a squeeze. Yet the dealers were in no

---

witnesses] by agreeing to stipulate that the dealer trade, for all Respondents, if they want it that way, is an important factor in their business.

"The greater the importance of the dealer the more probable it is that they defer to the wishes of their dealers, as they have done, and as we approve for them to do." (*Record*, Transcript p. 26024.)

"*Trial Examiner Norwood:* I do not think there is any evidence to the contrary that the manufacturers — the main part of their business, the substantial part is through dealers; that it is a diversified business; that it is more substantial for that reason, goes through many small sources, and docs not subject him to violent reactions in the matter of quantity, as between one year and another.

"We have gone into that. We know all about that."

"*Mr. Paulson:* I do not think there is anything more clear in the case than that we should not go into the fine percentages of this proposition." (*Record*, Transcript p. 28572.)

98 *Cement Institute*, 37 FTC 87 (1943), pp. 125–276.

99 *Record*, Transcript p. 26068.

position to complain about this, since their only economic function in such sales was the private one of protecting cement manufacturers from the unsettling effects on prices of direct sales to large contractors. It is little wonder that an executive of Southern States testified, "I hope sincerely I will be able to organize my business so I will never have to take a contract and have nothing but dealer business."[100]

A policy of protecting dealers was initiated in 1913 when manufacturers withheld from contractors the minimum (dealer) price quotation on all orders below 7500 barrels (about 24 carloads), subsequently raised to 15,000 barrels. During 1914 and 1915 a more stringent policy was adopted generally, that of quoting contractors five additional cents per barrel, irrespective of quantity. At the May 1915 meetings of the Association of American Portland Cement Manufacturers the Committee on Trade Conditions reported:

> It is believed that the principle of making higher prices to consumers and contractors than are made to dealers is correct, and that there has been a material improvement in the situation in territories where this practice has been followed. It is, therefore, believed that the practice should be general in all territories and that all companies follow the same practice. . . .
>
> Therefore, the Committee recommends that it be established as a custom in quoting contractors and consumers to add not less than five cents per barrel to the dealer's price.[101]

Minutes of the Cement Manufacturers Protective Association meeting in 1916 noted that all of its members were practicing the trade custom of quoting dealers and contractors on a different basis.[102] Moreover, in 1919 the Committee on Trade Conditions of the Portland Cement Association published a booklet of trade practices which included a recommendation for the continued maintenance of a price differential between the dealer and contractor.[103]

The differential was increased to ten cents late in 1916. Ten years later, following the leadership of Lehigh, the practice was adopted of quoting the same price to dealer and contractor, but offering a ten cent discount to the dealers. During the ensuing

[100] *Ibid.*, Transcript p. 37544.
[101] *Ibid.*, Commission Exhibit 3193.
[102] *Ibid.*, Commission Exhibit 3234.
[103] *Ibid.*, Commission Exhibit 3192.

period of rapid highway construction, however, when there were huge orders for cement by contractors, the dealer discount was "abused." Some dealers chiseled on the discount when soliciting sales to contractors, and the "less scrupulous" manufacturers organized "phony" dealers to cut prices by shading the discount margin. Moreover, during 1930–31 some manufacturers began to sell directly to contractors at dealer prices — and below. As a result of such underhandedness dealer discounts were finally abandoned by 1931. Thenceforth, a flat price was to be quoted to all buyers, and manufacturers had to experiment with a new plan of dealer protection. The policy which emerged with respect to contractors was one of refusing them direct sale for work located entirely within cities and towns where there were dealers.[104] Article XI of the NRA Code for the cement industry (approved on November 27, 1933) which contained such a provision of market classification reflected the new prevailing practice.[105] However, the Article was suspended in January 1934, following the refusal of the Consumer's Advisory Board to permit any classification of buyers in the Code.

The rash of price concessions which broke out temporarily in Indiana and Mississippi during the latter part of 1938 was attributed primarily to direct sales to highway contractors.[106] Here is another possible explanation for the discontinuation of sealed bid purchasing of highway cement requirements by many state governments after identical sealed bids became universal in the summer of 1932. All testimony relating to secret prices during the Commission hearings showed that concessions were made much more frequently to contractors than to dealers. The differential marketing power possessed by the contractors is forcefully described in the testimony of two cement executives:

Charles L. Hogan, president of Lone Star — : "Well, the dealer trade is scattered throughout the United States, almost in every little hamlet or village there is a dealer and the total amount which individual dealers buy

104 Railroads and the federal and state governments had long held the privilege of purchasing at the dealer price. In the late twenties this privilege was also extended to concrete products manufacturers and central mixing plants. These buyers could still buy directly irrespective of location.

105 *Record*, Commission Exhibit 585 Q–S.

106 *Ibid.*, Transcript p. 34657.

with the exception of a few in the larger cities is not — I mean the total amount for a year is not great enough to warrant any one going in and making them secret prices.

[*One paragraph omitted.*]

"Such big cities like New York, Boston, Chicago, we have from our experience been led to believe that certain dealers have been given special prices. We have never made any special prices to dealers. Never done that. Made special prices to contractors, because in that case the contractor has a job, he is the only buyer on the job, and he may not have another job for a long time and you are making him that special price for just that one job; whereas, if you gave it to a dealer, it would be a continual operation throughout the year. We don't do it." [107]

Chester A. Brooke, vice-president of Monarch — : "Well, I would say this, that the contractor, where this business is so highly competitive, the contractor is buying cement for a particular job, and when he is through, why, we are through with that obligation; whereas, you sell a dealer at a price less than the published price, you have to continue it or usually lose a customer." [108]

Manufacturers' sales representatives lavishly entertained large contractors doing city work and provided them with technical assistance in the hope of inducing them to specify particular brands of cement when ordering from dealers or central mix operators. The contractors, however, being price conscious, would specify a particular brand only when prices were identical for all brands. Consequently, it was extremely difficult for a manufacturer to keep secret any price concession made to a contractor via a dealer or ready-mix operator. When a manufacturer failed to receive via the middleman an order "promised" by a contractor, he suspected a price concession; and the secret price was likely to be discovered, met, generalized in accordance with the formula, and forced to be continued openly in the future. Such a synthetic system of "price reporting" undoubtedly increased confidence that all manufacturers would respect the pricing formula.

Subsidiary Cooperative Practices

1. Standardization of terms of sale

Beginning with the earliest trade association, efforts were made from time to time to publish standardized terms of sale:

[107] *Ibid.*, Transcript p. 34659.

[108] *Ibid.*, Transcript p. 42358.

cash discounts, package charges, refunds for returned bags, and the requirement that buyers who requested bin testing of cement (by commercial laboratories) pay the cost.

2. Protection of dealer territories

In 1915 the Committee of Trade Conditions of the Association of American Portland Cement Manufacturers recommended that dealers be quoted the dealer price for shipments destined for their home town only. Four years later this practice was also recommended in a pamphlet of the Portland Cement Association, and was subsequently adopted generally. On the basis of the limited treatment of this practice in the *Record*, one might be tempted to believe that cement manufacturers were solicitous merely of the welfare of their dealers, but it seems likely that the manufacturers were equally concerned with their own welfare. Dumping by a dealer into rival territories at reduced margins undoubtedly produced the kind of demoralization among dealers which would make them want to bargain with manufacturers for price concessions.[109]

3. Suppression of quality competition

In order to prevent price concessions by manufacturers of inferior cement and also in order to minimize rising costs due to non-price competition, repeated efforts were made by industry associations to standardize the product and discourage rivalry based on alleged superior quality. With price identity as the major objective, in 1904 the Association of American Portland Cement Manufacturers adopted standard minimum quality specifications. Said one producer at this early meeting, "This will certainly give us a common ground in the cement business on which we can meet, and will enable a standard, uniform article to be made at a uniform price." [110] And with the cost-increasing effect of quality competition in mind, the 1929 Code of Ethics of the Cement Institute declared it to be an unfair trade practice to make and sell portland cement which exceeded the existing

[109] And at least one manufacturer so argued. *Ibid.*, Commission Exhibit 971–9 A–B.

[110] *Ibid.*, Commission Exhibit 3235U.

standard specifications set by the American Society for Testing Materials. Fineness of grind (contributing to strength) constituted the principal technique of rivalry over quality. Although many manufacturers violated the industry's code by producing "standard" cement substantially in excess of the minimum specifications, institutional advertising by associations stressed the "standardized" nature of the product, and individual producers refrained from advertising the fact that their brands exceeded the standard.[111] Representatives of the United States Public Roads Administration and of the Bureau of Standards testified during the hearings that prior to the marketing of "high-early-strength" cement the strength of the various brands of "standard" cement had differed by as much as 50 to 100 per cent. Fineness of grind constituted the major difference in these two lines of portland cement, the standard and the "high-early-strength." Witnesses testified before the Commission, furthermore, that after the C–1 Committee of the American Society of Testing Materials in 1930 had approved "high-early-strength" specifications (which produced a cement which was to sell at a substantial premium) the wide variance in quality of "standard" cements was reduced somewhat. Moreover, despite the objections of consumer groups, cement manufacturers persuaded the C–1 Committee to reduce the minimum fineness requirements for "standard" cement, thus further lessening the possibility of substituting one of the two types of cement for the other.[112]

4. Collective boycott of dealers handling imported cement

Imported cement never exceeded 2 per cent of domestic production during any one year of the thirties, yet imports threatened certain markets at East Coast ports and those inland points within an economical trucking radius. Until the summer of 1932 the combined effect of the 1930 tariff of 22 cents per barrel and the decline of domestic prices discouraged imports even on the East Coast. When producers in the Lehigh and Hudson valleys advanced their base prices 29 cents per barrel in August 1932, the basing-point formula was modified so that unchanged deliv-

[111] *Ibid.,* Transcript pp. 48348, 48425.
[112] *Ibid.,* Transcript pp. 48325–6, 48345, 48348, 48375, 48420.

ered prices in the metropolitan area of New York could meet foreign competition. However, at the end of December 1932, prices were advanced in New York City to reflect the controlling base mill price. In order to discourage the importation of foreign cement into New York and Boston, a collective boycott of all dealers handling imported cement was organized. Dealers were informed that if they handled the foreign product, they would be denied American cement, which most government projects specified. From 1933 to 1935 a rotating system of espionage by manufacturers' representatives was used to check dealers' trucks.[113] Handlers of the imported product were "blacklisted" and domestic cement was denied them until such time as they petitioned a committee of manufacturers for reinstatement and agreed to discontinue sale of foreign cement.[114] The eastern boycott collapsed, however, in 1935. The National Portland Cement Company had just begun production in the Lehigh Valley and in order to find an outlet for its product offered to sell to any dealer. The firms in the eastern area, forced to compete with imported cement, instituted lower port prices, and established a complicated pattern of slightly higher zoned prices at surrounding points in order to discourage dealers at ports from trucking cement inland. Leading companies which issued the complex "depressed price schedules" in July 1935 (after the demise of NRA) and the subsequent revisions during 1936 and 1937, either notified the Cement Institute of these zoned price lists or submitted them directly to competitors prior to the public announcement.[115]

5. *Cooperative checking and cancellation of surplus specific job contracts*

Because there was usually an excess capacity, cement manufacturers were eager to make sales and so readily committed themselves to dealers for specific job contracts. Dealers, desiring

[113] *Ibid.*, Commission Exhibits 1160–A–F, 1161–2; Transcript pp. 7409, 7413–15, 7434–35, 7811, 7817, 7920.

[114] *Ibid.*, Commission Exhibit 1176, Transcript pp. 7717–19, 7724–25, 7728, 7805–06, 7752–60, 7993–94, 23865.

[115] *Ibid.*, Commission Exhibits 210–C–I, 276–A–D, 308–B, 593–D, 286–C, 326–A–B, 867–U–Y, 870–13–B, 922; Transcript pp. 24603–05, 27293, 28175, 28357–60, 28418.

to hedge against possible price increases, traditionally oversubscribed their requirements for cement by duplicating contracts for a "specific" construction job with several manufacturers. Should the price remain stable or decline, the dealer would merely cancel his surplus "contracts." Manufacturers never filed suit to enforce these contracts, because such action would have resulted in loss of good will and future sales. The specific job "contracts" therefore were tantamount to options to buy. In a rising market the dealer would exercise all of his options at the contract price thereby securing large stocks of cement for his general trade at a price below the new and higher delivered price announced by the manufacturers. The constant threat of lower prices made very difficult the initiation of a price increase, save at times of very strong demand.

The purpose of cooperative checking and cancellation of redundant contracts for a specific job was to combat this dealer speculation and thus facilitate price increases. Such contracts between manufacturers and dealers in the cement industry were used to allow a contractor to receive his cement requirements at a ceiling price for a special job which might last for several months. If the quoted delivered price declined, the contractor would receive the remainder of the cement contracted for at the reduced price. But if the quoted price advanced, he would still pay only the price agreed upon. A particular job contract was made between the manufacturer and dealer for a specific quantity of cement which the dealer had engaged to supply to a contractor.

To combat the one-sided speculation by dealers, manufacturers undertook collective action to eliminate the duplication of specific job contracts. This was one of the most important activities of the Cement Manufacturers Protective Association, prior to its voluntary dissolution in 1922, as well as of the Cement Institute, organized in 1929. Specific job contracts were reported daily by manufacturers to the Cement Institute; subsequently field checks of dealers were made by representatives of the Institute; and duplicate contracts were canceled at meetings of the Institute.[116] The Cement Institute's service was abandoned in

[116] *Ibid.*, Commission Exhibits 1018A, 137A. The latter exhibit told of the elimination of 6 million barrels of duplicated contracts in the Northeast (New England and Middle Atlantic states) between November 1, 1929 and January 8, 1930.

May 1931 when prices were declining; it was revived in 1933 prior to its authorization in the NRA Cement Code; and was again abandoned in September 1936 as part of a general policy of retrenchment.

The Supreme Court in 1925 had condoned the collective contract checking and cancellation as a means of preventing "unfair trade tactics" by dealers.[117] But in a tightly rigged oligopolistic market, the one-sided speculation by buyers may have been very desirable from the point of view of consumers, since it was one of the few means of weakening understandings among the producers which lead to upward prices.

6. Dissemination of individual company statistics on production, shipments, and stocks

Until its demise in 1922 the Cement Manufacturers Protective Association distributed to its membership statistics on clinker production and stocks, and on cement production, shipments, and stocks — identified by individual companies. When the Cement Institute was established in 1929, it renewed the dissemination of the same statistics. Since government agencies distributed similar data, grouped by production districts as well as nationally, there is little doubt that the purpose of distributing individual company data was to bolster confidence that firms were adhering to the pricing formula. The validity of this contention is confirmed by a memorandum from the head of the Institute's statistical service to its general manager dated April 2, 1936:

> I have no knowledge as to the value the reports have to the companies. However, they are issued in the belief that they will help the companies by eliminating their suspicions in connection with what their competitors are producing and shipping since they get the facts. . . .[118]

7. Informal trading of shipments to obtain higher mill nets

In order to reduce the financial losses inherent in cross-hauling under the basing-point system of pricing, cement manufacturers from time to time effected a cooperative exchange of shipments so that each firm would realize a high mill net. The *Record* does not disclose the full extent to which the practice of

[117] *Cement Mfrs. Protective Ass'n, et al.* v. *U.S.*, 268 U.S. 588, 596 (1925).
[118] *Record,* Commission Exhibit 2879.

shipping for each other's account developed, but scattered references in exhibits and testimony suggest that the volume of traded shipments was not inconsiderable. Sometimes sales were "swapped" immediately, while on other occasions credits were obtained for future reciprocity. Writing to his Penn-Dixie headquarters in September 1929, a sales representative in Des Moines remarked: It is reported that Atlas is shipping some for Ideal; Northwestern shipping for Ash Grove and Ideal; and Lehigh is shipping for Marquette. We are the only ones, I believe, shipping for Hawkeye.[119] A representative of Louisville Cement testified that his company had arranged an exchange with Universal Atlas, whereby the latter would ship 50,000 barrels to the Indiana Roads Commission in Valparaiso in northern Indiana for the account of Louisville, while Louisville would ship to the Roads Commission at Lafayette in central Indiana 40,000 barrels for the account of Universal Atlas, thereby reducing the amount of freight to be absorbed.[120] In 1937 the cement division of Pittsburgh Plate Glass, with its mill in central Ohio, arranged to have a northern Ohio cement company truck cement in bags bearing the Pittsburgh label to fill a large order at Republic Steel's Cleveland plant.[121] Undoubtedly, difficulties in arranging commensurate mutual advantages occasionally hindered or delayed exchanges, as illustrated in a letter of May 1931 prepared by the assistant of the president of the Lawrence Portland Cement Company, which possessed one mill in Maine and one in the Lehigh Valley:

> On Wednesday of last week I had lunch with Walter Wing and Druckenmiller of the Penn-Dixie Company and suggested that we trade cement — we to furnish jobs which they have in Massachusetts and they to furnish the jobs which we have in New York from their Portland Point [New York] mill. They would make a savings of 8¢ a barrel on freight and we would make a saving of 23¢ to 25¢ a barrel. At first they wanted to exchange contracts but I told them that we weren't interested in it and then they wanted to split the difference of the saving and I told them flatly that we weren't interested in that either. They then agreed to think it over and let me know.

119 *Ibid.*, Commission Exhibit 2867.

120 *Ibid.*, Transcript pp. 13239–42.

121 *Ibid.*, Transcript pp. 37777–78. Had Pittsburgh Plate Glass made the shipment directly, a very low mill net would have been realized since the order specified truck delivery.

To date I have heard nothing more from them. They happen to have about a 50,000 barrel job and so have we and it would be a nice piece of business as I figured it to swap cement.[122]

Not only did the informal exchange of shipments permit cement manufacturers to increase their earning power by reducing the wastes of cross-hauling, but adherence to the basing-point system may have been somewhat bolstered thereby. In absence of this trading, some firms might have been tempted to shade prices in their home market in order to increase their share of high mill net business.

Summary: The Development of Defensive Monopoly by Imperfect Competition

An effective basing-point system developed slowly in the cement industry. Serious setbacks were experienced occasionally until the summer of 1932 when basic elements were finally established which enabled adherence to a basing-point pricing formula and encouraged it. During the period of the NRA Cement Code (effective from December 7, 1933 to May 27, 1935), price filing was required as well as a five day waiting period before price changes could be made effective. In all other respects, however, the Code Authority simply built upon established trade practices which already had achieved an effective open price system by "formula" without the formalities of price filing and waiting periods.[123] And the death of NRA left the basing-point system functioning in the cement industry much as it had for more than a year before the establishment of the Cement Code.

The beauty of the basing-point system for the cement industry was that it entailed virtually no *overt* collusion, once the rules of the game had been well established. True, the circulation of common freight rate books (as well as certain subsidiary features) involved continuing overt collusion. But the plan to adhere to a delivered pricing formula could be easily and almost

122 *Ibid.*, Commission Exhibit 1159–B.

123 Commenting upon the NRA, John Treanor (president of Riverside Cement) wrote to John M. Clark on August 27, 1935: "Personally, I have not been seriously interested in waiting periods, or in any other contraptions. Without these, once the principle of *openness* is established, I believe a decent standard of commercial morality will develop." *Ibid.*, Commission Exhibit 553–3D, 3E.

automatically, followed once trucking was controlled and direct sales to large contractors were curtailed. The growth of the big chain companies (largely accomplished through acquisition) inevitably increased the proportion of mill capacity where a mutual obligation to price systematically was strongly felt. Moreover, because the geographically diversified chains possessed a powerful enforcement weapon (the ability to apply punitive bases systematically), independent mavericks were likewise induced to adhere to the common formula.

Defensive monopoly being the objective of the cement industry, the kind of imperfect, but effective, collusion inherent in rigid adherence to a formula price fulfilled the limited objectives of price stabilization. Greater perfection of collusion through agreements on inter-area base mill prices was never sought, and apparently never contemplated. The ultimate in collusion through the establishment of a formal authority to divide market territories was out of the question, both administratively and legally. Interpenetration of markets and excess capacity had accompanied the growth of the industry. The older established firms had a vested interest in perpetuating their positions which brand preferences, friendly dealers, and contractor good will had established; they were prepared to retreat from rival markets only when freight absorption became excessive. Moreover, all firms desired to diversify the markets serviced by particular mills in order to stabilize their production and sales in the face of geographic fluctuations in demand.

In the absence of any industry-wide plan, interpenetration of markets served to induce price cutting at particular destinations. Collective interest called for the adoption of a rigid system whereby the geographic pattern of prices should be known. The basing-point system provided this objective and so protected the industry from competitive undermining of the price level. Moreover, once the system became institutionalized, the imperfectly collusive mechanism could continue to be employed without showing any of the conventional earmarks of conspiratorial behavior. But the historical development of marketing practices in the cement industry bears witness to appreciable overt and tacit collusion in establishing a common pricing formula, as has been extensively documented in this chapter.

CHAPTER V

Market Behavior Under the Basing-Point System

Establishment of Basing Points

1. Momentum in the movement toward a universal multiple base system

A single basing point, Lehigh Valley plus, was established in the cement industry around 1902. Between that year and 1940, the last year for which data are available, an increasing number of mills in the industry came to adopt independently a base mill status. The principal reason why firms established additional bases was that they might market a larger proportion of their production in the territory of maximum mill nets. This they hoped to do by discouraging the penetration of distant mills. Discussion of the extension of basing points will begin with and largely concern sections of the country other than that of the Pacific Coast. Mills in that area were sheltered from production centers to the east by the thinly populated states of Arizona, Nevada, and Idaho, where little or no productive capacity existed.

By 1910 base prices had been established at two mills in southern Indiana and eastern Missouri belonging to Lehigh Valley companies and at mills in southeastern Kansas and southeastern Tennessee belonging to independents; but the Lehigh Valley continued to provide the base price for all points in the Northeast, the upper South, and in Ohio and Michigan for at least a few more years. The *Record* suggests, however, that during this period unsystematic pricing by mills west of the Allegheny Mountains occasionally developed, as some of them shaded the Valley delivered price and others temporarily established base prices in order to increase sales in their high mill net territories.[1] By 1915 formal base prices were established at Hudson,

[1] *Record,* Transcript pp. 38575–91.

New York, Universal, Pennsylvania (near Pittsburgh), and Fordwick, Virginia, in order to discourage, by means consistent with the basing-point formula, shipments from mills concentrated in the Lehigh Valley. And additional base prices were established at mills located in Michigan, northern Indiana, Illinois, and Iowa to discourage, in a systematic manner, shipments from other midwestern production centers. Of some 104 mills outside the Pacific Coast area in 1915, however, 29 were still more than 50 miles from a base mill.[2]

By 1920 base mills were established in the industry's hinterland — Alabama, Texas, and Minnesota — and a few additional bases were set up at intermediate locations in the East and Middle West. By 1925 eleven additional base points had been established, and by July 1937 (when the Federal Trade Commission filed its complaint) there were nineteen more (including base points at Great Lakes silos). The overwhelming number of base points instituted after 1920 were at mills or silo points belonging to chain companies. Map 3 shows the location of mills and base points in the area east of the Pacific Coast, as of the time of the complaint in 1937. There were 44 basing points, and 99 of the area's 139 mills (representing 80 per cent of its productive capacity[3]) were located at or within 50 miles of the base points. The situation in 1937 is somewhat understated, however, since 9 of Michigan's 10 mills were temporarily operating (for the year) under a zone price, so that the previously controlling base price had been converted into a delivered price for almost the entire state. By 1940 several additional base prices had been installed, primarily at chain mills already operating within a 50-mile radius of existing bases, with the result that 112 of the 139 mills outside the Pacific Coast area were at or within 50 miles of a base point. In the Eastern Trunk Line territory (most of the area east of the Mississippi and north of the Ohio rivers) the difference in cost between a 5-mile and a 50-mile rail haul during the latter thirties amounted to about 15 cents per barrel of cement,[4]

[2] *Brief for Respondents,* Appendix A, Vol. I, p. 364, *FTC* v. *Cement Institute,* 333 U.S. 683 (1948).

[3] *Ibid.,* p. 363.

[4] *Record,* Respondent Exhibit 2899. The freight rate for 5 miles was approximately 22.5 cents per barrel and for 50 miles approximately 37.5 cents.

Map 3. Portland Cement Basing-Points in the United States, Excluding Washington, Oregon and California, 1937

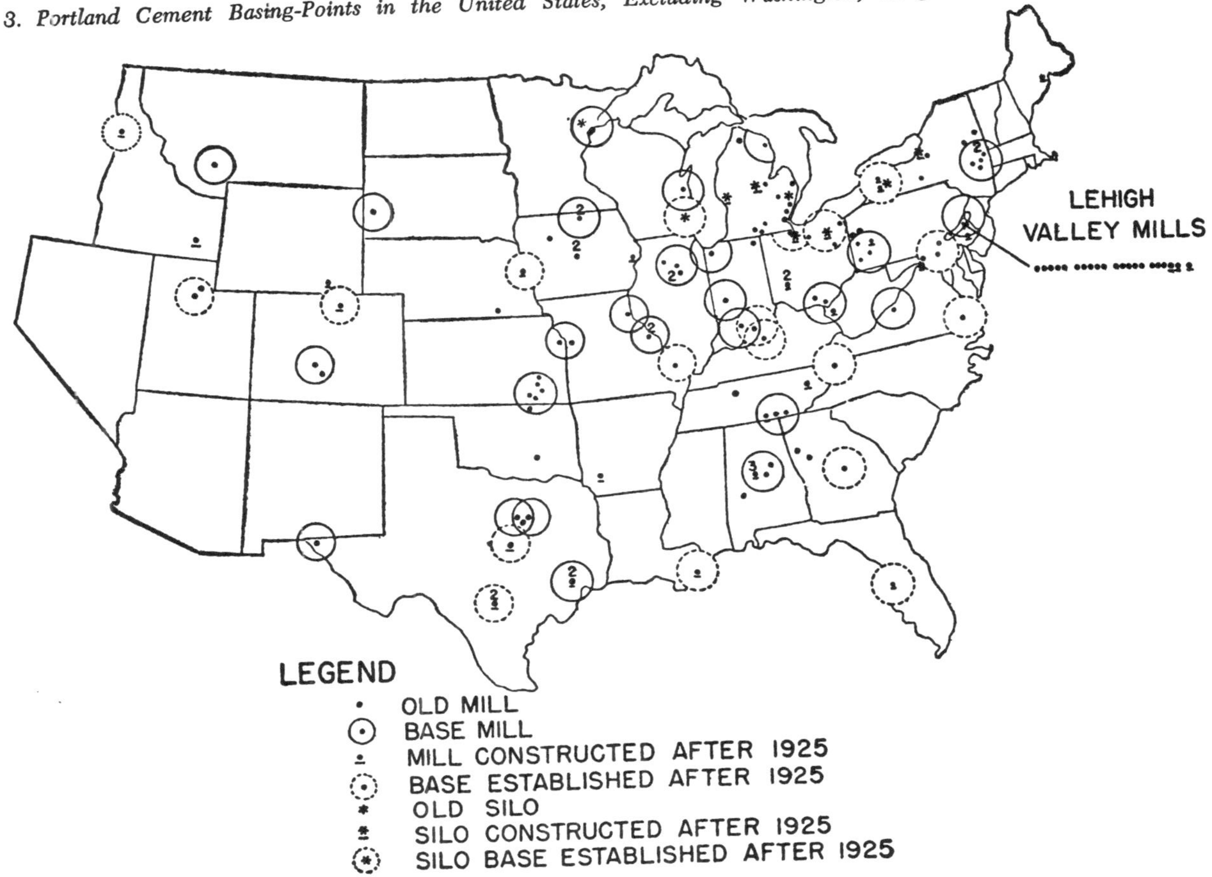

with base prices running about $1.60 per barrel.[5] Non-base mills located within the 50-mile radius of a base were not collecting large phantom freights, yet the failure of these mills to become additional base points undoubtedly simplified the use of common freight rate factors.[6]

Most of the twenty-seven non-base mills outside the 50-mile radius of a base point were admittedly located in the more sparsely populated market areas. However, a few major market centers continued to be served with delivered prices which included substantial amounts of phantom freight. Establishment of base prices at non-base mills would have reduced prices in near-by areas: an Osborn, Ohio, mill in the Springfield-Dayton-Cincinnati area; a Des Moines, Iowa, mill and a Nashville, Tennessee, mill in those cities, respectively; an East Fultonham, Ohio, mill in Columbus; a Rockmart, Georgia, mill in Atlanta; an Okay, Arkansas, mill in Little Rock and in Shreveport, Louisiana; and a Jamesville, New York, mill in Syracuse.

On the Pacific Coast virtually every mill was a base point by 1932, but the development of base prices themselves can best be treated by dividing the region into three sections. (1) In southern California, a zone delivered pricing system was initiated by the Riverside Company in 1927 because trucking was the prevailing form of transportation in the Los Angeles metropolitan district. The system of zone prices (with mountains, deserts, and farming belts serving to separate the zones) was followed by the other three firms with mills in the area, and the use of zoned delivered prices continued throughout the thirties. In quoting prices to central California, Arizona, and Nevada, however, a basing-point system was used, with two of the five mills serving as base points. (2) Prior to 1929 all six mills in northern California were quoting prices on a base mill at Davenport, California. In that year the Cowell mill applied the Davenport base to its own and each of the other four mills. With all mills having the same base price, the action had the effect of creating a freight equalization system on sales in northern California. (3) In Washington and Oregon six

5 Had uncontrolled trucking been permitted, the freight cost differential between a 5-mile and 50-mile haul would have been greater because of the substantial trucking economies on very short hauls.

6 *Record*, Commission Exhibits 970–4H, 975–19K.

of the seven mills were quoting base prices in the twenties, and the seventh joined them in 1932.

2. Reasoning of companies concerning base or non-base status

There was nothing to prevent mills in the cement industry from establishing base prices. Producers in older centers were unable to "persuade" firms in newer areas (better situated with respect to certain markets) to continue their non-base status or to maintain base price differentials at these locations in consideration of the heavy excess capacity in the more established producing areas, as has been alleged to be the case in the steel industry. For example, during the thirties many Lehigh Valley producers withdrew as regular marketers in the Buffalo, New York, area, partly because of the establishment of base prices in mills of the area and partly because of an inability to meet the service of controlled truck delivery offered by local producers. The freedom to select mill status was acknowledged by the Commission in its Findings: "The number and identity of base and non-base mills change from time to time. A base mill may, for the reasons its management considers sufficient, become a non-base mill, and similarly, a non-base mill may become a base." [7]

Additional base prices were established most frequently at mills close to high density markets in order that these markets might become as economically unattractive as possible to mills much more distantly located. It is true that when a new or a reduced base price was first set up, the most distant sellers did not usually retreat immediately. Because of expensive sales expenditures made to cultivate this market by establishing good will with dealer and contractor, many of the distant mills remained in the market until convinced that the lowered price had been made a permanent policy by the initiator. With the passage of time, mills absorbing extensive freight cost discovered that their mill nets in this market offered little toward overhead, after reckoning incremental selling as well as production expenses; then they retired permanently, leaving the market to be penetrated only by less distant rivals. The gradual retreat of rivals from territory placed under the control of a new base mill was illustrated

[7] *Cement Institute,* 37 FTC 87 (1943), 148, Par. 7 (b).

during the Commission hearings by the experience of the Lone Star Company in New Orleans.[8] When Lone Star opened a new mill at New Orleans in 1927, ten to a dozen competitors were soliciting business in the territory, presumably from mills located in Alabama, Tennessee, Arkansas, and Texas. Although Lone Star installed a base price, only reluctantly did its rivals retreat, and not until the latter 1930's was the number of its regular competitors in the territory reduced to two or three.

Another, but less frequent, reason for establishing base prices, as revealed in the *Record,* has been the wish to quote a reduced price to win the award of a specific large construction project and yet to make the price reduction in accordance with the "ethics" of the basing-point system. The Thomaston, Maine, mill became a basing point for the first time in 1938 so as to win a contract for 105,000 barrels of cement for the construction of a dam at Mattawamkeag, Maine. The buyer had threatened to use imported cement for the project, and rather than make an unsystematic special quotation, the Lawrence Portland Cement Company cut its price by quoting a base price at its Maine mill.[9] The same procedure was followed by the Penn-Dixie mill at Kingsport, Tennessee, in October 1935, when quoting a reduced cement price to Tennessee-Eastman which was planning to purchase 100,000 barrels of cement for a new chemical plant at Kingsport. By offering the reduced price to Eastman through adopting a base price, Penn-Dixie was assured of the business without breaching the common pricing formula of the industry.

Political considerations undoubtedly explained the establishment of seventeen additional base mills between 1937 and 1940. The Federal Trade Commission complaint against the cement industry had been filed during the summer of 1937, and industry leaders probably wished to reduce public censure by eliminating phantom freight. Nine of these additional bases were established at mills belonging to chains (Ideal, Lehigh, North American, Lone Star, and Medusa) already located very close to existing bases. Characteristic of the base-price installations during this period was that made by one of the lesser chain com-

[8] *Record,* Transcript pp. 32640–41.
[9] *Ibid.,* Transcript pp. 8219–21.

panies, Medusa. In July 1939 Medusa set up bases at five of its mills: York, Pennsylvania, about 75 miles from the Lehigh Valley base; Wampum, Pennsylvania, about 30 miles from the Pittsburgh base; Bay Bridge, Ohio, about 40 miles from silo bases at Cleveland and Toledo; Silica, Ohio, about 10 miles from the Toledo silo base; and Dixon, Illinois, about 30 miles from the La-Salle base. In reply to the Burns-Clark questionnaire in 1935 Medusa had offered no reason other than "individual company policy" to explain the non-base status of most of its mills.[10] But in testimony before the Commission an executive of Medusa explained its establishment of the 1939 base prices as a means of giving its mills "a geographical advantage they had not theretofore enjoyed." [11] The sudden flash of intuition which led Medusa to discontinue its former policy of self-abnegation was not disclosed.

The industry's leading policy maker had long advocated a base price for each mill, or at least for each production territory. The Lehigh Company believed that much of the criticism of the cement industry resulted from the high mill nets collected by isolated non-base mills, and it expressed these views in reply to the Burns-Clark questionnaire in 1935:

> The Lehigh Portland Cement Company has always believed that each mill or producing district should be a basing point. We believe that such a price structure would dissipate much of the criticism of the industry's pricing methods.
>
> Given the same percentage of operation, manufacturing costs the country over do not greatly vary. There are some districts in which for natural reasons costs are somewhat lower than in others, such as districts 1 and 4 [Lehigh Valley area and Michigan]. There are other districts where, because of the climatic conditions or high freight charges for coal and raw materials, manufacturing costs are somewhat higher, such as districts 10 and 12 [Rocky Mountains and Pacific Northwest]. However, the chief cause of the variations of costs as between districts is the fact that there are marked fluctuations from year to year in consumption of cement in certain sections of the country.
>
> By and large, however, the establishment of a base price at every mill or group of adjacent mills would unquestionably result in a more even level of delivered prices the country over. While it is true that more basing points

[10] *Ibid.*, Commission Exhibit 970–11.
[11] *Ibid.*, Transcript pp. 40569–70.

are recognized in the cement industry than in many other industries which have adopted the so-called multiple price basing system, nevertheless the staggering of these bases has been purely arbitrary and has resulted in wide gaps in certain areas. If we were to trace the maximum mill nets at every plant location under the present price structure, the graph would indicate high peaks at certain mills located between far distant basing points, and low broad valleys.

Under the method which we favor the picture of the price structure of the industry would represent an undulating plain. Under such a price structure it would be impossible for a manufacturer to take advantage of his isolated location by not establishing a base price at his mill, and thereby obtain a mill net which has no relationship to his manufacturing costs.[12]

The reasons for mills retaining their non-base status appear to fall into four categories. (1) Most non-base mills were located quite close to (within 50 miles) an existing base, and these mills (as well as the base mills) could avoid the calculating of freight rates destinations, while incidentally collecting some minor phantom freights. Such an explanation was suggested by an official of a company located at West Winfield, Pennsylvania, which possessed a 4-cent-per-barrel rail freight advantage over the Universal, Pennsylvania, base, about 30 miles away.[13] (2) There were a few stand-by mills of multi-plant firms which were closed in slack years, and these were maintained on a non-base status (e.g. Ideal's mill at Concrete, Colorado, Lone Star's mill at Spocari, Alabama, and Riverside's mill at Oro Grande, California). (3) There were a few mills less desirably located with respect to primary markets than the base mills which established the price. A good illustration is provided by a mill at Glens Falls, New York, about 75 miles north of a group of mills in the Hudson Valley. The mills at the Hudson Valley base were much closer to major markets at Albany, New York City, and Boston. High mill nets could probably be earned on only a small proportion of the sales of a non-base mill such as the one at Glens Falls. (4) There were some very favorably located mills. Situated between a base point and a major market, these non-base mills were able to collect high mill nets (including phantom freight) and extra profits on a large proportion of their sales. The mill at West Conshohocken,

[12] *Ibid.*, Commission Exhibits 967–6E, F; 16 A, B.
[13] *Ibid.*, Commission Exhibit 970–4H; Transcript p. 27942–44.

Pennsylvania, on the outskirts of its major consuming market, Philadelphia, calculated prices until 1937 on the Lehigh Valley base, 50 miles further away. Having neither sufficient capacity to supply the entire Philadelphia market, nor a sufficient freight advantage to drive the many Lehigh Valley producers out of the big city market, for about a decade the mill quoted prices on the Lehigh Valley base and pocketed the advantages of its favorable location on as many sales as it could win by non-price competition. A few other non-base mills were even more favorably located with respect to somewhat smaller city markets at Springfield-Dayton, Ohio; Des Moines, Iowa; Nashville, Tennessee; Columbus, Ohio; Atlanta, Georgia; Syracuse, New York; and Little Rock, Arkansas — Shreveport, Louisiana.[14]

The long continued presence of non-base mills in the cement industry, including those within a 50-mile radius of base points, was really a consequence of the delivered price policy of refusing sales to trucks controlled by buyers. Had non-base mills offered to load buyers' trucks at a posted price equivalent to the maximum mill net realized on rail shipments (entailing deduction of the minimum switching charge) they would, in effect, have been converted into minor base mills controlling at least a small bit of territory. Moreover, had such mills reduced their posted mill price in order to offer consumers in a wider area the direct and indirect saving of buyer trucking, their base price status would have become somewhat more than minor — although frequently their prices would continue to exceed sub-

[14] It is interesting to compare Arthur Smithies, "Aspects of the Basing-Point System," AER, 32:723 (December 1942). On the basis of abstract reasoning and simplified assumptions, Smithies argued that a "non-base position is at best a *pis aller*" of high cost producers who would really prefer to charge more, and that phantom-freight charging mills are not simply exploiting monopolistic power within their area. This universal apologia for the non-base mill cannot be accepted, although it seems to fit the facts in cases (2) and (3) above. Most of the mills in group (4) were efficient mills in terms of production costs, as well as location, and for long periods they collected high mill nets in important sales territory close to their mills, under the umbrella of prices established at more remote bases. Of course, such mills may have more closely maximized profits by remaining non-base mills, but it would appear that these mills could have established base prices and still have earned higher profits than many mills at the base points. One purpose of outlawing non-base mills in the 1945 *Staley* decision (324 U.S. 746) was to force mills with locational monopoly to share at least part of their advantage with local buyers.

stantially base prices in the surrounding areas. The fact is that buyer trucking, prior to its elimination, was found to be disruptive from the individual vantage point, as distinct from the collective interest, at only those mills which simultaneously sought to maintain their non-base status. The non-base mill at Nashville, Tennessee, had accommodated trucking by charging buyers who hauled in their own trucks the formula delivered price *minus* the rail freight from Nashville to destination. By attempting to collect from those buyers close to the mill higher mill nets than from those 30 to 50 miles away, the mills frequently incurred arbitrage. Buyers' truck shipments were diverted from the allegedly more distant destinations into areas where higher mill nets were being quoted. The Nashville mill not only found its mill net in the city pulled down, but it was confronted with complaints from dealers in the city.[15] Had it established a posted mill price (base price) to buyers' trucks, the arbitrage problem and dealer discontent would not have developed. Base mills which quoted only this posted price to truckers were not disturbed by an arbitrage problem. When they absorbed freight (that is, reduced mill nets) in order to penetrate a market controlled by a distant rival, they quoted destination prices, *rail* delivery.

3. *Making Known the Base Prices*

Base prices have not been published, save for a limited few in the construction trade journal, *Engineering News-Record*, nor have they been circulated regularly among members of the industry. Each concern individually collected base prices by subtracting known freight factors to various mills from destination prices "found in the field". Where uniform mill nets were derived from a number of destination price quotations at particular mills, these mills were deemed to be basing points. Each company maintained a list of the derived base-mill prices prevailing in the territory which it served. The Federal Trade Commission in its findings, after admitting that neither base prices nor delivered prices were generally exchanged, added:

> No such exchange is needed in the successful operation of the multiple-basing point delivered price system. When a corporate respondent makes a

[15] *Record*, Commission Exhibit 976–10T.

change in its base price, written delivered-price quotations reflecting this change are usually sent to all customers. Through common customers and through salesmen in the field, information concerning this change reaches the other respondents selling cement in that area almost immediately. Examination of a reasonable number of the new price quotations reveals the pattern followed and thus discloses the base price change made. Notices of price increases are usually sent five days in advance of the effective date thereof; and in the case of a decrease, customers are usually given the benefit of the decrease on shipments made during the five days preceding the decrease.[16]

The practice of "broadcasting" delivered price quotations had long been used by many manufacturers to keep the company's brand name before customers. These "broadcasts" were not confined to periods of price changes, and dealers at all times acted as open information posts for price quotations. When non-base mills intended to become base mills, they merely broadcast their new delivered-price quotations to dealers who would then be governed by the new base. And when punitive bases were applied, the dealers in the affected area were supplied with quotations based on the unsystematic mill net which had been realized by the maverick's mill. And the punitive base remained effective until such time as the disciplining mill in the area was willing to withdraw its quotations.

Price Leadership, Inter-Base Price Movements, and Adherence to the Formula

1. Price leadership

A system of multiple price leadership existed in the cement industry under the basing-point system. So long as it adhered to the formula, any firm at a single plant location could automatically exercise price leadership by lowering or raising its base price. If a firm raised its base price sufficiently high, or left it unchanged when surrounding base prices were sufficiently reduced, its base price became ineffective, and it assumed the status of a non-base mill. In practice, however, most base-price changes were initiated by one of the chain mills. Production tended to be heavily concentrated in certain areas, and firms in the immediate

[16] *Cement Institute,* 37 FTC 87 (1943), p. 178, Par. 9 (e).

area customarily used the base price announced by the leader, while base mills in surrounding areas as a rule synchronized changes in their own base prices with those of the leaders (although these latter mills sometimes would delay in following upward, or decline to follow downward with their own base prices). In answer to the Burns-Clark questionnaire in 1935, the Alpha Portland Cement Company, a chain concern, stated: "Changes usually have been made by one of the chain mills. Lehigh Portland Cement Co. has probably made more changes than any other." [17]

The Federal Trade Commission did not attempt to determine who were the leaders in particular regions, but, after examination of price announcements, exhibits, and testimony of executives, the writer believes that the following shows the pattern of leadership as it existed in various areas. (1) In the Northeast, Lehigh appears to have been the leader on the basis of its price setting for the Lehigh Valley, Hudson Valley, and Union Bridge, Maryland.[18] (2) In western Pennsylvania, Universal Atlas provided the only basing point as late as 1937. (3) In Ohio, Lehigh with a grinding plant at Cleveland seems to have shared the leadership with Alpha's plant on the Ohio River.[19] (4) In Illinois, Indiana, Iowa, Wisconsin, and Kansas, Lehigh and Universal Atlas were said to be "the recognized leaders of the industry." [20] (5) In the St. Louis area, Alpha reported that it shared the leadership with Missouri.[21] (6) In the Southeast, Lone Star, Lehigh, and Alpha all seemed to play the role at one time or another in the base-price movements in the pivotal Birmingham area.[22] (7) Huron and Universal Atlas were the recognized leaders in Michigan.[23] (8) There was no clear evidence of leadership in the Rocky Mountain area, but with Ideal possessing about 70 per cent of the area's capacity, it was truly a dominant firm. (9) Riverside was considered to be the southern California leader,[24] and Cowell (now extinct) and Calaveras were named as

[17] *Record,* Commission Exhibits 968–8X, 9W; 970–16H, 975–9P, 20G.
[18] *Ibid.,* Transcript pp. 26897–926. [19] *Ibid.,* Transcript pp. 11346–47.
[20] *Ibid.,* Transcript p. 13383. [21] *Ibid.,* Commission Exhibit 975–4Q.
[22] *Ibid.,* Transcript pp. 23128–29; Commission Exhibits 975–11Y; 975–6B.
[23] *Ibid.,* Commission Exhibit 967–5N.
[24] *Ibid.,* Commission Exhibits 967–9N; 967–10U.

leaders in northern California.[25] There was insufficient information by which to judge leadership in either the Pacific Northwest or Texas.

Leadership downward in base-price movements has usually followed an outburst of unsystematic cutting of the formula price in the area. Because the leaders were the most vocal advocates of "ethical" pricing, they met widespread price cutting in their areas by lowering the base prices of their mills. Leaders at adjoining base-mill production centers generally followed the first leader, so as to maintain the existing interbase relationship. On a few occasions prior to the summer of 1932, base prices were successively and markedly reduced until the leaders were convinced that the unruly concern had suffered the consequences of unsystematic pricing sufficiently and had adhered to the formula for a reasonable period of time. When the leader was satisfied that other firms in the region were effectively disciplined, the base price was raised by one or more stages. In answering the Burns-Clark questionnaire in 1935, Lehigh explained that its base-price reductions in the Birmingham, Alabama, and La Salle, Illinois, regions had been made primarily because of the prevalence of unsystematic pricing.[26] The firm also explained the logic of its price leadership at Union Bridge, Maryland, in 1932, which raised the delivered prices in Baltimore and the District of Columbia:

> This advance in price followed a period of extremely intense and drastic competition in the market area served by this mill. After prices had been on this level for over a year we reached the conclusion that if an advance were made to a level which somewhat approached costs, such an advance would be generally observed and maintained.[27]

Short run base-price policy by a leader was thus concerned mainly with inducing other firms in the area to comply with the formula price. Once the formula was adhered to, longer run considerations ruled the selection of a base price. The four most important factors usually cited by leaders in explaining base-price selection, under stable marketing conditions, were: (1)

[25] *Ibid.*, Commission Exhibit 968–11W.
[26] *Ibid.*, Commission Exhibits 975–11X, 11K.
[27] *Ibid.*, Commission Exhibit 968–2G.

changes in cost conditions, (2) prices of competing construction materials, (3) discouragement of sales by more distantly located mills in the natural market territory of the base mill, and (4) discouragement of the construction of new mills in the area.

2. Inter-base price movements

Movements in base prices controlling adjoining marketing territories indicate a marked stability in inter-base relationships at all times, and a stability that was especially pronounced after July 1932. Chart 2 shows the base prices in existence at six important base mills for which data are continuously available during the period from 1925 to 1940. Discussion of the inter-base movements can be more conveniently handled by treating separately the four consuming regions covered by Chart 2.

(1) In the northeastern coastal area, the base prices at Lehigh Valley and Hudson, New York, moved almost simultaneously throughout the 17-year period, although a 10-cent differential was maintained at the Hudson Valley mills over prices at the Lehigh mills for most of the period. Additional data, covering a more limited period, show that the base mill at Union Bridge, Maryland, maintained a constant price differential of 25 cents above the Lehigh Valley base during 1929-30 and of 10 cents during 1933-37. The similarity of movement at the East Coast bases reflects, of course, the leadership and price policy of the Lehigh Company, facilitated by its ownership of a mill in each of these centers.

(2) The Universal base, close to Pittsburgh, moved in almost perfect sympathy with that of Lehigh Valley about 300 miles to the east. The most important exception was the four-month lag in effecting a 20-cent-per-barrel advance at Universal, following that by Lehigh Valley in the summer of 1932. This lag was undoubtedly a consequence of the troubled price situation in Ohio, where a price decline began and ended at a somewhat later date than in the Lehigh Valley. It was not until December 1932 that Lehigh made a significant advance in its base price at Cleveland, and likewise Alpha at its plant in southern Ohio. After Universal joined Atlas in 1929, it acquired eastern plants in both the Lehigh and Hudson valleys, but Univer-

SELECTED BASE PRICE MOVEMENTS, 1925-1940

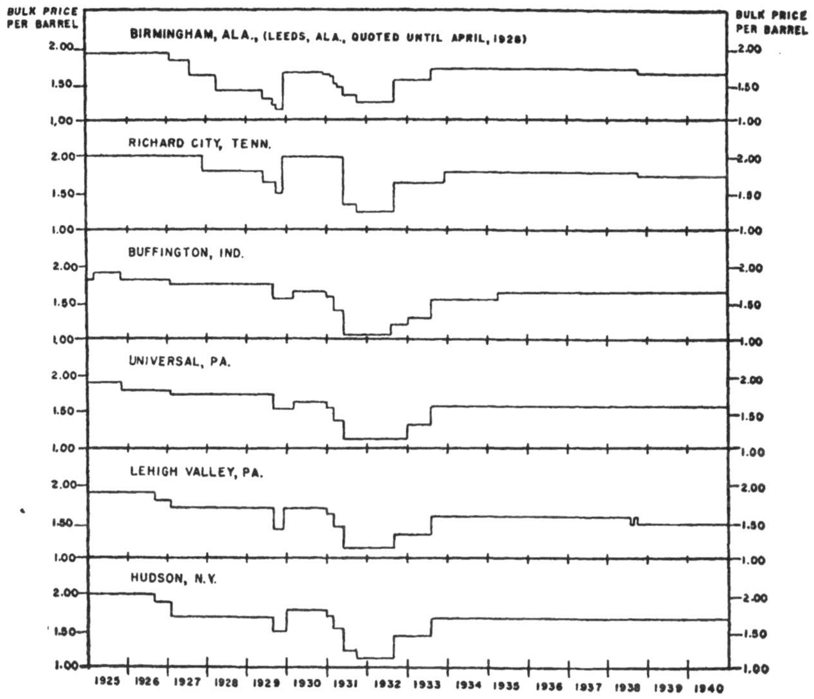

SOURCE: ENGINEERING NEWS-RECORD AND RECORD, COMMISSION EXHIBIT 1185 C-D

Chart 2

sal Atlas's base-price policy at its western Pennsylvania mill still appeared to respond to the leadership of Lehigh in adjoining territories. In reply to the Burns-Clark questionnaire in 1935, Universal Atlas stated that all of its base-price changes at the Universal, Pennsylvania, mill followed similar changes announced at adjoining bases.[28]

(3) The base-price movements at the huge Buffington, Indiana, mill of Universal Atlas, although much like those at the Universal base, were primarily influenced during 1931-35 by four large cement mills operating in the La Salle, Illinois, area, about 70 miles west of Chicago. For almost the entire period pre-

[28] *Ibid.*, Commission Exhibits 970–13N; 975–3G; 975–2B, 3H, 14V.

ceding 1931 the La Salle leader followed the base-price changes at Buffington, maintaining a base price 10 cents a barrel higher. By the end of March 1931, however, Lehigh had reduced its base price at La Salle from $1.75 to $1.05, in order to force Marquette (with a large mill at La Salle) to universalize the reduced mill net which it had accepted on unsystematic bids to the Illinois highway department. Universal Atlas met these initial reductions in base price at its Buffington base. Marquette was again penalized in May of 1932. (The term punitive base cannot be strictly applied since Lehigh was operating in the same location, and therefore penalized itself equally at this mill.) Marquette had stolen another huge highway contract for the State of Illinois by bidding unsystematically, and was forced to drop its base price another 25 cents per barrel to 80 cents. Buffington ignored this latter temporary price depression at La Salle, and left its own base unchanged. However in the middle of July when the La Salle base was increased to $1.20 per barrel, Buffington followed making its base price identical. (The increase in the base price at La Salle, Illinois, as well as the removal of a punitive base at Marquette's Cape Girardeau, Missouri, mill were announced on the very day that Marquette agreed to rejoin the Portland Cement Association.) The Buffington mill followed three additional base-price increases made at La Salle by Lehigh between December 1932 and March 1935, and thereafter the base prices of the two mills remained identical through the end of 1937 at least. Other data show that the Lone Star mill near Indianapolis established base prices which were very similar to those at Buffington between 1929 and March 1931, and after that date quoted changes in base prices identical with those at Buffington at least through 1940.

(4) Inter-base movements in the South diverged somewhat from the above pattern, Birmingham being the major production center and basing point. Sharp base-price reductions were made in that area during 1927 and early 1928 in response to outbreaks of secret prices and unsystematic sealed bids on highway contracts which occurred long before such price cutting had seriously infected other areas. Acquisition by chain companies of two of the area's "outlaw" plants (described in the preceding chapter)

led to a temporary stabilization of the Birmingham base price in 1928, at a level much below those in other areas. But they were reduced again in 1929 in an effort to systematize the price cuts which once more had been quoted to a highway commission. The Birmingham base was raised sharply late in 1929 and the new level maintained until 1931 when a series of reductions were made, possibly in an effort to protect its marketing territory from excessive invasion from a Cape Girardeau mill whose base had been punitively reduced to $1.00 by May 1931. The summer of 1932 found the price situation well stabilized in Birmingham, as in most of the rest of the United States, and the Birmingham base price was increased. In the surrounding territory, however, the base-price behavior differed markedly from pivotal Birmingham. At Penn-Dixie's mill at Richard City (southeast Tennessee) the base price followed very sluggishly the reductions at Birmingham. In the periods of price stability preceding 1927 and following the summer of 1932 this mill maintained a constant 10 cent differential above Birmingham. However, in 1927, when this expanded to 40 cents, almost a year passed by before the Richard City base was reduced. Again in the spring of 1928 the differential increased to 40 cents, but Richard City continued to maintain its base price until the middle of 1929 when Birmingham reduced its base once more. Richard City followed suit to a degree but maintained a 35 cent differential. It copied Birmingham's sharp rise of 50 cents at the end of 1929, continuing the 35 cents differential through most of 1930. It is possible that in the early spring of 1931 it temporarily became a non-base mill as the differential increased to 55 cents when Birmingham reduced its base once more and Richard City failed to follow. In the middle of May 1931, however, it reduced its base by 65 cents to a par with Birmingham, and remained identical with the latter until the summer of 1932 when it followed the Birmingham lead but restored the "traditional" 10 cent differential.

Another Penn-Dixie mill at Clinchfield, Georgia, for which data are available only for the period 1929–37, evidenced base-price behavior similar to that at Richard City, i.e., it followed the advances at Birmingham but lagged behind on the decreases. Two other base mills, much more distantly located but sharing many markets with the Birmingham producing district, maintained base prices at a high and constant level throughout the 1929–32 period of Birmingham price gyrations. The Tampa, Florida, mill (belonging to the Cowham Engineering Group) maintained a base price of $1.85 per barrel, while the New Orleans mill (belonging to Lone Star) maintained one of $1.65 during this time. Of course, the Florida mill was a relatively isolated producer, while the New Orleans mill was somewhat sheltered on the west from price instability, because Texas producers (who employed controlled trucking in the middle twenties) passed through this period of turmoil with their base prices virtually unchanged.

Very few base-price changes were made after 1933. During the ensuing period of strict adherence to the basing-point system, there was little evidence that base-price reductions were initiated at established mills in an effort to discourage penetration of local markets by mills more distantly situated. Although many newly constructed mills were converted from a non-base to a base status in order to decrease the number of rivals soliciting sales in their natural markets, most subsequent base-price reductions were made to eliminate the effects of unsystematic pricing and to discourage new outbursts of it.

The cement industry modified its basing-point formula on a few occasions. The purpose was to stamp out unsystematic pricing by means which avoided the great cost entailed in applying strictly the rules of the system. One technique employed a "dual base," the reduced base price being restricted to a particular geographic area. To meet "openly" and in a "non-discriminatory" manner price disturbances which erupted in Ohio during the spring and summer of 1931, Lehigh established a very low base price at its Cleveland grinding plant, applicable to points in Ohio but not to New York State which was serviced by Lehigh's Buffalo mill. In 1931 Alpha restricted to the Virginia-North Carolina line the application of its Ironton, Ohio, base, so as not to depress prices in Tennessee served by its Birmingham, Alabama, mill. That same year Lehigh temporarily applied dual bases at its mills in the Lehigh Valley and at Union Bridge, Maryland, with the lower base prices applying only in the New Jersey and District of Columbia-Maryland areas, respectively, the territories of rampant price concessions.

Flat statewide zone prices have also been applied temporarily. Early in 1931 Alpha set a single delivered price for the state of Ohio in an effort to meet widespread sporadic price cutting. However, the experiment was unsuccessful, and after a few months Alpha substituted punitive bases at the mills in East Fultonham and Osborn, Ohio. For fifteen months during 1937–38 Huron set a flat delivered price for almost the entire lower peninsula of Michigan. This zone price grew out of a Wabash-Aetna feud in which Wabash had applied a punitive base at the Bay City mill of Aetna, and Huron was caught as a bystander. A Huron representative testified to having set the flat price in an effort to terminate the Wabash-Aetna disturbance, but the zone price was discarded when Huron decided that the experiment was not a sound marketing method.[29] The zone pricing system in use in southern California has already been mentioned, but it was both graduated in structure and lasting, being in continuous use since 1927.

"Arbitrary" (special) prices have been employed at various times to meet foreign competition. They were applied from time to time to ports in the North Atlantic coast region. Since there were no commodity rail rates on cement to the interior from these points, the special delivered prices were "feathered out" for about thirty miles into the interior suburbs so as to protect dealers in suburban markets from those in the ports who otherwise might have attempted to truck cement to higher priced areas inland. At South Atlantic ports, however, where commodity rail rates did exist, the industry installed special basing points. Freight rates were added to these port bases in accordance with the standard formula.

As a result of the use of dual bases, zone prices, and port prices from time to time, delivered prices at particular cities have varied more than can be explained by mere movements in base prices.

[29] *Ibid.*, Transcript pp. 33667–70.

3. *Adherence to the pricing system*

With the exception of the widespread price cutting between 1930 and 1932 (most severe in 1931), an observer gets the impression from both Commission testimony and exhibits that members of the industry adhered well to formula prices. Two surveys conducted by the Federal Trade Commission confirm the impression that little secret price shading occurred.

The Commission examined 60,000 invoices sent by manufacturers to dealers in twenty-one cities and covering varying periods between 1927 and 1929, when the cement industry was operating at between 73 and 85 per cent of "practical capacity." Total sales amounted to 22,000,000 barrels of cement and the invoices indicated extreme uniformity in selling terms and prices. In thirteen of these cities (including such metropolitan centers as New York, Philadelphia, Cleveland, Pittsburgh, St. Louis, Birmingham, and Washington, D.C.) compliance with the formula was shown in 100 per cent of the cases. Only in Detroit (plagued by trucking earlier than were other areas) was there a marked price divergence involving a number of competitors over a considerable period of time. Yet even in that city, 88 per cent of total volume covered showed an adherence to formula.[30]

During the hearings the Commission subpoenaed invoices of respondent manufacturers to dealers for the month of April 1938 to test the degree of uniformity. Again a high degree of uniformity was found. Yet the survey was made during a year when industry members alleged that a fairly large amount of price cutting had broken out. The coverage of the survey was admittedly limited, qualifying invoices being confined to those urban communities which had received shipments from more than one respondent manufacturer. Consequently the invoices covered only 580,000 barrels shipped to dealers in some 250 cities and towns in 40 states and the District of Columbia. Nevertheless, in 11 of these states and in the District of Columbia prices were identical in all cases. In 16 states, such identity existed in 95 per cent or more of the cases, while in only 6 states was it shown

[30] Federal Trade Commission, *Price Bases Inquiry* (Washington, 1932), pp. 57–59.

to be less than 90 per cent. And the degree of divergence which did exist may have been partially accounted for by the inclusion of some invoices covering shipments on incompleted specific job contracts taken at a lower price, or by changes in base prices in some areas during the month.[31]

The uniformity of transaction prices as revealed by the invoices was indeed great, and contrasts strikingly with pricing conditions in the steel industry during 1939, shown in a study made by the Bureau of Labor Statistics.[32] The appreciable shading of prices in steel led to the suggestion that the basing-point formula was "honored in the breach."[33] That the pricing formula was much better observed in cement is partly to be explained, the writer believes, by the industry-wide policy of sheltering the dealer in marketing, so that the hard bargaining contractors could rarely buy directly from the cement manufacturer.

With respect to bids to the federal and state governments, counsel for the Cement Institute accepted the Commission's findings that sealed bids of cement manufacturers were usually identical.[34]

In the case of commercial sales, most executives testified that their firms were "ethical" companies which eschewed price shading. The testimony of Lawrence's sales manager was typical. He denied price cutting and said, "We try to maintain a one-price policy."[35] Ash Grove's president also did not want to "be charged with being a chiseler by quoting a lower price."[36] It should be remembered that appreciable price cutting below the formula was confined mainly to 1930–32, and that the minor amount of price shading in 1937 and 1938 was made primarily on direct sales to highway contractors. A few company representatives

[31] *Brief in Support of the Complaint,* Vol. I, Part II, p. 40, *Cement Institute,* 37 FTC 87 (1943).

[32] See Carl Kaysen, "Basing Point Pricing and Public Policy," QJE 63:289–314 (August 1949). On page 298 he summarized in tabular form a 1943 B.L.S. study, *Consumers Prices of Steel Products,* which study in turn had been prepared for the use of the Office of Price Administration and the War Production Board.

[33] T.N.E.C. *Hearings,* Pt. 27, p. 14146.

[34] *Brief for Respondents,* Appendix A, Vol. II, pp. 704, 875, *F.T.C.* v. *Cement Institute,* 333 U.S. 683 (1948).

[35] *Record,* Transcript p. 7130.

[36] *Ibid.,* Transcript p. 13694.

testified to having initiated some secret prices, but most firms which admitted cuts below list prices indicated that they had good reason to believe that rival companies had already initiated concessions. Some executives of smaller companies stated that they had frequently offered concessions after 1933, but offered no documentary evidence as to their extent. Efforts of counsel for the Commission to learn the amount of the alleged frequent secret price cutting were thwarted by a general dodging by company representatives during the cross-examination. The following answer is typical:

> Only this, that [deviations] are being called to my attention from time to time. I have not any specific case in mind at the present moment. If I had time, I could undoubtedly pick out cases, such as I have stipulated here in the stipulation.[37]

Lone Star was the only chain which admitted to having deviated from its one-price policy during the 1931 "price war." No evidence was offered concerning unsystematic price cutting by such chain companies as Alpha and Penn-Dixie. While a representative of Universal Atlas specifically denied having cut prices,[38] a Lehigh agent elaborated at great length upon the company's "one-price" policy and the method it chose to meet difficult competitive situations. Extracts from this testimony are worthy of extensive quotation:

> . . . For 20 years prior to that time [1930] we had been operating as a one-price — in a one-price policy, by which I mean that we published our quotations and sold in all cases only at those published quotations. We thought that that was the only sound way to do business, and adhered to it.
>
> *[One paragraph omitted]*
>
> During the latter part of 1930 and the early part of 1931 we found a tremendous increase in the number of situations such as I have described where we were unable to sell at our published prices because our competitors were offering our customers price concessions below their published prices. Because we were unable to meet those price concessions in individual cases but wanted to handle our business by open quotations, and in an open way, as we had in the past, we made a number of reductions in our prices,

[37] *Ibid.*, Transcript pp. 36055–56, see also e.g. Transcript pp. 42351–56, 47951–52, 36360–62, 42174.

[38] *Ibid.*, Transcript pp. 13043–45.

quoting prices on steadily reduced base figures at our mills; all in an effort to reach a level of prices at which we could sell.

[One paragraph omitted]

The reductions we had made, figuring on our own mills, had, as I said, brought our prices very much below cost. We were still, however, unable to sell our product in a great many instances. At that time, still in an effort to arrive at prices which we could make openly and which we could sell at, we began in the spring of 1931 to quote prices which reflected base figures at some of the mills of our competitors from which we had found the greatest number of secret price concessions to emanate. In doing this the base figures were in no case lower than the base figures of our nearest mills, nor were they lower than the base figures reflected by sales of substantial volumes of cement by those companies.

By and large our action was governed by two considerations: First, we had competition to meet and we had to meet it. Second, we wanted to make our prices open, to maintain those prices publicly, and to treat our customers all in the same manner so that we might hold the same reputation for fair and open dealing that we had tried to build up.

[One paragraph omitted]

. . . The effect was to reduce our destination prices over the whole area covered by that plant. In many cases a good portion of that area had not been as adversely affected by competitive price concessions as other portions of it. The effect was, of course, to reduce prices in some cases over a territory larger than what — larger than that in which we had discovered price concessions.

[One paragraph omitted]

[We covered this large area] simply because we were making our prices publicly and openly, and when we reduced our prices we reduced them to all our customers in the territory concerned.

[One paragraph omitted]

[After quoting base prices at mills of competitors] there was a gradual change in the situation, so that we began to get business. Prior to that action competitors were able to make prices in certain territories secretly and still obtain higher prices from the trade, either in the same market, perhaps, or in adjacent markets, but with our quotations made publicly those competitors very quickly found that they could no longer get business at varying prices, but must take the price covered by our published quotations.

As time went on we found that the secret price concessions gradually began to clear up and we did begin to get a considerable volume of business at our published prices.[39]

[39] *Record*, Transcript pp. 26894–904.

And it might be added, when other producers demonstrated their adherence to the basing-point formula, Lehigh was prepared to lead off with base-price increases at its many mills throughout the country during the summer of 1932.

Excess Capacity, Prices, and Profits (*A historical and analytical treatment*)

In a book written in 1908 a government geologist and cement expert selected 1907 as the year of incipient maturity for the portland cement industry. Having observed a marked slowing down in the annual rate of increase in cement shipments in 1907 after a decade of rapid expansion, Edwin C. Eckel wrote:

> . . . it seems fairly safe to say that the American cement industry reached a distinct turning point in the latter part of 1907, and that from now on the matter of output must be handled differently. Hereafter we may expect that the cement production will be related very closely to general business conditions; that in times of prosperity we may temporarily fall behind in capacity; but that the approach of business depression will be marked either by a radical decrease in cement output or by its alternative — which is general demoralization in the trade.[40]

In retrospect it appears that Mr. Eckel saw the picture clearly. Cement production was still to expand greatly over the course of time; but the rate of expansion has been slower, and an upward trend in cement demand could not be counted upon to offset the effects of periodic depressions. In fact, with the exception of the decade following World War II when cement supply was tight, excess capacity developed well ahead of the "approach of business depression."

Figures showing the excess capacity for the period preceding 1948 are given in Table 6. Capacity estimates for the cement industry, as for most industries, involve the use of elusive concepts and imprecise measurements, and where calculated they are usually published in terms of "theoretical" quantities. To a certain degree, daily output can be increased beyond the engineering specifications designed to minimize average total costs. Moreover, some plants are more antiquated in terms of location and production costs than are others. Ideally, installed-capacity

[40] E. C. Eckel, *Portland Cement Industry*, (*supra*, IV, fn. 67), p. 31.

ratings should be presented in a schedule showing potential supply at various specified price levels. In practice, price levels are ignored and capacity is generally calculated on the basis of the total amount each existing plant could produce during a year if operated continuously at the customary daily rate, after allowance for necessary shutdowns for repair. Portland cement manufacturers have reported figures of "theoretical capacity" annually to the Bureau of Mines (and its predecessor the United States Geological Survey). Based upon "maximum utilization" (365 days per year) of plant equipment with "maximum demand" and favorable labor, fuel, and transportation conditions, the reports allow only for repair and other unavoidable shutdowns. Edwin G. Nourse and his associates believed that capacity reports may have been overstated both because allowances for repair shutdowns were somewhat underestimated and because of a natural desire to discourage the construction of additional plants by existing or potential companies.[41]

But they recognized that in an industry like cement a much more important factor inflated calculated theoretical capacity when compared with practical capacity: the seasonality of construction activity, particularly in regions characterized by cold winters, limits severely the possibility of producing at theoretical annual capacity, even in the absence of excess structural capacity. In most producing regions demand falls off sharply during the winter months. Continuity of production is partly maintained by building up inventory; but because of the high capital costs involved in constructing and maintaining silos, storage bottlenecks usually develop before spring and plants either shut down completely or reduce the number of kilns operated during a portion of the year. After studying production records from 1911 to 1929, Nourse and his associates found that in the ten years of lowest excess capacity average daily production constituted but 83 per cent of daily production during the peak month in each year. They therefore concluded that a 17 per cent deduction should be made from theoretical capacity to allow for seasonal variation, and to arrive at practical capacity.[42] The deduction

[41] E. G. Nourse, *America's Capacity to Produce* (Washington, 1934), pp. 23f.
[42] *Ibid.*, p. 124.

Table 6

Capacity and Production of United States[a] Portland Cement Mills, annually, 1909–1955

Year	Theoretical capacity	Practical capacity (90% theoretical capacity)	Production	Percentage of practical capacity utilized
	millions of barrels			%
1909	93.5	84.2	65.0	77.2
1910	97.7	87.9	76.6	87.1
1911	112.5	101.2	78.5	77.6
1912	110.0	99.8	82.4	82.6
1913	115.0	104.3	92.1	88.3
1914	115.0	104.3	88.2	84.6
1915	129.8	116.8	85.9	73.5
1916	134.0	120.6	91.5	75.9
1917	136.8	123.1	92.8	75.4
1918	137.6	123.8	71.1	57.4
1919	134.1	120.7	80.8	66.9
1920	146.4	131.8	100.0	75.9
1921	144.4	129.9	98.8	76.1
1922	146.2	131.6	114.8	87.2
1923	161.8	145.7	137.5	94.4
1924	175.1	157.6	149.4	94.8
1925	193.6	174.2	161.6	92.8
1926	215.3	193.8	164.5	84.9
1927	227.1	204.4	173.2	84.7
1928	243.7	219.3	176.3	80.4
1929	258.9	233.0	170.6	73.2
1930	270.0	243.0	161.1	66.3
1931	271.8	244.6	125.4	51.3
1932	271.3	244.2	76.7	31.4
1933	269.3	242.4	63.7	26.3
1934	262.7	236.4	77.7	32.9
1935	261.9	235.7	76.7	32.5
1936	255.5	230.0	112.6	49.0
1937	255.2	229.7	116.2	50.6
1938	255.7	230.1	105.4	45.8
1939	256.1	230.5	121.9	52.9
1940	253.8	228.4	129.8	56.8
1941	246.9	222.2	163.6	73.6
1942	248.2	223.4	182.1	81.5
1943	241.1	217.0	132.4	61.0
1944	238.9	215.0	89.9	41.8
1945	239.9	215.9	101.3	46.9

Table 6 (continued)

Capacity and Production of United States[a] *Portland Cement Mills, annually, 1909–1955*

Year	Theoretical capacity	Practical capacity (90% theoretical capacity)	Production	Percentage of practical capacity utilized
	millions of barrels			%
1946	239.8	215.8	162.3	75.2
1947	246.6	221.9	184.6	83.2
1948	251.7	226.5	203.0	89.6
1949	255.3	231.1	207.5	89.8
1950	264.4	239.1	222.8	93.2
1951	277.4	249.7	241.8	96.8
1952	279.9	251.9	245.2	97.3
1953	287.5	258.7	260.5	100.7
1954	294.3	264.9	268.7	101.4
1955	311.5	280.4	293.3	104.6

[a] Puerto Rico and Hawaii excluded.

Source: U.S. Geological Survey, *Mineral Resources of the United States,* and U.S. Bureau of Mines, *Minerals Yearbook.*

was probably excessive, however, because a very tight supply situation characterized only about five years of the period. The Bureau of Mines has also criticized the Nourse conclusion. It admitted that its published data on rated capacity somewhat overstated the annual rate of potential production but it believed that a 17 per cent discount was excessive.[43] The president of Universal Atlas, when testifying before a Congressional committee in 1936, estimated practical capacity to be about 90 per cent of the theoretical,[44] and this is the estimate which the writer has employed in calculating practical capacity in Table 6. The 10 per cent seasonal deduction is admittedly arbitrary but not unreasonable, since production actually exceeded 90 per cent of theoretical capacity in several producing regions between 1923 and 1927 [45] (as well as after 1948), and also on a national

[43] *Minerals Yearbook, 1934* (Washington, 1934), p. 779.

[44] *Record,* Commission Exhibit 2878J.

[45] While the U.S. Geological Survey reported great variability in the percentage of the theoretical capacity utilized among the producing districts (except for 1926 when data were not collected), the Illinois–Indiana–Kentucky area was reported as utilizing 95, 93, and 90 per cent of theoretical capacity in 1923–24–25, respectively; Eastern Pennsylvania–New Jersey–Maryland was reported as utilizing 92 and 91 per cent in 1925 and 1927; and Texas was reported as utilizing 90 per cent in 1923. To illustrate the variability, during 1924 when the percentage of

basis during the relatively strike-free years of 1953–55. Nevertheless, supply can probably be considered as relatively tight, with few pressures existing for producers to cut prices, when production exceeds 90 per cent of practical capacity or 81 per cent of theoretical capacity. Even practical capacity estimates, adjusted for the seasonal factor, tend to overstate the extent of a potentially elastic supply, since in the absence of a satisfactory price producers are under little compulsion to utilize that fraction of capacity which is based upon relatively obsolete equipment. Moreover, work stoppages in the cement and auxiliary (coal and railroads) industries have ordinarily coincided with high levels of cement demand, thus further curtailing the industry's effective capacity.

Average factory prices realized annually at United States portland cement mills for the period 1900–54 are presented in Table 7. A time series of realized mill prices for cement presents a fairly complex index which reflects more than the general changes in base prices at mills making standard portland cement. Also reflected are changes in the extent of freight absorption, the regional composition of demand, the product mix of portland cements, and the extent of concessions being granted below prices set by the geographic pricing formula. Although it is reasonable to believe that the volume of freight absorption increased appreciably as low rates of capacity utilization superseded periods of relatively tight supply, it is unlikely that the other three factors have ordinarily contributed significantly to the annual variations in average realized mill prices. It is true that both base and average realized prices are moderately higher in California and substantially higher in the Rocky Mountain and Pacific Northwest areas (presumably because of higher fuel costs) than in the remainder of the United States. But the great bulk of cement is regularly produced and sold in these latter areas where the level of both prices and average realized mill prices are much more uniform. Similarly, the problem of product

---

national theoretical capacity utilized reached 85.3 per cent (a peak for the twenties), California utilized only 79 per cent, Colorado–Utah 76 per cent, and Oregon–Washington–Montana 60 per cent. See the chapters on "Cement" in U.S. Geological Survey and Bureau of Mines, *Mineral Resources of the United States, Non–Metals* (Washington, 1923–27).

Table 7

Average Price Per Barrel, F.O.B. Plant, of Portland Cement Shipped from United States Cement Plants, annually, 1900–1955

Year	Price	Year	Price
1900	$1.09	1930	$1.44
1901	0.99	1931	1.11
1902	1.21	1932	1.01
1903	1.24	1933	1.33
1904	0.88	1934	1.54
1905	0.94	1935	1.51
1906	1.13	1936	1.48
1907	1.11	1937	1.45
1908	0.85	1938	1.45
1909	0.81	1939	1.47
1910	0.89	1940	1.46
1911	0.84	1941	1.47
1912	0.81	1942	1.53
1913	1.00	1943	1.57
1914	0.93	1944	1.59
1915	0.86	1945	1.63
1916	1.10	1946	1.72
1917	1.35	1947	1.90
1918	1.60	1948	2.18
1919	1.71	1949	2.30
1920	2.02	1950	2.35
1921	1.89	1951	2.54
1922	1.76	1952	2.54
1923	1.90	1953	2.67
1924	1.81	1954	2.76
1925	1.77	1955	2.86
1926	1.71		
1927	1.62		
1928	1.57		
1929	1.48		

Source: U.S. Geological Survey, *Mineral Resources of the United States* and U.S. Bureau of Mines, *Minerals Yearbook and Mineral Industry Surveys.*

mix presumably raises few difficulties. "General use," "moderate heat," and "air entrained" portland cements from a given mill usually sell at the same price, and these cements have rarely made up less than 94 per cent of all portland cements produced.[46]

[46] Moreover, during the period 1943–52, for which more detailed price data are available, the average realized price of *all* portland cements (including premium priced specialty portland cements) has maintained a fairly constant 3 cent differential over the average realization of the "bread and butter" cements. U.S. Bureau of Mines, *Minerals Yearbook, 1952,* Vol. I (Washington, 1955), p. 253.

Finally, there is no evidence that secret concessions have influenced significantly the reported variations in average realized price, except during 1930–32 when the basing-point system temporarily broke down, and prior to 1914 when the system had not been fully bolstered by implementing devices.

The summary of profits (average rates of net income after taxes to stockholders' equity) presented in Table 8 for the period 1919–55 is undoubtedly the weakest of the three statistical series. Not only are four different samples used to span the time period, but none of the four meets the test of randomness. Administrative convenience and availability of data undoubtedly dictated the selection of firms to be included, and the largest firms have been over-represented. Moreover, given the changing size of bite of the corporate income tax, our dependence upon after-tax-profits data limits long period comparisons of earning rates, unless the tax was primarily shifted. However, it is always hazardous to place too much reliance upon data based upon formal accounting statements,[47] and these profit series are offered merely as suggestive indicators, not as "facts."

The capacity utilization, price, and profit series are depicted in Chart 3, and will be noted by various periods below.

1. 1907–1913

Beginning with 1907 there was a slackening in the rate of the expanding demand for cement; but since there were only moderately difficult barriers to entry, new capacity continued to be built into the industry. Early efforts at price stabilization were largely unsuccessful. The courts disallowed the claims of the Hurry-Seaman patent which had underpinned a combined effort designed to control both capacity and price in the cement industry; and the very large number of single-plant firms discouraged adherence to a pricing formula. The result was a marked reduction from the average realized price of $1.11 per

[47] See J. S. Bain, "The Profit Rate as a Measure of Monopoly Power," QJE, 58:271–293 (February 1941), for an excellent discussion of the difficulties inherent in employing published accounting profit data as an approximator of economic profits.

Table 8

Annual Rate of Return After Taxes on Stockholders' Equity for Selected Samples of Cement Corporations, 1919–1955.

Year	Epstein [a] sample %	*Record* [b] sample %	Author's [c] sample %	National City [d] sample %
1919	8.1			
1920	8.5			
1921	7.1			
1922	13.3			
1923	18.6			
1924	15.0			
1925	15.0			
1926	13.2			
1927	10.8			
1928	11.4	10.2		
1929		7.2		
1930		6.9		
1931		–3.1 (loss)		
1932		–5.6 (loss)		
1933		–1.6 (loss)		
1934		2.6		
1935		0.6		
1936		6.9		
1937		4.7	6.2	
1938			3.5	
1939			6.6	
1940			7.0	
1941			8.9	
1942			7.5	
1943			4.8	
1944			2.2	
1945			3.0	2.5
1946				9.7
1947				12.2
1948				16.6
1949				18.1
1950				18.2
1951				14.1
1952				14.1
1953				14.7
1954				18.8
1955				20.3

[a] 21 cement companies with an average capitalization of $11.75 million on December 31, 1928.

[b] 50 cement companies representing 80 per cent of mill capacity operated by respondent manufacturers in *Cement Institute* case, collected by Price Waterhouse.

[c] 10 largest cement producers publishing financial data continuously during the period (Lehigh, Lone Star, Ideal, Marquette, Alpha, Penn-Dixie, Medusa, Riverside, Missouri and North American).

[d] Size of sample varies, ranging from a low of 23 companies for 1946 to a high of 33 companies for 1952.

Source: R. C. Epstein, *Industrial Profits in the United States*, pp. 240–242; *Record*, Transcript pp. 16614–18; *Moody's Industrials* and *Marquette Annual Report for 1953;* National City Bank, *Monthly Letter*.

barrel in 1907. Not until 1913 did it rise to as much as $1.00 per barrel, and by that year common freight rate books prepared by Alpha were being widely used and a system of dealer protection

THE ESTIMATED RATE OF PRACTICAL CAPACITY UTILIZATION, 1910-1955, ESTIMATED AFTER TAXES RATE OF RETURN ON NET WORTH, 1910-1955, AND AVERAGE REALIZED MILL PRICE, 1910-1955 IN THE UNITED STATES CEMENT INDUSTRY

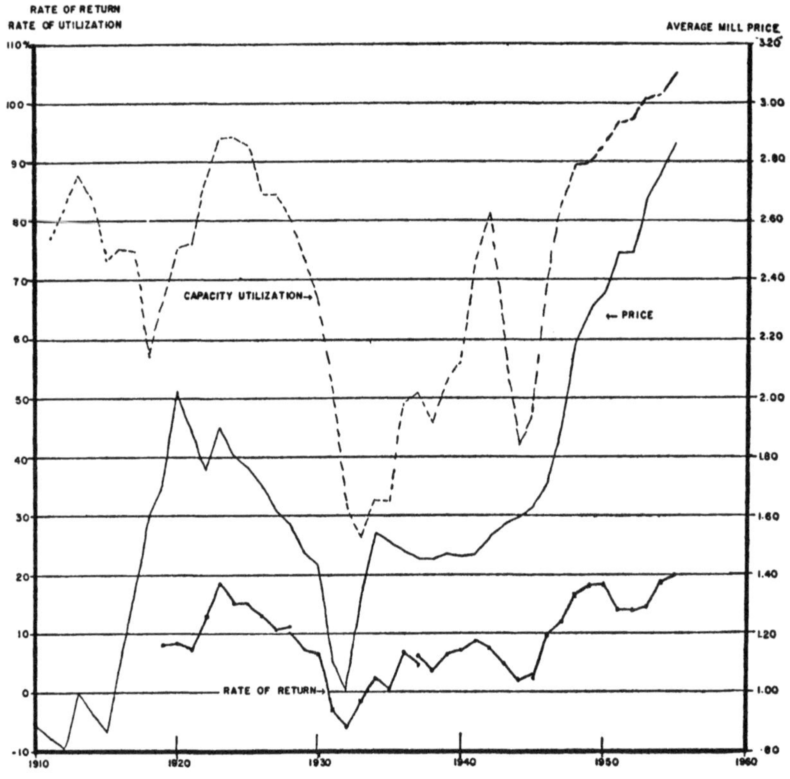

SOURCE: Tables 6, 7, and 8

Chart 3

was being instituted. The increase in average realized price in 1913 was undoubtedly facilitated also by an increase in demand for cement which raised the rate of operations to 88 per cent of practical capacity. Nevertheless, excess capacity continued to characterize the entire period. Only 77 per cent of estimated practical capacity was utilized in 1909; and although increased demand led to a 40 per cent increase in production by 1913, the growth in demand failed to eliminate the surplus since capacity also increased, by about 24 per cent during the same period.

2. *1914–1917*

The forces of stabilization were appreciably strengthened during this period. The number of multiple-plant companies was increasing significantly; contractors were excluded from obtaining the dealer price, irrespective of volume; and freight rate books and statistical data on shipments were formally circulated by regional associations in many areas of the country. The result was a stabilization of marketing conditions which permitted the average realized price, after a decline in 1914–15, to climb to $1.35 by 1917. Yet production remained below the 1913 level, save for the fractional increase in 1917. As might have been expected in the case of a well-stabilized market with only moderately difficult entry, additional capacity was attracted into the industry in quest of its "quota" of cement sales and profit. During this four-year period of non-expanding demand, capacity increased about 19 per cent, but the industry operated at only 75 per cent of practical capacity during 1917.

3. *1918–1919*

The two years which followed America's entry into World War I were years of maladjustment for the construction industry — and, therefore, for cement. That practical capacity utilized during 1918–19 fell to the 60 per cent range reflected the national allocation program which restricted construction activity during 1918 and the slow revival in construction planning and expenditures during the postwar year. Hence the extensive proportion of idle capacity during this period was by no means solely the effect of socially erroneous investment decisions.

The average realized price rose from $1.35 in 1917 to $1.71 by 1919, but it is impossible to judge by how much the higher prices were merely the result of the sharp inflation in wage rates, delivered fuel prices, and other material and equipment costs which characterized the period. An analysis of Census data shows that wage-labor and purchased material costs per barrel rose 75 per cent (from $0.80 to $1.40) between 1914 and 1919, while price increased 83 per cent (from $0.93 to $1.71). That the price behavior was noncompetitive in 1919, however, may be readily inferred from the fact that Epstein's sample of 21 cement firms averaged a return after taxes of 8 per cent on net worth, although the industry was operated at only 67 per cent of its capacity.

4. 1920–1925

The revival of peacetime construction in 1920 was accompanied by a continuation in the upward trend in cement demand with the result that about 100,000,000 barrels of cement were produced in 1920–21, entailing a utilization of about 76 per cent of the industry's practical capacity. Beginning with 1922 a tremendous building boom and cement demand were ushered in which were to increase the production of cement by about 60 per cent by 1925. Supplies of cement became very tight in some areas during this period of boom, and the national level of practical capacity utilized averaged over 90 per cent from 1922 to 1925.

Average realized price rose above $2.00 per barrel in 1920 (a level not to be reached again until the post-World War II inflation) before declining in 1921–22. Unit wage costs changed little during this period, but the temporary doubling in 1920 of wholesale bituminous coal prices undoubtedly contributed to the price increases, since the rate of return after taxes on net worth of the twenty-one sample cement manufacturers averaged but 8.5 per cent. But the development of "sound marketing procedures" — based upon a system of virtually all delivered prices, informational devices, and greater concentration in ownership — no doubt facilitated the price increases, considering the fact that only 75 per cent of capacity was utilized.

In 1919 the Department of Justice had initiated what was to be a series of antitrust suits against the regional trade associations operating in the cement industry. The basing-point system of pricing was not a direct issue in any of these suits. The joint collection and dissemination of various forms of marketing data (including freight rates from basing points) constituted the basis of the charge of restraint of trade. These inter-related suits were settled in a 1925 test case when the Supreme Court absolved the association of cement producers operating in the Northeast.[48] However, during the two years preceding this *Old Cement* decision by the Supreme Court, the legal status of several collective informational practices employed in the cement industry lay under a heavy cloud. In 1923 a district court had found the trade association activities of the same northeastern cement association to be a violation of the Sherman Act because they tended to limit production and create price uniformity,[49] and the association was voluntarily dissolved prior to the test decision in the highest court. But any marketing uncertainties temporarily introduced because of the unfavorable decision of the district court were drowned out by a groundswell of market demand already under way in 1923, which persisted throughout the entire period of litigation.

By the middle of 1922 a veritable boom was on, and the 87 per cent utilization of practical capacity recorded for the year would probably have been substantially greater but for the work stoppages in industries supplying fuel and rail transportation. Beginning with 1923 practical capacity began to expand quite markedly, increasing by about 42,000,000 barrels by the end of 1925, but production grew at an even faster rate, by drawing upon capacity formerly unutilized. The percentage of practical capacity utilized averaged about 94 per cent for the years 1923–25 indicating a fairly tight supply. Average realized prices rose sharply in 1923 reflecting a temporary general increase in base prices and, though declining in the following two years, continued to exceed the 1922 level. Profits after taxes averaged an estimated 16 per cent for these three years. But in the light of the high rate of capacity operation, this temporary high rate of profit was not inconsistent with competitive behavior.

[48] *Cement Mfrs. Protective Ass'n.* v. *U.S.*, 268 U.S. 588 (1925).
[49] *U.S.* v. *Cement Mfrs. Protective Ass'n.*, 294 Fed. 390 (S.D.N.Y., 1923).

5. 1926–1930

The housing boom reached its peak in 1925, but factory and highway construction continued to maintain the demand for cement. However, the annual increase in cement demand slackened sharply after 1925. In contrast to the 46,800,000-barrel expansion in production from 1922 to 1925, cement production in the peak year of the decade, 1928, was only 14,700,000 barrels (9 per cent) above the 1925 figure. Yet practical capacity had expanded by about 45,000,000 barrels (26 per cent) between 1925 and 1928, and practical capacity utilized fell to only 80 per cent in the year of peak production. Production declined by about 6,000,000 barrels in 1929 and another 9,000,000 the following year, bringing the 1930 figure back to the 1925 level. But practical capacity increased by about 14,000,000 barrels in 1929 and by an additional 10,000,000 barrels in 1930, so that only 73 and 66 per cent of practical capacity, respectively, were being utilized in these years.

Undoubtedly the vast expansion in redundant capacity during this period reflected partly the familiar cobweb phenomenon, a delayed and uncoordinated growth in response to a sharp profit boom,[50] and partly the ebullient optimism of the twenties. But it must also have resulted from the successful maintenance of price stability by the industry in the face of developing excess capacity. Moreover, potential investors must also have noticed that history was repeating itself between 1926 and 1927 when profits and prices were again being successfully stabilized despite the emergence of appreciable surplus capacity. Only about 85 per cent of practical capacity was utilized in 1926 and 1927, and yet the rate of return on net worth after taxes averaged about 12 per cent for the sample of twenty-one cement producers. Even during the three succeeding years of substantially lower rates of practical capacity utilization, the rates of return after taxes for fifty cement manufacturers (representing about 80 per cent of

[50] It seems unlikely that construction of cement plants during the twenties would have required more than a year, however, since Henry Kaiser was actually producing cement in 1940 at his new Permanente Cement Co. mill within six months after construction was begun.

national capacity) stood at approximately 10 per cent in 1928 and 7 per cent during 1929–30.

Average mill net realization at United States cement plants did decline about 19 per cent, from $1.77 to $1.44 per barrel, between 1925 and 1930; but technological improvements undoubtedly reduced operating costs [51] and cushioned most of the effect of lowered prices upon profits. Moreover, in 1930 key base prices (as reported by *Engineering News-Record*) were only 20 to 25 cents per barrel below 1925 levels, so that increased freight absorption must have accounted for about 30 per cent of the reduction in mill realization.[52] Save for sharp base-price reductions in the Birmingham, Alabama, area between 1927 and 1929, key base prices demonstrated unusual stability during the period when excess capacity was developing. Following some significant reductions during the summer and winter of 1926, most base prices remained unchanged until the summer of 1929. They were raised again that winter and held firm during the remainder of 1930.

Stabilization of prices in the cement industry was undoubtedly facilitated by the climate of opinion which prevailed in high governmental circles during the twenties. Not only had the open-price doctrine of Arthur J. Eddy [53] won the hearts of the Department of Commerce and the Trade Practice Conferences of the Federal Trade Commission, but apparently of the highest judiciary as well. Ruling that the government had not specifically charged agreement or understanding in the *Old Cement* [54] and *Maple Flooring* [55] cases, the Supreme Court proceeded not only to condone but also to applaud the circulation of statistical and

[51] During the twenties the installation of more modern equipment was facilitating a decrease in labor and fuel inputs per barrel of cement produced. Nicholas Yaworski et al. estimated that the coal equivalent of fuel consumed per barrel of cement declined from 186.5 pounds in 1919 to 159.3 in 1929 (*supra*, II, fn. 6), p. 76; George Perazich et al. estimated that output per man increased 29 per cent between 1923 and 1929 (*supra*, II, fn. 6), p. 89; and Frazer and Doriot reported that despite reduced rates of capacity utilized in 1929, Alpha's unit costs were 23 cents less than in 1923; North American's were 10 per cent less than in 1928, while Penn–Dixie's were slightly less than in 1928 (*supra*, IV, fn. 66), p. 295.

[52] According to testimony during the hearings unsystematic price concessions did not become significant until 1931.

[53] Arthur J. Eddy, *New Competition* (New York, 1912). 375 pp.

[54] *Cement Mfrs. Protective Ass'n.* v. *U.S.*, 268 U.S. 588 (1925).

[55] *Maple Flooring Mfrs. Ass'n.* v. *U.S.*, 268 U.S. 563 (1925).

marketing information which served to stabilize industrial prices.

During the late twenties cement companies in most regions continued to use common freight rate books. The freight factors from basing points to market destinations were distributed either by regional trade associations or by private rate bureaus. By 1930 the newly formed Cement Institute was establishing a comprehensive freight rate service.

Trucking, which had increased substantially in most sections of the country, suffered a temporary setback during the last half of 1929 when mills in most regions imposed a 15 cent premium on the loading of trucks. The newly imposed discrimination against truck shipments, together with cooperative cancellation of redundant specific job contracts during the fall and winter of 1929, as noted earlier, undoubtedly contributed to the successful establishment of upward prices at base mill locations during the early months of 1930.

The wave of acquisitions and the formation of geographically diversified chain companies were probably the most important factors in encouraging adherence to the basing-point formula during the last half of the 1920's. New entrants into the cement industry established thirteen of the twenty-two mills constructed between 1920 and 1925 and seventeen of the twenty-nine mills between 1926 and 1930. But the number of cement firms failed to increase by thirty, since eight of the new firms and at least fifteen of the old were absorbed during the decade — leaving a net increase of at most seven additional firms. The wave of mergers did more than merely offset the effects of the new firms: it helped to eliminate notorious pricing mavericks. (See Chapter IV.) Moreover, mergers facilitated the formation of geographically diversified chain companies which could both price selectively in particular base mill areas and apply punitive bases when necessary. When a newly merged chain combined selective base-price reductions with a punitive base at an isolated mill in Alabama, the wide publicity that followed must have discouraged independent firms in other areas from violating the pricing formula.

Society paid a heavy price for the cement industry's success in stabilizing prices in the face of excess capacity: that success encouraged further excess capacity. During 1926–28 when an excess of capacity was already developing, and the estimated rate of return on investment in the cement industry exceeded the average for all manufacturing,[56] plans were under way for additional breaking of ground. The repeated experience of profitable stabilization in the presence of excess capacity, of course, served to discount the risk entailed in portland cement investment and therefore encouraged the development of additional excess capacity. Put simply, there probably existed a reasonable expectation on the part of investors that they would not have to bear the full competitive penalty of extensive excess capacity. And this expectation proved substantially correct save for 1931–32.

6. 1931–1935

This period marked the advent of the Great Depression for the cement industry — a period during which a large amount of idle capacity was inevitable in view of the relatively low elasticity of demand for cement and the niggardly monetary-fiscal policy in force. But on top of the capacity idled by the depression there existed an estimated 60,000,000 barrels of practical capacity idled by excessive building[57] — or about 25 per cent of the average practical capacity of the period 1931–35. The deepening of the depression saw the rate of practical capacity utilization fall to 51 per cent in 1931 and to 31 per cent in 1932 before reaching the nadir of 26 per cent in 1933. And operations approximated only 33 per cent during 1934–35.

The basing-point system virtually collapsed in 1931 under the pressures of mounting excess capacity, and was not revived until the summer of 1932. Average realized price at cement mills fell 23 per cent between 1930 and 1931, from $1.44 to $1.11, and dropped to $1.01 per barrel for 1932. Although both the cost data and analysis provided in Chapter III suggest that the average realized price remained substantially above marginal costs, the sharp declines in price in conjunction with low volume operation

56 Epstein (*supra,* III, fn. 8), pp. 243, 285.

57 The estimate is based upon the difference between peak production in 1928 and practical capacity in 1934, by which year practical capacity had declined about 8,000,000 barrels from the 1931 peak.

led to widespread deficits. A sample of fifty cement manufacturers (representing approximately 80 per cent of the industry's mill capacity) showed an average rate of loss after taxes of 3 and 5½ per cent, respectively, for the years 1931 and 1932. Reductions in base prices in most areas east of the Rocky Mountains began during the winter of 1930–31, and, following a series of sharp drops during the spring, lowest figures were generally reached by the late spring or early summer of 1931. In addition, between April 1931 and May 1932 basing points were initiated at several isolated mills when the leaders applied punitive bases. As described earlier in this chapter, the series of sharp reductions in established base prices were effected by the leaders in order to halt the unsystematic pricing by the local independents. These reduced base prices at key production centers were maintained in most areas for over a year, until unsystematic pricing and uncontrolled trucking were eliminated. During the summer of 1932 Lehigh initiated a sharp increase in base prices at all of its base mills except Cleveland. These leads were followed both by all mills in the producing centers where Lehigh operated and by most local leaders in adjoining producing territories. Base prices for Michigan, southern Ohio, and western Pennsylvania showed no increase until Lehigh raised its base price in Cleveland at the end of 1932. The second round of base price advances in July 1933, following the drafting of a proposed NRA Code for the cement industry, brought most base prices back to the approximate level of 1929. And those established during the summer of 1933, save for some minor increases in the Midwest during the summer of 1935, remained virtually unchanged until the OPA approved some increases toward the end of World War II.

Three factors seem to explain the breakdown in adherence to the basing-point system during 1931. First, the huge cyclical decline in demand, combined with a previously developed structural excess capacity, encouraged a large amount of unsystematic price cutting. Many of the independents were slow to cut down on their production in the face of the Great Depression and attempted competitively to maintain their volume of shipments instead of merely their relative share in a declining market.[58] The

[58] This explanation was offered by the president of Universal Atlas, *Record*, Transcript p. 13043.

application of the principle of cutting production so as to operate with prices maintained at low break-even points often takes time, particularly for the less well financed, smaller producers. As a result, the formula was discarded in many sealed bids to midwestern state governments during 1931, and in most areas unsystematic price quotations were made to dealers and contractors both openly and secretly. Such unsystematic quotations, of course, reduced the certainty as to what prices would be quoted at particular destinations, and in self-defense many other "honorable" independents instituted unsystematic price reductions. The chains, in turn, attempted to wipe out the effects of such reductions by a series of sharp decreases in their own base prices, as well as by applying punitive bases. Second, the proportion of shipments by truck to total shipments greatly increased during 1931 and 1932, despite efforts in 1929 to restrict trucking through the application of a discriminatory 15 cent differential on the loading of trucks. Consequently, against the principle of the basing-point formula, a tremendous volume of cement moved into metropolitan markets at uncertain destination costs. Many buyers were able to bargain with more distantly located rail-shipping suppliers and obtain concessions substantially below the formula delivered price. Moreover, when several mills were within trucking range of a metropolitan market, the more distant mills made selective concessions from their posted truck price in an effort to maintain patronage in this market. It seems likely that price cuts resulting from efforts to meet uncertain destination costs inevitably induced deliberate violations of the formula in that part of the region beyond the economical trucking range. In the many areas plagued by uncontrolled trucking, base prices typically declined fifty cents or more per barrel (approximately 30 per cent) during the early thirties. By contrast, in Texas, where trucking had been effectively controlled in the late twenties, base prices either remained unchanged or were reduced a maximum of fifteen cents per barrel during the same troubled period. Third, a temporary breakdown in the system of dealer protection also developed during 1931. With the abandonment of speical dealer discounts went also much of the manufacturers' orderly marketing at open prices. There ensued a period of direct selling to large contractors "when competitive conditions required," ostensibly at the dealer price. Contractors were able temporarily to bargain directly with the manufacturers for price concessions, and thus to induce unintended violations of the pricing formula.

The following steps were taken during 1931–32 to develop renewed adherence to the basing-point delivered price formula, and to facilitate an increase in basing-point prices. First, during the spring and summer of 1931 the leaders made a series of sharp base-price reductions at production centers plagued by unsystematic pricing. The last of these reductions was typically maintained for about a year until the barometric price leaders felt confident that new increases would be followed religiously. In two selected areas Lehigh drastically reduced its base price to a level which must have been very close to marginal costs. Undoubtedly, the power demonstrated by geographically diversified cement companies of reducing their own base prices in a selective fashion also encouraged independent rivals to resume adherence to the basing-point formula. Second, between the spring of 1931 and the spring of 1932 several punitive bases were applied at isolated mills. The effect of these was not only to induce adherence on the part of the non-base mills which had been pricing unsystematically, but also to warn other isolated mills what they might expect should they violate the formula. Third, with the possible exception of some areas of the Rocky Mountains and Pacific Coast, by the summer of 1932 trucking had either been completely eliminated or, as in the Great Lakes region, fully regulated, with all truck shipments made in manufacturer-controlled trucks at published delivered prices. Base-price increases in the Lehigh and Hudson valleys during August 1932 were announced simultaneously with the elimination of trucking.[59] Fourth, new marketing plans providing general dealer protection were gradually formulated by the leaders and followed

59 It is likely that Huron's trucking policy at port silos led to Lehigh's establishing a 90 cents a barrel base at Cleveland. The first increase in the Cleveland base price was delayed until October 1932 (two months later than the general round of increases), following Huron's announcement that truck shipments would be made only in company controlled trucks and at delivered prices 5 cents higher than for rail delivery. The 80 cent base temporarily imposed by Lehigh at LaSalle, Ill. between May and July 1932 was probably a consequence of Marquette's having priced unsystematically on sealed bids to the State of Illinois.

by the independents. Bargaining and secret price concessions tended to disappear when cement manufacturers discontinued direct sales to contractors operating in urban areas.

Price stabilization prevailed for almost a year before representatives of the cement industry voted in June 1933 to have the Cement Institute serve as the agent to draw up and administer its NRA Code of Fair Competition. Prior to presidential approval of the Code in November, a second round of substantial base-price increases was begun in July 1933. During the period of the Code's legality (until the *Schechter*[60] decision in May 1935), 98 per cent of the United States cement productive capacity was represented in the Cement Institute, and filing of prices, combined with a waiting period of price changes, was in force during this time.

Some fairly important practices, old and new, were instituted under operation of the Code Authority, practices which were continued for varying periods by the Cement Institute after the demise of the Authority. (1) The development and distribution of common freight rate books were further extended to cover all areas except the Pacific Coast. (2) The destination-cost bid with a "control clause" was developed, and implemented, to assure uniform bidding to the federal government on shipments where land grant rates were involved. The Institute implemented the system by circulating "estimated" land grant rates among member companies, so that delivered-cost bids could be made identical. (3) The mutual circulation of individual company statistics concerning production, shipments, and stocks was re-instituted. (4) The specific job contract checking and cancellation was again jointly undertaken to eliminate excessive "options to buy" at ceiling prices, and therefore to facilitate potential increases in prices.

7. 1936–1940

Demand was stimulated somewhat during 1936–40 by a partial revival in business activity and a federal public works program. Production climbed to an average level of 117,000,000 barrels during this period, as compared with 74,000,000 barrels

[60] *A.I.A. Schechter Poultry Corporation* v. *U.S.*, 295 U.S. 495 (1935).

for the previous four years. Yet at the same time the average practical capacity utilized was only about 51 per cent. Base prices remained virtually unchanged, and only very minor fluctuations occurred in the annual average realized factory price. With the assistance of previously developed stabilizing practices, the basing-point formula was well adhered to, and the average realized factory price remained very close to $1.46 per barrel — just two cents below the 1929 average. That most base prices were not raised during these five years may well have reflected a political decision, since the Federal Trade Commission's anti-monopoly action against the cement industry was initiated in 1937.

Although our samples of profit data change in 1937 [61] and lose strict comparability, a conservative estimate suggests that profit after taxes probably yielded about 5 per cent on net worth of the cement industry for the five-year period. Such a rate of return was indeed socially excessive for an industry which utilized but 51 per cent of its practical capacity. But the 5 per cent rate of return is attributable only in part to the fact that prices had been maintained close to the 1929 level. Appreciable economies in fuel and labor had been achieved through the installation of relatively inexpensive mill equipment. At mills using coal exclusively, coal consumption per barrel of cement decreased 9 per cent between 1929 and 1939,[62] while average output per man-hour of employment in cement companies increased 38 per cent during the same period.[63] An exhibit submitted by Peerless during the Commission hearings showed its costs, excluding bond interest, to be 18 cents less per barrel in 1938 than in 1929, although it produced only half as much in the latter year [64] making unit accounting overhead costs inevitably greater. Society, therefore, was deprived not only of the price reductions which competition would have brought about under conditions of

[61] See Table 8, page 173.

[62] Bureau of Mines, *Mineral Resources of the United States, Non-Metals 1929* (Washington, 1932), p. 408; *Minerals Yearbook, Review of 1940* (Washington, 1941), p. 1123.

[63] Bureau of Mines, *Minerals Yearbook, Review of 1939* (Washington, 1940), p. 1142.

[64] Respondent Exhibit 2406 was excluded from the *Record*, since it was deemed irrelevant.

excess capacity, but also of further reductions in price resulting from the accumulated effects of technological changes.

Estimated capacity remained just about constant during this five-year period, after declining about 2.5 per cent between 1935 and 1936. The estimated 5 per cent average rate of return on net worth, although failing to encourage many marginal mills to leave the industry, was sufficiently modest to deter the entry of much additional capacity. Three new companies did begin operation during the period. A small mill was constructed in Puerto Rico in 1938 (a market supplied by American producers), and another at Houston, Texas. The major entry into the industry came in 1939 when Henry J. Kaiser began construction of a 2,500,000-barrel-annual-capacity mill in northern California, after being low bidder to supply a 5,800,000-barrel-cement contract for the construction of Shasta Dam. The entire output of the plant initially was to be used to supply this contract.[65]

8. 1941–1942

These first years of the defense program greatly stimulated the demand for cement in the construction of training and productive facilities for waging war. The large surplus capacity of cement permitted it to replace tight supplies of steel and lumber in many construction projects and this substitution demand supplemented the purely derived increased demand for cement. The average factory price remained stable during these two years. The administered price policy was undoubtedly assisted by the OPA during 1942 when tight supplies developed in a few regional markets. The great expansion in production and the rate of capacity utilization pushed up the estimated average rate of return to about 8 per cent for these two years. This rate would probably have been appreciably greater if there had been no opposing pressures in cost prices, particularly in wage rates and fuel.

The most remarkable feature of the period is this: in the face of the greatest demand that the industry had ever experienced, only 82 per cent of its practical capacity was utilized in 1942

[65] Bureau of Mines, *Minerals Yearbook, Review of 1939* (Washington, 1940), p. 1136.

when production reached 182,000,000 barrels. Even in this year of peak wartime construction, approximately 41,000,000 barrels of practical capacity were not utilized, and much of that in use had been built fifteen to thirty years earlier and, therefore, *prima facie*, neither necessarily in the best location for supplying the newer regions of large cement demand nor of the most modern and efficient design.

9. 1943–1945

During these three years the industry, for the second time in a generation, faced a condition of war-restricted construction activity, and hence suffered again from tremendous excess capacity, most of which can be attributed to conditions largely beyond its control. The estimated rate of return was squeezed down to an average of about 3 per cent for the period, as the decline in demand restricted production to about 50 per cent of practical capacity, and pressures of increased labor and material costs pushed up against the OPA price line. Many base prices at the beginning of 1945 were still at the 1940 level, but some advances were made in the spring and fall. Annual average mill realization increased only 12 per cent between 1940 and 1945. A number of firms closed shop during this period and sold their obsolete equipment for scrap or to South American companies, so that by 1945 practical capacity was about 7,000,000 barrels less than in 1942. It had in fact been declining at an average rate of about 2,000,000 barrels a year from the high water mark of 1931, and by the end of 1945 was 27,000,000 barrels (about 11 per cent) below the 1931 figure of 244,600,000 barrels.

10. 1946–1948

Under the pressure of pent-up demand for construction, the postwar era ushered in a veritable cement boom. Production climbed to 162,300,000 barrels in 1946 with 75 per cent of practical capacity being utilized. Shortages developed in 1947 when the first of a new series of production peaks (still piling up in 1956) was reached, with 184,600,000 barrels being manufactured and 83 per cent of practical capacity utilized, the highest percentage of utilization since 1927. The percentage of practical capacity operated in 1947 is misleading, however, since shipments fell short of demand for the year. Production was handicapped by fuel shortages, both oil and coal, by delays in obtaining repair parts, by freight car shortages for cement shipments which created bottlenecks in storage capacity, and by some strikes in cement mills. These handicaps resulted in severe temporary shortages in some areas and some gray-market selling.[66] They were somewhat lightened in 1948, and the industry was able to operate at 90 per cent of practical capacity and to produce over 203,000,000 barrels. Yet supply became even tighter in 1948, so that the greatly increased demand could not be fully met even by the increased output.[67]

Average mill realization climbed appreciably between 1945 and 1948, from $1.63 to $2.18, under the pressure of a cost inflation which characterized the entire economy. But the basing-point system was not employed to engineer a rapid hike in the price floor which would have continued to restrict output among producers. In fact, the industry appeared to practice great moderation in its administered pricing policy, permitting spot shortages to develop during 1947 and 1948 and rationing cement to buyers in shortage areas on an allocation rather than a price basis. Given the administered base price "ceilings," firms that sought to increase current profits reallocated their sales to reduce the amount of freight absorption. Some representatives of Lehigh Valley producers told me that in the fall of 1947 their firms began to discontinue sales to many parts of Virginia, since there was an unfilled market demand in areas controlled by the Lehigh Valley base price or at least in areas entailing lesser reductions in mill net. This action, moreover, took place prior to the Supreme Court's landmark *Cement* decision in April 1948.[68] That a moderate price and profit policy was being pursued in the face of a cement boom is also attested by data on the rate of return published by the National City Bank. Whereas the rate of return

[66] See Walter E. Trauffer, "Cement Review and Forecast — New Record Volume of Cement Output Strains Rapidly Growing Plant Capacity," *Pit and Quarry*, Vol. 40, No. 7:80 (January 1948).

[67] See "Never-Equaled Cement Production Is No Match For Record Consumption," *Engineering News–Record*, September 23, 1948, pp. 3, 10–11; and *Business Week*, September 4, 1948, p. 30.

[68] *F.T.C.* v. *Cement Institute*, 333 U.S. 683 (1948).

on net worth for the sample cement firms averaged 12.2 and 16.6 per cent in 1947 and 1948, respectively, the rate of return for all sample manufacturing concerns averaged 17.0 and 18.9 per cent for the same years.

During the summer of 1948, following the *Cement* decision, most cement companies announced that they would henceforth discontinue freight absorption and would sell at f.o.b. mill price. One probable immediate result was the easing of a difficult supply situation in scattered sections of the country. Many buyers, to whom shipments had been discontinued from distant mills because of extensive freight absorption and to whom adequate supplies were not provided by local mills, now found an additional source of supply reopened to them — at a higher price, to be sure, but one which they were very willing to pay. Of greater importance, average realized mill prices and profits could be increased by eliminating most freight absorption at this time while the alleged "blame" for such "profiteering" at the expense of buyers disadvantageously located could be placed on the shoulders of the Supreme Court and Federal Trade Commission.

Whether the Supreme Court's injunction against the basing-point system was really unequivocal, and whether the cement industry in abandoning freight absorption had also abandoned all market practices which would have prevented an easy future revival of a delivered price system (e.g., controlled trucking) are matters to which we shall return in the final two chapters.

CHAPTER VI

Economic Performance Under the Basing-Point System

Structural Misallocation of Resources

Serious consequences of the basing-point system in the cement industry are to be found in the long-run tendency to waste economic resources. Stabilization of the price level through use of a delivered-price formula has operated to induce and maintain long-run excess capacity; to mislocate the initial installation of capacity and retard its shifting geographically; to stimulate excessive cross-hauling and selling expenditures, while restricting arbitrarily the use of more economical media of transportation; and probably to decrease the entrepreneurial pressures, or incentives, to reduce operating costs.

1. Long-run Excess Capacity

Under an economic system of private enterprise, competition, when functioning effectively, is expected to induce a socially desirable allocation of resources between industries by offering rewards to or imposing penalties on risk-taking investors. Profits are held out to investors who enter industries where the price mechanism, in conjunction with forecasts of future conditions, suggests evidence of under-capacity. Investors who make the mistake of burdening an industry with excess capacity are threatened with losses. The public gains most when incentives of competition encourage sufficient foresight in the planning programs of investors, including corporate managers, so that resources will be prudently allocated and a normal return of profits will be reaped by firms operating at economic capacity in all lines of production. However, in a progressive economy, with ever-changing tastes and techniques, perfect foreknowledge of future requirements is clearly impossible, and some mistakes are inevitable. But if competition is effective, windfall profits made in areas where resources have been inadequately allocated will induce further investment into such sectors of the economy; while losses in areas where investment has been excessive will expedite the shifting of resources into other sectors where they will prove more valuable to society.

The very fact that losses sometimes occur under competitive price pressures indicates that mistakes have produced waste in resource allocation. But *ex post*, if the competitive price mechanism is manipulated to eliminate losses, mistakes once made in investment allocation will lead to further social waste; currently available output will be restricted and the shift of resources which would correct the basic maladjustment will be retarded. And *ex ante*, mistakes are more apt to be made if the prospect of loss is removed or minimized, as in industries where stabilization devices have proved effective in the past and are expected to continue to dull competition in the future.

The *ex ante* inducement to wasteful resource allocation is particularly powerful when cartel-like price stabilization shelters an industry characterized by relatively easy entry and periodic declines in demand. The basing-point delivered pricing formula, strengthened by the practice of dealer protection, provided the cartel-like mechanism by which the cement industry stabilized its price level when threatened with periods of excess capacity. As described chronologically in the preceding chapter, the cement industry was beset by careless expansion of capacity during most of the twenty years preceding the Great Depression. The success of a price stabilization scheme which had been put on a fairly firm base between 1913 and 1915 undoubtedly contributed to the exceedingly reckless expansion of capacity which took place during the last half of the twenties. Although the increase in demand showed signs of leveling off after 1925, extensive additions to capacity continued through 1930. The peak consumption year of 1928 employed only 80 per cent of the installed practical capacity, and only 73 per cent of practical capacity would have been employed in 1930, even had demand remained at the same level. Despite the temporary setback to the stabilization system during 1931 and part of 1932, investors' faith in the power of the basing-point system was justified by the price increases engineered in the summer of 1932. Moreover, modest profits were realized in every year of the decade after 1933, despite the fact that the cement industry was operating at about or substantially below 50 per cent of practical capacity. The capacity of the industry declined only 4 per cent during the entire decade of the thirties. Even during the boom year of 1942 only 82 per cent of practical capacity was utilized. It was not until 1948 that cement shortages developed in many areas, and production, limited to some degree by work stoppages and bottlenecks in auxilary industries, soared to about 90 per cent of practical capacity. Clearly the structural, or long-run, excess capacity which existed in the cement industry was both induced and perpetuated by the basing-point system.

It is unlikely, however, that mere competitive price flexibility could ensure the continuous operation of all relatively efficient mills at full practical capacity, even if there were no structural excess capacity. The typical cyclical declines in demand for cement have been too great relative to its price elasticity. Many plants would be forced to discontinue operations during great declines as effective competition pulled prices down toward a level of marginal costs which failed to cover operating (variable) overhead costs. But should future monetary and especially fiscal policy cushion declines in the derived demand for cement, price competition could lead to the continued full utilization of all relatively efficient mills, and only highly marginal mills would cease operations temporarily or permanently. Cutthroat competition would still inflict large losses on most, if not all, firms during the period of recession, because of the high proportion of overhead costs. But if the industry and the economy are basically healthy, the retained capacity will again be fully utilized after a moderate time lag and at prices sufficiently high over several cyclical peaks to keep average profits at a normal level over the long run.

Nevertheless, the threat of possible huge temporary losses during periods of business depression engenders private rationalizations for restrictive practices, employed or contemplated, to stabilize the industry. Such reasoning seems to forget that if investors are sheltered from losses in hard times, relatively easy entry would probably cause a surplus of capacity to develop during periods of high demand and profits, given the knowledge that "fair" depression-time returns on investment will be protected. In the last analysis consumers would be forced to pay high prices (averaged over the cycle) for this heavy cost burden of unused capacity. Arthur R. Burns has stated succinctly the dangerous consequences of permitting industries to protect themselves against declines in demand: "The stimulus to careful calculation of probable changes before investments are made is diminished; the burden upon purchasers of unanticipated reductions of demand tends to be increased."[1] And in contrast, Burns has compared the long-run results likely to follow effective competition:

> The risk of heavy losses, when demand declines, may deter investors from entering the industry until prices rise to a level offering a normal return after allowing for the probability of these losses, i.e., in the longer run investors seek to pass these greater risks of loss on to purchasers in higher prices. If there are prospects of high profits during periods of deficient plant capacity, and investors take these prospects into account, the risks of loss may be counted against the chance of abnormal gains. However, by increasing the penalties of investment based upon inaccurate forecasts of demand this policy intensified the stimulus to careful forecasting.[2]

Our tentative conclusion, based upon both the experience of the cement industry and economic analysis, is that private restrictive practices which prevent any real and substantial price competition in cement during the short run appear very likely to aggravate the long-run misallocation of resources. Admittedly, competition can be quite brutal at times, but collusive action to resist its effects is likely only to weaken the incentives to distribute investment among industries properly, and to force consumers to pay excessively for prolonged maintenance of unutilized capacity. However, some economists challenge this reasoning and offer two lines of economic defense for short-run stabilization practices during depression, both of them based on an alleged contribution to superior resource allocation in the long run. The writer, however, believes that he can refute these arguments.

[1] A. R. Burns, *The Decline of Competition* (New York, 1936), p. 534.
[2] *Ibid.*, p. 533.

First, it is argued that where an industry is composed of a limited number of firms operating with highly specialized equipment, the most efficient firms are not always in the best position to withstand the financial drain caused by cutthroat competition, and some are forced into bankruptcy. Less efficient concerns may still be able to continue operations if they have larger financial reserves or superior access to credit and capital markets.[3] (But this argument applies as well to farmers operating under unlimited pure competition during periods of excess capacity.[4]) To the extent that an industry is really over-expanded for the long run, some productive units will of course have to leave the industry, and capitalization written down. In this process a certain amount of bankruptcy and reorganization may be inevitable. But the best located and the most technically efficient plants will still have potentially lower costs even if a transfer of ownership has occurred; and, if price competition persists, these plants should continue in operation or in maintenance while those with more marginal physical facilities are gradually forced out. It is true that managerial factors may be as important as physical factors in determining firm efficiency, and that superior managerial units may disappear for liquidity reasons during a depression. But if society believes that the financial battle, waged by cutthroat price competition, is an unsatisfactory method of weeding out managements, the most efficient remedy would be for the government, through some quasi-Reconstruction Finance Corporation, to make loans available to efficient firms financially disabled but with excellent prospects of making repayment in the future. The administrative task would admittedly be a difficult one. But the alternative usually proposed, stabilizing price controls where quality is relatively standardized, not only weakens the competitive pressures which encourage a more efficient allocation of resources but also tends to promote selectively those particular firms most skilled in the arts of non-price, salesmanship

[3] Daugherty et al., *supra*, III, fn. 3, p. 558.

[4] L. G. Reynolds, "Cutthroat Competition," AER, 30:738–739 (December 1940); "But where producers are few the processes of readjustment are more spectacular, the movement of prices is more violent and unpredictable, and personal animosities are more bitter. Beneath these differences, however, the results of competition are the same. As marginal producers are eliminated, the downward pressure on prices is relieved . . ."

competition. Not only do such forms of competition raise costs, but success in a salesmanship which maintains or increases a firm's share of the market may lack as much correlation with operational efficiency as does financial strength. Even under cyclical cutthroat price competition, the superior efficiency of those firms with the best locations, technology, and operational management will lessen their losses relative to the others. Therefore, should the public wish to temper the selective pressure of imperfect capital markets, loans by a government lending agency to distressed but deserving firms would appear the best remedy. And, of course, a counter-cyclical monetary-fiscal policy, including public works, designed to maintain public income and employment at reasonably high levels during periods of low private construction activity, would serve both directly and indirectly to keep the demand for products like cement from declining below a tolerable level.

Second, it has been suggested that cyclical excess capacity and cutthroat competition may force an excessive scrapping or inadequate maintenance of an industry's resources. Huge losses may cause the dispersal of economically useful equipment and organization which will have to be reassembled later at tremendous additional costs. John W. F. Rowe, for example, has contended that in the case of industries without general excess or obsolete capacity *in the long run,* society might gain if restrictive schemes maintained surplus capacity in good condition during depressions.[5] Resources would be husbanded by obviating any frantic reconstruction of plant facilities and assembling of new supervisory personnel upon revival of demand, and lower long-run average prices to consumers should result. However, the weight of this argument, when applied to the cement industry, may be questioned for two reasons.

(1) To believe that firms confronted with extremely low prices and great losses during periods of cyclically unutilized capacity will scrap or undermaintain economical production units assumes that they take very short-run views in their investment policy.

[5] J. W. F. Rowe, *Markets and Men* (New York, 1936), ch. 10, and "Some General Economic Aspects," in W. Y. Elliot, et al., *International Control in the Non-Ferrous Metals* (New York, 1937), ch. 3.

It seems more probable that most business concerns will take a much longer view (as discussed in Chapter III), and will attempt to realize the greatest possible income over time by maintaining temporarily a substantial amount of unutilized capacity, particularly if an adequate revival of demand is expected soon. This longer view would seem to be supported by the reasoning of John M. Clark who also has advocated the tempering of competitive price pressures to steady cyclically unstable industries. But in contrast to Rowe, Clark assumes that in times of depression too many marginal production facilities will be maintained and that over the course of the cycle normal profits will not be earned in industries where price behavior approximates the purely competitive.[6] Clearly these two reasons for advocating restriction upon price competition contradict one another, although if either overly-pessimistic or overly-optimistic expectations are held generally by producers during a particular depression, one or the other hypothesis may explain a given set of historical events. The writer tends to minimize the likelihood of excessive scrapping and believes that producers in the industry, including those who take over bankrupt firms, will anticipate a revival in demand and so adequately maintain a substantial plant capacity in spite of possibly huge short-run losses. The prospect of very high, if temporary, prices and profits during prosperity years, sufficiently high over the course of the average cycle to more than compensate for depression deficits, will ordinarily be incentive enough.

(2) Moreover, for reasons of geography and oligopoly, it is likely that many mill nets in the cement industry will remain somewhat above short-run marginal costs during depression, even without a formalized pricing system. Although cement mills are rarely separated by great distances, the geographic dispersion of most of them (the Lehigh Valley, Hudson Valley, eastern Kansas, and Birmingham groups constituting some notable exceptions), creates a varying amount of spatial differentiation so that most producers enjoy a minor degree of "monopolistic" price control. If mill prices should fall to a sufficiently low level, the barrier of transportation costs would make it unprofitable for out-

[6] J. M. Clark, "Toward a Concept . . . ," AER, 30:250–251 (June 1940).

side mills to invade the local portion of a mill's natural market. Assuming that strategic considerations do not lead an outsider to absorb freight with mill nets below marginal costs, a mill would have a "monopolistic" hold over a limited area in its locality. Assuming, heroically, complete independence of price cutting behavior, the theoretical lower limit to base price cutting by an isolated mill would be the price at which additional sales (by enlarging the "monopolized" zone) would fail to cover the cost of the general reduction. Even at this potential lower limit to the posted price at the isolated mill, many sales would evidently be made at mill nets above marginal cost. Consequently, there would be some contribution to operating overhead in many mills even during the most ruinous competition.

Actually, prices in the cement industry will hardly fall to the level set by the assumption of purely independent behavior. A market environment could scarcely exist (or be created by public policy) which would eliminate all price-cutting inhibitions because of a mutual recognition of interdependence. Mere technical economies of plant scale relative to the size of regional cement markets guarantee a somewhat limited number of producers and *some* self-restraint in price behavior. This is not to suggest that during a cyclical decline in demand prices would not become cutthroat and force large short-period losses upon firms in the industry if collective marketing systems were prohibited. But during a depression prices would not ordinarily fall to the marginal cost level for grouped mills or to a level somewhat above marginal costs for isolated mills.

To the extent that "competitive" losses in the cement industry would be somewhat less during depression than if prices always equaled marginal cost, Rowe's fear of excessive scrapping of equipment and organization could be mitigated. By the same token, however, should expectations of future revivals in demand prove correct, effective, but impure, price competition would tend inevitably to maintain a certain degree of excess capacity. Likewise, a somewhat higher average price would accompany this structural excess capacity over the course of the cycle than if prices were based strictly on marginal cost. But the waste in the persisting excess capacity would tend to be insignificant when compared to the large scale structural surplusage characteristic of the cement industry for approximately forty years prior to 1948.[7]

2. Mislocation and retardation in the shift of the geographic distribution of capacity

The undesirable locational consequences of the basing-point system are less serious in the cement industry than in industries where there is a dynamic locational relation between producers and fabricating consumers. In the steel industry, for example, not only are some fabricators encouraged to locate close to basic steel producers so as to reduce transfer costs where steel scrap wastage is appreciable, but under its old basing-point system the industry offered an artificial incentive to fabricators to set up near those production centers where the lowest base-mill prices prevailed. The geographic price structure in steel tended to influence over time the density of the steel fabricating market in various areas of the country, and in turn the developing fabricator market influenced the expansion of basic steel production in rival areas of the country.[8] Such dynamic locational considerations are virtually non-existent in the cement industry, since practically all cement is "fabricated" into concrete at the site of the ultimate consumer market. Even concrete-product plants (block, slabs, pipe, and so on) tend to be market-oriented because of the great weight of water and aggregate (sand and gravel) incorporated in it. Markets for portland cement are not affected by the location of the mills and by the base-price structure of the industry, except to the extent that high transport costs encourage the substitution of rival materials in markets remote from any cement mill.

Nevertheless, there is evidence to support the proposition that

[7] Carl Kaysen, by assuming the demand for investment goods to be more elastic during booms than busts, has argued that a moderate amount of structural excess capacity in investment goods industries would not constitute a waste, but rather an asset, to society. By reducing the bottleneck problem during later stages of recovery, the greater available supply of investment goods would serve to promote a somewhat higher total level of national investment and income over the cycle. See *supra*, V, fn. 32.

[8] See G. W. Stocking, *Basing Point Pricing and Regional Development* (Chapel Hill, N.C., 1954), Chapters 4 and 5 and Appendix A.

some undesirable locations will be chosen by cement producers, and a socially inefficient, geographic distribution of capacity will be perpetuated under a basing-point system that works well. The basing-point system reduces the penalty for mistakes by stabilizing base prices at a level high in relation to marginal costs and by facilitating systematic dumping from excess capacity areas. Jacob Viner aptly expressed this theory while testifying before the Commission:

> Also a system of that sort which provides an umbrella for the badly located plant and the high cost of the plant would lessen the penalties in prospect before an entrepreneur in badly locating his plant or designing it. He would still have the incentive to have his plant located as well as possible, but he would know he is in an industry which wouldn't immediately oust him if he failed to exercise good judgment in handling the situation.[9]

Market data are not available by which to attempt a systematic evaluation of individual locational decisions made under the basing-point system, but one very obvious oversight in decision-making is clear. During the late twenties additional mills and increments to existing mill capacity were being installed well in excess of natural market requirements in such areas as the Lehigh Valley, Alabama, and Tennessee. At the same time no mills existed nor were any being built in either North or South Carolina although annual consumption in the area averaged 4,000,000 barrels between 1926 and 1928, and over 2,000,000 barrels during the depression years of 1936–38. Even with some shipments from mills adjacent to the Carolina borders, an efficient mill of 1,500,000 barrels of theoretical capacity (1,350,000 of practical capacity) could have been easily supported by the Carolina market, and substantial freight savings to most markets would more than have compensated for the slightly greater fuel costs involved in operating in the coastal limestone area. The state of North Carolina, dismayed over the high delivered prices of cement for its highway program, reflecting partly high base-mill prices but primarily high freight additions, on various occasions during the thirties and forties considered the construction of a state cement plant. And finally, in 1948 a cement plant was constructed in the Carolinas. It is not the writer's intention, how-

[9] *Record,* Transcript pp. 15695–96.

ever, to suggest that profit-maximizing was sufficiently dulled by security under the basing-point system so that poor judgment characterized most locational decision-making. Many mills were installed during the twenties in areas of obvious deficit capacity, such as New Orleans, Tampa, Norfolk, and Thomaston, Maine, to name some outstanding examples.

Nevertheless, two marketing practices inherent in the basing-point system operate in some degree to reduce private incentives to expand in large deficit capacity areas that lack a cement mill. The first is stabilized freight absorption which interacts with the functional relation that exists between plant scale and production economies, to encourage excessive geographic concentration in the distribution of mill capacity. During periods of growing demand and capacity expansion many existing cement producers, desiring to make but modest capital commitments, find it more to their advantage to add 200,000 or 500,000 barrels of annual theoretical capacity to their existing mills (by supplementary quarry, kiln, and grinding equipment) than to erect a new mill of comparable cost in a deficit capacity area. While expansion of capacity of existing mills would not lead to diseconomies in production costs and might offer some minor economies, the marked diseconomies of a new small-scale mill would more than offset the savings in transportation costs. In locating a new mill in deficit areas (except very isolated areas), 1,000,000 to 1,500,000 barrels of annual theoretical capacity must be built in order to achieve sufficient economies of scale. Given the expectations generated by an effective basing-point system, producers who expand capacity at existing locations can expect to dispose of much of their surplus capacity output by means of systematic freight absorption, where necessary. In turn, the very development of surplus capacity in certain established areas, in conjunction with the threat of systematic dumping, is likely to deter the erection, by others, of some new mills of efficient size in deficit areas. Whereas the expectation of unsystematic pricing would discourage excessive expansion at established locations and encourage alternative expansion in deficit areas, the basing-point system does just the opposite. Some large market areas, as a consequence, denied the advantage of a cement mill in their territory, continue to pay high destination prices for cement shipped from a great distance. Although it is impossible to estimate the strength of the locational bias resulting from the interaction of the basing-point system and economies of scale, there is evidence of such a bias. Between 1925 and 1930 theoretical capacity was expanded in the eastern Pennsylvania-New Jersey-Maryland area by 12,000,000 barrels, three quarters of which took place at the existing mills of some fifteen companies. Although demand was strong in the Middle Atlantic and New England states during the first few years of this period, much of the developing surplus production probably flowed into southern Virginia and North Carolina, and delayed the construction of new mills and lower destination prices in the Roanoke, Virginia, area.[10] That the basing-point system contributed to excessive concentration of production centers by encouraging a series of capacity increases at existing locations, is also attested by the testimony before the Capehart Committee in the fall of 1948 of an independent cement manufacturer located in the Lehigh Valley area:

> A year ago this time, anticipating a good demand for cement, I went to our board of directors with the recommendation that we increase our capacity by replacing a kiln with a larger one. This would have the effect of increasing our capacity by about 200,000 barrels a year, or 11 per cent . . . . We placed orders for the equipment at once, but final delivery could not be made until late 1948.
>
> After the Supreme Court decision and the issuance of the Federal Trade Commission interpretations, I had only one course; that was to go back to our board and tell them that, because the situation had now become so uncertain, we should give up our idea of increased capacity and cancel the orders for the material.[11]

The second practice was that controls upon trucking, and especially its outright elimination, reduced the advantage, relative to established mills, of locating new mills in deficit areas close to large metropolitan markets. In regions where trucking was completely banned (the typical situation), a new mill could

[10] One was finally built in the Roanoke area in 1951.

[11] *Study of Pricing Methods,* Hearings before a Subcommittee of the Committee on Interstate and Foreign Commerce, United States Senate, 80th Cong., 2d Sess. (1948), pp. 782–83.

expect to be plagued by extensive freight absorption since long-haul rail rates on cement were not appreciably higher than short-haul rates. During the late 1930's rail-freight charges on a 300-mile haul were less than twice those on a 50-mile haul, while rates for 200 miles were only two or three times those for 5 miles; and short-haul rates made up no trifling proportion of base prices. With base prices ranging from $1.50 to $1.90 per barrel in the territory east of the Rocky Mountains, rail rates on a barrel of cement in the various freight territories ranged from 18½¢ to 37¢ on a 5-mile haul and from 32⅗¢ to 48¢ on a 50-mile haul.[12] Rates on contract trucking and costs of private trucking of cement are not generally available, but even the notoriously high common carrier truck rates established by a few state commissions were below rail rates on hauls under 50 to 75 miles. Moreover, trucking provided additional savings by eliminating the extra haul from the rail siding to the job site, an extra cost sometimes as expensive as a direct truck shipment from mill to job site. Had trucking not been eliminated, established mills outside an area could have continued to penetrate the local markets of a potential newcomer only by making appreciable reductions in their mill nets. Had buyer trucking continued, a new mill could have expected fewer distant mills to penetrate the local market and take for itself a greater share of it. Even in the few regions where there was a controlled trucking service, the cost of short-haul transportation remained a little higher than with buyer trucking and the freight absorption required of penetrating mills was somewhat reduced.

By eliminating a key source of unsystematic reductions in destination prices, the control of trucking also made it difficult for a new mill to win sales where it was not previously known.[13] In this broad view, the entire basing-point system, bolstered by the threat of punitive base prices after the early thirties, must have deterred a firm from establishing new mills in areas where it had not previously sold. If a potential new entrant was also to be shut off from making unsystematic delivered price quotations on commercial business freighted by rail and on sealed bids to

[12] *Record,* Respondent Exhibit 2899.

[13] An exception would exist where the mill is constructed by a firm which had been marketing in this area from a distant mill.

governmental agencies, how could the firm hope to gain an adequate volume of sales without tremendous additional capital outlays for selling.

More than logic supports the proposition that the basing-point system retarded a desirable shift in the geographic distribution of cement capacity. In the period following 1936, when cement consumption in the South was increasing at a much faster rate than in the nation as a whole, there was a marked delay in shifting productive capacity toward that area. Mills are not completely immobile. Several companies which discontinued operations sold their mills and equipment to South American and Australian enterprises,[14] while many chains, when scrapping a plant, move usable equipment (kilns, crushers, grinders, quarrying apparatus, et cetera) to one of their other mills. During the mid-thirties Marquette suffered from tremendous underutilization of its 5,000,000-barrel mill at La Salle, Illinois, being surrounded by several mills in the immediate vicinity and in adjoining states, and seriously considered building a new plant near Vicksburg, Mississippi, with the surplus equipment. A trade journal reported that Marquette had found an adequate quarry site, was confident of the region's growth as a cement market, and appreciated the fact that Mississippi had not a single mill while Louisiana and Arkansas had but one each.[15] After commenting upon and analyzing the Marquette announcement, the editor of the journal concluded, "We firmly believe that the next few years will see the construction of many small, modern plants to serve sales areas not already served by existing plants." [16] However, Marquette never moved to make two mills out of its overbuilt LaSalle plant, nor did others build; and the editor's prophecy was proved false.

As Table 9 illustrates, the upward trend in consumption in the South became quite marked after 1936, yet southern productive capacity remained virtually unchanged until 1948 when a new mill was completed in South Carolina. Total shipments received (cement consumption) by southern states relative to southern mill practical capacity substantially exceeded the per-

[14] *Rock Products* (June 1942), p. 68 and (June 1948), p. 95.
[15] *Ibid.*, (June 1936), p. 30. [16] *Ibid.*, pp. 29–30.

centage of total United States shipments to total United States practical capacity during every year after 1936. Moreover, excepting 1944–45, wartime years of restricted consumption, cement consumption in the South substantially exceeded the practical capacity of its mills during the period 1941–48. A major clue to the retardation in the expansion of southern capacity, however, shows up in the comparison of total shipments received by southern states and those made by southern mills, each expressed as a percentage of practical capacity of those mills. Even in years when supplies at the mills were not especially tight (total southern shipments constituting less than 90 per cent of southern practical capacity), southern markets were being substantially invaded from the North. Both intensive sales cultivation and dumping probably developed under the basing-point system with northern mills winning a considerable share of the markets in the upper South; with Tennessee, Georgia, and Alabama producers laboring in Louisiana, Mississippi, and Florida; and with both groups feverishly applying their selling techniques in the Carolinas.

It must be recognized, however, that some significant reshuffling of regional capacity did take place despite this retarding tendency. While capacity declined about 6 per cent for the nation as a whole between 1938 and 1948, practical capacity in the eastern Pennsylvania-New Jersey-Maryland producing district declined about 35 per cent (50,400,000 to 35,000,000 barrels) and in Michigan about 26 per cent (17,500,000 to 12,800,000 barrels). Moreover, in two producing districts, with greatly expanding construction activity but relatively isolated from rival centers of surplus capacity, practical capacity substantially increased — rising 38 per cent in Texas (9,400,000 to 14,400,000 barrels) and 30 per cent in California (20,200,000 to 26,300,000 barrels). However, the 8 per cent increase in southern practical capacity (23,900,000 to 25,700,000 barrels) during these same years was small in comparison to the regional growth in cement consumption.

Had sufficient uncertainty moved the industry to substantial price cutting, competitive pressures could have led the management of cement firms, or the new purchasers of bankrupt firms,

Table 9

Cement Shipments Received and Made by Mills In Nine Southern States[a]: Comparisons with Practical Capacity[b], 1936–43, 1946–48[c]

	1936	1937	1938	1939	1940	1941	1942	1943	1946	1947	1948
	(millions of barrels)										
Shipments received by southern states	11.8	13.4	14.5	15.3	17.0	26.0	30.7	23.9	25.8	27.0	28.8
Shipments made by southern mills	9.9	11.1	12.0	13.5	14.9	20.4	21.9	18.4	19.4	21.8	23.8
Practical capacity of southern mills	23.0	23.3	23.2	23.2	23.2	22.1	22.2	21.7	23.0	23.4	25.7
	(%)										
Shipments made by southern mills as percentage of southern mill practical capacity	43.0	47.6	51.7	58.2	63.8	92.3	98.6	84.4	84.3	93.2	92.7
Shipments received by the South as percentage of southern mill practical capacity	46.1	57.5	62.5	65.9	73.2	117.6	138.3	110.1	112.2	115.4	112.1
Shipments in the United States as percentage of United States practical capacity	49.0	50.6	45.8	52.9	56.9	73.6	81.6	61.1	74.9	83.2	89.7

[a] Alabama, Florida, Georgia, Louisiana, Mississippi, North Carolina, South Carolina, Tennessee, Virginia.

[b] Practical capacity, as explained in Chapter 5, is estimated to be 90 per cent of the theoretical capacity reported by the Bureau of Mines.

[c] The years 1944–45 have been omitted because of war restrictions placed upon construction activity and derived cement demand.

Source: U.S. Bureau of Mines, *Mineral Yearbook*, 1937–1948.

to shift some of the surplus northern capacity to those deficit production areas of the South where available supplies of lime material made economical production feasible. But the basing-point system sustained not only a high price level but also systematic freight absorption, both of which operated to the particular advantage of excess capacity producers.

A better locational pattern would not necessarily be furthered, however, by a system of uniform f.o.b. mill prices. Uniform f.o.b. mill pricing would indeed sharply delineate market boundaries, and thereby induce more careful initial decisions as to location and more rapid relocation in the light of changing markets. But, for reasons to be discussed in the next chapter, although uncertainties and competitive pressures might well be greater under uniform f.o.b. mill pricing than under the basing-point system, it is questionable whether the average level of geographic prices would be much closer to a competitive level than under the latter system. Consequently, a tendency might develop under uniform f.o.b. mill pricing to locate an excessive number of small mills in sheltered geographic markets of small size. When compared with the distribution of plant capacity under conditions of effective price competition, the increased transportation economies of excessively decentralized capacity would not fully compensate for the loss of scale economies. The geographic distribution of cement capacity would in all probability be preferable to that which develops under a basing-point formula pricing system, but would it be sufficiently better under the uniform f.o.b. mill formula?

Intermarket penetration, per se, does not bring about a better production-cost transportation-cost locational adjustment than does nondiscriminatory f.o.b. mill pricing. On the contrary, intermarket penetration plays a role only *when unaccompanied by common use of a pricing formula,* thereby contributing to price competition. It is the existence, or prospect, of effective competitive pressure on the price level which should lead toward a superior balancing of production and transportation economies when new mill capacity is being planned. And it is effective price competition which should hasten the continued relocation of mill capacity toward the optimum geographic distribution, as it shifts unpredictably in response to secularly changing market and technological trends.

3. Excessive cross-hauling; excessive selling expenditures; restriction of truck transportation economies

Excessive cross-hauling is admittedly a qualitative term connoting that there is a "proper" amount of intermarket penetration. Unfortunately this cannot be defined quantitatively. What the writer has in mind is the amount which will provide buyers with economically useful alternative sources of supply. When sufficient uncertainty and independence exist in the marketing process, additional sources of supply enable buyers to bargain for price concessions and quality improvements in times of excess capacity. But the mere multiplication of suppliers who offer to sell allegedly identical quality at the same prices over extended periods of time, offers little real advantage to the buyer. Under the basing-point system as practiced in the cement industry, interpenetration usually increased costs by overstimulating the use of expensive transportation services. Since the basing-point system protected a high price level relative to marginal costs, firms absorbed considerable amounts of freight in seeking additional sales that promised to contribute to overhead costs. Yet in times of general excess capacity the advantage to one mill constituted a disadvantage to another; and when the interpenetration became reciprocal, the net effect was a great increase in transportation costs and waste. Except for the convenience of faster delivery or the greater assurance of having a source of supply should shortages be expected, the buyer had no special reason for purchasing from the local supplier rather than from a distant seller. With quality largely standardized, with construction schedules planned well in advance, and with the usual excess capacity in the industry, the buyer cared little about the individual seller.

Extensive cross-hauling under the basing-point system was primarily a phenomenon of excess capacity. When demand declined or when expansion in demand failed to keep pace with that of capacity, firms throughout the industry strove to maintain at least their past share of the regional market without breaking down the price level. Firms would naturally have preferred to supply a large proportion of their local markets, net revenues being greatest there, but mutual respect for and enforcement of the formula, the quest for more stable operations, and self-defense forced firms to reach out into less profitable areas. In the first place greatest effort would undoubtedly be devoted to winning business in the most profitable (local) markets, but largely through salesmanship. Mills which had been tempted to make unsystematic price concessions to capture sales, found their base prices reduced by the imposition of punitive bases, or by selective reductions in base prices by a chain mill operating in the same territory. Respect for the formula, thus fostered, discouraged use of the price weapon. Second, because of the constant shifting in geographic demand, firms believed it desirable to cultivate and supply more distant dealer markets at all times and to some degree, so as to insure themselves against a future inadequate local market demand when construction declined temporarily at home. Sales forces were shifted about in more distant markets to meet changes in construction activity. Third, under the pressure of excess capacity, mills which dumped cement systematically in markets of rivals so that the latter lost part of their local markets, compelled them, in turn, to practice reverse penetration in self-defense.

No precise estimate has ever been made of the "unnecessary" freight burden that resulted from the use of the basing-point system in the cement industry. To attempt such an estimate would require knowing the destination of all shipments at least by counties, the freight rates from all mills to destinations at least averaged by counties, and the productive capacities and cost conditions of all mills. Then one might set a benchmark of minimum freight costs under a central, perfectly administered system of uniform f.o.b. mill prices, and "unnecessary" freight would be all freight realized in excess of the standard. That such a study has never been attempted is understandable since the costs would be very great and the benefits limited, especially if it be agreed that some degree of unsystematic interpenetration may be "necessary" in promoting an effectively competitive level of cement prices.

Two less ambitious studies, employing different methods, have suggested that "unnecessary" hauling under the basing-point system was appreciable in the cement industry. A Federal Trade Commission study, although erring somewhat on the high side, made what was probably a fairly reasonable estimate of the "unnecessary" transport burden for the year 1927.[17] The Commission obtained the average maximum mill net and the average mill realization on total shipments from each of 117 mills in the industry, covering 141,000,000 barrels, or 81 per cent of the cement shipped during the year. When the weighted average mill net reduction of 24.3 cents per barrel was applied to all cement shipments in 1927, the "unnecessary" burden was placed at $42,000,000 for the year. Since the estimated average *maximum* mill price at both base and non-base mills was $1.864 per barrel during 1927 while estimated average mill realization was only $1.621,[18] the average maximum price was 15 per cent higher than necessary to maintain the same average realized price and profit level in the industry. Even had the Commission's estimate of unnecessary transportation been exact, and had the savings under uniform f.o.b. mill pricing been fully passed along, consumers in all geographic areas would not have gained equally. Because non-base mills and high base-price mills were taking reduced mill nets on most of their sales, while low base-price mills were making most of their sales at the maximum mill price, substantially larger reductions would have been made at the non-base and high base-price mills in comparison to those at other base mills under a system of uniform f.o.b. mill pricing.

There are several reasons, however, for believing that the Federal Trade Commission estimate of redundant transportation expenses, based on the average reduction in mill net, somewhat overstated the costs of cross-hauling. First, although the cement industry as a whole operated at only 84.8 per cent of practical capacity during 1927, mills in some sections of the country operated at higher rates, and during the seasonal peak these may not have been able fully to supply the demand in their natural market.

[17] FTC, *Price Bases Inquiry* (Washington, 1932), pp. 138–142.

[18] Since the Bureau of Mines reported an average mill realization on total shipments of $1.62 per barrel, it seems likely that the FTC estimate of average mill net reduction was quite reliable.

Base prices having been typically rigid during this period, excess capacity mills outside may have made some temporary shipments, priced according to the basing-point formula, into these under-supplied consuming areas. In such cases the reduced mill nets would not have involved uneconomical use of transportation. Second, although the Commission found a marked adherence to the pricing formula in 1927, any violations of the formula resulted in additional mill net reductions which did not constitute unnecessary transportation expenditures. Third, to the extent that reductions in mill net may have been necessary to meet foreign competition at coastal ports, unnecessary transportation may not have taken place, because foreign prices at the ports may themselves have reflected dumping and cross-hauling.

Although the unnecessary transportation cost for 1927 was undoubtedly overestimated by the Commission, we have no means of knowing whether it overshot the mark by *at least* one third, as suggested by John M. Clark.[19] However, one of the most striking features about the 24.3 cents per barrel estimate (15 per cent of the 1927 average realized mill price), is that it was so large during one of the more prosperous years in the industry's history: the industry operated at 84.8 per cent of practical capacity in 1927. Clark has also suggested,[20] and logic and experience bear him out,[21] that cross-hauling increases with depressed business and increased excess capacity. With the industry rarely operating at as much as 50 per cent of practical capacity during the thirties, and with price competition having been effectively eliminated in 1932, an extensive increase in unnecessary transportation would have been expected from practices which awarded markets on the basis of either selling ability or the "luck of the draw" on sealed bids. It would be interesting to have a similar estimate for some year of the middle or late thirties.

The second limited study of cement traffic was made by Paul E. Sweeney for the Board of Investigation and Research,

[19] J. M. Clark, "Basing Point," *Canadian Journal of Economics and Political Science*, 4:482 (November 1938).

[20] *Ibid.*

[21] *The Wall Street Journal*, on June 7, 1949, reported that many mills in the State of New York would delay in renewing freight absorbing sales so long as demand in the local market remained so high.

covering selected data for 1939 and 1941. Its conclusion was that cement was being transported indiscriminately during the period.[22] Using Bureau of Mines data for 1941 when the industry operated at 73.6 per cent of practical capacity, Sweeney studied gross interstate shipments of cement. Because many mills were located close to state boundaries, some of his findings lacked real significance, but not all. He found shipments moving from deficit producing states to surplus producing states, as well as many reciprocal long distance shipments between surplus states. Mills in Ohio were shown to have made substantial shipments to destinations in Illinois, and vice versa, all passing through Indiana, itself a surplus state with four producing mills.

Sweeney also made an analysis of carload traffic, including a record of the actual cement shipments from origins to destinations for one day in June 1939, as reported by Class I railroads. Four regional maps were prepared showing the origin and destination of all shipments within the Northwest, Great Lakes, Southern, and Western regions, as well as a national map showing shipments between the Official, Southern, and Western Freight territories. Indiscriminate cross-shipments appeared in virtually all areas save the Rocky Mountain region, where most mills were monopolized by a single concern. Moreover, some exceedingly long hauls passed through the territory of established mills. For example, a Lehigh Valley producer shipped to Birmingham; a Birmingham producer to Miami; a Kansas producer to Pennsylvania; and a New York producer to Nebraska.

Yet there is reason to believe that the wastes of cross-hauling at various times during the thirties were considerably reduced through cooperative action in handling shipments for one another's account. As reported in Chapter IV, the Commission discovered evidence which suggested that there may have been considerable "swapping" of sales orders between cement companies. Trades amounting to 50,000 and 100,000 barrels were recorded, permitting the reciprocating firms to realize substantially higher mill nets, while maintaining a high price level. Unfortunately, the Commission did not attempt to learn the full extent of the practice. Such anti-competitive exchange of mar-

[22] Sweeney, see *supra*, II, fn. 21.

kets, of course, reduced the wastes of cross-hauling and increased gross margins for producers. But since the consumer received no share of the savings, this method of reducing the costs of excessive cross-hauling had little social value.

The socially preferable means of lessening the wastes of unnecessary transportation is to be found through encouraging competitive forces which would reduce destination prices during periods of excess capacity. High base prices relative to marginal costs are necessary to permit extensive cross-hauling. Very distant mills could not afford to penetrate large sections of rival territories, unless posted mill prices were high enough to contribute to overhead even after considerable freight absorption. Had market penetrations taken place in an environment of uncertainty caused by non-collusive sealed bidding to governmental agencies, unsystematic price reductions at particular destinations, bargaining with large contractors, and optional trucking privileges, these very penetrations would have led to reductions of posted mill prices which, in turn, would have minimized the wasteful aspects of cross-hauling.

Excessive selling costs in marketing under the basing-point system constituted a surprisingly large proportion of the average realized mill price for a producers' good. According to a Federal Trade Commission study of forty-seven cement manufacturers, total costs of distribution exclusive of outward transportation averaged 16.28 per cent of the realized mill price in 1939.[23] Selling costs, to be sure, were spread over production representing but 53 per cent of practical capacity during the year. But for an industry which sells a relatively standardized producers' good to a relatively informed group of buyers such a large proportion appears unusually wasteful. This non-price rivalry operated, of course, as a counterpart to wasteful cross-hauling in the struggle of each firm to maintain or increase its share of the market.

Moreover, the cement industry's variant of non-price competition was peculiarly wasteful since there had developed a convention against quality-raising competition. As described in Chapter IV, the marketed product was guaranteed merely to

[23] FTC, *Report on Distribution Methods and Costs,* Part III, "Building Materials" (Washington, 1944), p. 47.

meet official minimum specifications in tensile strength and fineness. And although the raw materials and grinding equipment of various companies were such that their executives admitted to exceeding specifications by as much as 10 to 45 per cent, the fact was not publicized,[24] the industry deeming it an unfair practice to advertize or urge sales on a quality basis. Moreover, personnel in the regional offices of the Portland Cement Association gave contractors technical aid in the preparation of cement for various types of construction work, as part of the industry's promotional program. As a consequence, cement firms resorted to salesmanship and the provision of minor services such as those described by a cement company executive in the following testimony:

> Yes, we follow up all jobs very closely through different agencies and lettings. We send out word of these jobs to our salesmen who contact contractors in their territory; call their attention to these jobs and see if they are interested in bidding on them. If they are, the salesmen will take them to the site of the work, and if the man is interested at all in the job the salesman will then get them such information as he can for them, such as finding if there are raw materials; if aggregate is in the vicinity; the best place to get water; if the railroad has a siding there. If not, he will contact the railroads to see if they will put in a proper siding. Then, if the man decides definitely he will bid on the job, he will find out what the local conditions are for him. If he gets it, he will find out about machinery for the job. They will often know of second-hand machinery in the vicinity that can be used on the job.[25]

These services are not without value, but they could have been handled largely by the contractor himself with little effort or expense. And the general display of solicitude for good will in expense accounts for dinners, entertainment, gifts, and the like was undoubtedly costly.

The cement industry was aware of and concerned about excessive selling costs, and for years attention was given to the problem by the Committee on Elimination of Waste in Selling, of the Portland Cement Asssociation. A survey made by the Committee revealed that selling expenses had climbed 1½ cents per barrel between 1926 and 1928.[26] Although the industry operated

[24] See, e.g., *Record,* Transcript pp. 22865, 34949, 37425.
[25] *Ibid.* Transcript p. 26042.
[26] *Ibid.,* Commission Exhibit 971–2L.

at 84.7 per cent of practical capacity in 1926 as compared with only 80.4 per cent two years later, the latter year represented the greatest production year in the history of the industry prior to World War II, and the added selling cost, when applied to the 175,000,000 barrels produced during the year, amounted to approximately $2,000,000. Lavish entertainment of purchasers and users, and gifts to them, were condemned as unfair methods of competition in the Cement Institute's 1929 Code of Ethics [27] and in its July 1935 (post-NRA) Compendium of Established Terms and Marketing Methods.[28]

But the industry evidently found itself helpless in combatting excessive selling costs under a system of imperfect collusion, because the cost was the amount paid in return for stabilizing the price level. Selling expenses probably increased absolutely, as well as in relation to average realized price, during the depressed periods of the thirties — especially after the basing-point system was renewed in 1932. Many cement executives testified to the competitive need of enlarging their sales force during the thirties. As an example, the president of one company testified:

> The reason that I had to increase the sales force was because my district managers and my sales manager, whenever I would go after them to increase our sales, would claim that the other companies were increasing their sales force, and we were not getting as much business as I thought we ought to get. And from 1933, when I came there, to 1937, I put on six additional men. That is, I raised the sales force from 18 to 24, and since then we have made a number of changes to improve the quality of the force.[29]

Moreover, in 1936, after the sales manager of Aetna had been fired for failing to adhere to the basing-point system, the new sales manager wrote to his president explaining that he had hired many salesmen and that his selling expense per barrel had increased because "we are now merchandizing our cement according to the ethics of the industry." [30]

It is impossible to know just how much of the 1939 estimate of non-freight distribution costs represented wasteful selling.

[27] *Ibid.*, Commission Exhibit 138–N–U.

[28] *Ibid.*, Commission Exhibit 561.

[29] *Ibid.*, Commission Exhibit 971–2L.

[30] *Ibid.*, Commission Exhibits 20A–C, 37B, 42C, 44B, 45A–D, 909; Transcript pp. 519, 532–40, 815–19, 1015, 1054.

Even under conditions of effective price or quality competition, contacts must be established between buyers and sellers in order to present comparative offers as to prices, delivery dates, and sundry specifications, and to arrange orders. Salesmen perform many of these necessary functions. But in the cement industry, a large proportion of the selling costs undoubtedly represented social waste. Moreover, as the Federal Trade Commission has warned, in industries where the selling terms are fully standardized, sales competition threatens business ethics:

> . . . it is fraught with the possibility and dangers of commercial bribery because the appeal to buy which can not rest on price (in its broad sense) is apt to be based on some personal advantage to the purchasing employee or officer or to some other party in a position to influence the sale, instead of the actual buyer, or to the principal on the contract whose money is being spent.[31]

Like the remedy for excessive cross-hauling, the most desirable means for reducing selling wastes would be to attack the various elements which enable successful operation of formula pricing. Competition in selling there still would be. But with a lower price level, a smaller selling territory, and greater uncertainties as to rivals' intentions, costs of selling are likely to be greatly reduced and more or less confined to provision of the minimum necessary information and the offer of more attractive terms.

It is impossible to estimate the increased transportation cost imposed upon consumers by the restrictions placed upon the trucking of cement. Some inferences, however, can be drawn from scattered portions of the *Record.* Over 95 per cent of the shipments from the Universal Atlas mill near Pittsburgh moved by truck during 1931, and it was estimated in a Universal Atlas inter-office memorandum that the economical trucking radius, as gauged by alternative rail rates, was as much as 70 miles during 1930–31.[32] A New Jersey producer of ready-mix concrete testified that he had incorporated a company to truck cement from Lehigh Valley mills to his plant, a distance of 60 to 75 miles,

[31] FTC, *Price Bases Inquiry* (Washington, 1932), p. 27.
[32] *Record,* Commission Exhibits 2653C, 1320.

at costs 50 per cent less than if by rail.[33] The fact that the 15-cent-per-barrel truck differential (close to 10 per cent on base prices) imposed in most areas during 1929 failed in its objective of deterring trucking, also bears witness to the economies of short-haul trucking. Even in the Great Lakes area, where trucking of a controlled variety continued, the non-competitive truck rates of common carriers or of company-franchised contract carriers were below rail rates within a 30 to 50 miles radius. Many buyers undoubtedly would have continued to ship at still greater savings in these areas had they been permitted to arrange their own trucking.

In most areas of the country (as described in Chapter IV) trucking was eliminated completely, and buyers were denied not only the advantage of competitive truck rates, but also the economies of delivery direct to the job site. During the Commission hearings nearly all companies stressed the inconvenience, extra cost, and lack of facilities for handling trucking. The cost factor, along with a policy of dealer appeasement, constituted the principal elements in the industry's apologia for the virtual elimination of trucking. Yet, in replying to the Burns-Clark questionnaire in 1935, the manufacturers rarely gave the inconvenience of truck loading as a reason for eliminating trucking; the principal one offered was "market stabilization."[34] Furthermore, since numerous mills had shipped over 50 per cent of their cement by truck, the allegation of inconvenience and significantly greater loading costs must be viewed skeptically. The general manager of the non-respondent Cowell firm testified during the hearings that there was no disadvantage whatsoever in the loading of trucks as compared with railroad cars at his mill.[35] And during a visit at the Valley Forge mill on the outskirts of Philadelphia, the writer was told that no difficulty save of price instability had been experienced in the loading of buyers' trucks. It may well have been that some mills located at a distance from metropolitan consuming markets found the cost of small-scale truck loading slightly greater than rail car, but it is exceedingly

[33] *Ibid.*, Transcript pp. 7622, 7624, 7654–55.

[34] See *Brief for Respondents*, Appendix C, pp. 23–35, 149–157, *Aetna Portland Cement Co.* v. *F.T.C.*, 157 F.2d 533 (7th Cir. 1946).

[35] *Record*, Transcript p. 8777.

unlikely that any attendant additional cost approached the 15-cent-per-barrel premium uniformly imposed in most areas to deter truck shipments.

To the extent that greater loading and invoicing costs were actually entailed in shipping by buyers' trucks rather than in rail cars or company-controlled trucks, some price differential would have been justified. But cement manufacturers never attempted a careful estimate of the differential cost. Had the manufacturers imposed merely a premium justified by such costs, substantial savings from short-haul transportation would undoubtedly have continued to be realized by consumers. But, of even greater importance to consumers, vital links of the pricing formula would have been broken. Many buyers would have had an opportunity to bargain with more distant mills for price concessions; and uncertainties and disharmonies resulting from price concessions to buyers within the economical trucking range of rival mills would have encouraged some offering of unsystematic delivered price reductions even in territories dependent upon rail transportation.

4. Probable reduction in incentives for increasing production efficiency and innovation

Average output per-man-hour in cement companies increased from 1.63 barrels in 1928 to 2.81 barrels in 1948, or at an average compounded annual rate of increase of 2.65 per cent. This rate of productivity improvement compares not unfavorably with the average for the entire national economy. Still, there is no way of knowing what the rate of increase would have been had the competitive pressures been greater. Although it is generally held in the United States that competitive behavior increases the likelihood of developments in efficiency and innovation, some economists, and most notably the late Professor Schumpeter, have held that stabilizing practices promote development by minimizing the risks entailed. The evidence is far from clear, but prevailing practices in the cement industry would appear to support the correctness of the general opinion.

In the first place, most innovations in product use and improvement, as well as in technological changes in productive processes, have not come from individual cement firms. Most research to encourage greater use of cement was carried on by the Portland Cement Association, supported financially by a great many of the manufacturers; while the bulk of the research for improving plant technology by developing modifications of existing equipment and auxiliary devices for improving kiln and grinding operations, was performed primarily by cement machinery manufacturers (e.g., Traylor, Allis-Chalmers, Babcock & Wilcox). It was mainly the adoption by the mills of achievements of the machinery makers which reduced the labor and fuel requirements per barrel of cement in the period after 1920. Had the competitive pressures on price been greater, firms probably would have been under far greater compulsion to reduce costs by adopting more rapidly and more extensively the technological modifications which promised to lower production expense. How much difference it would have made, no one knows.

The proposition that the very defensive philosophy permeating the industry influenced the selection of managerial personnel is plausible, but by no means provable. Operating under a system of formula pricing, skilled marketing policy was undoubtedly of far greater importance and concern than efficiency in production and operation. And the cultivation of buyer loyalties through superior salesmanship was considered the ethical method for maintaining or enlarging markets. It is not surprising, therefore, that top executives in cement firms were generally chosen from among former sales managers.[36] Moreover, the success of the chief executives was probably gauged by their ability to develop and maintain superior selling organizations rather than by their ability to improve the administrative and productive organization directed at reducing costs, or by their skill in forecasting the best sites for the location of mills. With cooperation protecting prices at a level well above existing marginal costs, profits could be increased more readily by enlarging the volume of sales than by reducing the costs of production.

[36] E.g., Blaine Smith, the former sales manager of Universal, was made the president of newly merged Penn–Dixie in 1926 and during the thirties was recalled to become president of Universal Atlas. Moreover, when Aetna came under industry attack for its free-wheeling price cutting, the board chairman of Aetna in 1937 hired the sales manager of Consolidated to become president.

Productivity and efficiency relationships between product outputs and factor inputs can hardly be taken as fixed even in the short run, although they are conveniently assumed to be such in static economic theory. Where competitive pressures attack the profits of an industry, management is forced to exert itself to discover means to cut costs and to increase the general efficiency of operations, and it is often discovered that more output can be obtained from the current combination of productive factors. Discussing these considerations, Melvin Reder has written:

> The extent to which the principle of profit maximization can be ignored will depend on the market position of the firm. If the firm is a quasi-monopolist, it may be able to allow considerable inefficiency while showing a satisfactory operating statement. But if it is in a fiercely competitive situation, it may be unable to stand any inefficiency whatsoever. It is when operating profits turn to losses that management discovers how much inefficiency it has been tolerating and strives to eliminate it.[37]

The basing-point system indeed softened the profit-reducing pressures of declines in demand, and the shocks of sharp losses which may be needed to bring about the elimination of inefficiency occurred only if and when the system broke down.

Another tenet of the competitive "faith" is that new firms and growing small firms, less hidebound and bureaucratic, may bring a breath of fresh air to a tradition-minded industry. Again it is difficult to weigh the significance of this element. But it has occasionally proven sufficiently important so that many practices which would retard the development of new firms and the growth of small firms, have been declared contrary to public policy. Effective enforcement of the basing-point system by geographically diversified mills during the early thirties probably deterred the growth of small firms and the entry of new firms in deficit producing areas during the late thirties and early forties. With all forms of price advantage eliminated, and with punitive bases or selective base-price reductions threatening the unsystematic marketer, markets tended to be apportioned by the basis of superior salesmanship and long standing buyer-supplier relations.

[37] M. Reder, "A Reconsideration of the Marginal Productivity Theory," JPE, 55:453 (October 1947).

Under such circumstances, breaking into a new market or expanding a market position already held was extremely difficult. Moreover, economies of scale in non-price marketing probably operated to the advantage of the large chains, since from their scattered mills they could minimize both cross-hauling and duplicated selling efforts.

Cyclical Under-utilization of Resources

If we accept the Keynesian proposition that favorable investment opportunities are periodically inadequate for the total volume of planned savings and that the resulting reduction in investment spending forces a multiple contraction in national income and employment, it can be argued that noncompetitive stabilization of product prices accentuates the under-utilization of a nation's resources during periods of depression. Noncompetitive stabilization of gross margins high above average variable costs maintains savings, especially gross business savings. With respect to the latter, there is little reason to believe that a modern Say's law will operate during depression to funnel these savings back into the expenditure stream in industries where excess capacity is developing and profitable investment opportunities are further reduced. In the absence of price stabilization, the share of disposable income in gross national product would rise, giving an upward shift to the consumption function which ameliorates the cyclical declines in effective demand.

The writer suggests that stabilization of cement prices through the basing-point system accentuated under-utilization of resources primarily outside the cement industry. Effective price competition would not have prevented the contraction of cement output and employment which accompanied depression. During most of the thirties, to be sure, average realized price was stabilized at a level which was approximately twice the marginal costs. And although the intermediate-period price elasticity for cement was far from the extreme inelasticity which characterized the very-short-period demand, it was unlikely to be high. Even if cement output and employment during depression would have been appreciably greater under purely competitive price behavior, the expansion in output would scarcely have corresponded to the reduction in price. Moreover, with prices of substitute building materials unchanged, most of the output expansion in cement would have been offset by declines in other building materials. Hence the major effect of noncompetitive pricing in the cement industry during depression was the continuance of revenues substantially in excess of costs. This excess of revenues during the thirties did not reflect a high rate of return on the total equity of stockholders, but rather the fact that capital consumption (depreciation) allowances and "moderate" investment returns on an inherited structural excess capacity were being realized during a period of marked cyclical under-utilization. Even in the unlikely case where most, if not all, net earnings would have been distributed to stockholders, the gross savings of cement firms would have remained appreciable during depression. With profitable investment opportunities severely reduced in the cement industry by the presence of overwhelming excess capacity, most gross savings resulting from price stabilization primarily constituted leakages from the income stream. When such leakages flowed into the cement industry they reduced aggregative effective demand and therefore accentuated the under-utilization of resources in *other* sectors of the economy.

Should public policy promote effective price competition in the cement industry, gross margins and gross savings would be greatly reduced during a depression. How effectively the economy would be stimulated by the reduced absorption of funds by cement firms would depend upon how purchasers of cement utilized the income transfers. Cement is primarily used in the fabrication of producers goods. So far as these are employed in the private sector of the economy, the immediate fabricators (contractors) or the ultimate users of the producers goods, if able to avoid effective competition, might use the cost reductions to increase their own gross margins and thus enlarge their own net absorption of funds. Therefore, we cannot say *a priori* that a net diminution in society's savings would be effected, unless competition or regulation in the utility field can be made so effective among the fabricators or users of producers goods requiring cement that the price reductions are passed on to the public.

However, in a depression the largest demand for cement is likely to be from the federal, state, and local governments for their public works programs — public buildings, housing projects, highways, and conservative projects. The effectiveness of public spending programs in raising national income and employment will be all the greater if cement prices are competitive. With gross margins on cement greatly reduced, the prospect of governmental funds leaking to a great extent into idle gross savings of cement corporations will be similarly reduced. A given amount of government spending will support a greater expenditure for direct or indirect labor if the price and gross profit margin on cement are reduced.[38] Labor probably can be assumed to have a higher marginal propensity to consume than the typical stockholder, although statistical evidence is not unequivocal on this point, and undoubtedly has a higher propensity to spend out of the additional income, than the cement firms would have spent for investment out of the transferred income during a period of excess capacity. With consumption increased more than investment decreased, the demand for products in general will increase and the multiplier effects on national income and employment of deficit government spending will be that much greater. Therefore, an increase in competitive pressures on cement prices will shift the income distribution during depression and increase the buying power of labor. This increase in effective demand could then be expected to play a role in alleviating the under-utilization of resources in industry generally. Granted, gross business savings generated in the cement industry do constitute but a small percentage of total gross business savings; but this suggests the advisability of encouraging the extension of effective price competition to industry generally.

The proposition being advanced by the writer for alleviating the under-utilization of resources during a depression neither suggests that society should strive for price flexibility in all

[38] Such was the theory of Harold L. Ickes, Secretary of the Interior Department, who told a Senate Committee after complaining about identical bids in the cement industry, "If we have a certain sum of money with which to build projects in order to give work to the unemployed, the result of paying high prices for materials means fewer men put to work." *To Prevent Uniform Prices, Hearings,* Committee on Interstate Commerce, United States Senate, 74th Cong., 2d Sess., p. 289.

markets, nor that it should confine public policy to anti-monopoly measures in the effort to increase flexibility of gross margins. In the first case, it is assumed that union activity will prevent, and desirably so, any significant reduction of wage rates during a future depression. Pegged wage rates will set a lower limit to possible flexibility in cement and other industrial prices. A price floor is desirable as one way of reducing the danger of a cumulative contraction of business activity that would result from deflationary wage-price spirals. Labor union activity, which monopolistically stabilizes wages, can probably be expected to limit price declines in most industries, while competitive pressures would operate in product markets to squeeze gross margins and reduce the opportunity to save, particularly in the corporate sector.[39]

In the second case, the writer looks to the use of a compensatory monetary and fiscal policy by the federal government, including large scale public works programs, to provide the bulk of the income which will generate expenditures and so maintain tolerably high levels of demand and employment during periods of business depression. Easy money and extensive deficit spending would be necessary to make up for the residual excessive saving which would still persist in the household and corporate sectors. Expanded public works programs would be necessary both to stabilize output and employment in the erratic construction goods industries, and to prevent the economic suicide of many firms in other industries with cost and demand conditions similar to those of cement (as discussed in Chapter III), if they were forced to operate under effective competitive pricing in an otherwise laissez-faire economy. But if greater competitive pressures narrow gross margins in industry, and thereby reduce the flow of money into idle balances during depression, smaller governmental expenditures will be needed to limit unemployment

[39] No unanimity of opinion exists among economists concerning the effects of cyclical price behavior and income redistribution upon the level of economic activity. But a sub-committee of the Committee on Public Issues of the American Economic Association (Milton Friedman dissenting) has endorsed similar views with respect to market policy. "Stability of the wage level does not imply that the level of prices must remain rigid; profit margins can and should vary through the cycle." See "The Problem of Economic Instability," AER, 40:537 (September 1950).

to specified levels. In such cases the inevitable fiscal intervention by centralized government during periods of depression into the private sector of the economy may be comparably reduced.

Moreover, with industrial stabilization achieved at tolerable levels of aggregate demand through public commitments, there should be a healthier climate for initiating private investment expenditure which may shorten the period of depression. It may well be that, in the past, efforts by individual industries to stabilize their profits by collusive practices have perpetuated the depressed state of private investment by encouraging a widespread business psychology of defensive security rather than of aggressive creativity.

CHAPTER VII

Remedial Proposals and the Cement Case

Alternatives to Basing-Point Formula Pricing

The basing-point formula of delivered pricing has been criticized in previous chapters because it stifled effective competition between sellers in the cement industry and contributed toward waste in the allocation and utilization of resources in the whole economy. The formula essentially provided a simple system by which those cement firms who were *unwilling* to behave competitively were protected from uncertainties as to "correct" destination prices. Also disciplinary enforcement of the pricing rule was an easy way to discourage deliberately initiated price cuts by small mavericks. Advance knowledge that price cuts by a mill at particular destinations would be made unprofitable because the mill net reduction would be immediately generalized for its entire market, made the minority *unable* to compete.[1] In brief, voluntary use of a delivered-price formula established a known environment in which firms could avoid unintentional price cutting, while its involuntary application compelled smaller firms to surrender a competitive flexibility in their pricing policy. The result in either case was price stabilization.

Having condemned the basing-point system as it operated in the cement industry, we must ask what alternatives are possible. And, in response to changing conditions of the market, which one is most likely to induce the greatest uncertainty and competitive pressures upon price. Three approaches will be discussed: first, uniform or non-discriminatory f.o.b. mill pricing; second, f.o.b. mill pricing exclusively — the sellers being free to vary selec-

[1] Clair Wilcox states: "Effective competition requires substantial independence of action . . . each must be *able* and *willing* constantly to reconsider his policy and to modify it in the light of changing conditions of supply and demand" (italics added). T.N.E.C. Monograph #21, "Competition and Monopoly in American Industry," p. 8.

tively their f.o.b. mill prices, and the buyers being free to arrange their own transportation under all circumstances; and third, a general attack on formula pricing which includes the requirement that the sellers offer buyers the opportunity of arranging their own transportation when prepared to pay the established or posted base price at the mill, *although* sellers would be free to quote delivered prices exclusively when absorbing freight. (The third alternative eliminates the threat of spoiling the local market through diversion-in-transit which exists under the second.)

(1) Uniform f.o.b. mill pricing has usually been associated with Frank A. Fetter, its strongest advocate,[2] but has also been vigorously supported by Vernon A. Mund,[3] Fritz Machlup,[4] George J. Stigler,[5] and Walter B. Wooden.[6] There are many reasons for believing that this system of non-discriminatory pricing, which would eliminate freight absorption, is much preferable to the non-competitive basing-point formula. As employed in the cement industry the latter provides such a high degree of certainty as to prices that virtually all incentives for price competition are eliminated.

Uniform f.o.b. mill pricing increases the uncertainty in three respects. First, punitive action, to discipline "disorderly" uniform f.o.b. mill pricing at an isolated mill, would be far more difficult and costly than with the routine use of punitive bases under the basing-point system. To compel maverick mills at isolated locations to refrain from making temporary reductions in mill prices in order to win a large order, regional leaders would have to reduce drastically their own mill price or to build a competing plant in the area where the independent mills are located. Because retributory action would be less certain, isolated enterprises would feel freer to establish their mill prices independently. Second, reactions of rivals to reductions in posted mill prices

[2] F. A. Fetter, *Masquerade of Monopoly* (New York, 1931); *idem*, "Exit Basing Point Pricing," *AER*, 38:815–827 (December 1948).

[3] V. A. Mund, *Open Markets* (New York, 1948); *idem*, *Government and Business*, 2d ed. (New York, 1955), chs. 17 and 18.

[4] F. Machlup, *The Basing-Point System* (Philadelphia, 1949).

[5] Stigler, *supra*, III, fn. 21.

[6] W. B. Wooden, "The Concept of Unlawful Discrimination as It Applies to Geographical Price Differences," *Georgetown Law Journal*, 37:166–182 (January 1949).

would be less predictable than under the basing-point system, and there would be greater incentives for most mills to reduce their posted prices. Under the basing-point formula such an inducement is virtually nullified by the certainty that, in the face of unutilized capacity, delivered-price reductions will be met by all penetrating competitors, with the possible exception of some very distant suppliers. It is not simply the absence of advance announcement of pricing responses by rivals which increases the incentive to initiate price reductions under uniform f.o.b. mill pricing, but also the real possibility that some rivals may actually ignore such reductions. With several competitors typically surrounding a mill (or mill group) at different distances and in different directions, a reduction in mill price will enlarge the total market of the initiating mill by appreciably more than the loss of market suffered by any one rival. Given the asymmetrical distribution of gains and benefits, the price reducer may not have to anticipate an immediate equivalent, or even any, mill price reduction by all rivals in each surrounding producing center. At times of softening in the general demand for cement there would appear to be, *at least initially,* a greater temptation to reduce mill prices since the reactions of rivals are much less predictable. Nevertheless, in the event that several experimental mill price reductions are met, in greater or lesser degree, so that most efforts to expand markets at the geographic margin are nullified, a price stalemate may be expected. Certainty gained from experience, rather than by formula, may periodically make fairly rigid the price structure and price level. Price flexibility, in response to general changes in market demand, may not be much greater than under the basing-point system. Third, somewhat countering the tendency toward a stalemate in relative mill prices, as well as the average level, would be the frequent shifting of construction activity and cement demand between areas. That the geographic shifts in demand may be fairly considerable was indicated in Chapter III. Taken in conjunction with uniform f.o.b. mill pricing, they can be expected to force mills with little or no demand in their local area to reduce prices so as to expand their markets. Such temporary variations in mill prices could be expected to prevent the price structure from hardening, and the fluctuation of relative base prices to have some salutary effect in lowering the price level. Still, the writer is inclined to doubt that the greater uncertainty resulting from shifting geographic demand and relative mill price differentials will induce sufficient reduction in the price level in times of general unutilized capacity. A system of pricing would still persist.

It is true that uniform f.o.b. mill pricing would eliminate most of the *excesses* in selling expenditures and cross-hauling by completely eliminating interpenetration, save where sluggish adjustment of relative mill prices in times of boom permitted the charging of premium prices in markets with a temporary deficit productive capacity. Market areas would be completely divided, save in perimeter markets where the blanketing of freight rate charges brought several sellers together, or where mills in the same production center operated with grouped freight rates to all destinations, with the possible exception of the most immediate local market areas. Buyers could also obtain all of the advantages of trucking if the uniform f.o.b. mill selling were genuine. By permitting diversion in shipments, *bona fide* uniform f.o.b. mill pricing would hinder a producer at an isolated spot from displaying marked favoritism (in terms of quality specifications or speed of delivery) toward consumers in border areas where rival producers were met on a price basis. Furthermore, those growing markets with no cement mills could be expected to get new ones and to obtain lower destination cement prices, much sooner than under the basing-point system. Yet even if all of the savings in unnecessary transportation and selling expenditures were passed on to consumers, through greater competitive pressures, the public might be still better off under a less systematic form of pricing.

Unless average gross margins were greatly reduced under the uniform f.o.b. mill system of market sharing, there would still be inducements to considerable excess capacity. Prices on the average might still be expected to be too high over the course of the business cycle, and the flexibility of the price level too little. With the price level substantially shielded there would be a tendency toward the construction of an excessive number of unduly small mills dispersed through protected market areas (as discussed in Chapter VI). And in a few consumption areas where mills with highly concentrated local markets have very thin markets in the outlying regions, mill prices could actually be higher than under the basing-point system. In these cases where freight-absorbing penetration is outlawed, base prices need not be held down to minimize invasions of the local market by distant mills.

Experience in the industry during 1931 suggests that the degree of uncertainty might be far greater and mill price reductions more extensive if firms were permitted to penetrate rival territories, but without formulas to predict the systematic matching of prices. Until various measures were taken to revive the use of the basing-point delivered-price formula, unsystematic price discriminations provided effective competition and brought about base price reductions. During this period prices did not cover average costs, and, according to the industry, the disorderly pricing was "cutthroat and ruinous." In fact, one of the principal advocates of non-discriminatory f.o.b. pricing has urged uniform mill net pricing as a means of lessening the rigors of competitive price reductions:

> It is undoubtedly true that "discriminatory" competition among producers of standardized commodities, separated by substantial freight costs, may become destructive and ruinous. That is a strong reason why legal prohibition of discrimination at the point of production is necessary. The term "price cutting" rarely means a uniform reduction of prices for all customers, for a seller will not "cut" prices on business in areas where he will get it in any event. Rather it is almost certain that delivered prices will be "cut" in particular local areas, or to particular customers, in a discriminatory way.[7]

But if real competitive pricing is desired, the channels through which price reductions generally appear in oligopolistic markets in times of changing demand must be kept open; and this means unsystematic discrimination. Selective price reductions may indeed be used strategically by powerful rivals against particular local markets of independents, in the form of punitive bases or some more subtle disciplinary attack. The threat of such action may have been the primary concern of the advocate of uniform mill net pricing quoted above. But the remedy for predatory or coercive sharpshooting is a vigorous enforcement

[7] Mund, *Open Markets*, pp. 259–260.

of the Clayton Act against major concerns using *systematic* patterns of discriminatory pricing whenever there appears probable a substantial lessening of competition.[8] Admittedly there is the risk that administrative difficulties, conservatism, or inertia will, for a time, permit more than the border line cases of disciplinary attack, but the risk must be accepted.

One requirement of uniform f.o.b. mill pricing does provide some administrative appeal. Not only would it eliminate *one* form of economic coercion, that employing freight absorption, but it would also simplify the removal of many socially undesirable features of the basing-point system of formula pricing. All that would be required for enforcement would be to show that two buyers, purchasing from a particular mill at the same time, were charged different mill prices. Should other remedial efforts prove abortive, because of administrative or judicial failure to overcome the resistance of a limited number of sellers, and should it also be politically impossible to increase the number of sellers through dissolution proceedings, the requirement of uniform f.o.b. mill pricing might prove the only practicable alternative to the basing-point system. However, such a gloomy prospect seems to the writer unwarranted, at least in the case of the cement industry.

In summary, a uniform f.o.b. mill pricing system merely removes *some* of the worst features of the basing-point system. The real danger of truly noncompetitive price behavior has not yet been attacked. A formula which divides exclusive market areas fairly systematically merely replaces one that systematically matches prices in overlapping markets. Any law or regulation which imposes a formula for dividing market areas is scarcely the best policy for promoting effective competition.

(2) F.o.b. mill pricing exclusively, with the seller given freedom to vary his f.o.b. mill prices and the buyer to arrange his own transportation under all circumstances, has been advocated by Paul E. Sweeney[9] and, at one juncture, by staff members of the Federal Trade Commission.[10]

[8] See this writer's "Geographical Pricing Policies and the Law," *Journal of Business of the University of Chicago*, 27:211–224 (July 1954).

[9] Sweeney, *supra*, II, fn. 21.

[10] T.N.E.C. Monograph #42, "The Basing Point Problem," esp. pp. 9, 138–139.

As set forth by Sweeney, such a requirement would, among other things, offer purchasers the opportunity to arrange their own delivery from the mill in trucks. With the transportation charges in buyers' trucks, private, leased, or contracted-for, being unknown, the trucking option would destroy the certainty of destination costs and, hence, the systematic character of "meeting competition." A mill which attempts to invade deeply the market of a rival would be forced to estimate what f.o.b. mill price must be quoted to a distant buyer in order to equalize the destination cost of cement transported from a local mill in trucks controlled by the buyer. Superficially, complete elimination of delivered prices would appear to offer very great opportunities for sporadic and unsystematic dumping by cement mills into each other's territory, thus generating competitive pressures to reduce the price level. Such was the argument presented by Sweeney. But, upon closer examination, a requirement of compulsory selling at the mill is seen as very likely to bring an end to much of the very penetration necessary to generate the desirable uncertainties.

Because a seller could *never* control the delivery of his product, his markets could not be easily separated. Diverted shipments would discourage sellers from discriminating in favor of buyers who claim that they plan to use the cement in the natural market of a rival mill. A few major diversions of cement tonnage, resold by "arbitrage operators" at a greatly reduced destination price in the natural market of the supplying mill would break down the supplier's posted mill price. Moreover, with buyers taking possession of cement at the mill in all cases, diversions could result whether the buyer shipped by rail or truck. A producer would seldom attempt to penetrate rival markets when the end result could be like a planned reduction in the posted mill price. Compulsory f.o.b. mill pricing would most assuredly encourage voluntary acceptance of uniform f.o.b. mill pricing, save for the special and probably infrequent cases when a guarantee could be obtained that the purchaser would not divert the shipment into the seller's natural market. Such "voluntary" acceptance of uniform f.o.b. mill pricing appeared to be both the expectation and desire of the Commission staff as recommended to the T.N.E.C. Uncontrolled trucking can destroy a delivered price formula, but a method must and can be more skillfully planned that will create uncertainties in the transportation factor without simultaneously destroying incentives to interpenetrate markets.

Exclusive f.o.b. mill pricing, in effect, depends upon the diversion hazard for the generation of uncertainty. But the individual seller will probably avoid the diversion dilemma facing him by accepting voluntarily marketing practices which approximate uniform f.o.b. mill pricing. Nevertheless, the possibility of occasional instances of penetration, despite the diversion threat, encourages the opinion that this technique of social control is superior to uniform f.o.b. mill pricing, although inferior to a comprehensive assault upon formula pricing.

(3) A general attack upon formula pricing has been advocated by many economists, although they have rarely spelled out in detail methods of implementing this attack. Three economists seem to the writer to have been most important in developing this general approach — John Perry Miller,[11] Corwin D. Edwards,[12] and George W. Stocking.[13] None of these economists is opposed to freight-absorbing delivered prices which facilitate interpenetration of markets, but they all urge the use of public policy to discourage systematic adherence to a formula.

This writer has advocated as one of the most important techniques for encouraging unsystematic pricing the requirement that sellers offer buyers the option of purchasing at a bona fide f.o.b. mill price and then of arranging their own transportation to destination.[14] A bona fide f.o.b. mill price would be the *posted base*

[11] J. P. Miller, *Unfair Competition* (Cambridge, Mass., 1941), pp. 160–193.

[12] C. D. Edwards, *Maintaining Competition* (New York, 1949), pp. 189–192; *idem*, "The Effect of Recent Basing Point Decisions upon Business Practices," *AER*, 38:828–842 (December 1948).

[13] G. W. Stocking, "The Economics of Basing-Point Pricing," *Law and Contemporary Problems*, 15:159–180 (Spring 1950); *idem*, *Basing Point Pricing and Regional Development*, Chs. 1, 8, and 9.

[14] See "Geographical Pricing Policies and the Law," *Journal of Business of the University of Chicago*, 27:211–224, esp. pp. 214, 215 (July 1954); *idem*, "Inert Antitrust Administration: Formula Pricing and the Cement Industry," *Yale Law Journal*, 65:1–22 (November 1955). The f.o.b. mill price option has also been suggested, but without development of a complete rationale, by E. B. George, "The Law and Economics of Basing Points," Part III, *Dun's Review*, November 1948, p. 22; Carl Kaysen, "Basing Point Pricing and Public Policy," QJE, 63:313 (August

mill price effective at the plant, save for any *legitimate* cost differential which can be justified in the loading of the product into buyers' transportation equipment as compared with other carriers. Great merit would inhere, the writer believes, in a statutory requirement compelling sellers in industries which produce approximately standardized goods to offer such a bona fide option to buyers. The trucking option, as specified, would not induce diversion-in-transit and arbitrage unless sellers in particular circumstances voluntarily chose to offer a mill price to buyers' trucks below the required posted base mill price. The required trucking option therefore would not destroy the ability of sellers to separate markets on delivered-price sales that entailed rail transportation, and interpenetration of markets would be preserved. But, as discussed at length in Chapters I and IV, destination costs within the economical trucking range of mills would be uncertain, and mills seeking to penetrate such markets would not know exactly what delivered price to quote in order to equalize the destination costs of the distant buyer who can arrange his own truck transportation from a local mill. In bargaining with buyers possessing the trucking option, penetrating mills would be urged to beat competition.

The uncertainties confronting the penetrating mill do not result simply from having to consider more complex tariff schedules, as would be the case if the distant buyer were offered only the opportunity of shipping in trucks controlled by the seller in addition to rail transportation. The crucial uncertainties would stem from the sellers' ignorance of transportation costs in those instances when buyers controlled their own truck shipments. Contract truckers usually must file minimum rates with a public agency, but the filed minima are characteristically below the actual negotiated rates, which remain unknown. The amounts charged by the supplier of leased trucking services are even more unknown, since the lessor is not subject to rate filing. And, whenever the buyer utilizes private trucking, an estimate of trucking costs is still more baffling.

1949); D. F. Pegrum, "The Present Status of Geographic Pricing," *Journal of Marketing*, 15:434 (April 1951); and G. W. Stocking, *Basing Point Pricing and Regional Development*, pp. 3–4, 188.

As discussed at length in Chapter IV, uncontrolled trucking was extremely unsettling to the cement industry during 1929–32, and ultimately drastic measures were taken by the industry to eliminate it or control it. While it is impossible to attribute the collapse of the basing-point system during 1931 entirely to trucking, cement executives uniformly castigated it as being a powerful destabilizer, and upward price leadership immediately followed the control of trucking. Moreover, John M. Clark wrote in 1938 that a requirement of posted f.o.b. mill pricing concurrent with delivered pricing would be the least desirable of all alternatives to the basing-point system because it would create *excessive* price competition:

> But the greatest effect of such a plan would be on the pricing structure, and the greatest factor in this effect would be the uncertainty of the delivered cost of goods to any buyer. Sellers would be exposed to that form of unfair competition which results when buyers can pretend to have a cheaper alternative source of supply than is really open to them. Prices on rail delivery would be reduced to meet the real or supposed cost of truck delivery; and these reductions, not being open and general, would be the sort which tend naturally to develop into cutthroat competition, driving prices below costs . . . . Where trucking rates are standardized and known, most of the legitimate economies of trucking can be secured without introducing secrecy, chaos, and cutthroat competition into the pricing system.[15]

What the *Record* before the Commission fails either to support or refute, however, is the hypothesis that cutthroat price competition, when induced within the economical range for trucking, will tend to spread to the many remaining areas dependent upon rail. But the writer is convinced that the development of numerous pockets of price cutting, when induced by uncontrolled trucking, would tend appreciably to increase uncertainty and disharmony in the cement industry and thereby to encourage the initiation of unsystematic price reductions, either secretly or openly, in territories where otherwise a formula price would have been used. Even should unsystematic pricing fail to spread perceptibly to these other areas, buyer trucking could be expected to contribute significantly to price flexibility in most large metropolitan markets, most of them being located within

[15] J. M. Clark, "Basing Point Methods of Price Quoting," *Canadian Journal of Economics and Political Science,* 4:487 (November 1938).

economical trucking range from a cement mill. Hence, unless ownership concentration should grow to such a level that mills would voluntarily refrain from penetrating markets of rivals contaminated by uncontrolled trucking, the requirement of the trucking option, as described herein, should forcefully encourage unsystematic pricing. And the degree of oligopolistic self-restraint necessary to forego such unsystematic penetrations would be so great that, were it ever exercised, it would with little difficulty convince the courts of the need for dissolution.

But in analyzing a general attack against formula systems of pricing let us direct our attention to the process of litigation. Not only might antitrust litigation be used to restore uncontrolled trucking, but also to pursue several other approaches to combat formula pricing as it has operated in the cement industry. Five avenues will be explored. First, some advantages should flow from an attack upon overt collusive activity. Although this study does not emphasize persistent overt collusion, it recognizes that the Commission *Record* gave evidence of the occasional use of informal inter-company meetings to iron out common marketing policies, and suggested that not infrequently rival salesmen and executives had discussed the prices which would be quoted on particular jobs or an occasional sealed bid. Any diminution of cooperatively determined marketing policy and pricing decisions should be socially advantageous. Next, the elimination of the common use of centrally distributed "official" freight rate books is also desirable. Rail freight factors are very complicated, and mistakes in calculating freight rates to the less frequently quoted stations and rail sidings could lead to occasional unintentional price cutting. Should the unsystematic quotation relate to a construction job entailing a large cement contract, subsequent uncertainties and disharmonies might well induce one or more of the aggrieved competitors to initiate retaliatory price cuts. Again, the elimination of overt activity in cooperative reporting, checking, and cancellation of specific job contracts (options to buy) should increase the difficulty of initiating price increases while the market is soft. And the elimination of the collection and dissemination of individual company statistics concerning production and shipments might undermine faith in rivals. One could not be sure that others were not chiseling and attempting to procure an excessively large share of the market during dull periods.

Even these minor attacks against collectivism would be desirable. With reduced confidence in the trade ethics of rivals, uncertainties would be somewhat greater, and firms more prone to shade particular delivered prices. But the basing-point system proper would be unaffected, should the will to adhere remain strong.

A second attack could be against identical quoting on sealed bids since it constitutes clear-cut evidence of an implicit understanding to employ a pricing formula. It could be attacked as constituting inherent collusion, an unfair method of competition, and/or price discrimination which substantially lessens competition. The most literal jurists could scarcely consider rigid adherence to formula prices on sealed bids to be within that mystical realm of redemption — good-faith meeting of competition — when there exists no *known* price to meet. If independent bids could be enticed by the federal and state governments (and many state governments would resume direct purchase if independent bids could again be obtained), a powerful force would be at work to undermine seriously the basing-point system. During depression periods the federal and state governments are major purchasers of cement for reclamation, highway, and other public works programs. The uncertainty and conflict engendered when low bidders win large public cement awards might induce some independent price behavior in the more regular commercial channels. Price cutting is frequently contagious. Nevertheless, were cement firms determined to suppress even this degree of uncertainty, there could be secret agreements to develop procedures for the rotating or sharing of low bids. Such collusive behavior would clearly be illegal and would be subject to heavy fines, if it were proved that the agreement violated a standing order. But public relief from such oppression could not be obtained prior to the inevitable, time-consuming process of judicial enforcement of the antitrust laws. Assuming, however, that new forms of collusion would not replace the outlawed formula-price bidding, there would be a powerful force to encourage price reductions during any future softening of the market.

A third attack could be made upon any activity, individual or collective, intended to force adherence to a common pricing formula. Punitive bases or similar patterns of systematic, discriminatory price attacks, where the effect is to discipline pricing mavericks, should be declared an unfair method of competition and/or a discriminatory method of lessening competition substantially. Independent producers, lacking the power derived from diversified market positions and financial strength, would thus feel freer to price unsystematically than they did after the early thirties. Whether independents would care to utilize such freedom from threatened harassment, however, is unpredictable. Moreover, far fewer independents exist today than in the early thirties.

A fourth attack could be made on those formula-implementing devices which, though collusively established, require no overt cooperation to maintain. Controls over both trucking and direct sales to contractors fall into this category. The decontrol of trucking will be examined first, emphasis being placed on the legal and administrative problems.

The collusively developed practice of making *all* sales at delivered prices originated during the first decade of the century. During a period of shortages in rail transportation following World War I, trucking was welcomed at several mills. By the middle twenties competitive pressures had spread the buyer trucking option to virtually all other mills.[16] But during the latter twenties in Texas, and during 1932 in most other areas, trucking was collusively eliminated or controlled. Once established, trucking controls could be maintained without resort to renewed collusive activity, just as oligopolistic expectations of a "kinked" demand curve sufficed to deter open reductions in base prices, although previously price leadership or other forms of cooperation may have established the current price. In fact, the *Record* shows scarcely any cooperative activity in this sphere after 1932.

Should an antitrust order be sustained which required the cessation of specific practices founded upon collusion, such as the

16 The few mills which apparently never offered trucking were in the deep South and belonged to chain companies which opposed the unsettling effects of trucking.

refusal to sell at posted prices to buyers' trucks, the order could undoubtedly be made enforceable. But a protracted legal battle must be expected, since no current agreement supports the continued agreement. Respondents would undoubtedly argue that *individual* company policy dictates their proscriptions against trucking, or at least buyer trucking. Witnesses would undoubtedly testify anew, as they did during the thirties before the Commission, that buyers' trucking interferes with the plant routine, the trucks are too expensive to load, or that the mills are not equipped to load them. Of course many mills would indeed no longer be equipped to load trucks, since the special loading ramps were dismantled when trucking was eliminated in the early thirties. To secure enforcement of an order directed solely at the collusive elimination of buyers' trucking, the antitrust agency would have to contend that compliance with the order requires that the respondents take affirmative action if the continuing effects of the earlier collusion is to be eliminated. The incorporation of collusive phraseology in an antitrust injunction could produce significant administrative consequences. This matter will be returned to in both this and the concluding chapter. At this juncture, we shall merely point out the most effective way to combat those trucking restrictions which are used to maintain a common pricing formula. Let the restrictions be labeled unfair methods of competition and compel *each* firm to offer a bona fide posted base price to buyers who wish to do their own trucking from a mill. An agency like the Federal Trade Commission, which must draw up negative orders, might order respondents *individually* to cease and desist from refusing buyers the opportunity to purchase at the posted mill price, save for cost-justified loading differentials, and to arrange their own transportation. In such form the order would be virtually self-enforcing. Uncontrolled trucking would become a reality immediately without protracted litigation.

A similar administrative problem confronts an attack on the commonly adopted practice of refusing to sell directly to contractors doing urban work, notwithstanding their qualification on a quantity basis. The historical development of the standard classification of customers has been described in Chapter IV. The purpose of this marketing plan was undoubtedly to avoid direct quotations to large contractors, who were in a position to bargain for secret price concessions because their large purchases of cement for specific jobs came sporadically and at changing locations. As suggested in Chapter IV, the refusal of producers to sell directly to large contractors doing construction work in highly dense markets, probably explained the rarity of secret concessions in the cement industry. It seems reasonable that an increase in such unsystematic pricing to contractors could contribute significantly to eroding a rigid pricing formula. An order designed to soften hardened distribution channels will also run into delays, however, if phrased in the language of "collusion." In the course of compliance proceedings each respondent would undoubtedly argue that its refusal to sell directly to contractors stemmed from individual company policy and solicitude for dealers' good will rather than from agreement. An alternative order directed at individual respondents, however, could effect an immediate elimination of the arbitrary classification of customers which bolsters a pricing formula.

A fifth, direct attack could be one upon the practice of adhering rigidly to a delivered-pricing formula. Such an approach would most usefully supplement all of the others. The purpose of the direct assault upon persistent adherence to formula delivered-pricing would be to encourage unsystematic departures from the formula on commercial sales, identical bidding to governmental agencies presumably being eliminated under simpler tests of conspiracy. Required departures from the pricing formula would increase uncertainty as to rivals' future quotations and thereby encourage additional departures, in turn inducing flexibility into the base-price level.

The basing-point delivered-price formula is inherently artificial and lacks the earmarks of effective competition. Common adherence requires that rivals never undercut the formula in order to insure a sale in a penetrated market where a rival prevails as the price leader. But even more artificial is the requirement that producers shall never quote unsystematically below their own base price plus published freight within their natural market where their prices are being met by others, while they consistently accept systematically lower mill nets in rival territories. Certainly a reduced delivered-price quotation to a particular home market would be met subsequently by others, but in most cases only after a very large sales contract has been won by the first mill. Such persistent self-denial of individual marketing opportunities makes clear that rivals are pursuing a common plan of action.

Formula delivered pricing, established by statistical market data, could be challenged under any of three antitrust principles. First, rigid adherence to an arbitrary pricing formula could be shown to imply an industry-wide collusion to achieve price stabilization, in violation of both the Sherman and Federal Trade Commission acts. Second, rigid adherence to a formula restrains price competition and could be ruled an unfair method of competition, violating the Federal Trade Commission Act. Third, geographic price discrimination in accordance with a formula could be declared systematic discrimination which substantially lessens competition among the sellers, in violation of the Robinson-Patman Act. In effect, compliance with an injunction against continued use of the system would require that companies involved take independent, competitive steps to depart from the formula. Were the Courts to approve unequivocally any or all of these alternative views of formula pricing, and could the orders be effectively enforced by the administrative and judicial processes, a landmark victory would be won in the battle against noncompetitive oligopolistic marketing of relatively standard commodities.

Assuming no enforcement problem, the direct attack upon rigid adherence to a geographic pricing formula could usefully supplement the four previous approaches to the formula pricing problem combined. Those approaches seek to increase uncertainty in the industry by altering indirectly the marketing environment. Of the several elements included in the four groups, the decontrol of trucking appears the most important, and the attack on sealed identical bidding to come next. Nevertheless, to the extent that uncertainties released by unsystematic pricing in areas affected by trucking and competitive sealed bidding failed to spread to other areas, the direct attack in these other territories could constitute an added weapon. Uncontrolled trucking and non-identical sealed bidding might easily be sufficient in themselves to force flexibility into mill base prices, and therefore inevitably to reduce prices on commercial sales outside an economical trucking radius. Yet, if the decontrol of trucking were not pressed, the direct assault upon adherence to formula pricing in general, including sealed bids, would have to serve as the principal weapon against the basing-point system.

Difficult administrative problems will inevitably face remedial action to enforce court orders which outlaw rigid adherence to a pricing formula whenever the enjoined industry is sufficiently determined and concentrated in structure to avoid more than token compliance. Unlike specific orders directed against overt collusion, identical sealed bidding, controlled trucking, and so on, orders requiring the entire industry to cease adherence to a common pricing fomula lack clarity and self-enforcement. An administrative agency would have to make a time-consuming statistical study of market price quotations, possibly including transaction prices, to detect not merely identical prices, but the presence or absence of adherence to a formula over time. Standards would have to be set up showing *how much* rigidity or variability in the geographic pricing pattern would constitute violation or compliance. Just how much open or secret "beating of competition" (unsystematic pricing) would sellers have to engage in, to meet the standards of compliance? And how little variation from the pricing formula might the reviewing courts accept as constituting compliance? A lessening of compliance activity would follow if reviewing courts accepted mere "token" departures as meeting the obligation to desist from adherence. Yet, unless one defines "token" departures as those which are sufficiently few and predictable to permit substantial maintenance of a pattern and of the industry's base-price level, it will be almost impossible to locate the boundary between contrived and independent departures. The major administrative and legal difficulty, however, is likely to be procedural. Every time that an industry is believed to have fallen anew into pricing rigidity, time-consuming research study and legal proceedings will precede any possible relief. The order against adherence to a formula would not be self-enforcing.

The Federal Trade Commission and the Cement Case

That the attack on formula pricing under the basing-point system was made by the Federal Trade Commission rather than by the Antitrust Division, and that a laborious and detailed record to demonstrate agreement among producers was compiled by the Commission, stems from an adverse decision in the *Cement Manufacturers Protective Association* case.[17] In this predecessor case the basing-point formula for delivered pricing had not been challenged directly nor had the Court ruled gratuitously upon the basing-point system. The Antitrust Division's complaint had not explicitly charged agreement, but held that the exchange of specific job contract information, individual company statistics, and common freight factors resulted in concerted action to bring about a uniformity and stability of prices. Although the Department of Justice had not submitted a detailed record to support an inference of collusion, District Judge Knox believed the record showed a restraint of trade by concerted action, and he affirmed a decree prohibiting the collective activities.[18] Three Supreme Court justices agreed, but the majority of that Court overruled the District Court on grounds that the government had not specifically charged agreement or understanding and that the record failed to show concerted action which restrained trade. The Court reasoned that common circularized freight rate books, used in conjunction with basing points for quoting prices, merely permitted greater economy and prompter quotations, thereby facilitating competition. The Court relied heavily upon the testimony of "distinguished economists in support of the thesis that in the case of a standardized product sold wholesale to fully informed professional buyers as were the dealers in cement, uniformity of price will inevitably result from active, free and unrestrained competition." [19] The Court did recognize that uniformity of price may be "the result of agreement or understand-

[17] *Cement Mfrs. Protective Ass'n* v. *U.S.*, 268 U.S. 588 (1925).
[18] *U.S.* v. *Cement Mfrs. Protective Ass'n*, 294 F. 390 (1923).
[19] *Cement Mfrs. Protective Ass'n* v. *U.S.*, 168 U.S. 588, 605 (1923). In fact only one economist, Thomas Adams, had testified. The Justice Department had not bothered to engage another economic "expert" to demonstrate the limitations of Adams' propositions.

ing, and that an artificial price level not related to supply and demand of a given commodity may be evidence from which agreement or understanding or some concert of action of sellers may be inferred,"[20] but it argued that the record merely showed concerted action in the gathering and dissemination of pertinent information but failed to demonstrate "any effect on price and production except such as would naturally flow from the dissemination of that information in the trade and its natural influence on individual action."[21] The majority of Supreme Court justices in 1925 needed tutoring in the theory of collective action to minimize oligopolistic uncertainty and an economic record which would demonstrate the consequences of such collective action.

Beginning with 1933, save for a letup during the NRA, the Commission was besieged with complaints from the President, the secretary of interior, and state governors and highway department officials concerning identical sealed bids. Governor Horner of Illinois was among the first to urge the Commission to stop treating the 1925 Court decision as a stultifying precedent, since the particulars of the situation could probably afford relief under the Federal Trade Commission Act. The Department of Justice subsequently adopted the same position. Attorney General Homer Cummings in a letter to the President on April 26, 1937[22] stated that the more flexible administrative remedies of the Federal Trade Commission were better suited to handle the problem of identical sealed bidding and the basing-point system, since in the case of steel the Department of Justice had been unable to produce "sufficient evidence admissible in civil and criminal litigations to make advisable proceedings in court under the Antitrust Acts, *as they have been construed by the courts*" (italics added). On July 2, 1937, less than three months after the attorney general's letter to the President, the Federal Trade Commission issued its complaint against the cement industry.

20 *Ibid.*, p. 606. 21 *Ibid.*

22 White House press release of April 27, 1937. The attorney general concluded his letter by recommending that a committee to study the antitrust laws be established for the reason that court interpretations had devitalized the laws by imposing on the government impossible burdens of proof. The Temporary National Economic Committee grew out of the attorney general's recommendation.

The Commission had taken a long time in assuming the important anti-monopoly function. The enfeebling dictum in the *Gratz* case,[23] the first test of the Commission's authority, may have been largely responsible for its having adopted a "safe" policy of concentrating primarily upon unfair dealings between competitors. But the Commission's administrative authority received a much needed lift in 1927 from *Federal Trade Commission* v. *Pacific States Paper Trade Association*.[24] In that case the Supreme Court said:

> The weight to be given to the facts and circumstances admitted, as well as the inferences reasonably to be drawn from them, is for the Commission. Its conclusion that the habitual use of the established list lessens competition and fixes prices in interstate territory cannot be said to be without sufficient support.[25]

In 1934 the Commission's findings were vested with further prestige in *Federal Trade Commission* v. *Algoma Lumber Co.*[26] There the Supreme Court stated that, in passing upon the question as to whether a finding has evidential support, a reviewing court is not authorized to "make its own appraisal of the testimony, picking and choosing for itself among uncertain and conflicting inferences.[27] Finally, the Court in an opinion later that year, accorded unaccustomed respect to the expertness of the Commission in *Federal Trade Commission* v. *R. F. Keppel & Co.*[28] These three decisions were of great help in overturning the *Cement Manufacturers Protective Association* decision [29] and in obtaining relief much more substantial than that which had been denied the Department of Justice in 1925.

The Commission framed its complaint as against an agreement among producers to use and implement formula pricing, and proceeded to assemble a massive record to demonstrate the charge. But it apparently hoped that the evidence and inferences used to support a charge of concerted action might also sustain

23 *Federal Trade Commission* v. *Gratz*, 253 U.S. 421 (1920).
24 *Federal Trade Commission* v. *Pacific States Trade Ass'n*, 273 U.S. 52 (1927).
25 *Ibid.*, p. 62.
26 *Federal Trade Commission* v. *Algoma Lumber Co.*, 291 U.S. 67 (1934).
27 *Ibid.*, p. 73.
28 *Federal Trade Commission* v. *R. F. Keppel & Co.*, 291 U.S. 304 (1934).
29 *Cement Manufacturers Protective Ass'n* v. *United States*, 268 U.S. 588 (1925).

an anti-monopoly charge of "unfair competition," even if they were not sufficient to constitute a violation of the Sherman Act, as interpreted in 1937. Agreement to use the basing-point formula was to be the heart of the Commission's charge, although a supplementary charge, primarily for purposes of framing a cease-and-desist order, attacked the substantial lessening of competition which resulted from systematic price discrimination.

Count I charged respondents with violating the Federal Trade Commission Act by maintaining a combination to restrain price competition, which combination entailed mutual understanding or agreement to employ the basing-point pricing system and specified practices for making the system effective.[30] Count II rested chiefly on the same allegations of fact set out in the first count, but it charged that the basing-point system violated the Robinson-Patman Act because it resulted in systematic price discriminations which destroyed price competition between respondents.[31]

The record, as is well known, was exceedingly long: about 49,000 pages of testimony and 50,000 pages of exhibits. The Commission, which contributed approximately half the bulk, undoubtedly felt compelled to make a very strong case. The case was presented in a highly sophisticated form, demonstrating during the hearings a clear understanding of formula pricing. Commission counsel carefully analyzed the inferences of collusion to be drawn from controls over trucking and identical sealed bidding, and quickly demolished the respondents' argument that each separate destination constituted an independent market with a competitively determined price. If so, he asked, why were prices in each of these separate destination markets always linked together by the long-haul freight rate formula from a controlling base mill? The Commission also introduced extensive statistical evidence to demonstrate that price behavior in the cement industry, particularly the price increases in 1932 and 1933 (prior to the NRA) and the rigidity which characterized most of the base prices between 1933 and 1937, were not consistent with competitive behavior. Testimony by economists for the Commission,

30 *Cement Institute*, 37 FTC 87, 102–112.
31 *Ibid.*, 117.

while technically correct, was not particularly helpful,[32] since the analysis was generally confined to pure competition; but it did refute the misleading economic doctrine offered by the defendants' economist in 1925.

In its 1941 brief before the Commission the Commission staff prepared an excellent exposition of formula pricing and an impressive digest of supporting evidence from which collusion could be inferred.[33] However, counsel for the Commission failed to follow the "formula" track when it came to proposing a cease-and-desist-order.[34] Counsel relied almost entirely on the price discrimination attack of Count II in its quest for effective relief. Fearing that respondents would continue to "meet" competition, even if the combination alleged in Count I were dissolved, Commission counsel argued that by upholding Count II: "The difficulty of determining whether respondents were continuing their combination in some other form would be easily and mathematically solved by ascertaining whether the systematic price discrimination now practiced has continued." [35] But the concept of system used to define illegal price discrimination in Count II appeared to differ from the concept of system used to infer agreement in support of Count I. In conjunction with the latter a *system of pricing* connoted use of a *common* pricing *formula.* But as used in the Count II portion of the 1941 brief, "systematic" discrimination apparently connoted merely a "system" of mill net variations resulting in "identical delivered price quotations." [36] Even if substantial independence in price behavior had produced many breaches in the price structure tending to destroy the formula *system* of predictable prices, persistent freight ab-

[32] Testimony by economists for the Cement Institute was less than helpful. Every industry practice was interpreted as constituting nothing more than the inevitable consequence of imperfect competition. It was denied that any of the practices might lead to inferences of collusion. The Cement Institute economists were correct, of course, in stating that the market structure in the cement industry was characterized by imperfect competition, and that simple conclusions drawn from pure competition theory lacked relevance under these circumstances. But the attempt to explain every practice and event in terms of "rationalistic" imperfect competition appeared incredible. At the minimum, the parroting of "imperfect competition" to explain complex phenomena was as tame and meaningless as an offer to explain the current price level by the equation of exchange, $MV = PT$.

[33] *Brief in Support of the Complaint, Cement Institute,* 37 FTC 87 (1943).

[34] *Ibid.,* Vol. I, Part I, p. 60.

[35] *Ibid.* [36] *Ibid.*

sorption to meet competitors' price cuts would produce identical delivered prices and "systematic" discrimination. Certainly identical sealed bids, by sellers located at varying distances from destination, would indicate adherence to some *formula system.* But counsel did not distinguish identical sealed bids to government agencies from identical prices quoted to commercial buyers. The interpretation urged by the Commission counsel apparently assumed "systematic" discrimination to be present on commercial sales whenever identical destination prices resulted, even if each seller was practicing discrimination to meet identically delivered prices previously reduced unsystematically by rivals below a formula price, while each seller had reduced delivered prices at several destinations unsystematically below a formula price, delivered quotations which were subsequently met identically by rivals.

The term systematic discrimination, if used as a counterpart to pricing under a commonly used delivered-price formula, means one thing. But as used in counsel's brief, systematic discrimination apparently meant the constant and reciprocal acceptance of widely varying mill nets necessary to meet identically the lower delivered prices of rivals. The mere frequency of identical delivered prices, rather than their derivation by formula, constituted the culprit. And counsel for the Commission concluded his brief in support of Count II as follows: "Unless that discrimination be removed its counterpart in identical delivered price quotations will survive."[37] Hence, he sought to destroy the basing-point system by eliminating persistent price discrimination.

Walter B. Wooden was counsel in charge of the Commission's case. A skillful, scholarly attorney and a disciple of Frank A. Fetter, he believed firmly that non-discriminatory pricing constituted the only satisfactory alternative to the basing-point system. He realized that there were clauses in the Robinson-Patman Act which prevented the achievement of uniform f.o.b. mill pricing, but he hoped to obtain a Court-affirmed Commission order which would induce firms to confine penetrations to a few exceptions. Wooden clearly understood the argument of his sym-

[37] *Ibid.*

pathetic critics who advocated remedial action to encourage disorderly interpenetration, or unsystematic pricing, but he doubted the wisdom of their prescription and subsequently labeled them iconoclasts.[38]

The Robinson-Patman Act constitutes a legitimate vehicle for combatting price discrimination which substantially lessens competition among the sellers, since the problem of proving overt collusion is bypassed. But if the attack is to be made upon formula pricing, as this writer recommends, systematic discrimination should be viewed as the counterpart of pricing in accordance with the basing-point or any other *formula system* of delivered pricing, or as the consequence of efforts to enforce adherence to a formula. Of course, the greater the weight attached by the courts to statistical price data in drawing inferences of collusion or unfair competition under the Federal Trade Commission Act, the less need there would be to rely upon the controversial Robinson-Patman Act.

In any event, the Commission's Findings as to the Facts and Conclusions, and its Order to Cease and Desist, of July 17, 1943, could be interpreted (although they need not be) as having accepted the Commission counsel's recommendation with respect to the price discrimination count. The Findings and the Order fail to make clear whether systematic price discrimination is confined to the mill net counterparts of *formula systems* of pricing. The bulk of the Findings furnishes evidence in support of the charge of an agreement to use and maintain adherence to the

[38] See W. B. Wooden, "The Concept of Unlawful Discrimination as It Applies to Geographical Price Differences," *Georgetown Law Journal*, 37:171–174 (January 1949). He referred to three types of economists: (1) the "orthodox school" which employed the principle of indifference of classical economics; (2) the "rationalistic school" which employed the concept of imperfect competition to judge a pricing practice or a price structure by the standard of alleged business need, tending to rationalize the status quo; and (3) the "iconoclastic school" which criticized "the alleged 'ivory tower' concepts of perfect competition by which the orthodox school tests a price or a price structure, and particularly is critical of the principle of indifference, apparently considering price discrimination a more or less normal expression of competition. In this it seems to lean toward the rationalistic school of imperfect competition. But it vigorously rejects any complete rationalization of monopoly and monopolistic pricing under the concept of imperfect competition. It would condemn monopoly and monopolistic pricing by objective tests such as price rigidity and uniformity but would not accept the principle of indifference as of any value in reaching an economic judgement." (*Ibid.*, p. 173).

basing-point system's pricing formula. These findings in support of Count I of the complaint make impressive reading, and the inference of concerted action is, to the writer, unmistakable. The Commission used great restraint in developing its findings and was careful not to overdraw its case.[39] If anything, it appears to have understated it. The consequences of unsystematic pricing could have been expressed more forcefully. The implicit collusion, inherent in rigid adherence to an arbitrary formula, might have been hammered home with greater vigor, with less emphasis placed on overt symptoms and activities. Instead of demonstrating merely the "perfection" of the pricing formula when presenting extensive listings of identical sealed bids, involving numerous bidders, numerous simultaneous destinations, and/or numerous decimal points, the data could have been used to develop the argument of implicit collusion. Even the carefully documented record showing the cooperative elimination and control of buyers' trucking failed to explain the destructive effect of uncontrolled trucking upon the pricing formula, to present evidence showing a relationship between base price advances and the elimination of uncontrolled trucking, and to develop a theory of collusion based on controls placed upon trucking. But then, the *Cement* case was the first of a series of multiple-basing-point cases, and the desire to set a more modest, but firmly established, precedent may explain the direction taken in the Commission's Findings of Facts.

Findings concerning Count II, the systematic price discrimination charge, constituted but 2 paragraphs and 3½ of the total 176 pages of Findings and Conclusions.[40] A portion of Paragraph 24 (b) refers to the discrimination of mill nets as forming a "systematic pattern that is the mathematical counterpart of the delivered-price pattern resulting from the multiple basing-point

[39] The Commission made no effort to hide the variability of participation in the overt collective activities: "Some of the respondents have been parties to substantially all of these activities; other respondents have participated to a lesser degree, or been mere followers, adopting and supporting the practices of their more active associates; and a few respondents have from time to time, for various reasons, participated only reluctantly in some of the practices, and have occasionally opposed for a time particular instances of group actions." See *Cement Institute* 37 FTC 87, 144 (1934) Paragraph 6(a).

[40] *Ibid.*, p. 254–257.

delivered price system, which system is an expression of the effort of each respondent seller to match the delivered prices of other respondent sellers."[41] The emphasis upon *pattern* and *basing-point delivered price system* could be interpreted as confining the concept of systematic discrimination to a mirror image of the mill nets of a common formula of pricing. Yet the additional phrasing "to match the delivered prices," taken in conjunction with subsequent expressions in the Findings, might also be made to include within the elastic expression "system," the mere frequent endeavor to quote identical prices. That the Commission *may* have intended to define the concept of "system" very broadly could be drawn from the following passage in Paragraph 24 (d):

> The systematic variations in mill nets resulting from respondents' pricing system are conditioned upon and are in proportion to the failure of the respective respondent sellers to make due allowance in their delivered prices for differences in their actual cost of delivery.[42]

The construction of the Commission's Order to Cease and Desist, considering counsel's interpretation of the order before the reviewing Circuit Court (see page 254), suggests that the Commission had adopted the counsel's view that effective relief would be obtained primarily by prohibiting price discrimination which resulted in identical prices. Such an inference may be drawn from the failure of the Commission to prohibit respondents *individually* from refusing to quote an f.o.b. mill price equal to the posted base price effective at each plant (save for any extras related to additional costs) and refusing delivery at the mill to buyers who wish to use their own means of transportation.[43] The principal features of the Commission's order are the following:

> It is ordered that . . . corporate respondents . . . and their respective officers, agents, representatives, and employees, . . . in connection with the . . . sale . . . of portland cement in interstate commerce do forthwith cease and desist from entering into, *continuing*, cooperating in, or carrying out any *planned common course of action*, understanding, agreement, combination, or conspiracy between and among any two or more of said respondents or

41 *Ibid.*, pp. 254–255. 42 *Ibid.*, p. 256.

43 In connection with the weaknesses of a much later order (1951) issued by the Commission against the steel industry, George W. Stocking has noted the same failure of the Commission to attack directly individual controls placed upon buyers' transportation. See *Basing Point Pricing and Regional Development*, p. 188.

between any one or more of said respondents and others not parties hereto, to do or perform any of the following things: *[Italics added]*

1. Quoting or selling cement at prices calculated or determined pursuant to or in accordance with the multiple basing-point delivered price system; or quoting or selling cement pursuant to or in accordance with *any other plan or system which results in identical price quotations or prices for cement* at points of quotation or sale or to particular purchasers by respondents using such plan or system, or which prevents purchasers from finding any advantage in price in dealing with one or more of the respondents against any of the other respondents. *[Italics added]*

2. In connection with or aid or support of any plan, system, acts or practices prohibited in paragraph 1 above

(a) Refusing or declining to quote or sell cement at the location of the producing mill *at a price effective at such location. [Italics added]*

(b) Refusing or declining, when quoting or selling cement at a price effective at the location of the producing mill, *to allow purchasers to provide transportation by any means, at any cost, or to any place they may desire. [Italics added]*

[Subparagraphs (c), (d), and (e) concern the quoting of either delivered prices or varying f.o.b. mill prices systematically calculated to produce delivered costs identical with delivered costs derived from calculating the sum of the base price plus common-carrier transportation from differently located mills.

Subparagraphs (f) and (g) concern the collection of freights by systematically including freight factors other than the carrier actually employed.

Subparagraphs (h) and (i) concern practices which deprive the federal government of any benefits of land grant or other special transportation rates.

Subparagraph (j) concerns circulating of freight rate factors.

Subparagraph (k) concerns attempting to control the destination of shipments after title passes to the purchaser.

Subparagraphs (l) and (m) concern classification of customers and determining purchasers or classes of purchasers who may purchase directly from respondents.

Subparagraph (n) concerns circulating data which reveal individual production and shipments statistics to other corporate respondents.

Subparagraph (o) concerns boycotts of customers who purchase imported cement.

Subparagraph (p) concerns the determination of discounts and other terms and conditions of sale.]

3. Discriminating in price between or among their respective customers by systematically charging and accepting mill net prices which differ by the amounts necessary to produce delivered costs to purchasers *identical with delivered costs* available to such purchasers through purchases *from other producers. [Italics added]*

[Paragraph 4 refers to using means substantially similar with the purpose or effect of accomplishing things prohibited by the order.] [44]

It should be noted that the entire order is conditioned by a "planned common course of action" preamble. The Commission in its brief before the Circuit Court explained that the more novel phrase "planned common course of action" would combat a *continuation* of the practices and devices which, originating in agreement, made effective the price-fixing combination — and added:

There is less uncertainty to individual business laymen whether they are pursuing a "planned common course of action" than there is whether they are parties to an "understanding, agreement, combination or conspiracy," which involve more elastic legal concepts.[45]

Although the preamble qualifying the prohibited practices is phrased consistently with the concept of implicit collusion, the principal weakness of the Commission order was that respondents might refuse to discontinue voluntarily particular, "individual" practices, such as controls over buyers' trucking. The Commission might well contend that compliance with the order demands positive action by respondents to demonstrate the abandonment of the continuing effects of planned common course of action. But respondents might persist in their rearguard action to preserve the formula by arguing that their continued individual decisions to control trucking were not really to perpetuate a pricing formula, but merely reflected individual "business necessity," based on avoiding having buyers' trucks "cluttering up the mill area." The dissimulation would undoubtedly fail; but only after further protracted litigation would relief be forthcoming. The Commission may have believed that if it could achieve its objective of compelling an approximation of uniform mill net selling, controls over trucking would either be unnecessary or voluntarily removed.

That the Commission considered Paragraph 3 (prohibiting systematic discriminations in mill nets which resulted in identical delivered costs) the heart of the remedy, may be judged by its

[44] *Cement Institute,* 37 FTC 87, 259–61 (1943).
[45] *Brief for Respondent,* p. 299, *Aetna Portland Cement Co.* v. *FTC,* 157 F.2d 533 (7th Cir. 1946).

vigorous defense in the brief before the Circuit Court. The cement producers had protested more strenuously against Paragraph 3 than against any other portion of the order; and the Commission made the following lengthy reply:

The obvious fallacy in petitioners' objection is that they are quite anxious to be permitted to continue doing just what they have been doing on the theory that it constitutes meeting an equally low price of a competitor in good faith and making due allowance for differences in cost of delivery. *This case will have been litigated in vain if petioners' views prevail on this subject, even though other provisions of the order were to stand.* For it is this systematic discrimination and failure to make due allowance for differences in cost of delivery that causes the identical matched delivered prices which petitioners insist are competitive. Paragraphs 1 and 2 of the order are applicable to petitioners *collectively* and to their use and support of the *basing point system.* Paragraph 3 is by its nature applicable *only* to the *respective* corporate petitioners, *but* to a *practice* which to the extent *used by all* would in effect recreate the system and have the same effect in *making delivered prices identical.*[46] *[Italics added]*

It is not quite accurate to allege that the Commission was seeking absolutely uniform f.o.b. mill prices. Delivered-price quotations, as such, were not prohibited. Nor were varied mill nets which made for neither matched identical prices nor a substantial lessening of competition. And the Commission had admitted in its defense of Count II that the Supreme Court in the *Glucose* cases [47] had not prohibited all freight absorption resulting in identical prices. But it did argue in its brief that the Supreme Court had not stated that respondents "may always absorb freight." [48] The Commission was apparently attempting to achieve the closest approximation to uniform mill nets as a judicial interpretation of the Robinson-Patman Act would permit.

The writer wonders if the Circuit Court majority dealt so harshly with the *Cement* case because the Commission had failed to make clear the distinction between behavior under the challenged systematic pricing formula and under unsystematic pricing practices. Non-discriminatory mill net pricing was the only

[46] *Ibid.*, pp. 301–302.

[47] *Corn Products Rfg. Co.* v. *FTC* 324 U.S. 726 (1945); *FTC* v. *A. E. Staley Mfg. Co.* 324 U.S. 746 (1945).

[48] *Brief for Respondent*, p. 200, *Aetna Portland Cement Co.* v. *FTC*, 157 F.2d 533 (7th Cir. 1946).

alternative, as the Court saw the basing-point problem. At an early stage in its long opinion, the Circuit Court discussed the Commission's order and reached the conclusion that it was intended to rule out any "system" which results in identical destination prices and, hence, required the sale of cement on an f.o.b. mill basis.[49] The Circuit Court specifically seized upon the Commission's interpretation of Paragraph 3 of the Cement Order to criticize the prohibition of "each individual respondent from absorbing freight even though done in good faith to meet an equally low price of a competitor." [50]

The Circuit Court was not prepared to affirm a Commission order which it believed would radically alter long-established geographic pricing practices, and so it launched into a severely critical attack both on the reasoning of the Commission's Findings and on the substantiality of the evidence supporting them. The Court relied heavily upon the *Old Cement* case and argued that in the absence of a demonstrated agreement to use the basing-point system the Commission's case was faulty. In this respect, it should be reported that the Court never referred to the Commission findings relating to the control of trucking, and, while mentioning punitive bases, merely stated that these were not imposed as a result of agreement among the respondents.[51] The Court was unwilling to infer common purpose from collective activities which had been undertaken, and even less willing to infer collusion from rigid adherence to the basing-point formula.[52] In the latter case, the Court may have been reflecting merely its aversion to non-discriminatory pricing which it viewed as the only alternative.[53]

The elusive concept of "system" which the Commission had employed in its brief, returned to haunt it in the Circuit Court's opinion. The Court complained that the Commission had failed to provide a "definition of the system of pricing which the Commission seeks to outlaw," [54] and it expressed its bewilderment as to how a "formula" method of pricing served to produce collusive price identities.[55] Confused as to the concept of system

[49] *Aetna Portland Cement Co.* v. *FTC*, 157 F.2d 533, 542 (7th Cir. 1946).
[50] *Ibid.*, p. 543. [51] *Ibid.*, p. 564.
[52] *Ibid.*, pp. 556, 558. [53] *Ibid.*, pp. 557–558.
[54] *Ibid.*, p. 561. [55] *Ibid.*, p. 562.

employed by the Commission, the Court believed that in the case of cement any pricing practice, whether used individually or in combination, would inevitably result in uniform prices, since price reductions would be met and identical prices result.[56] The Commission's findings and brief had failed to make clear to the Court that the lack of unsystematic breaches of the formula on commercial delivered prices (rather than the absence of identical prices) constituted the very thing needed for inferring a *system* of pricing and an agreement to adhere to a formula.

The Court's stated objections revolved primarily around the question of sufficiency of evidence supporting the Commission's general findings, and the logic of its reasoning in drawing inferences. Comparatively few of the findings had been challenged by respondents, and only one inconsequential finding was rejected by the Court as being unsupported by evidence.[57] The Court did offer two dicta amounting to concessions to the Commission. It stated that the record "may and possibly does disclose practices by some of the respondents which are prohibited."[58] It also questioned the collection of phantom freight on truck and water shipments and by non-base mills. And it suggested that identical sealed bids might imply collective action among the respondents concerned, although the Court was not prepared to link the evidence of identical bids with the general charge of combination.

Although the Circuit Court had unsparingly rebuked the Commission, and had ignored much supporting evidence in its findings, the very points of confusion and criticism in the Circuit Court opinion proved of inestimable value for the next step forward. With help from the solicitor general's office, the Commission prepared a highly effective and clarifying brief for the Supreme Court.

Charles Weston, the antitrust expert in the solicitor general's office, guided the preparation of the case, with Walter Wooden

[56] *Ibid.*, p. 568.

[57] *Ibid.*, p. 567, "Finding 20 (h) states: 'In general, dealers and ordinary purchasers are not aware of differences in quality among the brands of cement sold by different producers. The possession of such knowledge by these groups would tend toward making it impossible for respondents to maintain uniform prices for cement.' While the Commission refers to this finding at numerous points in its brief, it nowhere cites any evidence in its support."

[58] *Ibid.*, pp. 572–573.

serving as a subordinate.[59] The resulting brief was highly impressive from a legal-economic standpoint. The brief early emphasized that Count I alleged combination and that Count II adopted the allegations of combination made in Count I. The alleged illegal price discriminations were asserted to be an inevitable result of the respondents' agreement to use a pricing formula to prevent price competition among themselves.[60] Furthermore, it was specifically stated in the brief that a "planned common course of action" qualified all the prohibited practices. The charge of agreement was clearly identified with efforts to use and maintain formula pricing, and the challenged pricing *system* with adherence to a *formula* which obstructed competition.[61] The Commission suggested that previous Supreme Court interpretations of the Federal Trade Commission Act authorized the Commission to prohibit practices which operated to suppress competition irrespective of combination and agreement; but the point was not pressed, "since we believe that the Commission's order can be sustained on more clearly settled ground." [62] A sophisticated analysis of the record of identical sealed bidding was spotlighted to compel the inference of an agreement to maintain a pricing formula. Not only was it argued that the repeated identical bids implied collusion, but also that they constituted convincing evidence of an understanding to maintain a particular pricing system which would eliminate all price competition among the respondents. By bidding in strict accord with the formula each respondent was "affirming his participation" and

59 See letters dated July 7, September 18, October 13 and October 17, 1947 from Walter Wooden to Professor Fetter in the Frank A. Fetter Collection in the Indiana University Library. These letters described Wooden's loss of control in shaping the theory of the case to be put to the Supreme Court. The general correspondence of Professor Fetter between 1934 and 1948 reveals the strategic role played by him in formulating the Commission's *Cement* case through 1947. The correspondence shows the great respect accorded to Fetter's economic analysis and policy recommendations by Walter Wooden.

60 *Brief for Federal Trade Commission,* pp. 8, 36–37, *FTC* v. *Cement Institute* 333 U.S. 683 (1948).

61 *Ibid.,* pp. 39, 43, 124–125.

62 *Ibid.,* pp. 40–41. But in closing his oral argument before the Supreme Court, Mr. Weston offered another explanation, "Perhaps mistakenly we were somewhat hesitant in presenting this view or this application of the statute, because of the fact that the Commission's complaint and order were framed in terms of combination." See *Transcript of Proceedings,* p. 183, *FTC* v. *Cement Institute* 333 U.S. 683 (1948).

they "thereby implicitly assured each other that they would continue their prior observance of the pricing formula." [63] It was asserted that the pricing system, at least on sales to government agencies, would have collapsed had a few producers departed from the formula.

Furthermore, unlike the brief submitted to the Circuit Court, this one attempted to outline the economic effects intended by the Commission's order. The brief stated that the lower court had misapprehended its meaning, and had assumed incorrectly that the order prohibited all freight absorption. The Commission emphasized that a respondent would violate the provisions of the order only if it were a party to "planned common course of action, understanding, agreement, combination, or conspiracy." And the brief added:

> This is an essential qualification to the prohibitions of these paragraphs. The order therefore leaves each respondent free — provided he acts individually and with that variability in action respecting particular competitive situations which is characterstic of genuine competitive endeavor and a free market — to absorb freight in order to meet a competitor's low price or to sell at a delivered price.
>
> What the order does is to bar acting in concert in adopting, continuing, or implementing the multiple basing-point delivered price system or any similar system which necessarily operates to suppress price competition.[64]

Thus the brief prepared under Charles Weston's supervision affirmed the respondents' right to absorb freight to meet competition, however circumscribed the conditions. In contrast, the brief prepared for the lower court had been unusually silent on this contested issue.

The new brief went on to deny that the Commission had found the basing-point system per se to be illegal.[65] It noted that the Commission had disclosed collective action to implement and continue the system as well as rigid adherence. However, it also suggested that there existed many reasons for serious doubts as to whether a rigid basing-point system could be maintained in the absence of agreement.[66] Hence, the Commission believed that a rigid basing-point system might be found collusive.

[63] *Brief for Federal Trade Commission*, p. 53, *FTC* v. *Cement Institute*, 333 U.S. 683 (1948).

[64] *Ibid.*, p. 122. [65] *Ibid.*, pp. 122–123. [66] *Ibid.*, p. 123.

The brief carried further its discussion of the anticipated effect of the order upon freight absorption, by clarifying the concept of systematic discrimination:

The Commission's order does not forbid freight absorption as such nor do we anticipate that its practical effect will be to preclude freight absorption by sellers of cement. We do anticipate that the order will preclude mutual and common use of any pricing formula in which, as at present, freight absorption is systematic, frequently flagrant (in relation to sales price), and mutually practiced by all concerned.[67]

And the above paragraph was accompanied by the following footnote:

Section 2 (a) of the Clayton Act would not preclude freight absorptions different from the present systematic ones. Many such absorptions would not have the effect on competition which would make them unlawful and still others would be within the justification of Section 2 (b).[68]

An industry-wide freight absorption in adherence to a formula was clearly identified as the challenged *systematic* discrimination.

The Commission's brief had made extremely clear the nature of formula pricing from which the inference of collusion had been drawn, and it made as clear as possible (complete clarity being impossible) that freight absorption was legal so long as it did not fall into a pattern consistent with a rigid pricing formula. Yet Weston threw further light on the matter during his condensed oral rebuttal. Extending his economic argument beyond the confines of identical sealed bidding, which had been explored carefully in the brief, Weston clinched the case by pointing up a central question which respondents had never answered:

. . . why a producer never sold below his base price plus freight within his home territory when he was constantly, consistently, selling below base price plus freight outside his home territory, when he could increase sales by doing so.

The whole inference that necessarily follows is that they were preserving a consistent pattern.[69]

[67] *Ibid.*, pp. 124–125.
[68] *Ibid.*, p. 125, note 85.
[69] *Transcript of Proceedings*, pp. 180–81, *FTC* v. *Cement Institute*, 333 U.S. 683 (1948).

Furthermore, Weston emphasized that rigid adherence to a basing-point formula (or its occasional modification with a zone formula), and not merely identical prices, constituted the essential evidence of agreement. He argued that if the real market is at destination, as respondents claim:

It is curious that the market price at all destinations is exactly the price which the formula produces. What we rely on more than the identity in price in particular markets, is that it is made in the same way in all markets, with certain specified variations.[70]

When the Commission's case against formula pricing had finally been presented clearly, the Supreme Court, in a six to one decision, completely affirmed the Commission's Findings and Order. A reading of the Court's opinion in conjunction with the Commission's brief and oral argument before the Court reveals an extremely close similarity, possibly reflecting both the persuasive reasoning of Mr. Weston and the confidence which the high Court places in the "filtering action" of the solicitor general's office. Still, the order is not unequivocal because of the "planned common course of action" preamble.

Too much should never be read into a Court decision, let alone the dicta, but we shall offer a few observations for purposes of interpreting this specific injunction. At the very outset of its opinion, the Supreme Court made a cryptic comment on the issue of relief:

For the present it is sufficient to say that, if the order stands, its terms are *broad enough* to bar respondents from *acting in concert* to sell cement on a basing point delivered price plan which so eliminates competition that respondents' prices are *always* identical at any given point in the United States.[71] *[Italics added]*

The Court's key concept would appear to be "acting in concert," yet rigid adherence to a formula whereby prices are "always" identical would appear to indicate the very concerted action which the Court believed the terms of the order "broad enough" to prevent. Detailed discussion of the implications of the Commission's order came after the Supreme Court decided that the

[70] *Ibid.*, p. 181.
[71] *FTC* v. *Cement Institute,* 333 U.S. 683, 689 (1948).

Commission concluded properly that concerted maintenance of the basing-point system was an unfair method of competition,[72] and that systematic price discrimination violated the Robinson-Patman Act because it lessened competition substantially and failed to meet the exonerating defense of "good faith." [73] The Court asserted that the order's prohibitions forbade no activities except those which "if continued would directly aid in perpetuating the same old unlawful practices." [74] The Court emphasized that both it and the Commission denied the allegation that the terms of the order would prevent an individual producer from absorbing freight to meet the lower price of a competitor.[75] It further stressed, as had the Commission, that all provisions of the order were modified and limited by a preamble "directed solely at concerted, not individual activity on the part of respondents." [76] And the Court added, in answer to the respondents' objections, that the phrase "planned common course of action" in the preamble possessed a quite clear meaning:

> It is merely an emphatic statement that the Commission is prohibiting concerted action — planned concerted action. The Commission chose a phrase perhaps more readily understood by businessmen than the accompanying legal words of like import.[77]

The significance of the high Court's decision therefore appears to rest upon the weight of evidence needed to support an inference of concerted action. That the rigid behavior required for maintaining a common pricing formula will constitute sufficient evidence for inferring continued collusion appears unmistakable to this writer. Although the Supreme Court did not say so explicitly, several dicta support this position. The Court expressed doubt, even in the case of a standardized product, that prices would be identical everywhere and at all times in the absence of agreement — "the desire to sell will sometimes be so strong that a seller will be willing to lower his prices and take his

72 *Ibid.*, p. 720.

73 *Ibid.*, p. 726. The Court made clear that not only was phantom freight illegal under any basing-point system, but so was freight absorption under a multiple-basing-point system when systematic, as in the "cement basing-point system," p. 725.

74 *Ibid.*, p. 727.

75 *Ibid.*

76 *Ibid.*

77 *Ibid.*, p. 728.

chances."[78] The Court stated that the Commission was authorized to find participation in an understanding from the fact "that all of the respondents have sold their cement substantially in accord with the pattern required by the multiple basing-point system."[79] Thus it reaffirmed one of its modern opinions, that a finding of combination within the meaning of the Sherman Act could be made if evidence exists that parties who know that concerted action is contemplated and invited give adherence and participate.[80] Finally, and possibly with the intention of placing less stress on the formal aspects of "the invitation," the Supreme Court expressed the opinion that concerted action "which falls short of being a Sherman Act violation may constitute an 'unfair method of competition' prohibited by the Federal Trade Commission Act. . . . The Commission and the Courts were to determine what conduct, even though it might then be short of a Sherman Act violation, was an 'unfair method of competition' ".[81]

It does seem likely, as Milton Handler has suggested, that under the new regime of antitrust "there is added the affirmative obligation to compete actively and vigorously. The categorical imperative thus becomes 'thou shalt compete' rather than 'thou shalt not restrain competition' ".[82]

The writer, however, doubts if cement producers will feel legal pressure to compete actively unless the Commission initiates an ambitious program in the Courts to gain compliance. We must recall that substantial collective activity to adopt practices to implement the system had been undertaken in the past in the cement industry, but that most of these practices, once adopted, required no continuing collective activity. The Supreme Court reckoned with these activities, of course, in reaching its conclusions. As a consequence, there remains the possibility that respondents may interpret narrowly the "concerted action" prohibited by the Commission order, as affirmed by the Supreme Court. The typical firm in the cement industry may merely discontinue certain overt collective activities, such as the joint circulation of common freight rate books, individual company

78 *Ibid.*, p. 716. 79 *Ibid.*

80 *Ibid.*, p. 716, note 17. 81 *Ibid.*, p. 708.

82 Milton Handler, "Anti-Trust — New Frontiers and New Perplexities," *The Record* (February, 1951), p. 60.

statistics, and specific-job contract information; cease participation in a Cement Institute or any other meetings where the formulation of common marketing policies are discussed; and refrain from submitting sealed bids in accordance with any pricing formula or imposing formalized punitive bases. The elimination of all of these activities, especially identical sealed bids to governmental agencies, should constitute a substantial improvement. Yet, as discussed earlier in this chapter, if cement producers are determined to avoid price competition, the reforms in practices listed here may be insufficient. Not only must there be careful surveillance of the pattern of sealed bids to government agencies, but further antitrust litigation must confront those respondents who interpret the prohibition against "concerted action" excessively narrowly. They must be made to see that compliance with the Commission's order requires affirmative action.

CHAPTER VIII

Developments Since the Cement Decision and Policy Recommendations

Because of the persistent and uninterrupted boom characteristic of the cement industry ever since World War II, and because of the political strategy which dominated the pricing policies of delivered-price-system industries in the months immediately following the 1948 Supreme Court decision, it is impossible even at this time (January 1957) to see clearly the economic effects of the *Cement* decision upon pricing practices and market behavior in the industry. But there are strong reasons for believing that widely-heralded changes in marketing policies have been superficial rather than fundamental, and that, unless prevented by future antitrust action, the cement industry in most regions intends to restore the stabilizing features of the basing-point system for commercial sales substantially as they existed prior to the decision.

As was described at the close of Chapter V, the *Cement* decision came during a period of booming demand for cement. The percentages of practical capacity utilized during 1947–48 (shown in Table 6) are misleading in suggesting a redundance of effective capacity relative to demand. The period was plagued by production bottlenecks resulting from shortages in fuel, replacement parts, and transportation, as well as strikes in cement mills. In February 1948 cement supply was reported to be short by industrial purchasing agents who announced that the manufacturers had adopted a 15-cent escalator clause in cement contracts for specific jobs (replacing the traditional guarantee against price increases) and warned that cement prices were likely to rise through 1951.[1] As the immediate postwar handicaps to pro-

[1] *New York Times,* Feb. 19, 1948, p. 35. See also *Rock Products* (Mar. 1948, p. 151) for a discussion of the cement shortages during 1947 and the expected shortages during 1948 by the executive secretary of the National Ready Mix Concrete Association.

duction decreased, the practical capacity utilized rose to above 93 per cent in 1950. Further elimination of bottlenecks to capacity utilization, including expansions in storage facilities,[2] permitted practical capacity utilized to rise to above 97 per cent in 1951–52. Finally, the additional advantage of mild winters which permitted a longer construction season and reduced the storehouse bottleneck, enabled it to exceed 100 per cent in 1953, 101 per cent in 1954, and 104 per cent in 1955. Unlike the steel industry which was confronted with a mild decline in demand in 1949–50 and a more significant setback in 1953–54, the cement industry has continued to boom. Cement production and shipments have shown a continuing expansion every year through 1956. The nearest thing to an easing of tight markets occurred during 1953–54 when no serious or prolonged shortages were reported, except in the area of the New York and Ohio turnpikes — the principal manifestation of short supply in many local areas being higher prices of supplementary shipments from other areas rather than outright shortages.[3] By the late spring of 1955, however, severe shortages again developed in many areas, and producers renewed the rationing of shipments while gray markets again developed and substantial imports of foreign cement were made at premium prices.[4]

The dramatic changes in marketing policy announced by most cement firms in July 1948 were undoubtedly influenced by an organized political strategy, apparently initiated by the United States Steel Corporation to generate pressure for legislation to repeal the *Cement* decision.[5] Less than a week after

[2] Storage capacity has been greatly increased at most mills during the postwar period, so that mills may produce clinker and cement for longer periods during the winter lull in demand. Presumably it has become less expensive, relative to the capacity boom of the twenties, to meet the problem of seasonal variation in demand by the construction of greater storage capacity rather than by the installation of additional burning and grinding equipment. As a consequence, it will be necessary in the future to modify upward the rubric suggested in Chapter V (90 per cent of practical capacity) for gauging the presence of a relatively tight cement supply during those periods free of bottlenecks in complementary industries.

[3] The discussion of production and market conditions in the cement industry during the postwar period is primarily based upon W. E. Trauffer, "Cement Review and Forecast," *Pit and Quarry*, January issues 1948–57.

[4] *Wall Street Journal*, May 23, 1955, p. 1.

[5] "Adoption last week by several major steel companies of the f.o.b.-mill pricing system that the industry has vigorously opposed for the last quarter century, represented a gamble by the steel industry that unfavorable public and industrial

the Supreme Court's basing-point decision, Irving S. Olds of the Steel Corporation announced that corrective legislation would be essential if the decision should eventually become applicable to the steel industry.[6] The significance of the attack upon formula-price systems was all too apparent to operators of delivered-price systems, and a two-pronged plan was developed by the Corporation to publicize that uncertainties resulting from antitrust decisions required uniform mill net selling and to switch the pricing policies of United States Steel subsidiaries to meet this requirement. On this basis a new marketing policy would be introduced which, during the boom-time transition, would raise prices to distantly located buyers who would then demand that "clarifying" (nullifying) legislation be approved by the Republican Congress and President which it was anticipated would follow the November 1948 elections.

Although the majority of the Federal Trade commissioners quickly denied that the *Cement* decision forbade freight absorption,[7] and the *National Association of Manufacturers Law Digest* emphasized that the *Cement* decision merely prohibited concerted action to maintain a basing-point system,[8] legalistic prophets on the basis of judicial dicta could theorize about a future prohibition of freight absorption. Dicta in the *Cement* case suggested that constant acceptance of varying mill nets might fail to qualify under the "good faith" defense to a price discrimination charge, and dicta in the *Morton Salt* case[9] volunteered that the illegal effect on competition might be judged by a "reasonable possibility" in lieu of the traditional "reasonable probability." Hence, virtually any freight absorption *might* sometime in the future be judged as an antitrust violation. George W. Stocking

---

reaction eventually will spur Congress to legalize the basing-point method of computing prices — the practice just discarded under protest, by both the cement and steel industries." Mullaney, "Steel Ruling Seen as a Boomerang," *New York Times,* July 11, 1948, Sect. 3, p. 1F. See also "Basing Point Blues," *Wall Street Journal,* July 29, 1948, p. 1.

6 *New York Times,* April 28, 1948, p. 41.

7 Commissioner Lowell B. Mason, however, sabotaged his colleagues by publicly warning that only uniform f.o.b. mill pricing would henceforth be safe in the present state of the law. *New York Times,* May 23, 1948, Sect. 3, p. 1F.

8 "Trade Regulation under the Robinson-Patman and Federal Trade Commission Acts — Implications in Recent Decisions," June 1948, pp. 33–45.

9 *FTC* v. *Morton Salt Co.,* 334 U.S. 37 (1948).

has carefully analyzed these conjectures, and although admitting the existence of some uncertainty, expressed the opinion that the all-too-certain meaning of the *Cement* decision with respect to formula pricing constituted the principal target of the revisionists.[10]

During 1948 the steel shortage greatly exceeded the cement shortage both in magnitude and in impact upon the economy. Gray markets at the wholesale level were more prevalent in the steel industry, and many more consuming enterprises were strategically affected by the system of allocations used by manufacturers to distribute their product under a deflated, administered price level. Evidence also exists that many shipments had already been discontinued to consumers in areas where heavy freight absorptions were entailed.[11] As a consequence, the adoption of a complete, but temporary, break with the basing-point system in the steel industry would increase mill nets and profits while leaving base prices unchanged; and also the injured buyers would be squeezed by the increases in destination prices which put them at a disadvantage with many of their competitors. Moreover, given the pervasive shortage in steel and the system of voluntary allocations in operation, many established supplier-customer relationships could be maintained despite destination prices exceeding those formally available from rival producers more advantageously located. Finally, an "unclear" law, in need of clarification, could be made the scapegoat.

The lead in the pricing moves toward so-called f.o.b.[12] mill selling was taken by the United States Steel Corporation, first by its subsidiary in the cement industry and a week later in the steel industry, and was followed by most other producers in both of these industries. Undoubtedly it was the change in pricing policy in steel which induced Congress to report favorably upon Senator Capehart's resolution to investigate pricing practices,

[10] G. W. Stocking, *Basing-Point Pricing and Regional Development*, chapter 8.

[11] See Special Committee to Study Problems of American Small Business, U.S. Senate, 81st Cong., 1st sess., Report No. 44, *Changes in Distribution of Steel, 1940–47* (Washington, 1949).

[12] "So-called" f.o.b. mill is used advisedly, since buyers were rarely given the option of taking possession at the mill and arranging their own transportation.

rather than the *Cement* decision as such, or reactions in the cement industry to the decision.[13]

Marketing Announcements in the Cement Industry

Prior to the bombshell set off by Universal Atlas on June 30, 1948, only one cement manufacturer had offered a detailed statement of his intended marketing policy. In May, less than one month after the *Cement* decision, Marquette (which had recently become a medium-size chain) announced that nothing in the Supreme Court decision required a change in its sales policy. Emphasizing that the Commission order applied only to practices involving combination or agreement, and that the individual producers were free to absorb freight to meet lower prices of rivals, Marquette informed its dealers that: "if Marquette finds that its quoted price is higher at any destination than the price quoted by a competitor, it will be the company's policy to meet the lower price whenever it seems good business to do so." [14] This, of course, was a correct interpretation of the Supreme Court decision, although the company undoubtedly desired to interpret the concept of concerted action excessively narrowly. It probably assumed that industry-wide adherence to a basing-point formula might be perpetuated on commercial sales through the mere individual but literal meeting of the lower destination quotations by rivals as disclosed by advertising circulars or invoices in possession of dealers — and so the existence of a concerted system could be denied.

During the last week in May, without fanfare, the mills of the affiliated General Cement and Consolidated Cement firms (formerly known as the Cowham Engineering Group) began to ship cement on a so-called f.o.b. shipping point basis.[15] The news received no particular write-up in the press, no policy statement was reported, and presumably the objective was simply the elimination of profit-reducing freight absorption during a period

[13] For a good discussion of the politics and legislative maneuvers of the basing-point system protagonists, see G. W. Stocking, *Basing-Point Pricing and Regional Development*, chapter 8, and E. Latham, "The Politics of Basing Point Legislation," *Law and Contemporary Problems,* 15:272–310 (Spring 1950).

[14] *Pit and Quarry,* June 1948, p. 62.

[15] *Wall Street Journal,* July 1, 1948, p. 2.

of booming demand, when leaders in the industry were maintaining modest base prices in the mill areas of General and Consolidated.

Then, on June 30, 1948, Universal Atlas, the nation's largest cement manufacturer and the Steel Corporation subsidiary, shook the industry by announcing dramatically that, effective July 7, all sales would be at prices f.o.b. shipping point, or, if the customer desired, at delivered prices which reflected full transportation charges from the shipping point.[16] There were three distinctive features about the accompanying announcement. It failed to mention that the f.o.b. shipping point prices would not be available to buyers sending their own trucks to the mill — thus casting doubt upon the genuineness of the offer to sell at a posted f.o.b. mill price. What reason existed for denying buyers' trucking unless Universal Atlas contemplated future freight absorption, and therefore desired to preserve a cornerstone for future formula pricing? Also, Universal Atlas stated that it would have to abandon selling at delivered prices as low as those quoted by competitors because of the "recent decision of the United States Supreme Court sustaining a cease and desist order of the Federal Trade Commission."[17] In a subsequent paragraph dealing with freight absorption the company asserted that "the Supreme Court has decided that such a method can no longer be used as a regular practice."[18] It is clear that here the Steel Corporation subsidiary was relying upon isolated dicta and ignoring the decision which ran in terms of concerted action to maintain a pricing formula. Finally, suggesting that the uniform mill net pricing was the only legal alternative available and that most serious consequences would befall buyers, the company set the stage for political action to revise the antitrust law:

> Although Universal Atlas holds firmly to its conviction that the order of the Federal Trade Commission is economically unsound and wrong, the law as interpreted by the Supreme Court must be respected and carried out, regardless of the grave difficulties which may thus be created for many buyers and users of cement.[19]

[16] *New York Times*, July 1, 1948, p. 33.
[17] *Ibid.*
[18] *Ibid.*
[19] *Ibid.*

The *New York Times* reported that Universal Atlas' announcement had come as a "complete surprise" to other firms in the New York area and that no other leading company could be found whose policies were also being changed to a so-called f.o.b. pricing policy.[20] The *Wall Street Journal*, however, reported finding one other major company (which refused to be named) that had decided to quote full freight to destination, but that an official had stated that the firm still had the option to meet competition by freight absorption.[21]

Although most of the major cement chains (e.g., Lehigh, Lone Star, Alpha) did not switch to the so-called f.o.b. mill pricing method until July 9, 1948, or later,[22] by which time United States Steel and most other major steel firms had indicated their intention of abandoning freight absorption,[23] Penn-Dixie specifically stated that all sales would be in rail cars and that the firm would absorb freight in certain circumstances:

> This company will sell only wholesale, for rail shipment, in full carload lots, in bulk, paper or cloth. The company will quote and sell cement f.o.b. railroad cars at the mill or at the buyer's destination, but all sales will be made on the current mill price, plus rail freight to the point of delivery in the case of f.o.b. buyers' delivery, except for such variations in delivered prices as may be practicable and may be lawfully made.[24]

Adequate information is not available, but presumably most cement manufacturers discontinued freight absorption on the bulk of their sales during the month of July.[25] Only one major cement company was known to be adhering regularly to its old marketing policy.[26] On July 20 Marquette wrote to dealers reaffirming its policy statement of May 15, stating that it would continue to absorb freight whenever it was good business to do so. Desiring to preserve the valuable good will of its customers in its normal marketing area, the firm stated that it did not believe that the super-high level of demand justified charging its

20 *Ibid.*
21 *Wall Street Journal*, July 1, 1948, p. 2.
22 *Ibid.*, July 9, 1948, p. 3; July 14, 1948, p. 14.
23 *New York Times*, July 8, 1948, p. 31; *Wall Street Journal*, July 9, 1948, p. 3 and July 13, 1948, p. 3.
24 *New York Times*, July 2, 1948, p. 27.
25 *Pit and Quarry*, August 1948, p. 50.
26 *Ibid.*

customers more for Marquette cement than its customers' competitors paid for other brands.[27] Other firms may have made selective freight absorptions for similar reasons.

Contrary to the explanation in the Universal Atlas announcement of June 30, 1948, and the subsequent elimination of freight absorption by the bulk of the cement industry, the typical cement firm did not interpret the *Cement* decision as preventing the continuation or resumption of freight absorption. Of the fifty-five cement companies which filed compliance reports with the Federal Trade Commission in September 1948, thirty-seven stated definitely their intentions to absorb freight; fifteen either neglected or failed to describe clearly their intentions concerning the matter; while only three indicated that their interpretation of the order had the practical effect of preventing freight absorption.[28]

The widely publicized "Notice to the Staff: in re: Commission Policy Toward Geographic Pricing"[29] of October 12, 1948 should have cleared the air for the few cement producers whose compliance reports evidenced a reluctance to absorb freight. Two sets of "confusion" had been generated by the opponents of the Commission's attack upon formula pricing, one related to the Circuit Court's upholding of the *Rigid Steel Conduit* case[30]

[27] *Ibid.*

[28] Reported in R. A. Wallace and P. H. Douglas, "Antitrust Policies and the New Attack on the Federal Trade Commission," *University of Chicago Law Review*, 19:697 (Summer, 1952).

[29] Reproduced as Appendix B in G. H. Sage, *Basing-Point Pricing Systems Under the Federal Antitrust Laws* (St. Louis, 1951), pp. 331–347.

[30] *Triangle Conduit & Cable Co.* v. *Federal Trade Commission,* 168 F.2d 175 (C.C.A. 7th, 1948). The Circuit Court's opinion was affirmed one year later by a 4–4 decision in the Supreme Court, *Clayton Mark & Co.* v. *Federal Trade Commission,* 336 U.S. 956 (1949). This basing-point system case had been brought exclusively under the Federal Trade Commission Act. Not only had conspiracy been charged and found, but the Commission had also charged and found that each respondent had priced in accordance with the basing-point system with knowledge that its rivals did likewise and with the effect of lessening competition dangerously. Moreover, the Commission had not only ordered a cessation of the "planned common course of action," but it had also ordered *individual* respondents to discontinue quoting in accordance with a basing-point system for the purpose, or with the effect, of *systematically* matching delivered-price quotations. Opponents of *Rigid Steel Conduit* argued bitterly, however, that the decision prevented the concurrent undertaking of freight absorption by rival members of an industry.

Whatever the Commission may have meant by systematic freight absorption prior to 1947, the Commission's brief before the Supreme Court in the *Cement*

and the other to problems raised by the Robinson-Patman Act. The "Notice" emphasized again that the attack on delivered-pricing systems under the Federal Trade Commission Act was directed at formula pricing. It reaffirmed that a clear inference of collusion resulted not from the mere uniformity of prices which resulted from freight absorption, but from an industry-wide rigid adherence to a complex geographic price structure which was inconsistent with the immediate competitive interests of the enterprises which observed it.[31] The Commission explained that the concept of illegal "conscious parallel action" in the *Rigid Steel Conduit* case applied only to rigid adherence to an industry-wide formula, and that the reference to collusion was eliminated in order to simplify proof in basing-point cases.[32]

Turning to the applicability of the Robinson-Patman Act to geographic pricing problems, the Commission stressed its po-

---

case and the Supreme Court's opinion in that case made clear that *systematic* pricing was the counterpart of a rigid *formula* system of pricing. And the Circuit Court opinion in *Rigid Steel Conduit* relied upon the Supreme Court's *Cement decision*. The Commission's purpose in developing findings and an order which extended beyond an implied conspiracy to use a common pricing formula reflected a hope that the burden of proof in demonstrating non-compliance with a Commission order might be eased if the legal terms "conspiracy" and "common course of action" were eschewed.

In a nutshell, the *Rigid Steel Conduit* decision focused squarely upon a yet-to-be settled question of antitrust law. Must a record of economic evidence to demonstrate continued rigid adherence to a geographic pricing formula be supplemented by evidence of overt acts in order to find continued concerted action and non-compliance? If so, the developed concept of conscious parallel action to destroy geographic price competition would constitute an essential supplement to our antitrust arsenal. However, if we can assume that the courts would find illegal combination from the mere continued adherence to rigid formulas, the opinions of those economists and lawyers antipathetic to formula pricing differ over the wisdom of bringing such antitrust actions within the liberalized traditional framework of "implied understanding and concerted action" as against the novel concept of "conscious parallel action." Some believe that the legal concept of "agreement" has been overworked in antitrust, and that "agreement" should be retained for situations involving overt acts, while "conscious parallel action" demonstrating common purpose, as distinct from purely individual purpose, should be employed for attacking oligopolistic adherence to a pricing formula. Others, however, believe that the concept of "conscious parallel action" is treacherous and subject to abuse by commissions and courts which might carelessly examine the facts necessary for drawing inferences of common, as distinct from individual, purpose. The latter group would, therefore, prefer retention of the liberalized tradition of "implied understanding and concerted action" which forces the drawing of careful inferences.

31 Sage, *supra*, fn. 29, p. 334.

32 *Ibid.*, pp. 335–336.

sition that price discrimination was illegal only if it resulted in injuring competition. It explained that its interpretation of injury to competition in the context of geographic price discrimination was relatively conservative. Three reasons were offered why the Robinson-Patman Act would not bar unsystematic geographic price discrimination. First, efforts to get business from a competitor by sporadic price reductions were not regarded as illegally injurious to that competitor, unless the practice came to jeopardize the continuation of effective competition.[33] Hence, barring strategic discriminatory pricing by dominant firms, sellers were free to "beat" competition on freight absorbing sales. Secondly, sporadic and insignificant price concessions at particular destinations to particular buyers, although creating price differences between competing customers, would not constitute illegal injury to competition among buyers.[34] Hence, temporary price differences resulting from bargaining, at times of price changes, were not being ruled out. Thirdly, the Commission denied any intention of applying to geographic price discrimination cases the "reasonable possibility" criteria of injury to competition among buyers, merely because different mill nets were received by the seller. "The minimum determination of injury should be based upon ascertained facts that afford substantial probability that the discriminations, if continued, will result in extensive injury to competition.[35] The writer is convinced that the Commission's "Notice" correctly interpreted its administrative policy, and he knows of no Commission decision in any Robinson-Patman case where the findings of illegal discrimination have been based on evidence involving unsystematic discrimination.[36] Thus the Commission apparently left the door open for

[33] *Ibid.*, p. 342. [34] *Ibid.*, pp. 343–344. [35] *Ibid.*, pp. 344–345.

[36] Despite the failure of the Robinson-Patman statute to limit its prohibitions to price discriminations which substantially lessen competition, the Commission does not appear to have ever found violations of the Act where unsystematic price discriminations resulted in injury merely to "any person." Even the controversial *Detroit Standard Oil* case appears to have contained systematic discrimination — especially on the geographic level. The author's interpretation of the administrative (as distinct from judicial) history of the Robinson-Patman Act is shared by two of his colleagues, Professors Ralph Fuchs and Ivan Rutledge of Indiana Law School. In the writer's view, the most serious problem resulting from the administration of the Robinson-Patman Act has been the Commission's diversion of excessive antitrust resources from more basic anti-monopoly work.

extensive freight absorption, including the unsystematic reduction of delivered prices at particular destinations in the mill's natural market.

The Commission's "Notice" failed to stop legislation which would have seriously complicated antitrust attacks upon formula pricing,[37] but in June 1950 the President's veto did. However, during the spring of 1953, following an alteration in the membership of the Commission, the attitude of the majority toward the basing-point system evidently underwent a fundamental change, and the press responded lustily.[38] It was reported that most of the Commission supported proposed legislation modifying, first, the Robinson-Patman Act, so that "good faith" meeting of competition would constitute a complete defense to any charge of illegal price discrimination even where a substantial lessening of competition might result and second, indirectly, the Federal Trade Commission Act, so that independent freight absorption to meet competition, in the absence of conspiracy, could be legalized. In its explanation to Congress the Commission majority not only made no effort to define their concept of "individual freight absorption," but also failed to suggest whether or not they would infer conspiracy, in the absence of overt action, from market behavior which evidenced rigid adherence to a pricing formula on commercial or even government business.[39] The

[37] For a good discussion of the pitfalls of the vetoed legislation, see G. W. Stocking, *Basing-Point Pricing* (*supra VI*, fn. 8), pp. 181–184.

[38] *New York Times*, June 20, p. 21. "Change Reported in View on Pricing — F.T.C.'s New Attitude Toward Controversial Basing Point System Held Significant."

[39] Letter of June 16, 1953 to the Senate Committee on the Judiciary expressing the FTC majority and minority views on S. 1357 (Kefauver Bill) and S. 1377 (Capehart Bill), 83rd Congress (unpublished). The Capehart Bill would have added two new subsections to Section 2 of the Clayton Act.

"(g) In any proceeding involving an alleged violation of this section, it shall be a complete defence to a charge of discrimination in price . . . if the seller shows that his lower price . . . was made, regularly or otherwise, in good faith, to meet what the seller reasonably believed to be an equally low price of a competitor . . . *Provided,* That a seller shall not be deemed to have acted in good faith if he knew or should have known that the competitor's offer was unlawful.

"(h) It shall not be a violation of this Act for a seller acting independently, to sell at delivered prices, or to absorb freight regularly or otherwise to meet in good faith what the seller reasonably believed to be an equally low price of a competitor . . . Any price or pricing practice permitted by this or the preceding subsection shall not be prohibited under Section 5 of the Federal Trade Commission Act . . . *Provided* That nothing in either subsection shall make lawful any

bills were not enacted, but the implication to be drawn from the views of the Commission majority was that individual producers might "independently" meet the confirmed lower delivered prices of competitors, if there were no overt acts of cooperation, without fear of antitrust complications even if formula pricing were pursued in the process. As we shall see later, steel producers accepted the cue of the "New Commission" and restored the substance of a basing-point system during the lull in steel demand which began in the fall of 1953 and ran for a year. Subsequent anonymous comments by cement producers indicate that they were gratified by the apparent shift in governmental policy, although they would have preferred the adoption of permanent legislation.[40]

Most cement firms, however, seem to have continued to market most of their cement at prices reflecting full freight. Unlike the 1953–54 experience in steel, demand for cement has remained very strong relative to capacity, at least through the end of 1956. Although some modest increase in freight absorption probably occurred during 1953, it must have been rather insignificant judging by some of the anonymous comments of cement manufacturers as reported in January 1954:

> As long as we can continue to sell all our product without freight absorption, we will do so. When and if it becomes necessary to absorb freight to become competitive, we will do so.

---

contract, combination or conspiracy in restraint of trade or any act to monopolize, or conspiracy or attempt to monpolize, trade or commerce among the several States."

The Kefauver Bill would have amended section 2(b) of the Clayton Act.

"(b) . . . *Provided,* however, That unless the effect of the discrimination may be substantially to lessen competition or tend to create a monopoly in any line of commerce it shall be a complete defense for a seller to show that his lower price . . . was made in good faith to meet an equally low price of a competitor. . . ."

The minority Commissioners objected to the Capehart Bill not only because it weakened the price discrimination statute, but also because it modified the Federal Trade Commission Act and might have the effect of legalizing geographical pricing practices carried out as part of some systematic plan or formula. The minority urged adoption of the Kefauver Bill since "good faith" would remain a complete defence where the effect of a discrimination is limited to injury of competition with an individual concern, but it would not be a complete defence where the practice is of such proportions that the effect may be substantially to lessen competition or tend to create a monopoly."

40 W. E. Trauffer, "Cement Review and Forecast," *Pit and Quarry,* January 1954, p. 110.

. . . we have already found it necessary to some extent to meet in good faith the established lower delivered prices of competitors and will undoubtedly continue to do so to a limited extent in 1954.

We have lost some markets in the past by adhering strictly to an F.O.B. Plant Price Policy, but of course did not lose total volume because all of the product could be absorbed on an f.o.b. plant basis. We do, however, expect to absorb some transportation and, in fact, have done so to a minor degree . . .[41]

One major change in marketing form, if not substance, did occur in some regions of the country with respect to the transportation of cement. Although the American Trucking Association complained to Congress during the summer of 1949 that trucking was still being denied in eastern Pennsylvania and eastern New York,[42] and although it was reported in a trade journal that trucking was still refused during 1952 in the southern and central states,[43] it was also disclosed that trucking had substantially increased in California, where controlled trucking had been practiced during the thirties, and had been initiated in many new areas of the Middle West by 1953.[44] Undoubtedly the postwar increases in rail freight rates had encouraged some firms to offer truck service to reduce the destination costs on short hauls; and other firms in the immediate region found it expedient to follow suit. However, the published reports offered no indication as to whether the increased trucking moved at controlled freight rates, as had been the practice at mill and silo points along the Great Lakes during the thirties.[45] Were

[41] *Ibid.*

[42] Statement of Edgar S. Idol, general counsel, Hearings before the Select Committee on Small Business, H.R., 81st Cong., 1st sess., *Small Business Objections on Basing Point Legislation, Particularly S. 1008* (Washington, 1949), p. 106.

[43] W. E. Trauffer, "Cement Review and Forecast," *Pit and Quarry,* January 1953, pp. 119–120. Moreover, *Pit and Quarry* later reported that Lehigh's newly constructed mill although shipping only by rail had made "provision for loading trucks if this should become necessary." August 1953, p. 112.

[44] W. E. Trauffer, "Cement Review and Forecast," *Pit and Quarry,* January 1954, p. 113.

[45] An exception is provided by the relaxation of controls over buyer trucking at the mills in Colorado and Wyoming. In July 1949 the Commission filed a complaint alleging that since January 1947 Monolith and Ideal were violating the Robinson-Patman Act by charging truck buyers a premium of 20 cents per barrel over the posted (base) price at each mill, applicable on rail shipment. The Com-

buyers required to take truck shipments in carriers hauling at published rates, common carriers or trucks owned or under contract to cement manufacturers? Or, were buyers' trucks discriminated against by excessive mill price premiums so as virtually to exclude them? Were buyers thus being denied the opportunity of arranging their own truck transportation and hauling at uncertain costs, frequently substantially below the noncompetitive rates filed with state and national commerce commissions? Phantom freights were not the issue. The central question was this: Were cement manufacturers attempting to maintain definite destination prices by so controlling trucking that individual cement manufacturers could issue truck freight rate schedules to destinations served by the mills? If so, when demand eventually declines in relation to capacity and freight absorption is resumed on an extensive scale, a formula of clear-cut delivered prices will be available to prevent trucking from disrupting the basing-point system. To be sure, if buyers were permitted to arrange their own trucking, as repeatedly emphasized in previous chapters, uncertain transportation and destination costs would result, and a formula of destination prices within the economical trucking range would be destroyed. During the postwar boom when most firms were charging full freight to destination on most sales, such uncertain destination costs of course would have been immaterial. But if the industry expects a resumption of extensive interpenetration of markets in the future, it would have a great incentive to control trucking.

---

mission found, however, that between July 1948 and January 1949 the companies abandoned the practice complained of. Thereafter, the mills established a policy of selling only in carload lots in one loading operation (but more than one vehicle permitted) without premiums above the posted base price regardless of method of transportation. The companies expressly waived their right to attempt to justify the former price differentials since the practice objected to had been abandoned. See *Ideal Cement Co., Colorado Portland Division,* 47 FTC 1030 (1951) and *Monolith Portland Midwest Co.,* 47 FTC 1292 (1951).

It should be noted that these actions did not concern compliance with the FTC *Cement* order, which required, among other things, the cessation of any planned common course of action to restrict truck transportation. In fact, the new trucking policies of these firms probably continued to limit the impact of buyer trucking. Full carloads carry 400 barrels of cement, and if mills defined "carload lot" in terms of full carload (rather than minimum carload), only buyers who were prepared to send trucks capable of carrying (in a connected loading operation) at least 75 tons of cement would be serviced at the mill.

Department of Justice Closes the Denver Cement Case[46]

The Department of Justice had filed its own civil action against the cement industry in 1945, an action which was primarily directed toward effecting relief by removing controls over buyers' trucking. The complaint was similar to that of the Federal Trade Commission, although the emphasis was placed more clearly upon formula pricing and less upon freight absorption. The prayer for relief included provisions against collective activities substantially similar to those in the Commission order[47] and differed from that order only in two major respects. First, none of its provisions was concerned directly with price discrimination, and it could not possibly have been interpreted as challenging interpenetration of markets through freight absorption. Second, the Court was asked in Paragraph 6 to require *each defendant* to offer the buyer the choice between a delivered price and posted base price f.o.b. mill, with the buyer being given the opportunity to arrange his own transportation when purchasing at the posted mill price.[48] It should be stressed that Paragraph 6 was designed to destroy the delivered-price formula within the economical trucking range, while continuing the incentive for mills to absorb freight and interpenetrate markets on delivered-price sales. That is, mills were not to be required to offer to buyers' trucks mill prices equivalent to the mill nets received on freight absorbing delivered prices, a requirement which would have encouraged arbitrage and thereby have discouraged attempted market penetrations.

In all probability, filing of the 1945 Justice Department complaint reflected three sets of objectives. First, the Department wished to be ready to remedy a bad industrial situation were the Federal Trade Commission to lose its case in the courts. We must recall that only after 1947 was it clear that the Commission was not attempting to achieve a close approximation to non-discriminatory mill net pricing. Secondly, the Department strongly disagreed with the Commission concerning what

[46] Complaint, *United States* v. *Cement Institute,* Civil No. 1291, D. Colo., June 28, 1945. [47] *Ibid.,* pp. 21–22. [48] *Ibid.,* p. 20.

geographic pricing practices were most likely to induce a more competitive price behavior. The Department clearly believed in the merits of interpenetration of markets, particularly if some unsystematic freight absorption could be generated. Third, and most important, it was convinced that it had a potent provision in its request for relief which would be both extremely effective in breaking down formula pricing and *self-enforcing*. The Department was sure that relief which compelled each *individual* mill to offer to load and sell to any buyer's truck at the posted f.o.b. mill price would constitute not only effective relief,[49] but also relief which would be simple to enforce because no question of conspiracy would be involved.

It was agreed at the time when the Department of Justice filed its complaint that judicial proceedings would not begin until a final determination had been reached in the Commission's case. Following the reformulation of the Commission's case against formula pricing and affirmation of its re-interpreted order by the Supreme Court, Paragraph 6 of the Justice Department's request for relief, which would have required *each defendant* to offer the posted mill price to buyers' trucks, remained the only objective in the Justice suit not obtained. The defendants moved that the *Denver Cement* case be dismissed, but the Department objected and in 1949 the District Court denied the motion.[50] The Department of Justice continued its action in the belief that Paragraph 6 was necessary to procure an administratively workable order promising effective relief. Representatives both of the Department and of the cement producers have suggested to the writer that the Department was willing to settle for a consent decree along the lines of Paragraph 6,[51] but that the cement industry was determined in opposition. The trying

[49] Communication between the writer and Antitrust Division personnel has revealed that the Justice Department had a second objective in their attempt to free trucking from arbitrary controls. Destruction of the formula through uncertain destination costs constituted the primary purpose, but the Division also hoped that the concomitant elimination of protected dealer markets would increase competition at resale and indirectly increase pressures upon cement producers to make concessions.

[50] *United States* v. *Cement Institute, et al.*, 85 F. Supp. 344 (1949).

[51] The Department of Justice was evidently willing to modify the required posted mill price to buyers' trucks so as to allow for premiums which could be justified by cost differentials.

of the case, however, was delayed by the death of the trial judge and by the resignation of attorneys of the Department assigned to the case. Pre-trial conferences were finally scheduled in Denver for the summer of 1953, but the litigation ended on August 27, 1953 when the attorney general announced dismissal.[52]

In closing the *Denver Cement* case the attorney general announced that the Department of Justice had obtained information which indicated that practices in the cement industry had substantially changed. He noted that the Cement Institute had been disbanded, the circulation of freight rate books had been discontinued, substantial variation existed on bids for government contracts, and that the degree of uniformity in prices on sales to commercial buyers had materially lessened. He also asserted that "a majority of the cement companies now sell cement f.o.b. their mills, and permit transportation by truck, when requested to do so by the buyers." [53] Therefore he concluded that a court decree was no longer necessary and that the "existing order of the Federal Trade Commission, affirmed by the Supreme Court in 1948, appears to provide ample protection against a revival of the old practices." [54]

The writer contends that the closing of the Justice Department's *Denver Cement* case was a blunder, and that the accompanying public statement was at best misleading.[55] Given the prolonged cement boom which made the discontinuance of most freight absorption profitable, and given the objectives of political strategy which made the charging of full freight expedient, there is little wonder that the Justice Department inquiries disclosed a material reduction in the frequency of identical destination prices on commercial sales. It is strange, however, that the Department failed to understand or neglected to point out that formula pricing of the basing-point variety is primarily a reserve tool to be used to prevent a weakening in the price level whenever excess capacity develops. Furthermore,

52 *United States* v. *Cement Institute, CCH Trade Regulation Reporter,* Par. 66,090, (1953).

53 *Ibid.* 54 *Ibid.*

55 Two capable specialists in industrial organization, Joel B. Dirlam and Alfred E. Kahn, were deluded by the attorney general's announcement, citing its findings as constituting proof of the success of the FTC's Cement Order. See their *Fair Competition* (Ithaca, 1954), p. 128.

the Department made no effort to evaluate the reliability of its trucking information. It had never compiled a list of mills where buyers could send their trucks.[56] Nor had it investigated the transportation data on cement shipments collected regularly by the Bureau of Mines. Information assembled by the Bureau for 1952 shows that in nine out of nineteen cement producing districts there was little or no trucking.[57] Even these data, however, markedly understate manufacturers' restrictions on trucking in the other ten districts because in some districts there may have been trucking at a few but not all mills, and, even where trucking existed, it might have been controlled.

The author made a survey of cement manufacturers and of certain groups of commercial purchasers [58] during the year after the Department's case was closed. The findings showed that during the period 1953–54 uncontrolled trucking was, as a rule, being practiced only in the Rocky Mountain and Pacific Coast areas. Controlled trucking was prevalent from mills in western Pennsylvania, western New York, Ohio, Michigan, Indiana, Wisconsin, and southern Texas. In the remaining portions of the United States mills usually shipped cement by rail only. Of some 149 mills in the United States operated in August 1953 by 59 defendant companies in the Justice Department's suit [59] only

[56] Hoping to obtain information concerning the alleged emancipation of trucking in the cement industry, I requested from the Justice Department a list of mills to which buyers could send their trucks. The assistant attorney general, in a letter dated January 28, 1954, informed me that the Justice Department did not possess such information.

[57] Districts with little or no trucking of cement from cement mills during 1952 were the following: #1-eastern Pennsylvania and Maryland; #6-Illinois; #8-Alabama; #9-Tennessee; #10-Virginia, Georgia, Louisiana, South Carolina, and Mississippi; #11-Iowa; #13-Kansas; #14-western Missouri, Nebraska, Oklahoma, and Arkansas; #15-Texas (unpublished).

[58] Questionnaires were sent to purchasers (producers of ready-mix concrete and concrete products) in mill areas where cement manufacturers had been unwilling to respond or insufficiently clear in their responses to the questionnaires.

[59] The number of defendant companies had undergone some significant shrinkage since 1945 as attritions and acquisitions had occurred in the industry. In addition to 59 consolidated defendant companies, there were four other cement companies operating in the cement industry in the summer of 1953. Each of the non-defendant companies operated a single mill, resulting in a total of 63 companies and 153 mills. Of these four non-defendant companies, two practiced uncontrolled trucking, one controlled trucking, while the transportation policy of the fourth concern (owned by the state of South Dakota) has not been ascertained.

61 mills (41 per cent) shipped by truck, and only 25 mills (about 17 per cent) shipped by uncontrolled truck.

But let us examine the particular wording used in the Justice Department's assertion that "a majority of the cement companies now sell cement f.o.b. their mills, and permit transportation by truck, when requested to do so by the buyers."[60] Since the Department's announcement referred specifically to "companies" but ambiguously to "truck," how meaningful is the statement? Research, based on the period 1953–54, appears to support any one of the following different statements:

1. Thirty-eight of 59 defendant companies (64%) were allowing *at least some form* of truck transportation from *at least one* of their mills.
2. Thirty of 59 defendant companies (51%) were allowing *at least some form* of truck transportation from *each* of their mills.
3. Thirteen of 59 defendant companies (22%) were allowing *uncontrolled* truck transportation from *at least one* of their mills.
4. Eleven of 59 defendant companies (19%) were allowing *uncontrolled* truck transportation from *each* of their mills.

Evidently the attorney general had either relied upon unverified information concerning the trucking situation or been conveniently playing with words.

Non-discriminatory handling of buyers' trucking, as a consequence, is limited to a very few companies, and is found primarily in the Far West. Although buyers' trucking, if not controlled in the future, may increase price flexibility on the Pacific Coast, it will probably constitute a less significant factor in the Rocky Mountain region, whenever the eventual easing of demand comes, because the Ideal Cement Company, a multiple-plant concern, dominates that isolated area with about 75 per cent of the installed capacity. In other regions where uncontrolled trucking provided an important contribution to price flexibility during the early thirties, trucking is now either non-existent or controlled.

It may have been literally true, as the attorney general rea-

[60] *United States* v. *Cement Institute, CCH Trade Regulation Reporter,* Par. 66,090 (1953).

soned, that the standing order of the Federal Trade Commission *should* provide "ample protection against a revival of the old practices," but it did not follow that no court decree was necessary to require each individual defendant to sell cement at a posted mill price to buyers' trucks. The words of the preamble, "planned common course of action," conditioned all prohibitions of the Commission's cement order. The Old Commission (pre-1953) had failed to initiate action against respondents who had made no effort to discontinue refusing a mill price to buyers' trucks, a practice adopted earlier by concerted action. And the succeeding New Commission, apparently accepting a narrow interpretation of conspiracy ("planned common course of action"), was seemingly not prepared to challenge, in the absence of overt acts, either delivered-pricing systems evidencing a rigid adherence to formula pricing on commercial sales, or implementation of the formula through continued refusal to quote a genuine posted mill price to buyers' trucks. The Department of Justice, as a consequence, fumbled an opportunity to guarantee free trucking and thwart re-institution of the basing-point system.

That cement producers will attempt to reinstitute a basing-point system for commercial sales on a so-called "individual basis" can be gathered from the experience of the steel industry following September 1953. When the demand for steel fell off appreciably during a recession which lasted for more than a year, a modified basing-point system was resumed during the fall of 1953, in spite of a standing Commission consent order prohibiting "planned common course of action" to maintain such a system.[61] On commercial sales steel mills on an "individual basis" met the existing lower destination prices quoted by rivals, and there is every reason to believe that the resulting geographic pattern of prices on commercial sales reflected a formula of base price plus "published" freight to destination.[62] Every mill constituted a base mill, common freight rate factors were not being centrally distributed, and an estimated 53 per cent of steel

[61] *American Iron & Steel Institute,* 48 FTC 123, 152–54 (1951).

[62] L. Marengo, "The Basing-Point Decisions and the Steel Industry," *Papers and Proceedings,* AER, 45:509–522 (May 1955); S. M. Loescher, "Discussion," *ibid.,* 524–527.

tonnage was moved by trucks, but virtually all of the shipments were moving at "published" truck freight rates and in trucks controlled by steel producers.[63] It cannot be proved that buyers' private, leased, or contractor trucks were being discriminated against,[64] but the writer's survey of trucking in the cement industry suggests that such was the case. Furthermore, there is no indication that the New Commission initiated any compliance action against the resulting pattern of formula prices or the apparent continued "planned common course of action" to discriminate in sales against buyers' trucks. The steel industry's trouble-free experience in riding out the 1953–54 steel recession suggests that the cement industry will attempt to duplicate that experience sometime in the future, if there is no vigorous compliance activity on the part of the Federal Trade Commission.

Capacity Expansion 1948–1956

The uncertainty induced by the *Cement* decision and the possibility that a courageous Commission might some day challenge controlled trucking and the reinstitution of formula pricing, have undoubtedly contributed in some degree to two notable patterns of capacity expansion during the boom period following 1948. First, most new mills[65] have been constructed in areas remote from existing mills in the industry, and the deficit capacity situation of the South, described in Chapter VI, had been substantially corrected by 1952. Second, the reckless capacity expansion which characterized the latter twenties, described in Chapter V, has been replaced by a much more cautious expansion during the current boom.

Capacity expansion has come in two rather distinct phases since 1948, a gradual one through 1954 and a rapid one since then. Although most of it has continued to come from the enlargement of existing plant facilities, eighteen new mills have been or should by the end of 1957 be put in operation. Of the

[63] *Ibid.*, pp. 526–527.

[64] Continental Can Co.'s officer in charge of purchasing tin plate, however, informed me in December 1954 that he was certain that steel manufacturers would refuse to load trucks sent to steel mills by his company.

[65] New mills are defined to include only those mills constructed at locations new to the constructing firm, and thus exclude mill additions which duplicate or replace facilities at an existing mill location of the constructing firm.

ten new mills completed between 1948 and 1954, only one has been located close to existing rivals. That mill was built in the deficit South, close to Birmingham, by a crushed stone producer who branched out into the cement industry. Appreciable freight savings should have resulted in the local market areas of the other nine mills located in southwestern Virginia, eastern South Carolina,[66] northeastern Florida, southern Alabama, central Mississippi, southeastern Louisiana, southern Texas, west central Texas, and southern Arizona. Although the decentralization pattern has been less marked for the eight new mills constructed since 1954 (in operation or scheduled to be in operation by the end of 1957), most of them are located in areas separated from existing capacity. The five areas receiving their first cement mills are southern Florida, southwestern Louisiana, southeastern Texas, northwestern Ohio, and southeastern Wisconsin. The other three mills are in deficit markets close to existing mills, two in southern California and one in Detroit.

Nine of the eighteen new mills have been placed in the nation's former major deficit producing area, the South, previously defined to include Alabama, Florida, Georgia, Louisiana, Mississippi, North Carolina, South Carolina, Tennessee, and Virginia. During the period 1948–52 when six of the new plants were installed in the South, southern theoretical capacity increased 33.3 per cent (28,500,000 to 38,000,000 barrels of annual capacity).[67] Moreover, whereas consumption of cement in the southern states had greatly exceeded total shipments of southern mills during the period 1940–48 (see Table 9, page 206 of Chapter VI), cement consumption in the southern states by 1952 (33,800,000, barrels) was almost equaled by total shipments of southern mills (32,400,000 barrels).[68] Undoubtedly the decade of deficit productive capacity during the forties, combined with the continuing boom in southern cement demand, would have led to a substantial expansion of capacity in that region, even had the basing-point system persisted without challenge.

66 Construction of the South Carolina mill was begun prior to the *Cement* decision.

67 See Table 6, pp. 168–69, and U. S. Bureau of Mines, *Minerals Yearbook, 1952* (1955), Vol. I, p. 254.

68 *Ibid.*, pp. 249, 267.

But the uncertainties unleashed by the *Cement* decision most assuredly strengthened the incentives for making prudent decisions in locating new capacity and induced a more rapid expansion of southern capacity. Should greater flexibility in marketing practices and pricing characterize the period after the boom, wise locational decisions would prove all the more vital.

Expansion of cement producing capacity in relation to demand in the period following the *Cement* decision has been exceedingly moderate in comparison with that during the twenties (see Table 6). Both 1923 and 1948 were years of booming demand and tight supply, but whereas capacity expanded at an average annual rate of 8½ per cent between 1923–28, the corresponding figure for 1948–53 was only about 2¾ per cent. Consequently, although production increased about 25 per cent in each of these five-year periods, only 80 per cent of practical capacity was being utilized during 1928 while in 1953 the figure was 100 per cent. Furthermore, accompanying the modest decline in demand between 1928–29 was an additional 6 per cent increase in capacity, whereas the increase in demand between 1953–54 was attended by an increase in capacity of less than 2½ per cent. It must be recalled, however, that during the 1948–54 period production increased appreciably faster than did rated practical capacity. The gradual alleviation of supply shortages in complementary industries and the marked expansion in storage facilities permitted the utilization of practical capacity to rise from approximately 90 per cent in 1948 to 101 per cent in 1953 and 104 per cent in 1955. Nevertheless, demand grew so fast during those years that tight supplies and frequent shortages characterized the period. The sluggishness of the cement industry in expanding capacity at this time was criticized by many groups, including one of the trade journals serving the industry.[69] Only since 1954 has there been a rapid rate of capacity expansion, paralleling the rate of the twenties. During 1955 the rate was about 6 per cent, and it has been estimated that it would increase to about 8½ per cent during 1957.[70] But

[69] Editorial, "The Cement Problem," *Pit and Quarry*, August 1953, p. 145.

[70] W. E. Trauffer, "Cement — 1956 Tenth Consecutive Record Year," *Pit and Quarry*, January 1957, pp. 138, 144. Final capacity data for 1956 will not be reported by the Bureau of Mines until 1958.

given the spirited growth of demand, even this delayed but relatively rapid rate of capacity expansion failed to eliminate shortages during 1955-56. Provisional data suggest that practical capacity was undoubtedly operated above 100 per cent in 1956.[71] Moreover, in view of the 20,000,000 additional barrels estimated to be required in 1957 for the federal highway program,[72] the expected expansion of 27,000,000 barrels of practical capacity during the year may prove insufficient to eliminate shortages. And this, too, despite the fears reportedly held by cement executives that overcapacity was developing.[73] Consequently, the conservative expansion of the cement industry has continued to come under fire.[74]

The cautiousness of the cement industry has undoubtedly reflected the pessimism persisting since the overwhelming cyclical excess capacity during the Great Depression of the thirties, and the commonly held belief that the postwar construction boom would surely subside, or at least fail to sustain a rapid rate of expansion. But to the *Cement* decision must go part of the credit.[75] Uncertain concerning the nature of restrictive marketing practices which might be legally pursued if idle capacity should develop, and faced with the possibility that vigorous enforcement of the Commission order might induce effective price competition, the cement industry could not afford to expand as recklessly as it had during the twenties. At that time there was reasonable assurance that imperfect collusion, based on the rules of the basing-point system, would enable the industry to stabilize prices and profits, come what might. After 1948 a real possibility existed that a slackening of the growth of demand relative to growth in capacity might be accompanied by an erosion of the price level and a period of losses. On the whole it would appear that the increase in caution has been of benefit. Time may prove that the industry has been excessively pessimistic in gauging the

71 *Ibid.*

72 This estimate was prepared by the Bureau of Public Roads. See Select Committee on Small Business, H.R., 84th Cong., 2d sess., Report No. 2965, *The Portland Cement Industry: Supply–Demand Outlook,* p. 25.

73 *Wall Street Journal,* March 5, 1956, p. 1.

74 See e.g., Select Committee on Small Business, fn. 72, above.

75 Some would say "blame," emphasis being placed upon the boom period prices, profits, and shortages. But I believe that such a view is mistaken.

long-run growth of cement demand. But in a competitive system based upon decentralized decision making, it is generally assumed that fewer mistakes will be made when powerful incentives, including the penalty of losses for mistakes once made, condition the decision-making process.

As reported by the National City Bank, profits for twenty-seven to thirty-two cement producers during the period 1947–55 were very good, and in every year except 1948 and 1951 exceeded, usually substantially, the average rate of return after taxes on net worth for all manufacturing concerns surveyed by the bank.[76] Only during the period of price control (1951–52)

Year	*Net Income after Taxes as a Percentage of Net Assets*	
	Cement	*Total Manufacturing*
1948	16.6	18.9
1949	18.1	13.8
1950	18.2	17.1
1951	14.1	14.4
1952	14.1	12.3
1953	14.7	12.5
1954	18.8	12.4
1955	20.3	15.0

was the profit rate for this sample of the cement industry as low as 14 per cent, and in four of the eight years it exceeded 18 per cent. However, inflation has probably distorted the rate of return on the *replacement* value of net worth in the cement industry far more than in manufacturing as a whole. The useful life of a cement plant is long, exceeding twenty-five years, and an unusually high ratio of capital investment to sales prevails in cement manufacturing.[77] Moreover, the cement industry has been

[76] National City Bank, *Monthly Letter on Business and Economic Conditions,* April issues, 1949–56.

[77] The after-taxes rate of return on investment might have been as low as 6 per cent in 1954 for a new efficient size mill constructed in an "average" area where the industry leaders operated and which realized the same "average" mill prices as the leaders. This statement is based on data appearing in *The Portland Cement Industry: Supply-Demand Outlook,* Select Committee on Small Business, H.R., 84th Cong., 2d sess., Report No. 2965 (1955), pp. 37–41. Excluding Universal Atlas, profits after taxes for the next six largest cement producers averaged 40 cents per barrel, when the net property account for these six firms averaged $1.94 per barrel of rated annual capacity and the net price per barrel averaged $2.71. The House Committee reported that the estimated construction costs of ten companies planning new mills averaged $5.71 per barrel, and that no apparent correlation existed between the size of mill to be constructed and the estimated cost per barrel. Allowing for working capital, it was estimated that the cost of constructing and

operating at virtually full capacity throughout the entire period. The rate of return needs to be high during periods of boom to compensate for losses which will develop during periods of cyclical declines if society succeeds in inducing effective price competition.

In truth, the industry appears to have been administering a moderate price policy (possibly much too moderate) throughout most of the postwar boom, preferring to ration short supplies rather than to allow price, even approximately, to clear the market.[78] The probable explanation for this policy is that leading firms have sought to take advantage of the long-period elasticity of demand for their product with respect to competitive building materials and to hold on to the greatly enlarged markets for cement in the highway field as well as those which have developed in concrete block and reinforced, including prestressed, concrete construction. The administered, moderate price policy has probably not been pursued to discourage political harassment since the cement industry does not constitute a major political target during boom periods; shortages resulting from non-price rationing would produce greater political repercussion than would higher prices and profits. Nor has the moderate pricing policy been employed to deter entry, given the unsatiable demand at prevailing prices which eases access to markets. Moreover, new firms would be free to charge premium prices and, if the entrants were to locate in areas remote from present mill capacity, ill will would scarcely result in the long run from establishing a base-mill price higher than that of the distant suppliers.

---

operating a new mill would run about $6.71. Of course, the savings in variable manufacturing costs for a new mill might enlarge the after-tax profit of 40 cents per barrel, although the president of Lehigh has contended that such savings would be offset by the substantially higher depreciation charges. (Joseph S. Young, *A Brief Perspective of the Cement Industry*, a paper presented before the Financial Analysts of Philadelphia, November 3, 1955, p. 6.) The assumption that new firms would realize prices similar to the "average" price of the leaders is indeed questionable. By locating in a deficit supply area remote from existing mills, the new mill could simultaneously reduce destination prices in its local area and realize mill nets above the "average" of the leaders. Moreover, given the rather general cement shortage, a new mill located in almost any area could quote premium mill prices for the duration of the shortage, albeit at some sacrifice of consumer good will.

[78] See references cited in fns. 3, 4, and 73, of this chapter.

The substantial saving in freight charges to consumers could have been partly shared with the latter. The fact that no newly organized firm entered the cement industry between 1948 and 1956 (though one is scheduled to begin production by 1957) and the further fact that only two lateral new entrants from other industries appeared during the prolonged boom will be taken into consideration later.

Concentration, Mergers, and Entrance

Published data on concentration on a relevant, regional market basis are not available, but we do know that concentration on a national basis has increased to some extent since 1937 when the Federal Trade Commission filed its complaint against the Cement Institute. As shown in Chapter IV, the five largest cement producers possessed 39.0 per cent and the ten largest 54.5 per cent of total national theoretical capacity in 1937. Taking into consideration the corporate acquisitions made through June 1955 but employing their 1952 recorded capacities, the five largest cement producers possessed approximately the same percentage of the national total in 1952 (38.5 per cent), while the share of the largest ten had risen to 58.4 per cent. See Table 10.

If the unknown effects of new capacity constructed after 1952 are excluded, the leading firms which grew most rapidly during the period between 1937 and June 1955 were among those below the top three. The modest increase in the percentage of national capacity controlled by the ten leading producers reflects partly the outright attrition of a few independents prior to the end of World War II, but primarily it show the effects of acquisitions of independents by chains ranking below the top.

Several mergers have taken place both preceding and following the Celler Anti-Merger Amendment (December 1950). Between 1937 and 1950 the acquisitions represented mainly geographic diversification, but usually involved also a diminution of competition in an interregional market. Ideal, with two of its mills in southern Oklahoma and southwestern Arkansas, acquired Gulf at Houston, Texas, in 1940. Marquette, with a mill in north central Illinois, secured Hawkeye at Des Moines, Iowa, in 1940;

Table 10
Capacity of the Ten Largest Producers of Cement in the United States, 1952

Company [a]	1952 [b] Theoretical capacity (bbls.)		1952 Percentage of total
Universal Atlas	33,000,000		
Lehigh	22,000,000		
Lone Star	21,100,000		
Ideal	19,950,000		
General; Consolidated [c]	16,150,000		
Leading five		112,200,000	38.5
Penn-Dixie	15,170,000		
Marquette	12,650,000		
Alpha	11,100,000		
Huron; Wyandotte [d]	10,000,000		
Medusa	9,100,000		
Second five		58,020,000	19.9
Leading ten		170,220,000	58.4
Total for industry		291,680,000	100.0

[a] Includes the 1952 capacity ratings of firms acquired through June 1955.
[b] All theoretical capacity figures are from the *Pit and Quarry* Publications' map of portland cement plants in the United States prepared in November 1952. Total capacity reported by the U.S. Bureau of Mines for 1952 was only 279,900,000 bbls.
[c] Both firms are part of the former Cowham Engineering Co. Group, and have the same officers and headquarters.
[d] Wyandotte and Huron are commonly owned.

and, with another mill located in southeastern Missouri, in 1947 it added Hermitage at Nashville and Cumberland at Chattanooga, both in Tennessee. Universal Atlas, two of whose mills were near Chicago and Pittsburgh, in 1945 acquired Wabash near Dayton, Ohio. Finally, Penn-Dixie, with mills in the Lehigh Valley, in 1948 secured West Penn near Pittsburgh.

Following the Celler Amendment each of three of the concerns just mentioned acquired two additional cement producers. During 1954 Marquette obtained Southern States in northern Georgia, near its 1947 acquisition at Chattanooga, and also the Superior Cement Division mill of New York Coal Sales Company near Portsmouth, Ohio, an interregional competitor of the same mill. Penn-Dixie's acquisition of Petoskey in 1954 appears to have constituted solely geographic diversification, since the new mill in the northern portion of the lower Michigan peninsula was remote from any of its other mills. However, its addition, in 1955, of Federal near Buffalo, New York, eliminated an important interregional competitor of its 1948 acquisition in western Pennsylvania, and a lesser competitor, via water, of the Petoskey mill. In 1951 Ideal obtained Pacific with two mills in northern California and one in southern Oregon. This large addition not only provided geographic diversification but also eliminated an important interregional competitor of Ideal's mill near Salt Lake, Utah. Four years later Ideal acquired Spokane, located near Spokane, Washington, one of the very few interregional competitors of its mill at Trident, Montana. But later in the same year, when Ideal attempted to secure Superior, with two mills in western Washington, the Department of Justice threatened to bring injunction proceedings; and the Celler Amendment received its first, and successful, application in the cement industry.[79] A distinct series of significant acquisitions was initiated at the close of 1954 when American-Marietta, a prime example of conglomerate growth through mergers, added the first cement mill to its long and diverse line of building materials. After obtaining a mill at Martinsburg, West Virginia, from Standard Lime and Cement, American-Marietta acquired the new Alabama mill of Southern Cement in 1956 and Dragon Cement (formerly called Lawrence) which owned one mill in the Lehigh Valley

[79] *Pit and Quarry,* June 1955, p. 15. However, Lone Star acquired Superior early in 1957. Geographic diversification characterized this acquisition, since Lone Star had always operated east of the Rocky Mountains. Nevertheless, the acquisition may have prevented price competition in the Pacific Northwest since Superior was reported to have been closed down for three months for lack of orders (adhering to the basing-point formula?). See *Pit and Quarry,* February 1957, p. 26.

Moreover, several significant cement mergers have occurred since this manuscript was submitted for publication. Acquisitions eliminated the two remaining independents in the state of Washington, leaving but one in the Pacific Northwest. Northwestern and Olympic, which operated in the Seattle territory, were acquired respectively by Ideal (which had recently acquired one mill in western Washington and another in southern Oregon) and Permanente (which operated a distributing silo in the port of Seattle). A simultaneous merger of three widely separated cement firms resulted in the formation of one more major, geographically diversified chain in the industry; eighteen million barrels of annual capacity of Riverside (southern California), Peerless (Detroit, Michigan) and Hercules (Lehigh Valley) were consolidated to form the American Cement Corporation. Finally, the Flintkote Company, a producer of a broad line of building materials, extended its diversification by acquiring Kosmos Cement with a mill near Louisville, Kentucky. This last acquisition also contains elements of vertical integration since it is reported that Flintkote plans to use some of the acquired cement production in its asbestos products plants in New Orleans, Louisiana, and Chicago Heights, Indiana.

and one in Maine. Although only the Lehigh Valley and Martinsburg mills were engaged in inter-area competition with each other, the effect of the series of mergers was the creation of one more strong chain in the industry without increasing the alternative sources of cement supply which would have developed had American-Marietta achieved its desire for diversification by building new mills.

Where relatively few mills exist, a reduction in the number of interregional competitors would ordinarily constitute a substantial lessening of competition, a lessening which the Celler Amendment was clearly designed to prevent. But three other potentially serious consequences appear to flow from continued acquisitions in the cement industry, even when geographic or product diversification is the main consequence. First, the smaller cement producers (possessing but one or two mills) constitute the firms most likely to violate customary marketing rules — either because of less liquid positions, or a less extensive salesmanship program, or a slighter sense of mutual obligation to uphold established trade practices. As described in Chapter IV, the smaller producers were usually the ones who behaved independently until merged or disciplined by the imposition of punitive bases. By contrast, the chains were the strongest adherents to "ethical" marketing policies. The *Cement* decision should have the effect of minimizing the threatened application of punitive bases at least of the old style. But to the extent that independents are gradually acquired, fewer firms remain which might voluntarily exercise the greater freedom to market unsystematically. This consideration alone makes the acquisition of independent producers undesirable, even when there are no elements of geographically overlapping product markets.

Second, an equally important consequence of geographic or product diversification through acquisition is the substantial lessening of potential competition. In Chapter II it was shown that during recent years approximately $12,000,000 has been required to establish a new cement mill of efficient size. Certainly this requirement, although far from prohibitive, erects at least a moderate barrier to entry for a newly promoted company. Under the circumstances, lateral entry by a cement producer located in another geographic region or by a producer of a related product seems most likely.[80] Ordinarily a cement producer who desires to diversify geographically finds acquisition the easiest method of gaining access to a new territory. But this method, although possibly beneficial for the acquiring firm, creates fewer social benefits than self-growth which provides an important additional source of supply. Not only would geographic or product expansion by construction of a new cement mill add an additional firm in a marketing region, but frequently disturbances to established market shares would prevent rivalry from settling down into a routine pattern. A long-pursed company will, of course, frequently modernize and increase capacity at the newly acquired mill, thus providing some compensating advantages. But on the whole, competitive pressures are more likely to be promoted when expansion is limited to self-growth. Whether the Celler Amendment can eventually be made to prevent the acquisitions which substantially lessen potential competition is uncertain.

Third, geographic or product diversification through acquisition also increases the disciplinary power of leading chain mills over more specialized firms, without providing the compensatory social advantages of diversification through self-growth. The development of large, geographically diversified cement firms able to alter selectively their posted base-mill prices in various producing regions for disciplinary purposes (a practice difficult to

[80] Of the eighteen new mills constructed since 1948 (including those under construction and scheduled for completion by 1957), only one was developed by a newly promoted enterprise. Two were constructed by lateral entrants from related industries (one by a crushed stone producer near Birmingham, Ala., and one by an oil well cementing firm near Corpus Christi, Tex.) and two by cement producers invading new marketing territory. (Giant, a Lehigh Valley producer built a plant in South Carolina; Ideal, a Rocky Mountain and Southwest cement chain, one at Mobile, Ala.) The other thirteen mills were constructed in deficit areas by firms which had previously marketed in most of the new mill's territory from mills located at a greater distance.

Moreover, more recent trade reports indicate that eight of the twelve new mills completed or scheduled for completion during 1958–59 were constructed by a cement firm already marketing in most of its new mill's territory. Of the four new mills which increased the number of supply sources in all of their marketing territories, one (near Vicksburg, Mississippi) constitutes entry by a completely new firm; one (near Detroit, Michigan), an invasion of the American market by Swiss interests who operate numerous cement plants throughout the British Commonwealth; and two, vertical integration (in the Hudson Valley, New York, by a metropolitan New York crushed stone and ready-mix producer, and near Texarkana, Arkansas, by a natural gas producer).

counter effectively through the Sherman and Clayton acts) may very well deter not only unsystematic marketing behavior by existing firms but also potential entry by newly organized firms. Actually, the growth by acquisition of Universal Atlas, Lone Star, and Lehigh, as well as Alpha, Penn-Dixie, and Ideal, during the pre-1930 period has probably been a much more significant factor in deterring current invasions by newly organized firms than the increased diversification by merger of Marquette, Penn-Dixie, Ideal, and American-Marietta since 1940.

The period since World War II has seen only one newly promoted cement firm, scheduled to begin production by the end of 1957,[81] in spite of the prolonged period of boom and tight supplies since 1947. By contrast, a host of newly organized firms entered the cement industry during the twenties. Some explanation must be attempted. In all probability new firms have been discouraged from entering the cement industry by the same factors which deterred large capacity expansions by existing firms: First, fears that the postwar boom would not persist, coupled with knowledge of the effects of the Great Depression upon capacity utilization in the cement industry, and second, uncertainties concerning the effect of the *Cement* decision upon price stabilization practices, should there be another recession. In addition, although the capital requirements for entry are not prohibitive for a new firm, the effect of the progressive income tax has undoubtedly made the subscription of approximately $12,000,000 of risk capital more difficult than the $5,000,000 required during the twenties for a comparable mill. Yet the fact that one or more large diversified cement producers exists in virtually every section of the country (primarily a development of the late twenties) has probably contributed in some part to the lack of new firms during the recent boom.

That there has been no great outbreak of new firms, such as characterized the twenties, has of course been beneficial because a repetition of wasteful capacity has been prevented. Yet

81 Several announcements have appeared in the trade journals during the past five years disclosing plans of new entrants to establish mills in various sections of the country. Only one of these is scheduled to be in operation by the end of 1957, the Texas Portland Cement Co. at Orange, Tex. The others have thus far been unable to solve financing difficulties.

the almost complete absence of new firms has been equally disadvantageous. Not only has an opportunity (albeit a minor one) been lost to diffuse economic power in its broad political and social sense at the same time that the alternative sources of supply for buyers were increasing, but, and possibly more importantly, there has also been a reduced chance for the emergence of the unpredictable new entrant which supplies a necessary energizing and innovating force in an established industry.

It still seems that the *Cement* decision has facilitated the potential entrance of socially useful new firms. The mere judicial chastisement of the use of the punitive base should make it somewhat easier for new firms to gain access to markets through the adoption of less systematic pricing practices and less conventional marketing devices. Future disciplinary action, if undertaken, will have to be more oblique. But one can scarcely expect an epoch-making Supreme Court decision which was directed against a subtle form of imperfect, but effective, collusion to alter substantially the conditions of entry.

Policy Recommendations

The basing-point formula was primarily designed to stabilize the industry's price level in times of excess capacity. Because of a prolonged boom in cement which has yet to abate it is impossible now (January 1957) to tell how effective the *Cement* decision will prove in dispelling the imperfect collusion inherent in implementing and adhering to a geographic pricing formula.[82] The

[82] More recent economic data (April 1959), however, suggest that the cement industry stabilized itself admirably during the mild cement recession of 1957–58, when a modest level of excess capacity developed in the industry for the first time in a decade. As compared with 1956 when the industry, after taxes, earned 20.6 per cent on net worth (according to the First National City Bank sample) while operating at 100.8 per cent of practical capacity, the industry still managed to reap 15.9 per cent in 1957 and 16.0 per cent in 1958 while operating, respectively, at 86.9 and (an estimated) 86 per cent of practical capacity. From an all-time high of 312,200,000 barrels of domestic cement production in 1956, production declined to 292,900,000 in 1957 and 306,500,000 in 1958. Domestic cement practical capacity continued to rise from 309,700,000 barrels in 1956 to 337,000,000 in 1957 and an estimated (on the basis of theoretical capacity reports of the January 1959 issue of *Pit and Quarry*) 355,500,000 in 1958, undoubtedly undertaken in anticipation of a more rapid expansion of the Federal highway building program than actually occurred. Despite the emergence of this moderate amount of excess capacity, competitive pressures to reduce price were readily re-

diminution in overt cooperative activity, including the organized distribution of common freight books, should constitute some real advantage. In government business, the hazard of identical sealed bidding in accordance with the basing-point formula should greatly lessen its use, and even on some commercial sales non-identical bidding may be followed. When excess capacity again develops and sellers attempt to re-establish trade connections in freight disadvantaged territory, the reshuffling of buyer-seller relationships *may* also lead to some unsystematic dumping, and counter unsystematic price reductions. Yet the experience of the steel industry in 1953–54 suggests that a practice of so-called "individual" meeting of competition will perpetuate formula pricing on commercial sales.

In view of this situation seven policy recommendations are here offered that should discourage the potential return of imperfect collusion in the cement industry. Two of them call for immediate antitrust action to compel compliance with the spirit of the standing order where compliance has been resisted, so that it will be impossible for firms to reinstitute adherence to a geographic pricing formula when downward pressures on price are again created. Three recommendations concern continuous surveillance once freight absorption has been resumed on a large scale. The final two do not directly concern the *Cement* decision, but rather the broader public policies related to market structures and market demand.

1. Most importantly the Commission should act against controlled trucking. In most regions of the country respondents have failed to take affirmative steps to discontinue the past concerted action of refusing to quote the posted mill-base price to buyers' trucks. Paragraphs 2(a) and 2(b) of the *Cement* order prohibit the continuation of such "planned common course of action"; and the removal of discrimination against transportation by buyers' trucks would destroy a formula of known destination prices within an economical trucking range of cement mills.

---

sisted. Indeed, the average realized mill price continued to rise — from $3.05 per barrel in 1956 to $3.18 in 1957 and $3.25 in 1958. Moreover, between 1957 and 1958 only the Georgia-Florida producing district was reported by the Bureau of Mines to have experienced a decline in average realized mill price, and this decline was less than two per cent.

2. The Commission should insure that respondents actually discontinue the concerted action which denied direct sales to contractors when purchasing cement for large construction projects located within cities and towns. Paragraph 2(m) of the order prohibits any continued "planned common course of action" to classify buyers for direct sale. The Commission staff had failed to explain the reason for the denial of direct sales to large contractors, but evidence in the *Record* indicates quite clearly that the scattered, sporadic purchases of contractors for large construction jobs gave them unusual bargaining power for obtaining unsystematic price concessions. To be sure, resumption of direct sales to large contractors might not constitute quite the formula-weakening force of earlier decades, since many may find it more economical to continue to patronize the ready-mix concrete concerns for city construction jobs. Nevertheless, the writer believes that contractors handling large construction projects in cities and towns are still denied the opportunity of purchasing cement directly. It is therefore recommended that the Commission investigate this matter and demand that respondents comply with the standing order in regions where contractors purchasing in quantity continue to be denied direct sales.

3. The Commission should maintain a close watch over sealed cement bids and guard against any emerging patterns. When freight absorption is resumed on an extensive scale, the Commission should move quickly against any repeated identical quotations which constitute overwhelming evidence of agreement. Cooperating government agencies and the Commission itself should be on the watch for suspicious bidding patterns which suggest planned rotation of low bids or limited quota bids at staggered prices. When private construction activity lessens, governmental purchasing makes up a larger percentage of the total cement market, and price competition on governmental business may be expected to spread to unsystematic pricing in the commercial sector, as frequently happened during the early thirties.

4. The Commission should also be prepared to move quickly if complaints are received concerning alleged imposition of punitive bases or of more subtle forms of disciplinary discriminatory

pricing when freight absorption is resumed on a substantial scale. Admittedly, care will be necessary to distinguish between discriminatory pricing which contributes to competitive pressures and that designed to coerce mavericks into systematic pricing. But prompt investigation should at least deter dominant firms from undertaking the flagrant forms of disciplinary price discrimination applied during the early thirties, and should reduce the future threat and effectiveness of dominant firms in their attempts to police the geographic price structure.

The first four recommendations offered to the Commission are primarily concerned with restoring and preserving an environment more conducive to uncertainty in marketing and to unsystematic marketing behavior. The writer is convinced that these four policing activities by the Commission, in line with the terms of the order in the *Cement* case, should suffice to induce unsystematic pricing and a more flexible price level in the cement industry. However, in the event that they prove insufficient to destroy formula pricing, at least on commercial sales outside the economical trucking radius, a fifth remedy is available to the Commission.

5. As a last resort, the Commission could make an outright attack on failure to cease rigid adherence to a geographic price formula. In other words, it could voice the positive injunction "compete!" — make some real effort to "beat" competition within the natural market, or within a rival's market. Resort to this form of remedy may prove necessary outside the trucking radius of a mill, and even in all areas, if no action is taken to implement the first recommendation — to re-institute uncontrolled trucking. But because of the administrative weaknesses in the enforcement procedure (as described in Chapter VII) principal reliance should not be placed upon this technique.

6. Further mergers in the cement industry should not be permitted, save under the most extenuating circumstances. As previously discussed in this chapter, acquisitions involving pure geographic diversification are believed by the writer ordinarily to lessen potential competition almost as seriously as does increased concentration in local or inter-regional markets. If the current Celler Amendment is insufficient to halt further acqui-

sitions in the industry, a new anti-merger statute seems called for.

As discussed in Chapter II, large multiple-plant cement firms seem to the writer to possess little, if any, social cost advantage over the efficient size single plant and smaller chain operators. Therefore, without sacrificing efficiency, the dissolution of the larger chains, as well as the separation of Universal Atlas from its parent United States Steel, would undoubtedly contribute to a more competitive market structure, thus minimizing the policing job of the Commission. But for three reasons, no immediate antitrust restructuring is urged. First, under present judicial interpretation of the Sherman Act, the prospect for successful dissolution or divorcement in the cement industry is dim. Second, in terms of social priorities, the need to deconcentrate market structures is much greater in other industries, including some using a delivered-price formula, such as steel. Third, the implementation of the first four policy recommendations, supplemented by the fifth recommendation when, where, and if necessary, should be sufficient to achieve effective price competition in the cement industry, despite a large degree of significant concentration in regional markets and the relative disparity of power positions. However, only time and vigorous enforcement of the *Cement* order will tell.

7. Finally, if the foregoing reasoning is correct, that vigorous enforcement of the injunctions of the Supreme Court's *Cement* decision will promote unsystematic pricing and a fairly flexible price level, it is extremely important that the federal government also promote a vigorous counter-cyclical monetary and fiscal policy, including a public works program. The level of construction activity with its derived demand for building materials must be kept at tolerably high levels. The maintenance of demand for cement will keep competitive pressures from plunging prices to bankruptcy-inducing levels for prolonged periods. Private industrial groups in a democratic society can be expected to tolerate competitive insecurity only so long before trying to win legislative exemption from the antitrust laws. Substitute social controls, be they motor carrier style public utility regulation or NRA style self-regulation, have rarely been saluted for their

spirited dedication to the public, let alone consumer, interest. Yet by an apparently paradoxical reasoning, spirited antitrust action directed toward increasing competitive behavior may in the future constitute a force indispensable for guaranteeing adequate use of public measures to stabilize national income and demand for building materials at reasonably high levels.

Today public works programs are accepted in principle as a major instrument in counter-cyclical public policies, yet there exists a real danger that they will be "too little and too late." Many leaders in the business community apparently still abhor any substantial increase in governmental intervention, even for counter-cyclical purposes.[83] Such a view is most likely in industries where stabilization schemes of defensive monopoly enable firms to protect themselves reasonably well from the severe price and income insecurity which would otherwise accompany declines in demand. However, if through antitrust action competitive pricing pressures were to attend such declines, income insecurity could be ameliorated only by measures which increased demand for the product. In this situation many business leaders otherwise apathetic or antipathetic might be glad to give political support to ambitious compensatory governmental programs aimed at stabilizing construction activity and national income at relatively high levels.

[83] For an example, see *Business Week*, April 3, 1954, p. 28 which describes the refusal of Secretary of Treasury (and former steel industry executive) George M. Humphrey to agree that governmental deficits were desirable during the depression of the 1930's, while testifying before the Senate Finance Committee in 1954. For an explanation, J. K. Galbraith has suggested, "Even though the businessman might profit in a narrow pecuniary sense from the new role of government there was no chance that his prestige would survive intact," since "To share the prestige of decision-making is to lose prestige." *American Capitalism* (Cambridge, Mass., 1952), pp. 84–85.

Appendix

Works Cited

Index

Appendix

Portland Cement Plants in the United States, 1956

Source: *Pit and Quarry* publications.

Producing Plants

* Total annual capacity of all plants operated by this company.
† Plant scheduled to be completed during 1956.

ALABAMA

Birmingham

Alpha Portland Cement Co.
Wet process; 1,700,000 bbls.
Lehigh Portland Cement Co.
Wet process; 24,500,000 bbls.*
Lone Star Cement Corp.
Wet process; 1,800,000 bbls.

Leeds

Universal Atlas Cement Co.
Wet process; 33,000,000 bbls.*

Mobile

Ideal Cement Co.
Wet process; 2,400,000 bbls.

Ragland

National Cement Co.
Dry process; 1,750,000 bbls.

Roberta

Southern Cement Co.
Dry process; 1,100,000 bbls.

Spocari

Lone Star Cement Corp.
Dry process; 1,000,000 bbls.

ARIZONA

Rillito

Arizona Portland Cement Co.
Dry process; 2,500,000 bbls.

ARKANSAS

Okay

Ideal Cement Co.
Wet process; 1,350,000 bbls.

CALIFORNIA

Colton

California Portland Cement Co.
Dry process; 5,000,000 bbls.

Crestmore (P. O. Riverside)

Riverside Cement Co.
Dry process; 4,200,000 bbls.*

Cushenbury

† Permanente Cement Co.
Wet process; 2,000,000 bbls.

Davenport

Santa Cruz Portland Cement Co.
Dry process; 2,500,000 bbls.

Mojave

California Portland Cement Co.
Dry process; 2,400,000 bbls.

Monolith

Monolith Portland Cement Co.
Wet process; 3,500,000 bbls.

Oro Grande

Riverside Cement Co.
Dry process; 4,200,000 bbls.*

Permanente

Permanente Cement Co.
Wet process; 7,000,000 bbls.

Redwood City

Ideal Cement Co.
Wet process; 2,300,000 bbls.

San Andreas

Calaveras Cement Co.
Wet process; 3,250,000 bbls.

San Juan Bautista

Ideal Cement Co.
Wet process; 900,000 bbls.

Victorville

Southwestern Portland Cement Co.
Wet process; 5,000,000 bbls.

COLORADO

Boettcher (*P. O. LaPorte*)

Ideal Cement Co.
Dry process; 1,200,000 bbls.

Portland

Ideal Cement Co. (2 plants)
Wet and Dry process; 2,640,000 bbls.

FLORIDA

Bunnell

Lehigh Portland Cement Co.
Wet process; 24,500,000 bbls.*

Hookers Point (*P. O. Tampa*)

General Portland Cement Co. (Florida Div.)
Wet process; 15,000,000 bbls.*

GEORGIA

Clinchfield

Penn-Dixie Cement Corp.
Wet process; 15,800,000 bbls.*

Rockmart

Marquette Cement Manuacturing Co.
Dry process; 1,000,000 bbls.

IDAHO

Inkom

Idaho Portland Cement Co.
Wet process; 600,000 bbls.

ILLINOIS

Dixon

Medusa Portland Cement Co.
Dry process; 2,500,000 bbls.

La Salle

Alpha Portland Cement Co.
Dry process; 1,600,000 bbls.

Oglesby

Marquette Cement Mfg. Co.
Dry process; 4,250,000 bbls.
Lehigh Portland Cement Co.
Dry process; 24,500,000 bbls.*

INDIANA

Buffington

Universal Atlas Cement Co.
Dry process; 33,000,000 bbls.*

Limedale (*P. O. Greencastle*)

Lone Star Cement Corp.
Wet process; 2,600,000 bbls.

Mitchell

Lehigh Portland Cement Co.
Dry process; 24,500,000 bbls.*

Speed

Louisville Cement Co.
Dry process; 2,500,000 bbls.

IOWA

Davenport (Linwood)

Dewey Portland Cement Co.
Wet process; 2,750,000 bbls.

Des Moines

Marquette Cement Mfg. Co.
(Selling sub: Hawkeye-Marquette Cement Co.)
Wet process; 1,970,000 bbls.
Penn-Dixie Cement Corp.
Wet process; 15,800,000 bbls.*

Mason City

Lehigh Portland Cement Co.
Dry process; 24,500,000 bbls.*
Northwestern States Portland Cement Co.
Dry process; 2,500,000 bbls.

KANSAS

Bonner Springs

Lone Star Cement Corp.
Wet process; 2,100,000 bbls.

Chanute

Ash Grove Lime and Portland Cement Co.
Wet process; 2,100,000 bbls.

Fredonia

Consolidated Cement Corp.
Wet process; 3,450,000 bbls.*

Humboldt

Monarch Cement Co.
Dry process; 1,500,000 bbls.

Independence

Universal Atlas Cement Co.
Dry process; 33,000,000 bbls.*

Iola

Lehigh Portland Cement Co.
Wet process; 24,500,000 bbls.*

KENTUCKY

Kosmosdale

Kosmos Portland Cement Co.
Dry process; 2,000,000 bbls.

LOUISIANA

Baton Rouge

Ideal Cement Co.
Wet process; 2,150,000 bbls.

New Orleans

Lone Star Cement Corp.
Wet process; 2,200,000 bbls.

MAINE

Thomaston

Dragon Portland Cement Co.
Wet process; 2,000,000 bbls.

MARYLAND

Security (P. O. Hagerstown)

North American Cement Corp.
Dry process; 1,800,000 bbls.

Union Bridge

Lehigh Portland Cement Co.
Dry process; 24,500,000 bbls.*

MICHIGAN

Alpena

Huron Portland Cement Co.
Dry process; 10,000,000 bbls.

Bay City

Aetna Portland Cement Co.
Wet process; 2,000,000 bbls.

Cement City

Consolidated Cement Corp.
Wet process; 3,450,000 bbls.*

Detroit

Peerless Cement Corp.
Wet process; 1,750,000 bbls.
† Peerless Cement Corp. Plant #2
Wet process; 1,000,000 bbls.

Petoskey

Penn-Dixie Cement Corp.
Wet process; 15,800,000 bbls.*

Port Huron

Peerless Cement Corp.
Wet process; 2,000,000 bbls.

Wyandotte

Wyandotte Portland Cement Co.
Wet process; 1,200,000 bbls.

MINNESOTA

Duluth

Universal Atlas Cement Co.
Dry process; 33,000,000 bbls.*

MISSISSIPPI

Brandon

Marquette Cement Mfg. Co.
Wet process; 1,220,000 bbls.

MISSOURI

Cape Girardeau

Marquette Cement Mfg. Co.
Dry process; 1,800,000 bbls.

Hannibal

Universal Atlas Cement Co.
Dry process; 33,000,000 bbls.*

Prospect Hill

Missouri Portland Cement Co.
Wet process; 5,000,000 bbls.

St. Louis

Alpha Portland Cement Co.
Wet process; 1,900,000 bbls.

Sugar Creek

Missouri Portland Cement Co.
Dry process; 2,000,000 bbls.

MONTANA

Trident

Ideal Cement Co.
Dry process; 1,200,000 bbls.

NEBRASKA

Louisville

Ash Grove Lime and Portland Cement Co.
Wet process; 2,750,000 bbls.

Superior

Ideal Cement Co.
Wet process; 925,000 bbls.

NEW YORK

Alsen

Lehigh Portland Cement Co.
Dry process; 24,500,000 bbls.*

Buffalo

Lehigh Portland Cement Co.
Wet process; 24,500,000 bbls.*

Catskill

North American Cement Corp.
Wet process; 1,600,000 bbls.

Cementon

Alpha Portland Cement Co.
Dry process; 1,200,000 bbls.

Glens Falls

Glens Falls Portland Cement Co.
Wet process; 1,800,000 bbls.

Hamburg (P. O. Buffalo)

Penn-Dixie Cement Corp.
Wet process; 15,800,000 bbls.*

Howes Cave

North American Cement Corp.
Wet process; 1,500,000 bbls.

Hudson

Lone Star Cement Corp.
Wet process; 2,000,000 bbls.
Universal Atlas Cement Co.
Dry process; 33,000,000 bbls.*

Jamesville

Alpha Portland Cement Co.
Wet process; 850,000 bbls.

OHIO

Bay Bridge

Medusa Portland Cement Co.
Wet process; 1,250,000 bbls.

East Fultonham (P. O. Zanesville)

Columbia Cement Division
Pittsburgh Plate Glass Co.
Wet process; 1,850,000 bbls.

Ironton

Alpha Portland Cement Co.
Dry process; 1,200,000 bbls.

Middle Branch

Diamond Portland Cement Co.
Dry process; 1,450,000 bbls.

Fairborn

Southwestern Portland Cement Co.
Wet process; 2,250,000 bbls.
Universal Atlas Cement Co.
Wet process; 33,000,000 bbls.*

Painesville

Standard Portland Cement Division
Diamond Alkali Co.
Wet process; 1,900,000 bbls.

Paulding

† Consolidated Cement Co.
Dry process; 3,450,000 bbls.*

Silica (P. O. Sylvania)

Medusa Portland Cement Co.
Dry process; 1,600,000 bbls.

Superior

Marquette Cement Manufacturing Co.
Dry process; 1,250,000 bbls.

OKLAHOMA

Ada

Ideal Cement Co.
Wet process; 2,250,000 bbls.

Dewey

Dewey Portland Cement Co.
Dry process; 2,400,000 bbls.

OREGON

Gold Hill

Ideal Cement Co.
Wet process; 650,000 bbls.

Lime

Oregon Portland Cement Co.
Wet process; 500,000 bbls.

Oswego

Oregon Portland Cement Co.
Wet process; 1,800,000 bbls.

PENNSYLVANIA

Bath

Keystone Portland Cement Co.
Wet process; 3,000,000 bbls.

Penn-Dixie Cement Corp.
Dry process; 15,800,000 bbls.*

Bessemer (Lawrence Co.)

Bessemer Limestone & Cement Co.
Wet process; 1,800,000 bbls.

Broadhead (P. O. Bethlehem)

National Portland Cement Co.
Wet process; 2,000,000 bbls.

Cementon

Whitehall Cement Mfg. Co.
Dry process; 2,200,000 bbls.

Coplay

Coplay Cement Mfg. Co.
Dry process; 2,000,000 bbls.

Egypt

Giant Portland Cement Co.
Dry process; 1,860,000 bbls.

Evansville

Allentown Portland Cement Co.
Dry process; 2,300,000 bbls.

Fogelsville

Lehigh Portland Cement Co.
Dry process; 24,500,000 bbls.*

Martins Creek

Alpha Portland Cement Co.
Dry process; 2,500,000 bbls.

Nazareth

Lone Star Cement Corp.
Dry process; 2,300,000 bbls.
Nazareth Cement Co.
Dry process; 2,200,000 bbls.
Penn-Dixie Cement Corp.
Dry process; 15,800,000 bbls.*

Neville Island (P. O. Pittsburgh)

Green Bag Cement Division
Pittsburgh Coke and Chemical Co.
Wet process; 1,800,000 bbls.

Northampton

Dragon Portland Cement Co.
Dry process; 1,800,000 bbls.
Universal Atlas Cement Co.
Wet process; 33,000,000 bbls.*

Ormrod

Lehigh Portland Cement Co.
Dry process; 24,500,000 bbls.*

Penn-Allen (P. O. Nazareth)

Penn-Dixie Cement Corp.
Wet process; 15,800,000 bbls.*

Sandts-Eddy (P. O. Easton)

Lehigh Portland Cement Co.
Wet process; 24,500,000 bbls.*

Stockertown (P. O. Nazareth)

Hercules Cement Co.
Dry process; 2,800,000 bbls.

Universal

Universal Atlas Cement Co.
Dry process; 33,000,000 bbls.*

Wampum

Medusa Portland Cement Co.
Dry process; 1,600,000 bbls.

West Conshohocken

Allentown Portland Cement Co.
Wet process; 2,100,000 bbls.

West Winfield

Penn-Dixie Cement Corp.
Wet process; 15,800,000 bbls.*

York

Medusa Portland Cement Co.
(York Gray Plant)
Wet process; 1,250,000 bbls.
Medusa Portland Cement Co.
(York White Plant)
Wet process; 500,000 bbls.

SOUTH CAROLINA

Harleyville

Carolina Giant Cement Co.
(Division of Giant Portland Cement Co.)
Wet process; 1,800,000 bbls.

SOUTH DAKOTA

Rapid City

South Dakota Cement Co.
Wet process; 2,500,000 bbls.

TENNESSEE

Cowan

Marquette Cement Mfg. Co.
(Selling Sub. Cumberland Portland Cement Co.)
Wet process; 980,000 bbls.

Kingsport

Penn-Dixie Cement Corp.
Wet process; 15,800,000 bbls.*

Knoxville

Volunteer Portland Cement Co.
Wet process; 2,000,000 bbls.

Nashville

Marquette Cement Mfg. Co.
(Selling Sub. Hermitage Portland Cement Co.)
Wet process; 990,000 bbls.

North Chattanooga

General Portland Cement Co.
(Signal Mountain Division)
Wet process; 15,000,000 bbls.*

Richard City

Penn-Dixie Cement Corp.
Wet process; 15,800,000 bbls.*

TEXAS

Corpus Christi

Halliburton Portland Cement Co.
Wet process; 1,400,000 bbls.

Eagle Ford (P. O. Dallas)

General Portland Cement Co.
(Trinity Division)
Dry Process; 15,000,000 bbls.*

El Paso

Southwestern Portland Cement Co.
Dry process; 1,500,000 bbls.

Fort Worth

General Portland Cement Co.
(Trinity Division)
Wet process; 15,000,000 bbls.*

Harrys (P. O. Dallas)

Lone Star Cement Corp.
Wet process; 2,300,000 bbls.

Houston

Lone Star Cement Corp.
Wet process; 2,100,000 bbls.
Ideal Cement Co.
Wet process; 1,320,000 bbls.
General Portland Cement Co.
(Trinity Division)
Wet process; 15,000,000 bbls.*

Longhorn

Longhorn Portland Cement Co.
Wet process; 2,500,000 bbls.

Maryneal (P. O. Sweetwater)

Lone Star Cement Corp.
Dry process; 2,500,000 bbls.

Cementville

San Antonio Portland Cement Co.
Wet process; 2,000,000 bbls.

Waco

Universal Atlas Cement Co.
Dry process; 33,000,000 bbls.*

UTAH

Devils Slide

Ideal Cement Co.
Wet process; 1,800,000 bbls.

Salt Lake City

Portland Cement Co. of Utah
Wet process; 350,000 bbls.

VIRGINIA

Fordwick

Lehigh Portland Cement Co.
Dry process; 24,500,000 bbls.*

Lone Star (P. O. Cloverdale)

Lone Star Cement Corp.
Dry process; 2,200,000 bbls.

South Norfolk

Lone Star Cement Corp.
Wet process; 1,200,000 bbls.

WASHINGTON

Bellingham

Olympic Portland Cement Co., Ltd.
Wet process; 900,000 bbls.

Concrete

Superior Portland Cement, Inc.
Wet process; 1,800,000 bbls.

Grotto

Northwestern Portland Cement Co.
Wet process; 600,000 bbls.

Irvin (P. O. Spokane)

Ideal Cement Co.
Dry process; 650,000 bbls.

Metaline Falls

Lehigh Portland Cement Co.
Dry process; 24,500,000 bbls.*

Seattle

Superior Portland Cement, Inc.
Wet process; 1,000,000 bbls.

WEST VIRGINIA

Manheim

Alpha Portland Cement Co.
Dry process; 850,000 bbls.

Martinsburg

Standard Lime & Cement Co.
Wet process; 2,800,000 bbls.

WISCONSIN

Manitowoc

Manitowoc Portland Cement Co.
(Subsidiary of Medusa Portland Cement Co.)
Wet process; 2,000,000 bbls.

Milwaukee

† Marquette Cement Mfg. Co.
Dry process; 1,250,000 bbls.
† Universal Atlas Cement Co. (Grinding Only)

Superior

Huron Portland Cement Co. (Grinding Only)

WYOMING

Laramie

Monolith Portland Midwest Co.
Wet process; 1,000,000 bbls.

PUERTO RICO

Guaynabo

Puerto Rico Cement Corp.
Wet process; 1,400,000 bbls.

Ponce

Ponce Cement Corp.
Wet process; 2,700,000 bbls.

Distributing Plants

ALASKA

Anchorage
Permanente Cement Co.

Fairbanks
Permanente Cement Co.

CALIFORNIA

Alameda
Santa Cruz Portland Cement Co.

Bakersfield
Monolith Portland Cement Co.

Long Beach
Permanente Cement Co.

Los Angeles
Blue Diamond Corp.
Monolith Portland Cement Co.
Riverside Cement Co.

Redwood City
Permanente Cement Co.

San Diego
Riverside Cement Co.

Stockton
Santa Cruz Portland Cement Co.

DISTRICT OF COLUMBIA

Washington
Lone Star Cement Corp.

FLORIDA

Port Everglades, Ft. Lauderdale
Ponce Products, Inc.

HAWAII

Honolulu
Permanente Cement Co.

ILLINOIS

Chicago
Medusa Portland Cement Co.
Penn-Dixie Cement Corp.

INDIANA

Evansville
Kosmos Portland Cement Co.

LOUISIANA

New Orleans
Ideal Cement Co.

MICHIGAN

Carrollton
Huron Portland Cement Co.

Detroit
Huron Portland Cement Co.
Penn-Dixie Cement Corp.

Holland
Medusa Portland Cement Co.

Muskegon
Huron Portland Cement Co.
Universal Atlas Cement Co.

MINNESOTA

Duluth
Huron Portland Cement Co.

MISSOURI

St. Louis
Marquette Cement Mfg. Co.

NEW YORK

Buffalo
Huron Portland Cement Co.

Oswego
Huron Portland Cement Co.

OHIO

Cincinnati
Kosmos Portland Cement Co.

Cleveland
Huron Portland Cement Co.
Lehigh Portland Cement Co.

Toledo
Huron Portland Cement Co.

OREGON

Portland
Oregon Portland Cement Co.
Permanente Cement Co.

TENNESSEE

Memphis
Marquette Cement Mfg. Co.
Missouri Portland Cement Co.

UTAH

Salt Lake City
Ideal Cement Co.

WASHINGTON

East Pasco
Permanente Cement Co.

Seattle
Permanente Cement Co.

WISCONSIN

Green Bay
Huron Portland Cement Co.
Universal Atlas Cement Co.

Milwaukee
Huron Portland Cement Co.
Medusa Portland Cement Co.
Penn-Dixie Cement Corp.
Universal Atlas Cement Co.

Superior
Huron Portland Cement Co.

Works Cited

* Significant Contributions to the Basing-Point Controversy

Publications of the United States Government

* Attorney General's National Committee to Study the Anti-Trust Laws, *Report* (1955).

Bureau of Mines, *Minerals Yearbook*, Various years.

Congress, House of Representatives, Select Committee on Small Business, *The Portland Cement Industry: Supply-Demand Outlook*, 84th Cong., 2d sess., Report No. 2965 (1956).

——— *Hearings, Small Business Objections on Basing Point Legislation, Particularly S. 1008*, Select Committee on Small Business, 81st Cong., 1st sess. (1949).

Congress, Senate, *Hearings on S. 4055, To Prevent Uniform Prices*, Committee on Interstate Commerce, 74th Cong., 2d sess. (1936).

——— *Hearings on Senate Resolution 241, Study of Pricing Methods*, Subcommittee of the Committee on Interstate and Foreign Commerce, 80th Cong., 2d sess. (1948).

——— *Report No. 44, Changes in Distribution of Steel, 1940–47*, Special Committee to Study Problems of American Small Business, 81st Cong., 1st sess. (1949).

Congress, Temporary National Economic Committee, *Hearings*.

——— *Monograph* No. 13, "Relative Efficiency of Large, Medium-Sized, and Small Business." (1941).

——— *Monograph* No. 21, "Competition and Monopoly in American Industry." (1940).

* ——— *Monograph* No. 42, "The Basing Point Problem." (1941).

* Federal Trade Commission, "Notice to Staff: In re: Commission Policy Toward Geographic Pricing Practices." Oct. 12, 1948. (Mimeographed)

* ——— *Price Bases Inquiry; The Basing-Point Formula and Cement Prices* (1932).

——— *Report on Distribution Methods and Costs*, Part III, Building Materials (1944).

Geological Survey, *Mineral Resources of the United States*, Various years.

* National Recovery Administration, *Report on the Operation of the Basing Point System in the Iron and Steel Industry*, 5 vols. (1935).

Books and Articles

* Ackley, Gardner, "Price Policies," *Industrial Location and Natural Resources* (National Resources Planning Board, Washington, 1943), pp. 302–317.

Alderfer, Evan B. and Herman E. Michl, *Economics of American Industry,* 2d ed. (New York, 1950). 716 pp.

Avery, William M., "First Published Report of American Experience with Suspension Type Preheater," *Pit and Quarry,* Vol. 47, No. 1: 88–90 (July 1954).

Axe, E. W. & Co., *Cement Company Common Stocks in 1947* (New York, 1947). 31 pp.

Bain, Joe S., "Economies of Scale, Concentration, and the Conditions of Entry in Twenty Manufacturing Industries," *American Economic Review,* 44:15–39 (March 1954).

——— "The Profit Rate as a Measure of Monopoly Power," *Quarterly Journal of Economics,* 55:271–293 (February 1941).

* Barloon, Marvin J., "Institutional Foundations of Pricing Policy in the Steel Industry," *Business History Review,* 28:214–235 (September 1954).

* Bliss, Charles A., "Some Field Notes on Freight Absorption," *Harvard Business Review,* 26:656–670 (November 1948).

Boulding, Kenneth E., "In Defense of Monopoly," *Quarterly Journal of Economics,* 59:524–542 (August 1945).

Bowles, Oliver, *The Stone Industries,* 2d ed. (New York, 1939). 519 pp.

Bowman, Waldo G., "Never-Equaled Cement Production is No Match for Record Consumption," *Engineering News-Record,* 141:3, 10–11 (September 23, 1948).

Buckbee, J. C., "Volume Delusion in the Cement Industry," *Rock Products,* Vol. 35, No. 9: 30–32 (May 7, 1932).

* Burns, Arthur R., *The Decline of Competition* (New York, 1936). 619 pp.

Chamberlin, Edward H., *The Theory of Monopolistic Competition,* 5th ed. (Cambridge, Mass., 1946). 282 pp.

* Chamber of Commerce of the United States, *Economic Institute on Delivered Pricing and the Future of American Business* (Washington, 1948).

* Clark, John Maurice, "Basing Point Methods of Price Quoting," *Canadian Journal of Economics and Political Science,* 4:477–489 (November 1938).

* ——— "Imperfect Competition Theory and Basing-Point Problems," and "Rejoinder," *American Economic Review,* 33:283–300 (June 1943) and 33:616–619 (September 1943).

* ——— "The Law and Economics of Basing Points: Appraisal and Proposals," *American Economic Review,* 39:430–447 (March 1949).

* ——— "Machlup on the Basing-Point System," *Quarterly Journal of Economics,* 63:315–321 (August 1949).

——— "Toward a Concept of Workable Competition," *American Economic Review,* 30:241–256 (June 1940).

* Comment, "Conscious Parallelism — Fact or Fancy?", *Stanford Law Review,* 3:679–699 (July 1951).

* Comment, "Price Systems: The Basing-Point Issues," *Yale Law Journal*, 58:426–456 (February 1949).

* Daugherty, Carroll R., Melvin G. de Chazeau, and Samuel S. Stratton, *The Economics of the Iron and Steel Industry* (New York, 1937). 2 vols.

* de Chazeau, Melvin G., "Public Policy and Discriminatory Prices of Steel: A Reply to Professor Fetter," *Journal of Political Economy*, 46:537–566 (August 1938).

* Dewey, Donald J., "A Reappraisal of F.O.B. Pricing and Freight Absorption," *Southern Economic Journal*, 22:48–54 (July 1955).

Dirlam, Joel B. and Alfred E. Kahn, *Fair Competition* (Ithaca, 1954). 307 pp.

Eckel, Edwin C., *Cement Materials and Industry of the United States* (Washington, 1905). 395 pp.

——— *The Portland Cement Industry From a Financial Standpoint* (New York, 1908). 93 pp.

Eddy, Arthur J., *The New Competition* (New York, 1912). 375 pp.

* Edwards, Corwin D., "The Effect of Recent Basing Point Decisions Upon Business Practices," *American Economic Review*, 38:828–842 (December 1948).

* ——— "Geographic Price Formulas and the Concentration of Economic Power," *Georgetown Law Journal*, 37:135–148 (January 1949).

* ——— *Maintaining Competition* (New York, 1949). 337 pp.

Ehrke, Kurt, *Die Uebererzeugung in der Zementindustrie von 1858–1913* (Jena, 1933). 480 pp.

Epstein, Ralph C., *Industrial Profits in the United States* (New York, 1934). 678 pp.

Fellner, William J., *Competition Among the Few* (New York, 1949). 328 pp.

* Fetter, Frank A., "Exit Basing Point Pricing," *American Economic Review*, 38:815–827 (December 1948).

* ——— *The Masquerade of Monopoly* (New York, 1931). 464 pp.

* ——— "The New Plea for Basing-Point Monopoly," and "Rejoinder to Professor de Chazeau's Reply," *Journal of Political Economy*, 45:577–605 (October 1937) and 46:567–570 (August 1938).

Fraser, Cecil E., and Georges F. Doriot, *Analyzing Our Industries* (New York, 1932). 458 pp.

Galbraith, John K., *American Capitalism* (Cambridge, Mass., 1956). 217 pp.

* George, Edwin B., "The Law and Economics of Basing Points," 3 Parts, *Dun's Review* (Sept., Oct., and Nov., 1948).

Hadley, Earl J., *The Magic Powder* (New York, 1945). 382 pp.

* Handler, Milton, "Anti-Trust — New Frontiers and New Perplexities," *The Record* [of the Association of the Bar of the City of New York], 6:59–82 (February 1951).

* Hansen, Harry L., "Procrustean Economics: The Federal Trade Commission and Freight Absorption," *Harvard Business School Alumni Bulletin*, 24:129–131, 151 (Winter 1948).

* Head, Neil C., "The Basing Point Cases," *Harvard Business Review,* 26:641–655 (November 1948).

* Herbert, Bueford G., "Delivered Pricing as Conspiracy and as Discrimination: The Legal Status," *Law and Contemporary Problems,* 15:181–226 (Spring 1950).

Hilts, H. E., *The Manufacturing, Volume, and Costs of the Portland Cement Industry in the United States.* (Prepared by NRA Division of Research and Planning, Washington, 1938).

Hughes, H. H., and B. H. Bagley, *Minerals Yearbook 1934* (Washington, 1934), pp. 785–786.

* Johnson, William S., "The Restrictive Incidence of Basing Point Pricing on Regional Development," *Georgetown Law Journal,* 37:149–165 (January 1949).

* Kaysen, Carl, "Basing Point Pricing and Public Policy," *Quarterly Journal of Economics,* 63:289–314 (August 1949).

* Kittelle, Sumner S., and George P. Lamb, "The Implied Conspiracy Doctrine and Delivered Pricing," *Law and Contemporary Problems,* 15:227–257 (Spring 1950).

* Landon, Charles E., "Georgraphic Price Structures," *Law and Contemporary Problems,* 15:125–140 (Spring 1950).

* Latham, Earl, "Giantism and Basing-Points," and "Lament for Cement: Being an Answer to a Reply," *Yale Law Journal,* 58:383–399 (February 1949) and 58:1079–1089 (June 1949).

——— *The Group Basis of Politics* (Ithaca, 1952). 244 pp.

——— "The Politics of Basing-Point Legislation," *Law and Contemporary Problems,* 15:272–310 (Spring 1950).

Lesley, Robert W., *History of the Portland Cement Industry in the United States* (Chicago, 1924). 330 pp.

Loescher, Samuel M., "Discussion," in *Papers and Proceedings, American Economic Review,* 45:524–527 (May 1955).

* ——— "Geographical Pricing Policies and the Law," *Journal of Business of the University of Chicago,* 27:211–224 (July 1954).

* ——— "Inert Antitrust Administration: Formula Pricing and the Cement Industry," *Yale Law Journal,* 65:1–22 (November 1955).

* McAllister, Breck P., and Murray T. Quigg, "The Art of Selecting and Exploiting Half Truths: A Reply to Giantism and Basing Points," and "Rejoinder," in *Yale Law Journal,* 58:1068–1078, 1090–1091 (June 1949).

* McGee, John S., "Cross Hauling — A Symptom of Incomplete Collusion Under Basing-Point Systems," *Southern Economic Journal,* 20:369–379 (April 1954).

* Machlup, Fritz, *The Basing-Point System; an Economic Analysis of a Controversial Pricing Practice* (Philadelphia, 1949). 275 pp.

* Marengo, Louis, "The Basing-Point Decisions and the Steel Industry," *Papers and Proceedings, American Economic Review,* 45:509–522 (May 1955).

* Miller, John Perry, *Unfair Competition* (Cambridge, Mass., 1941). Ch. IX.
* Mund, Vernon A., "The Development and Incidence of Delivered Pricing in American Industry," *Law and Contemporary Problems*, 15:141–158 (Spring 1950).
* ——— "The 'Freight Allowed' Method of Price Quotation," *Quarterly Journal of Economics*, 54:232–245 (February 1940).
* ——— *Government and Business*, 2d ed. (New York, 1955). 738 pp.
* ——— "Monopolistic Competition Theory and Public Price Policy," and "Reply to Professor Clark," *American Economic Review*, 32:727–743 (December 1942) and 33:612–616 (September 1943).
——— *Open Markets* (New York, 1948). 272 pp.
National City Bank, *Monthly Letter on Business and Economic Conditions*, April issues, 1949–1956.
Neal, Alfred C., *Industrial Concentration and Price Flexibility* (Washington, 1942). 173 pp.
* Nelson, Saul, "Basing-Point Problems: Comment," *American Economic Review*, 33:620–622 (September 1943).
* Nichols, Alfred, "The Cement Case," *Papers and Proceedings, American Economic Review*, 39:297–310 (May 1949).
Nordberg, Bror, "Operates Kiln for Best Efficiency Rather Than Overcapacity," *Rock Products*, Vol. 47, No. 1:70 (July 1954).
——— "Producers Forecast Capacity Production in 1949," *Rock Products*, Vol. 52, No. 1:76 (January 1949).
Nourse, Edwin G., *America's Capacity to Produce* (Washington, 1934). 608 pp.
* Pegrum, Dudley F., "The Present Status of Geographic Pricing," *Journal of Marketing*, 15:425–435 (April 1951).
Perazich, George S., et al., *Mechanization in the Cement Industry*, WPA National Research Project, Report No. M–3 (Philadelphia, 1939).
Persons, Hubert C., *The Portland Cement Industry* (Boston, 1950).
"The Problem of Economic Instability," Report of Subcommittee of the Committee on Public Issues of the American Economic Association, *American Economic Review*, 40:502–538 (September 1950).
Reder, Melvin, "A Reconsideration of the Marginal Productivity Theory," *Journal of Political Economy*, 55:451–458 (October 1947).
Reynolds, Lloyd G., "Cutthroat Competition," *American Economic Review*, 30:737–747 (December 1940).
Rockwood, Nathan C., "Elements of Cost in a Barrel of Portland Cement," *Rock Products*, Vol. 43, No. 1:20–21 (January 1940).
——— "Chemistry Applied to Cement Manufacture," *ibid.*, Vol. 41, No. 8:32–36 (August 1938).
Rowe, John W. F., *Markets and Men* (New York, 1936). 259 pp.
——— "Some General Economic Aspects," in Elliott, William Y., et al., *International Control in the Non-Ferrous Metals* (New York, 1937), pp. 56–98.
* Sage, George H., *Basing-Point Pricing Systems Under the Federal Anti-*

trust Laws: A Legal, Business, and Economic Appraisal (St. Louis, 1951). 381 pp.

* Salera, Virgil, "Aspects of the Basing-Point System: Comment," *American Economic Review,* 33:900–902 (December 1943).

Schein, Nathan H., "1954 Cement Demand to Set New Record," *Pit and Quarry,* Vol. 47, No. 2:77–79 (August 1954).

* Simon, William, "The Case Against the Federal Trade Commission," *University of Chicago Law Review,* 19:297–338 (Winter 1952).

* ——— "The Fantasy of the Phrase 'Injury to Competition,'" *Law and Contemporary Problems,* 15:258–271 (Spring 1950).

* Smithies, Arthur, "Aspects of the Basing-Point System," *American Economic Review,* 32:705–726 (December 1942) and "Reply to Mr. Salera," *ibid.,* 33:902 (December 1943).

* Sorkin, Bernard R., "Conscious Parallelism," *Antitrust Bulletin,* 2:281–302 (January 1957).

* Stigler, George J., "A Theory of Delivered Price Systems," *American Economic Review,* 39:1143–59 (December 1949).

* Stocking, George W., *Basing-Point Pricing and Regional Development* (Chapel Hill, N.C., 1954). 274 pp.

* ——— "The Economics of Basing-Point Pricing," *Law and Contemporary Problems,* 15:159–180 (Spring 1950).

* ——— and Myron W. Watkins, *Monopoly and Free Enterprise* (New York, 1951), ch. VII.

* Sweeney, Paul E., "Economics of Cement Traffic Flow," Record Group No. 198, Board of Investigation and Research — Transportation. Unpublished volume placed in National Archives, Washington, in 1943.

Sweezy, Paul M., "Demand Under Conditions of Oligopoly," *Journal of Political Economy,* 47:568–573 (August 1939).

Topkis, Bernard H., "Labor Requirements in Cement Production," *Monthly Labor Review,* 42:564–577 (March 1936).

"Trade Regulation Under the Robinson-Patman and Federal Trade Commission Acts — Implications in Recent Decisions," *National Association of Manufacturers Law Digest,* June 1948.

Trauffer, Walter E., "Cement: 1956 Tenth Consecutive Record Year," *Pit and Quarry,* Vol. 49, No. 7: 138, 144 (January 1957).

——— "Cement Review and Forecast: New Record Volume of Cement Output Strains Rapidly Growing Plant Capacity," *Pit and Quarry,* Vol. 40, No. 7:80 (January 1948).

* United States Steel Corporation, *United States Steel Corporation T.N.E.C. Papers* (New York, 1940). 3 vols.

* Wallace, Robert A., and Paul H. Douglas, "Antitrust Policies and the New Attack on the Federal Trade Commission," *University of Chicago Law Review,* 19:684–723 (Summer 1952).

* Wilcox, Clair, *Public Policies Toward Business* (Chicago, 1955). Ch. VIII.

Wooden, Walter B., "The Concept of Unlawful Discrimination as It Applies to Geographical Price Differences," *Georgetown Law Journal,* 37:166–182 (January 1949).

* Wright, Joseph S., "Collusion and Parallel Action in Delivered Price Systems," *Georgetown Law Journal,* 37:201–216 (January 1949).

Yaworski, Nicholas, et al., *Fuel Efficiency in Cement Manufacture, 1909–35,* WPA National Research Project, Report No. E–5 (Philadelphia, 1938).

Young, Joseph S., *A Brief Perspective of the Cement Industry.* Paper presented before the Financial Analysts of Philadelphia, November 3, 1955. [A pamphlet]

Legal Cases

A. I. A. Schechter Poultry Corporation v. *United States,* 295 U.S. 495 (1935).

Aetna Portland Cement Co. v. *Federal Trade Commission,* 157 F. 2d 533 (7th Cir. 1946).

Cement Manufacturers Protective Association v. *United States,* 268 U.S. 588 (1925).

Clayton Mark & Co. v. *Federal Trade Commission,* 336 U.S. 956 (1949).

Corn Products Refining Company v. *Federal Trade Commission,* 324 U.S. 726 (1945).

Federal Trade Commission v. *A. E. Staley Manufacturing Co.,* 324 U.S. 746 (1945).

Federal Trade Commission v. *Algoma Lumber Co.,* 291 U.S. 67 (1934).

Federal Trade Commission v. *Cement Institute,* 333 U.S. 683 (1948).

Federal Trade Commission v. *Gratz,* 253 U.S. 421 (1920).

Federal Trade Commission v. *Morton Salt Co.,* 334 U.S. 37 (1948).

Federal Trade Commission v. *Pacific States Paper Trade Association,* 273 U.S. 52 (1927).

Federal Trade Commission v. *R. F. Keppel & Bro., Inc.,* 291 U.S. 304 (1934).

Maple Flooring Manufacturers Association v. *United States,* 268 U.S. 563 (1925).

Triangle Conduit and Cable Co. v. *Federal Trade Commission,* 168 F.2d 175 (7th Cir. 1948).

United States v. *Cement Institute et al.,* 85 F. Supp. 344 (1949).

United States v. *Cement Institute, CCH Trade Regulation Reporter* (1953).

United States v. *Cement Institute, Civil No. 1291,* D. Colo., June 28, 1945.

United States v. *Cement Manufacturers Protective Association,* 294 F. 390 (S.D.N.Y., 1923).

American Iron & Steel Institute, 48 FTC 123 (1951).

Cement Institute, 37 FTC 87 (1943).

Ideal Cement Co., Colorado Portland Division, 47 FTC 1030 (1951).

Monolith Portland Midwest Co., 47 FTC 1292 (1951).

Index

Acquisitions and mergers, 115–25, 180, 290–96, 299
Ada, Okla., 118, 128
Adams, Thomas, 243n
Aetna Portland Cement Co., 128n, 161, 215, 219n
Affleck, Benjamin, 105
Alabama, 41, 98, 106, 119, 120n, 121n, 144, 148, 180, 200, 205, 285, 292
Albany, N.Y., 52, 105, 150
Allentown Portland Cement Co., 310
Allis-Chalmers Manufacturing Co., 41n, 219
Alpena, Mich., 104
Alpha Portland Cement Co., 97–99, 107, 110n, 118, 120n, 121, 127, 128, 154, 156, 160, 161, 164, 174, 179n, 270, 291, 295, 305, 306, 308–10, 312
Alsen, N.Y., 117, 120n
Alternatives to basing-point pricing formula, 226–42
American Cement Corp., 292n
American-Marietta Co., 292, 293, 295
American Society for Testing Materials, 136
American Trucking Ass'n, 276
Antitrust suits, 176, 236–39, 243, 244, 263, 266, 269, 297, 300, 301. *See also* U.S. Department of Justice
Arbitrage, 10, 13, 73, 92, 93, 103, 104, 152, 232, 234, 278
Arizona, 143, 146, 285
Arizona Portland Cement Co., 305
Arkansas, 148, 204, 290
Ash Grove Lime and Portland Cement Co., 140, 163, 307, 308
Asphalt, 80–83
Ass'n of American Portland Cement Mfrs. (AAPCM), 94–98, 132, 135
Ass'n of Licensed Cement Mfrs. 38, 96, 97
Atlanta, Ga., 151
Atlanta, Ohio, 146
Atlas Portland Cement Co., 91–93, 96, 116–19, 140, 156, 157. *See also* Universal Atlas Cement Co.
Australian mills, 204

Babcock & Wilcox, 219
Bain, Joe S., 42, 43
Baltimore, Md., 155
Bargaining power of buyers, 2, 12, 26, 55, 73, 103, 104, 130, 131, 183–85, 234, 298. *See also* Buyers' transportation; Buyers' trucking; Contractors; Dealers
Base mills, 3, 5, 6, 8, 10, 11, 15, 18, 19, 21–23, 45, 81, 89, 92, 94, 125, 147–53. *See also* Non-base mills; Punitive base
Base prices. *See* Base mills
Basic Products Co., 106, 107
Bath, Pa., 103n, 120n
Bath Portland Cement Co., 117n
Bay Bridge, Ohio, 116, 149
Bay City, Mich., 128n, 161
Bellevue, Mich., 118
Bessemer Limestone & Cement Co., 107, 108, 120n, 310
Bethlehem, Pa., 103n
Bids. *See* Sealed bids; Control-clause-destination cost bid
Birmingham, Ala., 19n, 49, 117, 118, 120n, 127, 154, 155, 158–60, 162, 179, 197, 212, 285, 294n
Blomgren, Paul, 99n
Blue Diamond Corp., 56n, 313
Boettcher, Colo., 117
Bonner Springs, Kan., 118
Boston, Mass., 49, 134, 137, 150
Bowen, John C., 75
Boycott of dealers of imported cement, 25, 136, 137
Brooks, Chester A., 134
Buffalo, N.Y., 105, 117, 119, 147, 292
Buffington, Ind., 116, 119, 157, 158
Burns, Arthur R., 61, 110, 129, 194. *See also* Burns-Clark study
Burns-Clark study, 111, 120n, 149, 154, 155, 157, 217
Buyers of cement, 16, 53–57, 72, 84–86, 130
Buyers' transportation, 10, 11, 92, 93, 96, 101, 227
Buyers' trucking, 12, 13, 28, 151, 152, 231, 232, 235, 250, 253, 276–82, 284, 297; elimination of sales to, 102–11, 216–18, 239, 169, 283

Calaveras Cement Co., 56, 154, 306
California, 47, 48, 56, 106, 107, 110, 120n, 146, 154, 155, 161, 170, 187, 205, 276, 285, 292
California Portland Cement Co., 47, 305
Capacity utilization, 3, 65, 67, 71, 89, 102, 264, 265, 295; *1907–1913*, 172–75; *1914–1917*, 175; *1918–1919*, 175–76; *1920–1925*, 176–77; *1926–1930*, 178–81; *1931–1935*, 181–85; *1936–1940*, 185–87; *1941–1942*, 187–88; *1943–1945*, 188; *1946–1948*, 188–90; *1949–1956*, 284–90
Cape Girardeau, Mo., 127, 128, 158, 159
Capehart Bill, 274n, 275n
Capehart Committee, 202, 267
Carolina Giant Cement Co., 311
Castalia Co., 120n
Catskill, N.Y., 118
Celler Anti-Merger Amendment, 290–93, 299
Cement, consumption in U.S.A., *1880–1910*, 31n–32n; description of, 4, 31; domestic dominates markets, 31–33
Cement case (*FTC* v. *Cement Institute*). See especially Chapters VII and VIII
Cement Institute, 24, 61, 84, 99, 100, 109, 114, 135, 137–39, 163, 180, 185, 215, 247n, 280, 290
Cement Mfrs. Protective Ass'n, 98, 99, 101, 132, 138, 139
Cement Mfrs. Protective Ass'n v. *U.S.* See *Old Cement* case
Central Freight Ass'n, 45
Central Valley, Calif., 56
Chain mill cos., 5, 22–24, 38, 42, 43, 52, 53, 70, 98, 106, 107, 109, 115, 117, 119, 121, 122, 127, 142, 148, 153, 158, 164, 175, 180, 183, 209, 293–95, 300. *See also* Market structure
Chamberlin, Edward H., 2, 28
Chattanooga, Tenn., 291
Chicago, Ill., 49, 52, 88, 94, 105, 107, 109, 134, 157, 291
Chicago Statistical Bureau, 99
Chicago Heights, Ind., 292n
Cincinnati, Ohio, 120n
Clark, John M., 30, 61, 63, 68, 69, 111, 197, 211, 235. *See also* Burns-Clark study
Clayton Act, 231, 259, 274n, 295
Clayton Mark & Co. v. *FTC*, 271n
Cleveland, Ohio, 103–105, 107, 110n, 140, 149, 154, 156, 160, 162, 182, 184n
Clinchfield, Ga., 118, 159
Clinchfield Co., 118
Code of Ethics, 135, 215
Collusion, 13, 15, 17–19, 22, 23, 25–28, 57, 61, 76, 78, 112, 125, 126, 130, 142, 177, 194, 236–38, 241, 246, 247, 249, 250, 252, 255, 257–59, 272. *See also* Imperfect collusion
Colonial Sand and Stone Co., 56n
Colorado, 170n, 276n
Columbus, Ohio, 146, 151
Compendium of Established Terms and Marketing Methods, 215
Competition, 30, 116. *See also* Importation of cement; Unsystematic pricing
Concentration, 115–25, 153, 230, 236, 290–96, 299. *See also* Market structure
Concrete, Colo., 118, 150
Conshohocken, Pa., 48
Consolidated Cement Corp., 114, 120n, 121, 219n, 268, 291, 307, 308, 309
Consumer's Advisory Board, 133
Continental Can Co., 284n
Contractors, 94, 113, 130, 134; no direct sales to, 4, 25, 26, 29, 54, 55, 101, 175, 185, 238, 239, 298
Control-clause-destination-cost bid, 111–15, 185
Coogan, F. M., 98
Cooperative practice, 134–41
Coplay Cement Mfg. Co., 310
Corpus Christi, Texas, 294n
Costs, 2, 5, 27, 30, 32, 33, 36, 195, 196. *See also* Loading costs; Marginal costs; Overhead costs; Selling costs
Costs of cement, nature of, Chapter III
Cowell Lime and Cement Co., 146, 154, 217
Cowham Engineering Group, 120n, 121, 160, 268, 291n
Crapo, S. T., 105
Cross-hauling, 13, 42, 139, 191, 208–13, 216, 229
Cumberland mill, 291
Cummings, Homer (Attorney General), 244

Dakotas, the, 49
Dallas, Texas, 107

Dankel, J. L., 108, 120n, 121n
Davenport, Calif., 146
Davenport, Ia., 105
Davidson Coke and Iron Co., 40n
Dayton, Ohio, 291
Dealers, 25, 93, 94; protected, 55, 104, 129–34, 174, 183, 192. *See also* Market structure
Defensive monopoly, 3, 26, 27, 84, 141, 142, 219, 225, 301; quest for, Chapter III, esp. 83–86
Delivered prices, 6, 8–13, 15–17, 20–22, 29, 73, 84, 101–15
Demand for cement, 2, 5, 19, 22, 67, 89, 170, 187, 192–94, 208, 220, 228, 275, 286, 288, 289; demand conditions, 72–83; nature of, Chapter III
Denver, Colo., 49, 52, 53
Denver Cement case, 278–84
Des Moines, Ia., 46, 105, 118, 140, 146, 151, 290
Destination prices. *See* Delivered prices
Detroit, Mich., 46, 97, 103, 104, 107, 162, 285, 292n, 294n
Detroit Standard Oil case, 273n
Devil's Slide, Utah, 118
Dewey, Okla., 128
Dewey Portland Cement Co., 307, 309
Dexter Co., 118
Diamond Alkali Co., 40n, 309
Diamond Portland Cement Co., 309
Direct sales to highway contractors, 133
Dirlam, Joel B., 280n
Discriminatory pricing. *See* Unsystematic pricing
Distribution policy, 54
Dixon, Ill., 116, 149
Dixie Co., 118
Doriot, Georges, 179n
Dragon Portland Cement Co., 292, 307, 310
Dravo Corp., 56n
Duluth, Minn., 117, 119

Earnings. *See* Profit rate
East Coast area, 87, 96, 120n, 136, 144, 156
East Fultonham, Ohio, 146, 161
Eastern Trunk Line territory, 144
Eckel, Edwin C., 58n, 116, 166
Economies of scale, 2, 39–44, 47, 52, 55n, 56, 58, 198, 201, 221
Eddy, Arthur J., 179
Edwards, Corwin D., 233
Ehrke, K., 68n
El Paso, Texas, 47
Enforcement mechanism. *See* Punitive base
Enforcement problems, 241
Engineering News-Record, 152, 179
Entry conditions, 2, 19, 37–40, 44, 58, 90, 187, 192, 194, 289, 290–96
Epstein, Ralph C., 62, 66n, 176
Excess capacity, 5, 8, 9, 24, 28n, 55, 58, 59, 62, 63, 67, 68, 72, 73, 78, 81, 84, 85, 90, 102, 116, 126, 137, 142, 147, 166–70, 175, 181, 182, 188, 191–99, 208, 209, 213, 221–23, 229, 286, 287, 296, 297
Exit of mills, 60, 70, 72

Far West, 113, 282
Federal Co., 292
Federal Trade Commission, 75, 78, 91, 92, 94, 102, 105, 120–22, 127, 130, 131, 133, 136, 144, 147–49, 152, 154, 162–64, 179, 186, 190, 200, 202, 210–13, 216, 217, 231, 232, 235, 236, 239, 243–63, 266, 271, 274, 275, 278, 279, 284, 290, 298–300
Federal Trade Commission Act, 241, 249, 262, 266n, 272, 274
Federal Trade Commission, Briefs, 254, 256–59
Federal Trade Commission, Cement Order (to cease and desist), 4, 247, 249, 251–55, 258–60, 263, 269, 280, 283
Federal Trade Commission, Findings as to Facts and Conclusions, 249–51, 256, 260
Federal Trade Commission, "Notice to the Staff in re: Commission Policy Toward Geographic Pricing," 271–74
Federal Trade Commission v. *A. E. Staley Mfg. Co.*, 151n, 254n
Federal Trade Commission v. *Algoma Lumber Co.*, 245
Federal Trade Commission v. *Cement Institute* (1948). *See Cement* case
Federal Trade Commission v. *Gratz*, 245
Federal Trade Commission v. *Morton Salt Co.*, 266
Federal Trade Commission v. *Pacific States Paper Trade Ass'n*, 245

Federal Trade Commission v. *R. F. Keppel & Co.*, 245
Fellner, William J., 2, 26, 27
Fetter, Frank A., 227, 248, 257n
Flintkote Co., 292n
Florida, 34, 49n, 106, 120n, 121, 160, 205, 285
F.o.b. mill prices, 111–15, 226; exclusive, 231–33; uniform, 207, 209, 210, 226–31, 248, 254
Fordwick, Va., 117, 144
Frazer, C., 179n
Fredonia, Kan., 120n
Freight absorption, 5, 8–10, 13, 18, 19, 41, 73, 74, 76, 89, 103, 114–16, 126, 142, 147, 152, 170, 190, 198, 201, 203, 207, 208, 213, 227, 230, 231, 233, 247, 254, 258, 259, 261n, 266, 267, 269–72, 274, 275, 277–80, 297–99
Freight, common factors, 98–101; "unnecessary," 209–11, 213, 229
Freight rate ass'ns, 98
Freight rate books, common, 14, 15, 98–101, 141, 172, 175, 177, 180, 185, 236, 243, 262, 277, 280, 283, 284, 297
Freight Rate Bureau, 100
Freight rates, 6, 8, 9, 11, 14, 16, 18, 28, 44–46, 92, 229, 276. *See also* Land grant freight rates
Fuchs, Ralph, 273n
Fultonham, Ohio, 128

Galbraith, J. K., 301n
General attack on formula pricing, 233–42
General Portland Cement Co., 268, 291, 306, 311
Georgetown, D.C., 106
Georgia, 205, 285, 291
Giant Portland Cement Co., 294n, 310
Glens Falls, N.Y., 150
Glens Falls Portland Cement Co., 309
Government purchases, 16, 17, 29, 53, 54, 61, 81, 111–15, 133, 137, 159, 183, 185, 223, 236, 248, 258, 263, 280, 297, 298
Grand Haven, Mich., 104
Gratz case. See *FTC* v. *Gratz*
Great Lakes area, 46, 71, 104–106, 108, 109, 144, 184, 212, 217, 276
Greencastle, Ind., 118
Gulf Coast area, 34
Gulf Portland Cement Co., 290
Halliburton Portland Cement Co., 311
Handler, Milton, 262
Hannibal, Mo., 89, 91, 116
Harrys, Texas, 128
Hawkeye-Marquette Cement Co., 140, 290
Hercules Portland Cement Co., 62, 131, 292n, 310
Hermitage Portland Cement Co., 291
Hogan, Charles L., 133
Horner, Governor (of Ill.), 244
Houston, Texas, 107, 187, 290
Hudson, N.Y., 118, 143, 156
Hudson Cement Co., 56n
Hudson Valley (of New York), 19n, 88, 96, 119, 136, 150, 154, 156, 184, 197, 294n
Humphrey, George M., 301n
Huron Portland Cement Co., 104, 105, 107, 109, 110, 120n, 121, 150, 161, 184n, 291, 307, 312–14
Hurry-Seaman process, 33, 38, 96, 97, 172

Ickes, Harold L., 114, 223n
Idaho, 143
Idaho Portland Cement Co., 295, 306
Ideal Cement Co., 117, 121, 140, 148, 150, 154, 174n, 282, 290–92, 294n, 305–309, 311–14
Illinois, 45, 74, 92, 112, 119, 127, 144, 154, 158, 169n, 184n, 212, 290
Imperfect collusion, 2, 9–27, 30, 76, 142, 296, 297. *See also* Collusion; Oligopoly
Imperfect competition, 2, 141, 142
Importation of cement, 31, 32, 91, 136, 137
Independence, Kan., 118
Indiana, 45, 49, 52, 74, 92, 105, 109n, 112, 127, 133, 143, 144, 154, 169n, 212, 281
Indiana Roads Commission, 140
Indianapolis, Ind., 158
International Cement Co., 100, 118
Involuntary base. *See* Punitive base
Iola, Kan., 89, 117
Iowa, 74, 98, 105, 144, 154
Ironton, Ohio, 118, 160

Jamesville, N.Y., 107, 146
Job contracts, 25, 99, 137–39, 180, 185, 236, 263

Kahn, Alfred E., 280n

Kaiser, Henry J., 48, 56, 57, 178n, 187
Kansas, 19n, 74, 90, 98, 105, 116, 119, 120n, 143, 154, 197, 212
Kansas City, 49, 105
Kansas City Cement Bureau, 99
Kaysen, Carl, 199n
Kefauver Bill, 274n, 275n
Kentucky, 49, 94, 169n
Keystone Portland Cement Co., 309
Kilgore, Bernard, 84
Kiln burning, 32, 33, 35, 36
Kingsport, Tenn., 118, 148
Kingston, N.Y., 56n
Knox, District Judge, 243
Knoxville, Tenn., 128
Kosmos Portland Cement Co., 292n, 307, 313, 314
Kosmosdale, Ky., 128

Lafayette, Ind., 140
Lake Erie, 109
Land grant freight rates, 16, 113, 114, 185
La Salle, Ill., 118, 127, 149, 155, 157, 158, 184n, 204
Lawrence Portland Cement Co., 140, 148, 163, 292
Leeds, Ala., 118
Lehigh Portland Cement Co., 22, 75, 98, 101, 102, 109–11, 116, 117, 120n, 121, 127–29, 132, 140, 148, 149, 154–56, 158, 160, 164, 166, 174n, 182, 184, 270, 291, 295, 305–308, 310, 312, 314
Lehigh Valley (of Pennsylvania), 19n, 33, 39, 40, 48, 62, 71, 74, 87–98, 103, 105, 108, 109, 111, 116, 118, 119, 136, 137, 140, 143, 144, 147, 149, 154, 156, 157, 160, 184, 189, 197, 200, 202, 212, 216, 291–94
Little Rock, Ark., 146, 151
Loading costs, 6, 110, 218, 234, 239
Location, 2, 44–48, 55, 71, 74–76, 87–89, 286. *See also* Concentration
Lone Star Cement Co., 99, 106, 107, 117, 118, 120n, 121, 127, 133, 148, 150, 154, 158, 160, 164, 174n, 270, 291, 292n, 295, 305 307, 309–13
Long, "Bob" (of Lehigh), 108
Longhorn Portland Cement Co., 311
Los Angeles, Calif., 146
Losses, 83, 84, 86, 126, 193, 194, 197, 220
Louisiana, 204, 205, 285
Louisville, Ky., 292n
Louisville, Neb., 128
Louisville Cement Co., 140, 306

McKee (of West Penn Co.), 108
McKinley Tariff of 1890, 31
Machlup, Fritz, 227
Maine, 140, 293
Manheim, W. Va., 118
Manitowoc, Wisc., 46, 120n
Manitowoc Portland Cement Co., 312
Maple Flooring case (*Maple Flooring Mfrs. Ass'n* v. *U.S.*), 179
Marginal costs, 59–64, 68–70, 86, 184, 193, 198, 213
Market behavior, 3, 18, 70, Chapter V, 299
Market concentration, 52 and Table 1
Market sharing, 19, 60, 196, 294
Market stabilization, 24, 116, 129–34
Market structure, 2, 48–57, 142, 300. *See also* Chain mill companies; Concentration; Dealers
Marketing costs, 27
Marketing policy and practices, 60, 61, 93, 94, 96, 110, 265, 266, 268–77
Marquette Cement Mfg. Co., 121, 127, 128, 140, 158, 174n, 184n, 204, 268, 270, 271, 290, 291, 295, 306–309, 311–14
Martinsburg, W. Va., 292, 293
Maryland, 40, 41, 109, 119, 161, 169n, 202, 205
Mason, Lowell B., 266n
Mason City, Ia., 117
Materials Service Co., 56n
Mattawamkeag, Me., 148
Maule Industries, 56n
Medusa Portland Cement Co., 107, 116, 120n, 121, 127, 148, 149, 174n, 291, 306, 309, 310, 312–14
Mergers. *See* Acquisitions and mergers
Miami, Fla., 212
Michigan, 34, 45, 46, 52, 74, 87, 90, 97, 104, 105, 109, 120n, 143, 144, 149, 154, 161, 182, 205, 281, 291
Middle Atlantic states, 52, 53, 202
Middle West, 52, 95, 113, 116, 127, 128, 144, 276
Mill nets, 8–10, 13, 16–18, 32n, 93, 113
Miller, John Perry, 233
Milwaukee, Wisc., 52, 104
Minnesota, 104, 110, 144
Misallocation of resources, 191–221, 226
Mississippi, 133, 204, 205, 285

Mississippi River, 92, 144
Missouri, 74, 116 119, 143, 291
Missouri Portland Cement Co., 154, 174n, 308, 314
Mobile, Ala., 294n
Monarch Cement Co., 134, 307
Monetary-fiscal policy, 3, 61, 67, 86, 193, 224, 225, 300
Monolith Portland Cement Co., 305, 313
Monolith Portland Midwest Co., 312
Monopoly. *See* Defensive monopoly
Montana, 170n
Morgan, Arthur E., 128
Morton, Lindley, 120n, 121n
Morton Salt case. *See FTC* v. *Morton Salt Co.*
Multiple base system, 143-47, 250
Multi-plant firms. *See* Chain mill companies
Mundt, Vernon A., 227

Nashville, Tenn., 105, 146, 151, 152, 291
National Ass'n of Manufacturers Law Digest, 266
National Builders Supply Ass'n, 109
National Cement Co., 305
National City Bank, 189, 288, 296n
National Portland Cement Co., 137, 310
National Recovery Administration (NRA), 18, 85, 113, 114, 133, 137, 139, 141, 182, 185, 244
National Traffic Bureau, 99
Natural market, 6, 8, 17–19, 21, 73, 74, 125, 198, 210, 232, 240, 299
Nazareth, Pa., 118, 120n
Nazareth Cement Co., 310
Nazareth Traffic Bureau, 99
Nebraska, 212
Nevada, 143, 146
Neville Island, Pa., 106, 107
New Castle, Pa., 117
New England, 49, 52, 88, 202
New Jersey, 87, 105, 107, 161, 169n, 202, 205, 216
New Orleans, La., 46, 117, 127, 148, 160, 201, 292n
New York City, 88, 93, 97, 99, 105, 134, 137, 150, 162
New York Coal Sales Co., 291
New York State, 49, 87, 104, 105, 109, 110, 119, 140, 160, 212, 265, 270, 276, 281
Non-base mills, 3, 8, 23n, 103, 125, 127, 146, 153, 184. *See also* Base mills
Non-price competition, 25, 42, 43, 72, 73, 80n, 135, 136, 170, 171, 213, 216, 221, 229
Nordberg, B., 63n, 69n
Norfolk, Va., 100, 105, 106, 118, 201
North, the, 205, 207
North American Cement Corp., 148, 174n, 179n, 307–309
North Carolina, 160, 200, 202, 205, 285
Northampton, Pa., 92, 93, 96, 103n
Northeast area, 97-99, 143, 154, 161, 177
Northwestern Portland Cement Co., 312
Northwestern States Portland Cement Co., 140, 292n, 307
Nourse, Edwin G., 167, 169

Office of Price Administration (OPA), 182, 188
Official Freight territory, 212
Ohio, 40n, 45, 49, 52, 74, 104, 105, 109, 110, 120n, 140, 143, 154, 156, 160, 161, 182, 212, 265, 281, 285
Ohio River, 108, 144
Okay, Ark., 117, 146
Oklahoma, 116, 290
Old Cement case (*Cement Mfrs. Protective Ass'n* v. *U.S.*), 177, 179, 243, 245, 255
Olds, Irving S., 266
Oligopolistic restraint, 9, 19, 22, 26–29, 236
Oligopoly, 139, 241. *See also* Imperfect collusion
Olympic Portland Cement Co., 292n, 312
Omaha, Neb., 49, 53
Open-price doctrine, 85, 179
Options to buy, 138, 185, 233, 234, 236, 238
Orange, Texas, 295n
Oregon, 146, 170n, 292
Oregon Portland Cement Co., 309, 314
Oro Grande, Calif., 150
Osborn, Ohio, 120n, 128, 146, 161
Oswego, N.Y., 110n
Output, increased, 37, 69, 218, 222; reductions, 59
Overhead costs, 59, 60, 63, 64, 68–71, 193

Pacific Coast states, 14, 52, 53, 99, 110, 122, 143, 144, 146, 184, 185, 281, 282
Pacific Portland Cement Co., 292
Pacific Northwest, 149, 155, 170, 212, 292n
Painesville, Ohio, 128
Parks, Fred, 117n
Patent licensing price agreement, 93, 96
Peerless Cement Corp., 107, 186, 292n, 308
Penn-Allen Co., 118
Pennsylvania, 40n, 41, 45, 49, 74, 87, 88, 91, 105–107, 109, 119, 154, 157, 169n, 182, 202, 205, 212, 276, 281, 292
Pennsylvania-Dixie Cement Corp., 117n, 118, 120n, 121, 140, 148, 159, 164, 174n, 179n, 219n, 270, 291, 295, 306–11, 313, 314
Perazich, George, 179n
Permanente Cement Co., 48, 56, 178n, 292n, 305, 306, 313, 314
Petoskey Portland Cement Co., 291, 292
Phantom freight, 146, 256, 261n, 277
Philadelphia, Pa., 48, 80n, 93, 105, 108, 151, 162, 217
Pit and Quarry, 1, 2
Pittsburgh, Pa., 46, 88, 94, 96, 103, 105–109, 116, 119, 144, 149, 156, 162, 216, 291
Pittsburgh Coke and Chemical Co., 120n, 310
Pittsburgh Plate Glass Co., 40n, 140, 309
Ponce Cement Corp., 312
Ponce Products, Inc., 313
Pools, 27, 38
Portland, Colo., 118
Portland, Ore., 49
Portland Cement Ass'n, 94–98, 115n, 128, 132, 135, 158, 214, 219
Portland Cement Co. of Utah, 312
Portland Point, N.Y., 118, 140
Portsmouth, Ohio, 291
Premium on truck loading, 108, 110, 180, 183, 217, 218
Price competition, 3, 4, 12, 18, 67, 68, 72, 84, 108, 112
Price cuts, 5, 15, 17, 21, 23, 29, 59, 60, 92, 104, 112, 120, 126, 133, 142, 155, 198, 230, 235
Price discrimination. *See* Punitive base; Robinson-Patman Act; Unsystematic pricing
Price flexibility, 4, 81, 126, 282, 299
Price increases, 81
Price instability, 102
Price leadership, 8n, 18–22, 115, 117, 121, 153–56, 166, 184, 235
Price movement, inter-base, 156–61
Price reductions, 69, 79, 81, 89, 112, 125, 160
Price stabilization, 4, 13, 59, 81, 90, 97, 142, 181, 221, 295
Prices, 94, 166, 170–72; *1907–1913*, 172–75; *1914–1917*, 175; *1918–1919*, 175–76; *1920–1925*, 176–77; *1926–1930*, 178–81; *1931–1935*, 181–85; *1936–1940*, 185–87; *1941–1942*, 187–88; *1943–1945*, 188; *1946–1948*, 188–90
Pricing practices, *1900–1910*, 90–95
Profit rate, 43, 44n, 58–60, 65, 84, 172, 222, 288, 289
Profits, 3, 23, 27, 166, 172, 194, 288; *1907–1913*, 172–75; *1914–1917*, 175; *1918–1919*, 175–76; *1920–1925*, 176–77; *1926–1930*, 178–81; *1931–1935*, 181–85; *1936–1940*, 185–87; *1941–1942*, 187–88; *1943–1945*, 188; *1946–1948*, 188–90
Promoters, 90
Public works program, 224, 300, 301
Puerto Rico, 49n, 187
Puerto Rico Cement Corp., 312
Punitive base, 22–25, 29, 112, 115, 121, 125–29, 142, 153, 158, 161, 180, 183, 184, 209, 220, 226, 227, 230, 238, 255, 293, 294, 296, 298, 299

Quality competition. *See* Non-price competition

Rail transportation, 14, 92, 93, 281
Rapid City, S.D., 127
Raw materials, 33, 34
Ready-mix concerns, 55–57, 294n, 298
Recommendations, 4, 30, Chapter VIII, esp. 296ff. *See also* Remedial proposals
Reder, Melvin, 220
Reductions in incentives for efficiency, 218–21
Remedial proposals, Chapter VII. *See also* Recommendations
Republic Steel Co., 140

Retardation in geographic shifting, 199–208
Reynolds, L. G., 195n
Richard City, Tenn., 118, 159
Rigid Steel Conduit case (*Triangle Conduit & Cable Co.* v. *FTC*), 271, 272
Riverside Cement Co., 56n, 84, 106, 146, 150, 154, 174n, 292n, 305, 313
Roanoke, Va., 202
Robinson-Patman Act, 21n, 241, 246, 248, 249, 254, 261, 266n, 272–74
Rochester, N.Y., 96, 105
Rock Products, 2
Rockmart, Ga., 146
Rockwood, Nathan C., 63n
Rocky Mountain states, 14, 40, 44, 45, 49, 98, 99, 109, 110, 117, 149, 154, 170, 182, 184, 203, 212, 281, 282, 292n, 294n
Rowe, John W. F., 196–98
Rutledge, Ivan, 273n

St. Louis, Mo., 91, 118, 154, 162
Sales contracts traded, 25
Sales force, 93, 94, 219
Salesmanship, 196, 209, 214, 216, 220
Salt Lake, Utah, 292
San Antonio Portland Cement Co., 311
San Francisco, Calif., 57
Sandt's Eddy, Pa., 117n
Sandusky Portland Cement Co., 116. *See also* Medusa Portland Cement Co.
Santa Cruz Portland Cement Co., 57, 305, 313
Savings, 10, 44, 102, 104, 114, 290
Schechter case (*A.I.A. Schechter Poultry Corp.* v. *U.S.*), 185
Schein, Nathan H. 77
Schumpeter, Joseph A., 218
Sealed bids, 16, 17, 24, 29, 54, 112, 133, 163, 183, 184n, 203, 213, 236, 237, 241, 242, 244, 246, 248, 250, 256, 263, 297, 298
Secret quotations, 17, 24–26, 129–34, 164, 172, 185, 237, 240
Seller concentration, 5, 60
Selling costs, 42, 67, 191, 213–16, 229
Shasta Dam, 48, 56, 187
Sherman Act, 177, 241, 246, 262, 295, 300
Shipments, trading in, 139–41
Shreveport, La., 146, 151
Signal Mountain Portland Cement Co., 121
Silica, Ohio, 107, 149
Smith, Blaine, 219n
Smithies, Arthur, 151n
South, the, 49, 52, 88, 89, 113, 120n, 143, 158, 204, 205, 207, 212, 284, 285
South America, 118, 188, 204
South Atlantic area, 161
South Carolina, 200, 204, 205, 285, 294
South Chicago, 116
South Dakota Cement Co., 311
Southeast area, 52, 53, 71, 154
Southeastern Portland Cement Ass'n, 99
Southern Cement Co., 291, 305
Southern States Portland Cement Co., 132, 292
Southern Freight territory, 212
Southwest area, 49, 294n
Southwestern Portland Cement Co., 120n, 306, 309, 311
Speed, Ind., 128
Spocari, Ala., 118, 120n, 121n, 127, 150
Spokane, Wash., 292
Spontaneous coordination, incomplete. *See* Imperfect collusion
Standard Lime & Cement Co., 120n, 292, 312
Standardization, of contracts, 95; of discounts and terms of sale, 25, 134, 135; of selling, 94–98
Statistics, company distribution, 25, 99, 139, 175, 177, 185, 236, 244, 263
Stigler, George J., 74, 227
Stocking, George W., 233, 251n, 266
Storey, William, 114
Substitution, 19, 79–83, 86, 222
Sunnyvale Valley, Calif., 48
Superior, Neb., 118, 128
Superior Cement Division, 291, 292
Superior Portland Cement, Inc., 292n, 312
Supreme Court, 1, 4, 21n, 22, 99, 139, 177, 179, 189, 190, 202, 243–45, 254, 256, 257, 260–62, 264, 266, 268, 269, 279, 280, 296, 300
Sweeney, Paul E., 45, 46, 211, 212, 231, 232
Swett, B. L., 98
Switching charge, rail, 93
Syracuse, Ind., 116
Syracuse, N. Y., 105, 107, 110n, 146, 151

Tampa, Fla., 160, 201
Technological factors, 2, Chapter II, 59, 60, 68, 87, 88, 187, 218, 219

Temporary National Economic Committee (TNEC), 233, 244n
Tennessee, 41, 105, 120n, 143, 148, 200, 205, 285
Tennessee-Eastman mill, 148
Tennessee Valley Authority (TVA), 128
Texarkana, Ark., 294n
Texas, 49, 52, 106–109, 116, 118, 119, 120n, 144, 148, 155, 160, 169n, 183, 205, 238, 281, 285
Texas Portland Cement Co., 295n
Thomaston, Me., 148, 201
Toledo, Ohio, 104n, 105, 107, 149
Trade associations, 90, 91, 116, 134, 176, 177
Trade practices, regulated, 59
Trade Relations Committee, 95
Transportation costs, 5, 6, 19, 83
Traylor Engineering and Manufacturing Co., 41n, 219
Treanor, John, 84, 85
Triangle Conduit & Cable Co., v. *FTC.* See *Rigid Steel Conduit* case
Trident, Mont., 118, 292
Trinity Portland Cement Co., 107, 120, 121
Trucking, 102–11, 146, 162, 180, 183, 229, 277; controls on, 4, 6, 11, 14, 142, 202, 203, 235, 238, 246, 253, 255, 277, 281, 284, 297; decontrol of, 241, 278; uncontrolled, 11–13, 103, 183, 233, 235, 236, 242, 250, 281, 282, 299. *See also* Buyers' trucking
Tucson, Ariz., 47

Uncertainty, 79, 84, 93, 96, 101, 103, 126, 130, 132, 183, 226, 227, 229, 230, 233–35, 237, 241, 266, 267, 277, 284, 286, 287, 295, 299
Under-utilization of resources, 221–25
Union Bridge, Md., 117, 120n, 154–56, 160
U.S. Bureau of Labor Statistics, 78, 163
U.S. Bureau of Mines, 1, 41, 48, 65n, 77, 122, 167, 169, 212, 281
U.S. Bureau of Standards, 130
U.S. Department of Commerce, 77, 179
U.S. Department of Justice, 176, 243–45, 278–84
U.S. Geological Survey, 167, 169n
U.S. Public Roads Administration, 81n, 136
United States Steel Corp., 43n, 94, 105, 118, 119, 265–67, 269, 270, 300
Universal, Pa., 143, 150, 157
Universal Atlas Cement Co., 43n, 108, 109n, 119, 120n, 121, 140, 154, 156–58, 164, 169, 216, 219n, 268–71, 291, 295, 300, 305, 306, 308–14
Universal Cement Co., 105–107, 116, 117, 119. *See also* Universal Atlas Cement Co.
Unsystematic pricing, 4, 13, 17, 20–24, 29, 61, 73, 76, 90, 97, 98, 101, 106, 114, 125, 126, 155, 182–84, 201, 203, 209, 213, 220, 230, 232, 233, 235, 236, 238, 240–42, 248, 249, 256, 273, 274, 297–300
Utah, 170n

Valley Forge Cement Co., 48, 105, 217
Valparaiso, Ind., 140
Vicksburg, Miss., 204, 294n
Viner, Jacob, 200
Virginia, 98, 105, 109, 160, 189, 202, 285
Volunteer Portland Cement Co., 128, 311

Wabash Portland Cement Co., 128n, 161, 291
Waco, Texas, 117
Wall Street Journal, 84
Wampum, Pa., 149
Warner Co., 56n
Warrior Co., 127
Washington, D.C., 52, 105, 155, 161, 162
Washington State, 98, 146, 170n, 292
Wastes, 3, 4, 13, 26, 214
West, the, 88, 89, 91, 110, 212
West Conshohocken, Pa., 108, 150
West Penn Co., 108, 291
West Virginia, 101, 109
West Winfield, Pa., 150
Western Freight territory, 212
Weston, Charles, 21n, 256, 258–60
Whitehall Cement Mfg. Co., 310
Wing, Walter, 140
Wisconsin, 104, 110, 154, 281, 285
Wooden, Walter B., 227, 248, 249n, 256, 257n
Wyandotte Portland Cement Co., 107, 291, 308
Wyoming, 276n

Yaworski, Nicholas, 179n
Yocemento, Kan., 118
York, Pa., 116, 149
Youngstown, Ohio, 108, 120n

Bei Fragen zur Produktsicherheit wenden Sie sich bitte an:
If you have any questions regarding product safety,
please contact:

Walter de Gruyter GmbH
Genthiner Straße 13
10785 Berlin
productsafety@degruyterbrill.com